MAC OS X PANTHER HACKS™

Other Macintosh resources from O'Reilly

Related titles

Mac OS X Panther for Unix Geeks

AppleScript: The Definitive Guide

Running Mac OS X Panther

Mac OS X Panther in a Nutshell

Mac OS X Unwired

Learning Unix for Mac OS X Panther

Cocoa in a Nutshell

Hacks Series Home

hacks.oreilly.com is a community site for developers and power users of all stripes. Readers learn from each other as they share their favorite tips and tools for Mac OS X, Linux, Google, Windows XP, and more.

Macintosh Books Resource Center

mac.oreilly.com is a complete catalog of O'Reilly's books on the Apple Macintosh and related technologies, including sample chapters and code examples.

A popular watering hole for Macintosh developers and power users, the Mac DevCenter focuses on pure Mac OS X and its related technologies including Cocoa, Java, AppleScript, and Apache, just to name a few. It's also keenly interested in all the spokes of the digital hub, with special attention paid to digital photography, digital video, MP3 music, and QuickTime.

Conferences

O'Reilly brings diverse innovators together to nurture the ideas that spark revolutionary industries. We specialize in documenting the latest tools and systems, translating the innovator's knowledge into useful skills for those in the trenches. Visit *conferences.oreilly.com* for our upcoming events.

Safari Bookshelf (*safari.oreilly.com*) is the premier online reference library for programmers and IT professionals. Conduct searches across more than 1,000 books. Subscribers can zero in on answers to time-critical questions in a matter of seconds. Read the books on your Bookshelf from cover to cover or simply flip to the page you need. Try it today with a free trial.

MAC OS X PANTHER HACKS™

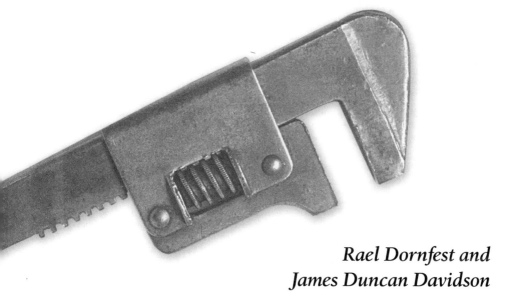

Rael Dornfest and
James Duncan Davidson

O'REILLY®

Beijing · Cambridge · Farnham · Köln · Paris · Sebastopol · Taipei · Tokyo

Mac OS X Panther Hacks™

by Rael Dornfest and James Duncan Davidson

Copyright © 2004 O'Reilly Media, Inc. All rights reserved.
Printed in the United States of America.

Published by O'Reilly Media, Inc., 1005 Gravenstein Highway North,
Sebastopol, CA 95472.

O'Reilly books may be purchased for educational, business, or sales promotional use. Online editions are also available for most titles (*safari.oreilly.com*). For more information, contact our corporate/institutional sales department: (800) 998-9938 or *corporate@oreilly.com*.

Editor:	Rael Dornfest	**Production Editor:**	Genevieve d'Entremont
Series Editor:	Rael Dornfest	**Cover Designer:**	Emma Colby
Executive Editor:	Dale Dougherty	**Interior Designer:**	Melanie Wang

Printing History:

June 2004:   First Edition.

Nutshell Handbook, the Nutshell Handbook logo, and the O'Reilly logo are registered trademarks of O'Reilly Media, Inc. The *Hacks* series designations, *Mac OS X Panther Hacks*, the image of a pipe wrench, "Hacks 100 Industrial-Strength Tips and Tools," and related trade dress are trademarks of O'Reilly Media, Inc.

Apple, the Apple logo, AppleScript, AppleScript Studio, AppleTalk, AppleWorks, Aqua, Carbon, Cocoa, Finder, FireWire, iBook, iCal, iChat, iMac, iPod, iSight, iSync, .Mac, Mac, Mac logo, Macintosh, PowerBook, Quartz, Quartz Extreme, QuickTime, QuickTime logo, and Rendezvous are trademarks of Apple Computer, Inc., registered in the U.S. and other countries. The "keyboard" Apple logo (⌘) is used with permission of Apple Computer, Inc.

Many of the designations used by manufacturers and sellers to distinguish their products are claimed as trademarks. Where those designations appear in this book, and O'Reilly Media, Inc. was aware of a trademark claim, the designations have been printed in caps or initial caps.

 This book uses RepKover,™ a durable and flexible lay-flat binding.

ISBN: 0-596-00718-3

[C]

Contents

Credits

About the Authors

Rael Dornfest is a maven at O'Reilly Media, focusing on technologies just beyond the pale. He assesses, experiments, programs, fiddles, fidgets, and writes for the O'Reilly Network and various O'Reilly publications. Rael is Series Editor of the O'Reilly Hacks series (*http://hacks.oreilly.com*) and has edited, contributed to, and coauthored various O'Reilly books, including *Mac OS X Hacks*, *Google Hacks*, *Essential Blogging*, and *Peer to Peer: Harnessing the Power of Disruptive Technologies*. He is also Program Chair for the O'Reilly Emerging Technology Conference.

In his copious free time, Rael develops bits and bobs of freeware, particularly the Blosxom weblog application (*http://www.blosxom.com*), is Editor in Chief of MobileWhack (*http://www.mobilewhack.com*), and (more often than not) maintains his Raelity Bytes weblog (*http://www.raelity.org*).

James Duncan Davidson is a freelance author, software developer, and consultant focusing on Mac OS X and related technologies. He is the author of *Running Mac OS X Panther*, the coauthor (with Apple Computer, Inc.) of *Learning Cocoa with Objective-C*, and the coauthor (with Michael Beam) of *Cocoa in a Nutshell*, all published by O'Reilly Media. Duncan is also a contributor to the O'Reilly Network (*http://www.oreillynet.com*), as well as publisher of his own web site, x180 (*http://x180.net/*).

In what sometimes seems like a previous life, Duncan was the creator of the widely used Apache Tomcat and Apache Ant and was instrumental in their donation to the Apache Software Foundation by Sun Microsystems. He was also the specification lead and author of two versions of the Java Servlet API and two versions of the Java API for XML Processing (JAXP). When he's not glued to a Mac hacking or writing, you can find Duncan out hiking the town or hanging out a local coffee shop.

Credits

The following people contributed their hacks, writing, and inspiration to this book:

- Mitch Chapman has been writing software professionally since 1984. Much of his work has involved Unix, X11, and C, but for the past five years Mitch has happily earned his keep with Python on a variety of operating systems. At home, he has found Mac OS X an ideal environment for a camera-toting Unix geek. When he isn't going blind in front of a computer monitor, Mitch is usually out hiking, flying, and taking pictures in the high desert near Santa Fe, New Mexico.

- Jason Deraleau (*http://tech.lifehertz.com*) has been a computer enthusiast since the Commodore 64. Having spent time focusing on DOS, Windows, Linux, and FreeBSD, his newest passion is the Macintosh and Mac OS X. Jason works as a Systems Administrator for a small manufacturing company and moonlights as an IT consultant and technical writer.

- Dan Dickinson (*http://vjarmy.com*) is the webmaster and CTO of Freeverse Software. His primary interests include weblog technologies, Beatmania IIDX, and all things Macintosh. His blog is updated frequently and often overzealously.

- François Joseph de Kermadec (*http://FJZone.org*) is currently a student and has been a Mac enthusiast for as long as he can remember. A fulltime Mac OS X user since the 10.0.4 release, F. J. began posting on the Apple Discussions in February 2002, where he enjoys helping fellow Mac users and writing user-contributed FAQs. An active member of many online and offline Mac communities, F. J. focuses on troubleshooting issues, switching "propaganda," and integrating Macs into educational workflows. He also contributes to various printed Mac publications, including the French magazine *MacAndCo*.

- Steven Frank cofounded Panic, an independent Mac software company. There, he helps develop Mac applications such as Transmit, Unison, and CandyBar. He maintains a weblog at *http://stevenf.com/*.

- Jennifer Golbeck is a Computer Science PhD candidate at the University of Maryland, College Park, where she studies complex systems. She likes to avoid any interactions that require leaving her two golden retrievers or changing out of pajamas, and ergo can be found conducting all of her business on *irc.freenode.net* using the nickname *golbeck*. Her other interests include marathon running, surfing, travel, and the Chicago Cubs.

- Kevin Hemenway, coauthor of *Spidering Hacks* and the original *Mac OS X Hacks*, is better known as Morbus Iff, the creator of disobey.com (*http://www.disobey.com*), which bills itself as "content for the discontented." Publisher and developer of more home cooking than you could ever imagine (such as the popular open source aggregator Ampheta-Desk, the best-kept gaming secret Gamegrene.com, the ever ignorable Nonsense Network, etc.), this is the seventh Hacks book he's been involved or mentioned in. Contact him at *morbus@disobey.com*.

- Peter Hickman started programming IBM mainframes far too long ago and was seduced by adventure games on VAXes and early CPM-based microcomputers. He got an entirely useless degree in Artificial Intelligence, went on to survive one dot-bomb, and is currently working as a programmer for Semantico (*http://www.semantico.com*), which specializes in online reference works and access control systems. When he's not programming or reading about programming, he can be found sleeping.

- Brian Jepson (*http://www.jepstone.net*) is an O'Reilly editor, programmer, and coauthor of *Mac OS X Panther for Unix Geeks* and *Learning Unix for Mac OS X Panther*. He's also a volunteer system administrator and all-around geek for AS220 (*http://www.as220.org*), a nonprofit arts center in Providence, Rhode Island. AS220 gives Rhode Island artists uncensored and unjuried forums for their work. These forums include galleries, performance space, and publications. Brian sees to it that technology, especially free software, supports that mission.

- Wei Meng Lee is a technologist and cofounder of Active Developer, a technology company specializing in hands-on training on the latest technologies. He is an established developer and trainer specializing in .NET, Macintosh, and wireless technologies. Wei Meng speaks regularly at international conferences and has authored and coauthored numerous books on .NET, XML, and wireless technologies. He writes extensively for the O'Reilly Network on topics ranging from .NET to Mac OS X. Wei Meng is also the author of *Windows XP Unwired* and *.NET Compact Framework Pocket Guide* (O'Reilly Media). He is also a contributor to the original *Mac OS X Hacks* and *Mac OS X Unwired* (O'Reilly).

- Chris Nandor (*http://pudge.net*) is editor of the Apple section and a developer for Slashdot (*http://apple.slashdot.org*). He is the maintainer of MacPerl (Perl for Classic Mac OS) and author of various Mac Perl modules.

- Matt Neuburg started programming computers in 1968, when he was 14 years old, as a member of a literally underground high school club, which met once a week to do timesharing on a bank of PDP-10s by way of primitive teletype machines. He also occasionally used Princeton University's IBM-360/67 but gave it up in frustration when one day he dropped his punch cards. He majored in Greek at Swarthmore College and received his PhD from Cornell University in 1981, writing his doctoral dissertation (about Aeschylus) on a mainframe. He proceeded to teach Classical languages, literature, and culture at many well-known institutions of higher learning, most of which now disavow knowledge of his existence, and to publish numerous scholarly articles unlikely to interest anyone. Meanwhile, he obtained an Apple IIc and became hopelessly hooked on computers again, migrating to a Macintosh in 1990. He wrote some educational and utility freeware, became an early regular contributor to the online journal TidBITS, and in 1995 left academe to edit *MacTech Magazine*. In August 1996, he became a freelancer, which means he has been looking for work ever since. He is the author of *AppleScript: The Definitive Guide*, *REALbasic: The Definitive Guide*, and *Frontier: The Definitive Guide*, all from O'Reilly Media.

- Erik T. Ray

- Ernie Rothman (*http://homepage.mac.com/samchops*) is an Associate Professor of Mathematics at Salve Regina University (SRU) in Newport, Rhode Island, where he is also Chair of the Mathematical Sciences Department. Ernie holds a PhD in Applied Mathematics from Brown University and held the position of Research Associate at the Cornell Theory Center in Ithaca, New York, before coming to SRU. His academic interests are in scientific computing, computational science, and applied mathematics education. As a longtime Unix aficionado, Ernie has enjoyed tinkering with Mac OS X since the day it was first released. Ernie has recently become interested in digital photography, especially of his Newfoundland dogs.

- Klaus Rutemöller (*http://macparts.de*) is a hobby programmer and freelance Mac technician. He is currently studying microelectronics at the University of Applied Sciences in Darmstadt, Germany. Klaus, who has used Macs since the age of five, is also an editor for *www.mac-tv.de*—a Web-TV station for Apple fans.

- C. K. Sample III maintains *3650 and a 12-inch* (*http://3650anda12inch. blogspot.com*), a weblog discussing the use of a 12" PowerBook G4 and a Nokia 3650. He is a doctoral candidate in English at Fordham University, focusing on 20th-century American and British literature, as well as 20th-century world literature, biblical studies, and critical theory. C. K. (Clinton Kennedy; no relation) works in Fordham's Department of Instructional Technology and Academic Computing as the Technical

Supervisor for the Fordham Graduate Center's North Hall Labs in Tarrytown, New York. His first "computer" was an Atari 400, and his first Mac was a PowerBook 5300CS. Originally from Jackson, Mississippi, C. K. currently lives in Bronxville, New York, with his fiancée, Kristin Landgrebe, and his pet Eclectus parrot, Misha, who just turned two years old.

- Mike Schienle has been on the Internet since long before Al Gore invented it. He started his career in the aerospace and defense industry in the early 1980s. His initial background was in image processing, remote sensing, and system administration of an ancient architecture once known as VAX. He has been using Macs since the day they took the Lisa computer out of his office in 1984. After 10 years of kicking shell scripts around, Perl became his language of choice, although he knows his way around several others. Mike runs Custom Visuals, LLC (*http://www.customvisuals.com*), a small company that dabbles in Internet applications, web site design/hosting, and database integration.

- Dori Smith is author of *Java 2 for the WWW: Visual QuickStart Guide*, coauthor (with Tom Negrino) of *JavaScript for the WWW: Visual QuickStart Guide*, and *Mac OS X Unwired*, and contributor to numerous print and online magazines. She is a frequent speaker at industry conferences and is Publisher and ListMom for the Wise-Women's Web Community. Dori is also a member of the Web Standards Project Steering Committee and maintains the Backup Brain weblog (*http://www.backupbrain.com*).

- Hadley Stern is a designer, writer, and photographer residing in Boston, Massachusetts. Hadley was born in London, England, relocated at age 4 to Singapore, then to Canada at age 10, and finally to America at age 22, where he met his lovely wife, Meiera. Hadley studied creative writing and western civilization and culture at Concordia University before studying graphic design at the Rhode Island School of Design (RISD). While at RISD, he began to pursue photography seriously, working in black and white and color and always experimenting with different techniques, including learning how to print Cibachromes. Since graduating from RISD, Hadley has worked as a professional designer at Malcolm Grear Designers, Rykodisc Records, and Razorfish. He has worked on corporate-identity projects, CD packages, web sites, flash banner advertising, and a wide variety of print collateral. Equally adept as both a print and interactive designer, he uses his technical knowledge of design production to further enrich his photography. He now works as a freelance designer, consulting with various clients. His personal site is *http://www.hadleystern.com*. Hadley also finds time to photograph, working in a variety of media, both digital and traditional. His current tools include a Canon EOS Elan IIE, Bronica ETRS, Graflex Speed Graphics, Canon S50, PowerMac G4, and a Jamcam. His work has been exhibited in Kentucky, Providence, Newport, and Kansas. Hadley has written for WebMonkey, *American Photo* magazine, and iPodLounge.com, and is the Publisher and Editor in Chief of AppleMatters.com. AppleMatters is a serious yet irreverent look at all things Apple. Covering opinions, news, and interviews, AppleMatters has done tremendously well since its launch over a year ago. Design, writing, photography—each informs the others.

- Ted Stevko (*http://www.plasticnoodle.com*) has been an illustrator, a programmer, a cartoonist, a network administrator, and a web designer...usually all at once. He started using Macs in 1989, helping to run a two-computer network for his journalism class while drawing cartoons and writing articles. Currently, Ted builds high-availability webservice applications in Java during the day, and at night he works on his award-winning comic strip, Soapbox (*http://www.soaptoon.com*).

- Chris Stone (*http://www.oreillynet.com/cs/catalog/view/au/783*) is a Senior Systems Administrator (the Mac guy) at O'Reilly Media, Inc. He's written several Mac OS X–related articles for the O'Reilly Mac DevCenter (*http://www.macdevcenter.com*) and contributed to *Mac OS X: The Missing Manual, Panther Edition* (Pogue Press/O'Reilly). Chris grew up on the San Francisco peninsula, went to Humboldt State University, and spent 10 years hidden away in the Japanese countryside before returning to California and settling in the North Bay area, where he now lives with his wife, Miho, and two sons, Andrew and Jonathan.

- Derrick Story is the Managing Editor for O'Reilly Network (*http://www.oreillynet.com*) and Mac DevCenter (*http://www.macdevcenter.com*), the latter of which he created in December 2000 for O'Reilly Media. His focus is on Mac OS X, digital media, and mobile computing. Derrick has authored the *Digital Photography Pocket Guide*, *Digital Video Pocket Guide*, and his latest, *Digital Photography Hacks* (O'Reilly). He also coauthored *iPhoto 4: the Missing Manual* (Pogue Press/O'Reilly). Derrick's professional experience includes more than 15 years as a photojournalist, former managing editor of Web Review, and a speaker for O'Reilly, CMP, and IDG conferences. He manages his online photo business, Story Photography (*http://www.storyphoto.com*), which specializes in digital photography and special events.

- Dave Taylor (*http://www.intuitive.com*) is a longtime tech expert who first logged into a Unix system in 1980 and used his first Mac in 1986. Author of 15 books, including *Wicked Cool Shell Scripts*, *Learning Unix for Mac OS X Panther*, and *Creating Cool Web Sites*, he's also a popular speaker and teacher. You can find all his latest projects and much more at his web site.

- Giles Turnbull (*http://gorjuss.com*, *http://gilest.org*) is a freelance writer based in Bradford on Avon, UK. He has written about the Internet and computers since 1997, but he is still searching for a decent email client. He had a great idea for a novel the other day.

- Phil Ulrich (*http://interalia.org/*) is a part-time indie software developer (for the Mac, of course!), part-time video editor for a nonprofit organization, and full-time student at Northern Kentucky University, double-majoring in Computer Science and Philosophy. In his nearly nonexistent free time, Phil is an avid video-game player and has been known to teach himself programming languages for fun.

- David E. Wheeler (*http://www.justatheory.com/*) is President of Kineticode (*http://www.kineticode.com/*), a content management and software development consulting company. He also serves as the maintainer and lead developer for Bricolage, an open source content management system built on Apache, mod_perl, and PostgreSQL. An active member of the Perl community and a speaker at the O'Reilly Mac OS X and Open Source conferences, David has contributed several articles addressing the needs of the serious Mac OS X–based Perl and Unix developer. David lives in Portland, Oregon with his wife, Julie, and two cats.

- Joar Wingfors (*http://www.joar.com*) is a Cocoa developer at Orc Software, a leading provider of technology for advanced market making, trading, and brokerage.

Acknowledgments

We would like to thank all those who contributed their ideas, tweaks, twiddles, hacks, and code to this book.

Dotting our t's and crossing our i's with vim and vigor was our copy editor, Brian Sawyer, who always eats, shoots & leaves *[and who let this sentence stand]*.

Watching our backs, technically speaking, was our technical editor, Erik Barzeski. The O'Reilly editors, production, product management, and marketing stuff—all are consummate professionals, hackers, and mensches.

Costello's Travel Café offered us a comfy couch, rich coffee by the cup, free WiFi by the byte, and didn't mind our taking the form of an incessant couch sculpture as the day wore on.

Rael

This book—and most of what I do, mind you—would simply not have been possible without the love, understanding, support, and beta testing of the members of Dornfest Household Labs: Asha, Sam, and Mirabai.

My extended family and friends, both local and virtual, watched me disappear slowly from site and iSight as the book went on, yet were standing there to greet me at the other end.

What you hold in your hands would not have happened, nor would it turned out anywhere near as well, without my coauthor and good friend, Duncan. (I'm still not crazy about his taste in music, I must admit.)

All the rest of my thanks go to everyone at my O'Reilly family. Particular kudos to Dale Dougherty for getting me started in all this editing nonsense in the first place, Laurie Petrycki for pointing the way though some of the prickly spots, and Tim O'Reilly, always my unflinching supporter, guide, and friend.

Props as usual to my virtual cube-mate, Nat Torkington, and peeps the world over.

Duncan

First and foremost, I'd like to thank my coauthor and friend, Rael. Not only did he bring me onboard as a full coauthor for this book after my contributions to the first volume, but he was also a joy to work with, even as we juggled the book with everything else in our busy lives.

Also, I'd like to thank Amy for dragging me off before the final hectic weeks of cranking out hacks to Mexico and Las Vegas; that road trip could very well have its own book written about it. It was a much-needed break. Chuck, editor of my other O'Reilly books as well as a friend, thanks for coming through with a couple of great hacks right in the nick of time.

In every book I've worked on, music gets credit. This one is no different. Top of the iTunes play list: Blue Man Group, The Crystal Method, BT, Paul Oakenfold, No Doubt, Groove Armada, Venus Hum, Filter, Fischerspooner, Thievery Corporation, Touch and Go, Black Eyed Peas, and Moby. And don't let Rael fool you; there's a bit of music there that I turned him onto, which he now likes.

And, of course, I thank all of my family and friends for their support and love.

Preface

Look left, then right. Whether you're in the office or a classroom, business meeting or café, hacker convention or design show, you're sure to exchange a satisfied grin with another Mac user.

There's a certain sparkle in the eye of a Mac person when within grasping distance of their PowerBook or G5 tower that's only increased by proximity to another equally zealous Mac type.

We Mac folk tend to move in and make ourselves at home more so than users of any other computer. The idea of merely tolerating the technologies in our midst is utterly foreign—sure you could just use your computer for Word processing or spreadsheets, but why? If you're going to spend quite so much time amongst windows and mouse-pointers, web pages and email messages, why not lose yourself in something that draws together these disparate bits into a cohesive, colorful, enjoyable whole?

The modern Mac is a wonderful combination of the power and flexibility of Unix with the ease of use that seems to be able to come only from One Infinite Loop in Cupertino. Regardless of your skill level—basic user, accomplished user, power user, or wild-eyed developer—you'll find many of the tools you need built right into the system. Because of this rich set of features, there's a way for almost everyone to dig and enjoy the system by hacking on it.

Combine this with the veritable cornucopia of third-party applications and cottage industry of customizations, tweaks, and hacks and you've a Mac to be reckoned with like never before.

Mac OS X Panther Hacks celebrates the Macintosh's adventurous spirit, inviting the citizen engineer on a quest of deeper discovery—both with the purpose of going further and simply enjoying the ride. *Mac OS X Panther Hacks* continues the tradition started with *Mac OS X Hacks*, sitting squarely at the peculiar confluence of deadly earnest optimization and creative (albeit sometimes wacky) tweaking you only seem to find on a Mac.

Why Mac OS X Hacks?

The term *hacking* has a bad reputation in the press. They use it to refer to people who break into systems or wreak havoc with computers as their weapon. Among people who write code, though, the term *hack* refers to a "quick-n-dirty" solution to a problem, or a clever way to get something done. And the term *hacker* is taken very much as a compliment, referring to someone as being *creative*, having the technical chops to get things done. The Hacks series reclaims the word, documents the good ways people are hacking, and passes the hacker ethic of creative participation on to the uninitiated. Seeing how others approach systems and problems is often the quickest way to learn about a new technology.

This collection reflects the real-world experience of those well steeped in Unix history and expertise, sharing their no-nonsense, sometimes quick-and-dirty solutions to administering and taking full advantage of everything a Unix Desktop has to offer. Add to that the experience of die-hard Macintosh users, customizing and modifying their hardware and software to meet their needs.

Each hack can be read easily in a few minutes, saving countless hours of searching for the right answer. *Mac OS X Panther Hacks* provides direct, hands-on solutions that can be applied to the challenges facing both those meeting the Mac for the first time and longtime users delving into Mac OS X and its Unix underpinnings.

How to Read This Book

You can read this book cover-to-cover if you like (we did, more than once), but for the most part, each hack stands on its own. If there's a prerequisite you ought to know about, there'll be a cross-reference to guide you on the right path. So, feel free to browse, flipping around to whatever section interests you most.

You'll notice the odd cross-reference to the previous version of this book, *Mac OS X Hacks* (sans the *Panther* bit)—for example, "Image Conversion in a Pinch" [Mac OS X Hacks, Hack #21]). While we did bring forward some things that have changed significantly between Jaguar and Panther, this book otherwise contains an entirely new crop of hacks. The cross-book cross-references are therefore only for interest's sake and not required reading for the current collection.

How This Book Is Organized

Mac OS X Panther Hacks goes beyond the simple tips and tricks—click here and drag there—to the more interesting hacks—bite-sized bits of truly useful functionality or otherwise rather interesting material you can manage in just a few minutes. It is divided logically (at least that was our intention) into several chapters:

Chapter 1, *GUI*

> Mac users have a long history of tweaking the Mac OS graphical user interface. This chapter looks at some of Panther's interface improvements and highlights the cottage industry of third-party menu tweaks, folder spindles, keyboard and mouse hacks, haxies, and Desktop widgets—a sight for sore eyes and a treat for mouse-weary hands.

Chapter 2, *Scripting*

> Mac OS X brings together the AppleScript scripting language and the world of Unix scripting. By interweaving Mac's own AppleScript with hacker heavyweights Perl, Python, and Ruby, we explore just what's possible when you put programming in the hands of mere mortals.

Chapter 3, *Web, Chat, and Mail*

> There have never been quite so many ways to interact with peers, family, friends, and virtual buddies than exist today on the Mac. With the built-in industrial-strength Mail client, state-of-the-art Safari web browser, and AV-enhanced iChat instant messaging, how could things possibly get any better? With a hack here, a tweak there, and a third-party plug-in or application thrown in every so often, you can make a great thing even better.

Chapter 4, *Multimedia*

> The Mac succeeds in bringing together the disparate components of your digital life with a suite of simple, powerful applications. There are, however, a lot of ways to draw outside of the otherwise nice, clean lines of your iLife. You find that there is more than enough hacking to keep you busy.

Chapter 5, *Gadgets and Hardware*

> Through WiFi and Bluetooth wireless networking, FireWire and USB drives, dongles, and devices, the Mac can exchange content and input with other Macs, Windows and Unix machines on the network, the PDA in your pocket, and even the cellphone in your hand. This chapter shows off just a few of the possibilities and explains the tech behind the magic.

Chapter 6, *Networking and Network Apps*

> The ubiquity of networking—both locally and worldwide—is driving Mac OS X to open its doors to an ever-widening collection of protocols, while stitching it all together in as seamless a way as possible. Between Apple's openness to interconnectivity and emerging third-party experiments and applications, there's a lot to love about Macintosh in the networked world.

Chapter 7, *Servers*

> Beneath the candy-coated shell of the Mac GUI beats the heart of a full-blown Unix server. This chapter flips all the right switches to turn up all that's already built into the Apache web server and steps you through installing, configuring, and bringing up your own Mac mail server.

Chapter 8, *Files and Backup*

> Files and folders lie at the heart of everyone's digital life. While using a filesystem has become all but second nature to us over the past few years of GUI computing, we still find ourselves struggling with the chore of storing, organizing, maintaining, and backing up our personal filestore. This chapter presents some potential solutions to common backup dilemmas and teaches you enough to extrapolate to suit your particular needs.

Chapter 9, *System Administration*

> We'd be flat-out lying if we said it didn't take a little system administration every now and again to keep your Mac running smoothly and reliably. This chapter covers maintenance and security, as well as using the Terminal and all those things you need to know to dig deeper into the Unix underpinnings of Mac OS X.

Conventions

The following is a list of the typographical conventions used in this book:

Italic

> Used to indicate new terms, URLs, filenames, file extensions, directories, and program names, and to highlight comments in examples. For example, a path in the filesystem will appear as */Developer/Applications*.

`Constant width`

> Used to show code examples, the contents of files, commands and options, or the output from commands.

`Constant width bold`

> Used for emphasis and user input in code.

Constant width italic
> Used in examples and tables to show text that should be replaced with user-supplied values.

Color
> The second color is used to indicate a cross-reference within the text.

Menu symbols
> When looking at the menus for any application, you will see some symbols associated with keyboard shortcuts for a particular command. For example, to open an old chat in iChat, you would go to the File menu and select Open... (File → Open...), or you could issue the keyboard shortcut, ⌘-O. The ⌘ symbol corresponds to the ⌘ key (also known as the "Command" key), located to the left and right of the spacebar on any Macintosh keyboard.

You should pay special attention to notes set apart from the text with the following icons:

> This is a tip, suggestion, or general note. It contains useful supplementary information about the topic at hand.

> This is a warning or note of caution.

The thermometer icons, found next to each hack, indicate the relative complexity of the hack:

 beginner   moderate   expert

Using Code Examples

This book is here to help you get your job done. In general, you may use the code in this book in your programs and documentation. You do not need to contact us for permission unless you're reproducing a significant portion of the code. For example, writing a program that uses several chunks of code from this book does not require permission. Selling or distributing a CD-ROM of examples from O'Reilly books *does* require permission. Answering a question by citing this book and quoting example code does not require permission. Incorporating a significant amount of example code from this book into your product's documentation *does* require permission.

We appreciate, but do not require, attribution. An attribution usually includes the title, author, publisher, and ISBN. For example: "*Mac OS X Panther Hacks*, by Rael Dornfest and James Duncan Davidson. Copyright 2004 O'Reilly Media, Inc., 0-596-00718-3."

If you feel your use of code examples falls outside fair use or the permission given here, feel free to contact us at *permissions@oreilly.com*.

How to Contact Us

We have tested and verified the information in this book to the best of our ability, but you may find that features have changed (or even that we have made mistakes!). For example, the 10.3.3 point update brought improvements that affected more than one hack in this book as we were wrapping it up. As a reader of this book, you can help us to improve future editions by sending us your feedback. Please let us know about any errors, inaccuracies, bugs, misleading or confusing statements, and typos that you find anywhere in this book.

Please also let us know what we can do to make this book more useful to you. We take your comments seriously and will try to incorporate reasonable suggestions into future editions. You can write to us at:

O'Reilly Media, Inc.
1005 Gravenstein Hwy N.
Sebastopol, CA 95472
(800) 998-9938 (in the U.S. or Canada)
(707) 829-0515 (international/local)
(707) 829-0104 (fax)

To ask technical questions or to comment on the book, send email to:

bookquestions@oreilly.com

The web site for *Mac OS X Panther Hacks* lists examples, errata, and plans for future editions. You can find this page at:

http://www.oreilly.com/catalog/0596007183/

For more information about this book and others, see the O'Reilly web site:

http://www.oreilly.com/

Got a Hack?

To explore Hacks books online or to contribute a hack for future titles, visit:

http://hacks.oreilly.com/

GUI
Hacks 1–12

Mac users have a long history of tweaking the Mac OS graphical user interface (GUI). Some regard the ever-improving Mac OS X GUI as a a breath of fresh air, panacea for all the ills of interface design over the years in a world dominated by dusty windows and quivering mice. Of course, there are others who don't agree and want to tweak the interface to meet their own particular needs and desires. And an entire industry has sprung up to service the needs of users everywhere who want to tweak their systems.

What almost everyone can agree on is that each iteration of OS X has brought vast improvements in how the interface looks, feels, and works. The first public beta of the system didn't have an Apple menu in the upper-left corner, which caused quite a stir. After much lamentation, Apple put it back for the 10.0 release. Mac OS X 10.1 and Jaguar brought further UI tweaks and polish. And the same holds true for Panther; back are the Labels of OS 9 (without many people even noticing that they were missing) and springy folders, re-enabling the ease of drag-and-drop navigation.

Still, the cottage industry of third-party menu tweaks, folder spindles, keyboard and mouse hacks, haxies, and Desktop widgets bends Mac OS X to its will. You're sure to find this chapter a sight for sore eyes and a treat for mouse-weary hands.

HACK #1

Enjoy the Animations

Mac OS X is full of little touches that, while sometimes silly, make the overall experience a little more fun.

About the first user interface flourish most users stumble across is the *genie effect*: the silky-smooth way that windows glide into the Dock when minimized—not unlike a genie into a bottle, as the name suggests. As cool as the genie effect is, it's not the only one available. Choose Dock → Dock Preferences from the Apple menu. In the Dock Preferences pane, shown in

Figure 1-1, you'll see an option labeled "Minimize using." By default, it's set to Genie Effect, but you can change it to Scale Effect.

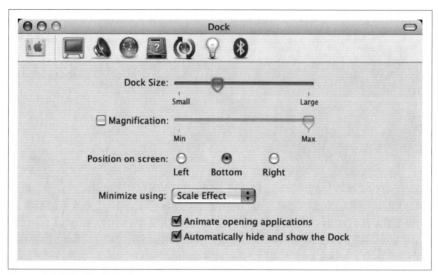

Figure 1-1. The Dock Preferences pane

The *scale effect* causes minimized windows to shrink as they zoom toward their position in the Dock, but it doesn't deform their shape as the genie effect does. If you have a slower Mac, you might find that using the scale effect slightly improves the performance of window minimization, because it is a little less taxing on the system. Even if you have a fast Mac, you might prefer the clean look of windows scaling toward the dock.

There's yet another minimizing effect, but it's hidden away and you can't get to it through System Preferences. It's called the *suck effect*. To enable this effect, open the Terminal (*/Applications/Utilities*), and type the following command:

```
$ defaults write com.apple.dock mineffect suck
```

Next, log out by choosing "Log Out <*Your Name*>..." from the Apple menu. When you log back in, the suck effect will be enabled. Minimized windows will have the appearance of being sucked into their spot in the Dock—perfect for all you Hoover lovers out there.

You can turn off the suck effect by going back to Dock Preferences and reselecting one of the other effects. You don't need to log out again.

Exposing Windows with Exposé

You're probably already familiar with the basics of the Exposé feature introduced in Panther. By default, briefly pressing F9 reveals all currently open windows, allowing you to select one by clicking it with the mouse. Pressing F10 does the same, but it reveals only the windows that belong to the currently active application. Finally, pressing F11 temporarily pushes all windows aside to reveal your Desktop.

But did you know you can also use Exposé as a funky application switcher? First, press F10 to view windows in your current application. Then, press Tab several times to cycle through all your open applications. Press Return to select the desired application when it comes around.

> If you're really bored at a conference, you can amuse yourself by switching between the various Exposé modes. It's great eye candy to occupy spare brain cycles. F9, F10, F11, F10, Tab, Tab.... Evidently, we've spent too much time going to conferences.

You can change the keys used to activate Exposé, and you can assign Exposé actions to extra mouse buttons (if you have them) by using the Exposé Preferences pane in System Preferences.

Watching in Slow Motion

This next trick is a bit superfluous, but it's great for impressing people when you are showing off your Mac. If you hold down the Shift key while minimizing a window or performing an Exposé action, the effect animations run in slow motion.

If you really want to blow people's minds, Shift-minimize a QuickTime Player window while a movie is playing in it. The movie will continue playing as the window slowly morphs into the Dock. For this to work, you'll need a Mac with a Quartz Extreme–capable video card. Any Mac produced within the last couple of years should be up to the task.

Trapping a Window

Now for something really weird. This hack requires a bit of preparation. First, for best effect, make sure you are using the genie effect for window minimization. Next, open a Terminal window and enter the following command, but don't press Return yet!

```
$ killall Dock
```

Remember not to press Return at the end, and make sure the D in Dock is capitalized.

Now, pick another window (any other open window will do) and Shift-minimize it so that it starts to glide slowly into the Dock. Quickly, while the window is still minimizing, switch back to the Terminal window and press Return.

You've just caused the Dock to restart in the middle of minimizing the window. The system, unsure of what to do without a Dock to put the minimized window into, just stops the minimization process cold, leaving a deformed, partially minimized window hanging out on your screen.

What's most amazing is that the deformed window remains fully functional. For example, if you do this trick on a TextEdit document, you can continue to type, edit, and scroll around in it as if nothing unusual were going on. This gives you some idea of the underlying power of the Mac OS X graphics subsystem.

To get rid of the odd window, just close it. If you find the close button is not accessible, use the keyboard shortcut ⌘-W. If all else fails, just quit the application. Don't worry; you can't damage anything with this trick. It's merely visual trickery.

—*Steven Frank*

H A C K   Spice Up Your Desktop
#2
Go beyond the Dock and menu extras to turn your entire Desktop into an information billboard.

The menu extras on the right side of your menu bar provide quick shortcuts to keep tabs on, and fiddle with, many aspects of your system. But, it has to be said, the widgets displayed there are pretty boring in their plain black motif. Also, because they are so small (16 or so pixels high), they can convey only the barest amount of useful information. Thankfully, taking up where menu extras leave you craving more, there are a few third-party applications that might just fit the bill.

Konfabulator

Billed as the tool that can "be whatever you want it to be," Konfabulator started out as a desire by Arlo Rose (who brought the world Kaleidoscope and theme-able interfaces for the original Mac OS) to display a cool battery monitor and the current weather on the Desktop. When Arlo teamed up with Perry Clarke, the result was a JavaScript engine that takes advantage of Mac OS X's Quartz rendering to display any kind of widget seamlessly on the Desktop.

When first downloaded from the Konfabulator web site (*http://www. konfabulator.com*; $25 Single User License, $500 Site License; fully functional time-limited trial available) and installed, it launches several of its built-in widgets, including an analog clock, a weather display, and a CPU meter. Figure 1-2 shows a few of these widgets.

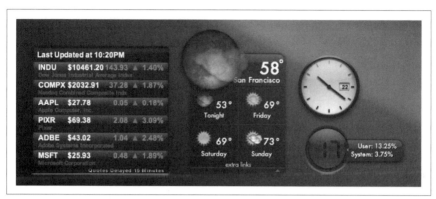

Figure 1-2. Some of Konfabulator's default widgets

But you aren't limited to the built-ins. From the get-go, Konfabulator is designed to allow people to write their own widgets. All you need is an XML file that points to various image resources to display, as well as the JavaScript code needed to drive the widget. And developers have gone crazy designing new widgets; there are over 600 listed on the Konfabulator web site. Figure 1-3 shows two of them.

```
Apr 22 21:28:19 localhost diskarbitrationd[115]: disk1s2    hfs      8E933103-1114-3045-96BE
-61403BD00ECD BetterWhatsGoingOn1-4    /Volumes/BetterWhatsGoingOn1-4
Apr 22 21:28:19 localhost diskarbitrationd[115]: disk1s2    hfs      8E933103-1114-3045-96BE
-61403BD00ECD BetterWhatsGoingOn1-4    [not mounted]
Apr 22 21:25:29 localhost kernel: jnl: write_journal_header: error writing the journal header!
Apr 22 21:25:29 localhost kernel: jnl: do_jnl_io: strategy err 0xd
Apr 22 21:25:29 localhost kernel: disk2s2: device is write locked.
Apr 22 21:25:29 localhost kernel: jnl: flushing fs disk buffer returned 0xd
Apr 22 21:25:02 localhost update_prebinding: update_prebinding started with cmd line:
update_prebinding -root / -files ./tempSensor
Apr 22 21:24:41 localhost diskarbitrationd[115]: disk2s2    hfs      68DE7DDE-2348-3053-A7CB
-217858AE721F Temperature Text    /Volumes/Temperature Text
Apr 22 21:24:41 localhost diskarbitrationd[115]: disk2s2    hfs      68DE7DDE-2348-3053-A7CB
-217858AE721F Temperature Text    [not mounted]
Apr 22 21:23:27 localhost kernel: jnl: write_journal_header: error writing the journal header!
Apr 22 21:23:27 localhost kernel: jnl: do_jnl_io: strategy err 0xd
Apr 22 21:23:27 localhost kernel: disk2s2: device is write locked.
Apr 22 21:23:27 localhost kernel: jnl: flushing fs disk buffer returned 0xd
Apr 22 21:23:25 localhost diskarbitrationd[115]: disk2s2    hfs      F88190A6-CAB5-3421-B6CB-
D797DFFBB4D8 Tail Chaser 1.0.1    /Volumes/Tail Chaser 1.0.1
Apr 22 21:23:24 localhost diskarbitrationd[115]: disk2s2    hfs      F88190A6-CAB5-3421-B6CB-
D797DFFBB4D8 Tail Chaser 1.0.1    [not mounted]
Apr 22 21:21:26 localhost kernel: jnl: write_journal_header: error writing the journal header!
Apr 22 21:21:26 localhost kernel: jnl: do_jnl_io: strategy err 0xd
Apr 22 21:21:26 localhost kernel: disk2s2: device is write locked.
```

Figure 1-3. Additional useful (and not so useful) widgets

The first, Tail Chaser, is possibly the most useful widget we've found; it shows you the last few lines of any log file you want. In this case, we're looking at the *system.log*. The second widget shown in Figure 1-3 is Satsuki, a little Japanese animation character that just hangs out on the Desktop and dances her heart out—very entertaining when you have some music cranked up on iTunes.

When setting up Konfabulator widgets, you should decide whether you want them displayed as floating windows or placed on your Desktop. There are advantages to each setting. If you set them as floating windows (the default behavior), you can interact with and layer them. However, when you activate Exposé, they'll either disappear or fly off the edges of the screen along with all the other windows. If, instead, you set them to be part of your Desktop, you can use Exposé's Show Desktop function (F11) to check up on everything quickly. This setting is especially useful for Tail Chaser.

Stattoo

If Konfabulator isn't your bag, but the idea of status information on your Desktop is still appealing, you might be interested in Panic's Desktop widget application: Stattoo (*http://www.panic.com/Stattoo/*; $12.95, trial version available). Instead of placing widgets willy-nilly across your Desktop, Stattoo displays a set of capsules in a neat row across your Desktop, as shown in Figure 1-4.

Figure 1-4. Stattoo's widgets, displayed in a row on the Desktop

Stattoo ships with capsules that can display the date, time, current weather, available disk space, and more. Unlike Konfabulator, you can't develop your own widgets for display, but if all you want is a nice, clean display of the weather and the current track playing in iTunes, it's a good solution.

iCal Viewer

iCalViewer (*http://www.icalviewer.com*; $11, trial version available) is another handy application for putting information on your Desktop. This simple application displays the various items on your calendar as boxes moving toward a yellow finish line that represents the current time. This gives you an idea of what's coming up in the next few hours or days. It can be run as a window on the Desktop, as shown in Figure 1-5.

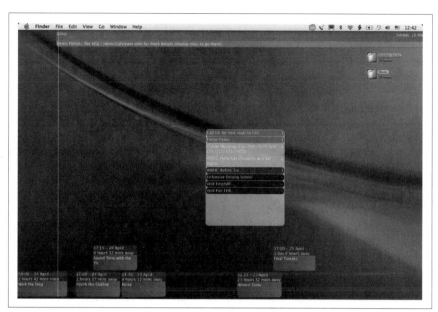

Figure 1-5. Using iCalViewer to display a calendar on the Desktop

For those who want a subliminal reminder of their calendar to appear while they happen to be talking on the phone, iCalViewer can even be run as a screensaver.

HACK #3 Use Labels Effectively

Labels aren't just for neat-freaks; they're also an effective way to keep track of what's in your queue.

It has been said that there are two types of people in the world: those who do and those who do not like Neil Diamond. In the Mac world, the great divide instead lies squarely between those who keep a uselessly cluttered Desktop or a pleasingly spare—yet no more useful—one.

The first group drags just about everything they are currently working on or use on a regular basis onto the Desktop, where those items will soon be mismanaged and forgotten as the virtual piles teeter and eventually fall. The problem is that beyond a certain point, having your files right there in front of you means only that you've hidden them in plain sight.

The second group fears the slippery slope of keeping things on the Desktop, preferring to keep projects well hidden in their *Documents* directory, perhaps even neatly organized by project. These folks use iCal's To Do list, an Omni Outliner document, or some folder named *Stack*, *Current*, or *To Do*. The problem here is one of out of sight, out of mind; without the constant reminder of what you have to get done, you can plumb forget what's in your stack.

I've always been of the latter sort. While I do realize the value of having my files right there on the Desktop, it all feels rather messy, with no real rhyme or reason. My feelings changed when I rediscovered a much-loved technology from Mac OS 9 that has returned in Panther: Labels.

Labels are those swatches of color you apply to files and folders, ascribing some meaning to them on the otherwise meaningless blank canvas of the Desktop. Labels can ascribe any meaning you wish: priority, timeliness, project, ownership, or what-have-you. Create your own coding system to suit the task at hand, stick to it, and you'll find that jumble less jumbled.

The Desktop Queue

I've taken to using my Desktop as a queue or stack of things with which I have to deal, as shown in Figure 1-6.

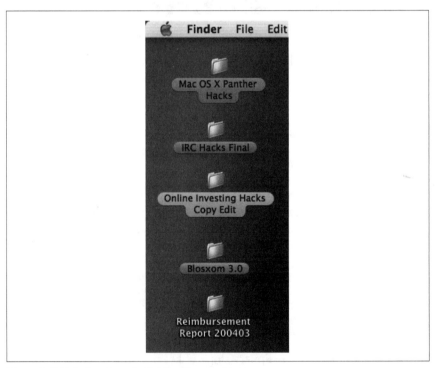

Figure 1-6. Labeling items in the Desktop queue

I attach a priority to each folder or file based on time, according to the following scheme:

Red
> Today or tomorrow

Orange
> This week

Yellow
> Next week

Purple
> Copious free time/personal project

Unlabeled
> Importantish, but not particularly timely

Anything a couple weeks or more out I tend to keep elsewhere, with a note in my iCal calendar. There's no sense needlessly cluttering your Desktop beyond a certain event horizon; this serves only to make you shy away from looking at your Desktop (there's so much to do in a month) and so break the system.

The Checklist

When I have a series of items to read through, I use color coding to indicate which items I've already read, which I'm currently working on, and which I've noticed some problem in or have a question on, as shown in Figure 1-7.

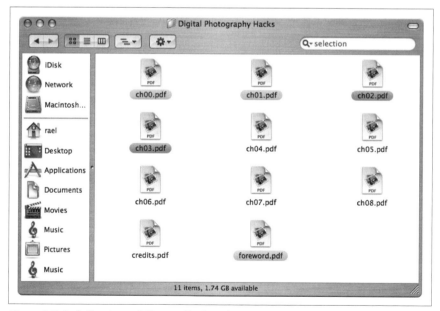

Figure 1-7. Labeling items differentially, based on status

In this case, these are my personal color choices:

Green
    Read/okay

Red
    Problem

Orange
    Question

Purple
    Currently reading

This scheme has served me rather well in editing books, reading chapter by chapter; building software, writing source file by source file; and keeping track of incoming/outgoing memos around a particular project.

The Collaborative Project

When you're working collaboratively with one or more people—as I did on this book—it is vital to keep a handle on who owns which document. While I could perhaps have assigned a different color to each contributor (assuming only seven, since that's the number of labels you have at your disposal), instead I chose just to keep track of what I owned, what was owned by my coauthor, and what was awaiting turnaround by a contributor (see Figure 1-8).

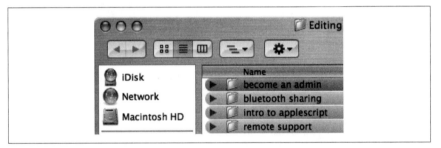

Figure 1-8. Keeping track of component ownership in a collaborative project

For colors, I chose:

Red
    Owned/locked by coauthor

Green
    Owned by me

Orange
    Awaiting contributor edits

While the switch between my owning something and assigning ownership to my coauthor was a manual process involving email, I could just as easily have used a shared .Mac folder and some other form of notification.

The ReadMe

How many times have you come across a folder filled to the brim with files yet sparking no memory of just what it was all about, how the files are related, and, indeed, whether it's even yours?

It's common practice among programmers to drop into every folder of any value a *ReadMe* (or *README* or *Read Me*) file that contains some semblance of explanation about just why this seemingly disparate collection of files is gathered together under one roof. But given enough files in a directory, you might well miss that *ReadMe*—at least until you've meandered through every other file in the folder.

Highlight a *ReadMe* in bright red to attract attention. Perhaps even prepend its filename with a space character so that the *ReadMe* rises to the top when the folder is viewed alphabetically (the default). Figure 1-9 shows the package folder for my Blosxom weblog; *ReadMe.txt* is on top and emblazoned in red.

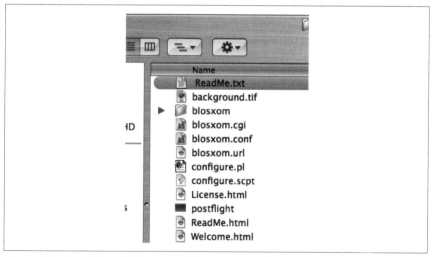

Figure 1-9. A ReadMe called out in red (trust us, it's red)

Label Labels

If you prefer, you can actually label your labels. Visit Finder → Preferences... → Labels and name your labels anything you like.

Because of the different ways I use labels in different contexts, I found this bit of functionality not particularly useful, as you can see in Figure 1-10, which shows my uninspired default label names (Red, Orange, Yellow, etc.).

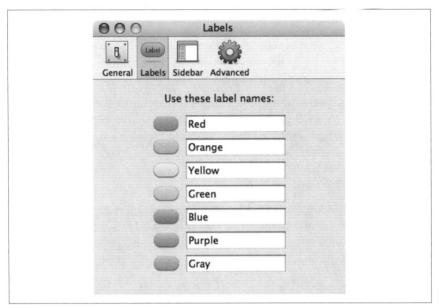

Figure 1-10. Labeling your labels

See Also

- "Label Your Mail" [Hack #37]

Launchers, or, Dial ⌘-Space M for Mail

Two Dock alternatives, LaunchBar and Quicksilver, put applications, URLs, contacts, and just about anything else you might want within easy reach from your keyboard.

"Holy Dock, Batman!" Cory (*http://www.craphound.com*) was aghast at my accretive Dock, chock-full of applications, minimized windows, and an Internet shortcut or three. If Dock bloat has got you down but you'd like to keep your favorite, most-used apps readily available, we have a couple of alternatives for you.

Quicksilver and LaunchBar are two of those rare apps that just about every alpha geek agrees are an indispensable part of the tricked-out OS X Desktop.

LaunchBar has been on our Desktops since Mac OS X 10.2 Jaguar and was featured in the original *Mac OS X Hacks* book. Quicksilver is the spunky new contender and has even the staunchest of LaunchBar loyalists considering their ⌘-space options.

Whichever you choose, you're just a keystroke or three away from your apps, files, favorite web sites, email addresses, and just about anything else you might want within easy reach. ⌘-space IE launches Internet Explorer, ⌘-space M switches me to Mail, ⌘-space NYT directs my browser to *The New York Times* on the Web (*http://www.nytimes.com*), and ⌘-space MOM brings up my mother's Address Book entry.

And it all starts with a ⌘-space. An engine powered by some adaptive algorithms jumps into action, suggesting matches for the keystrokes you type and what you chose as your preferred match to them last time. CO might suggest Console as the top choice the first time you give it a whirl, but choose Conversation [Hack #36] from the list and you've taught it not to make the same mistake twice.

Quicksilver and LaunchBar each are quite the Alt-Tab stand-in and afford fast switching between running apps. Assign single-character shortcuts to your oft-used apps—M for Mail, S for Safari, W for Microsoft Word, X for Excel—and you'll never visit the Dock between applications again.

While both Quicksilver and LaunchBar function in essentially the same fashion, each offers its own unique advantages—not to mention a distinct look and feel, something you'll care about given how much time you're bound to spend together.

Quicksilver

Act without doing;
work without effort.
Think of the small as large
and the few as many.
Confront the difficult
while it is still easy;
accomplish the great task by a series of small acts.

—*Lao-Tze (translated by S. Mitchell), quoted in the About Quicksilver documentation*

This isn't Ronco. I'm not an excitable friend from across the ocean with red hair and a bow tie and a British accent. You're not watching *Amazing Discoveries*.

But I swear, if you give me 10 minutes and follow my simple directions, you can go from merely using Mac OS X to owning it. I know, it sounds like more than a little dose of hyperbole. I wouldn't have believed it myself had I not tried Quicksilver (*http://blacktree.com/apps/quicksilver*) myself and had my jaw drop repeatedly.

The documentation of the app on the product's home page, which describes it as little more than a launcher akin to LaunchBar, does not do Quicksilver justice. It's more than a launcher; it's a powerful action engine. Let's give it a whirl!

Launch Quicksilver and walk through the self-explanatory setup wizard. Next, Quicksilver scans the standard data hotspots on your machine: your Address Book, iTunes Library, Applications folder, Desktop folder, and so on. It's creating a giant searchable version of your machine. In the future, this will happen automatically each time Quicksilver starts up.

All that's left is to set a few preferences. Press ⌘-, to bring up the application's preferences. On the Application tab, check "Start at login" and "Warn before quitting." Uncheck "Superfluous visual effects" if your machine is slow; you've got to admire any app that admits to some superfluous preferences. On the Command tab, change the hotkey if you have ⌘-space mapped to something else or just don't like the combo. Click the Activation field and type a new keystroke to set it. On the Update tab, turn on "Check for updates" if you want to be kept apprised of future Quicksilver updates. That should do it for now; close the Preferences window.

Preferences set, you should be about four minutes in at most. Let's start with some Quicksilver basics. Press ⌘-space (or whatever you chose as your hotkey combo) to activate Quicksilver. Press Esc to dismiss it. This should work regardless of which app you have in the foreground.

Search. Now, let's search for something. Activate Quicksilver and type a few letters of the title of a bookmark you visit often; they don't even have to be the *first* few letters. As you type, As shown in Figure 1-11, Quicksilver flicks through apps, bookmarks, addresses—anything matching what you've typed thus far. When the bookmark you're after appears, press Return. Bam! Your browser jumps to the fore and zips you over to the bookmarked site.

If what you were after didn't jump to the top and something else came up instead, wait a second and a list of all the matching results will appear below the Quicksilver bezel. Tap the down arrow, page down, use your scroll wheel, or just type some more letters to find the match you wanted.

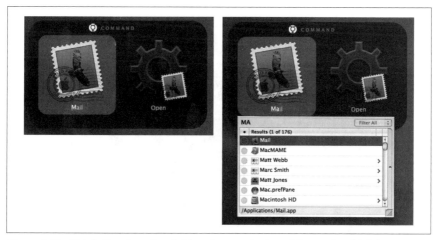

Figure 1-11. Quicksilver in action (left) and suggesting possible matches (right)

So it's a great launcher. But there's more, oh so much more.

Actions. Activate Quicksilver again Think of someone in your Address Book who has a Rolodex card full of data: business and home addresses, phone numbers, email addresses, and so forth. Type the first few letters of his first or last name (whichever is most distinctive). When he appears in the Quicksilver bezel, press the right arrow. Up pops the contents of his Address Book entry, as shown in Figure 1-12. Select an email address, hit Return, and you're composing a message to him. Choose a phone number and hit Return for an across-the-room-viewable representation of that number.

So, now we know that some items can have attached data. Neat! Now, let's take it even further. Make sure iTunes is running. Launch Quicksilver and start to type the word browse; a match titled Browse Music should come up. Hit the right arrow and you'll find yourself in what is essentially a keyboard-driven interface not unlike that of the iPod.

Files. Launch Quicksilver and type-and-hold the forward slash (/) for about one second. Your Macintosh HD appears. Hit the right arrow and you're browsing your hard drive. It's like Column View, only better. Hit the forward slash or right arrow to move forward, or use the question mark (?) or left arrow to move backward. Hit Return to open the selected item, or use any actions available to you, as discussed previously in this section.

Now, let's quickly explore the last few features before we run out of time.

Clipboard and Shelf. Launch Quicksilver and press ⌘-L to bring up the Clipboard, as shown in Figure 1-13. Anything you copy to the Clipboard ends

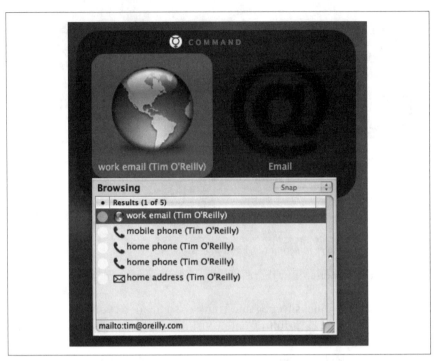

Figure 1-12. An Address Book entry found by Quicksilver

up here. Double-click any clipping to paste it into the application or document in the foreground—the equivalent of using Paste or ⌘-V.

Figure 1-13. The Quicksilver Clipboard

If the Clipboard doesn't appear to be remembering anything, visit the Clipboard Preference tab (⌘-space or equivalent → ⌘-, → Clipboard) and check Capture History and
Hide After Pasting. While you're there, you might want to
adjust the length of the Clipboard's memory (alter the number in the Capture History field).

Launch Quicksilver and type ⌘-Option-S to get to the Shelf, a pasteboard of
sorts. You can drag files, folders, bookmarks—anything drag-and-
droppable—to the Shelf for quick access. I haven't found the Shelf all that
useful, but you might.

Tweaking the Catalog. Press ⌘-space and then ⌘-; to access the Catalog of
resources that Quicksilver indexes and makes available to you. Explicitly
add something to the index, disable others, and poke about to see what
other sorts of things Quicksilver knows about. At the very least, the Catalog
provides some grist for your Quicksilver usage.

That should provide you with more than enough to chew on for some time.
When you're ready, be sure to dig into some of the unmentioned (*http://docs.
blacktree.com/*), advanced (*http://docs.blacktree.com/?page=Other+Hints*), and
untested (*http://docs.blacktree.com/?page=Untested+Features*) features of
Quicksilver. Some of the more advanced features include the ability to set
default search results, change Quicksilver's scores for items with certain
search terms, enable services to give you more actions for nearly everything,
and so on. The one downfall of the app is that it isn't well documented right
now (hence this hack), but the user forums (*http://forums.blacktree.com/
index.php?c=2*) are a great place to explore and share your discoveries.

At the time of this writing, Quicksilver is oddly devoid of any mention of
payment, despite the intense desire by anyone who uses it to pay the Black-
tree folks.

LaunchBar

LaunchBar (*http://www.obdev.at/products/launchbar*; $19.95 per seat for a
Home User license, $39 per seat for a Business User license; free evaluation
version available for download) is a much simpler app than Quicksilver. It
usually lives on the top-right edge of your Desktop and pops down from the
menu bar when called for, as shown in Figure 1-14. If you prefer it to appear
somewhere else, such as floating above the Dock or mid-screen like Quicksilver, just drag and drop it wherever you like.

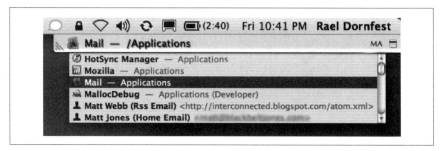

Figure 1-14. LaunchBar in action

Feeding LaunchBar's suggestions is a default set of folders, files, and applications to peek at upon startup. Each is associated with particular file types or attributes to memorize: all applications in Applications, HTML links in Internet Explorer Favorites, sound files in your Music folder, phone numbers and email addresses in Address Book and Eudora's email addresses, and anything in your Home directory. You can, and indeed should, alter this list (Configuration → Open Configuration or ⌘-Y), as shown in Figure 1-15, to suit your fancy and aid LaunchBar in its powers of suggestion.

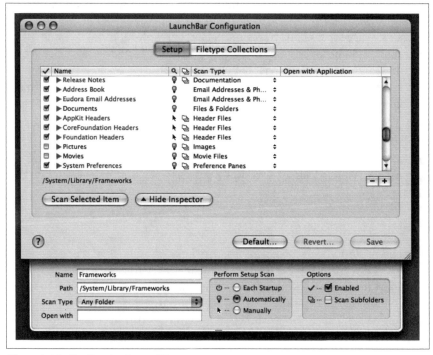

Figure 1-15. Configuring LaunchBar

LaunchBar is a commercial application (at the time of this writing, $19.95 for personal use or $39.00 per seat for business), but it sports a liberal evaluation license, the only constraint being the number of different items accessed via LaunchBar per session. While seven's the limit, you can actually go a little further if you don't mind the occasional nags. That said, it doesn't take long to decide that LaunchBar is a must-have application—unless, of course, you've already given your ⌘-space to Quicksilver.

Before you decide, though, there are still a couple more candidates to consider.

Butler

Butler (*http://www.petermaurer.de/nasi.php?thema=butler*; donateware, $18 recommended), aka *Another Launcher*, has been around for a while and undergone considerable development along the way. It's changed much more than just its name.

By default, pressing Control-space (yes, they bucked the ⌘-space trend) brings it to the front. Rather than stick to one corner of the screen, it takes center stage with a neat semitransparent window right in the middle, as shown in Figure 1-16.

Figure 1-16. Butler's main user interface window

Once again, using it is a case of typing an abbreviation, and in an instant Butler offers a list of choices for you. It offers integration with some of the built-in Apple applications and finds people in your Mail settings or Address Book. While iTunes is running, you can use Butler to start, stop, or skip tracks. Another swift key combo brings up a status window that shows what's playing and what rating you gave it. This window, like the system volume display, fades nicely in and out of view.

Butler reads bookmark files for every Mac browser (according to the documentation; I didn't have every Mac browser installed to test this out), so reaching any web site is as simple as remembering some letters from its name, although Butler does not appear to read bookmarked URLs.*

Butler really shines with its many user-configurable options, shown in Figure 1-17. Configuring which files Butler should scan is simple, and adding new hotkeys for specific actions is similarly easy. Already, dozens of pre-configured key combos are ready to use. To search Google, just press Control-space to activate Butler, then Control-Option-G to open a tiny text-entry box in your menu bar. Type your search, and then press Return. You can have dozens of combos like this, tailored to your personal habits.

Figure 1-17. Butler's preferences and configuration panel

If you prefer to use the mouse for some actions, Butler offers the choice of assigning *hot corners* to certain actions. If you wish, you can change the

---

* Does that sound odd to you? It might be a bit odd, but I'm one of those people who often remembers domains and email addresses better than I remember loved ones' birthdays. I sometimes search for web sites based on a domain or a path stub that sticks in mind.

Google search action to something like "Option-click in bottom-right corner" instead of the default keyboard combo.

By default, Butler runs without a Dock icon, so accessing basic functions is done via a small widget in the menu bar. This can also be changed to a small docklet that lurks in the top-left of your screen, as shown in Figure 1-18. For people with crowded menu bars, this might be helpful.

Figure 1-18. Butler's control docklet

Butler is a neat package with so much flexibility to offer it's hard to know where to start. Many users might find they need to spend several weeks using Butler to get it tailored perfectly to their needs.

The only apparent downsides are the lack of application-switching, which is so easy in LaunchBar, and the occasional, unwelcome presence of the infamous OS X spinning beach ball. Though the latter issue occurs on my G3 iBook, I suspect it wouldn't be as much of a concern on more up-to-date machines.

A Better Finder Launcher

A Better Finder Launcher (*http://www.publicspace.net/AbetterFinderLauncher*; $9.95 for a single user license, $24.95 with forever upgrade; $49.95 for a site license, $99.95 with forever upgrade; trial available), or ABFL, takes quite a different approach. The interface is split into different tabs, as shown in Figure 1-19, and it's up to you to flick to the correct one (using ⌘-arrow) depending on what you're looking for: applications, documents, or folders.

This is a bit of a disadvantage, because it adds another level of control that the other launchers don't require. Also, there's less flexibility in what you can type to find a particular item. You need to type the first few letters of the item's name, rather than any letters from the name. This works fine and quickly for things you know and use regularly, but if you want to dig out a file you haven't used for some time and can't remember the precise name you gave it, you're stuck.

A Better Finder Launcher is just a launcher, and it offers none of the bells and whistles of other applications covered here—no Finder replacement, no

Figure 1-19. ABFL's main interface window, after a search for items starting with "omni"

playlist browsing, no Address Book integration. But that's not necessarily a bad thing. Some people like applications that just do one thing, because they tend to do it well.

The settings and preferences are fairly limited, allowing you to add folders and file types you want scanned. There's no way to change the keyboard command used to initiate a new search; you're stuck using Control-⌘-L, a shortcut I found a little unwieldy.

—Dan Dickinson and Giles Turnbull

HACK #5 Wear Multiple Hats, Run Multiple Desktops

Stretch your screen real estate up to 100 times its size and organize different views of your workspace with virtual desktop software.

There's an old home-brew computer adage: "He with the most RAM wins." With RAM prices eminently affordable, CPU speeds accelerating, and disk space expanding at an alarming rate, the braggart's next frontier is monitor size—particularly of the flat-panel variety.

Not everyone can afford the 23" Apple Cinema HD Display (*http://www. apple.com/displays/acd23*). Even those of us spanning our 12" PowerBook screen across to a 17" Apple Studio Display (*http://www.apple.com/displays/ asd17*) could use a skosh more room from time to time—particularly when we're on the road and absolutely limited to our 12" display.

You can achieve some of the same effect (*wow!* factor not included) for as little as $0 with virtual desktop software. By emulating a number of separate desktops arranged (virtually, at least) alongside, above, and below one another, you can add quite a bit of elbow room, even on that otherwise rather teensy 12" screen. Think of it as an elastic waistband for your Mac, akin to those you find in jeans for people approaching 40.

Desktop Manager

At the top of the list for its feature-to-cost ratio is the rather plainly dubbed Desktop Manager (*http://wsmanager.sourceforge.net*; donateware, under the GNU Public License). In typical open source fashion, rather than touting the wonders of the app, smack dab in the middle of Desktop Manager's home page you'll find a rather uninviting, albeit friendly, warning:

> To implement virtual desktops, I've had to delve into the internals of OS X and reverse-engineer some functionality. There is no official way to implement virtual desktops (other programs have to do equally devious tricks). Consequently I appologise [*sic*] if this does weird things to your system but it works for me.

If you like, you can heed the warning and skip ahead in this hack to "Code-Tek VirtualDesktop." I didn't pay attention to the warning, though, and I have been enamored with Desktop Manager ever since.

Desktop Manager is a piece of work. You're allowed a seemingly endless number of desktops, all completely independent of one another. Applications live across individual desktops, so you can have a couple Safari windows here, four more over there, and so on. The pager, status bar, and/or current desktop name float in the corner of the desktop, as shown in Figure 1-20, allowing you to keep track of just where you are.

Figure 1-20. Desktop Manager's (from left to right) pager, menu bar, and desktop name

Sporting active edges, keyboard shortcuts, and pagers of various sorts, there's a navigation system for everyone. While I seem to be stuck in a bit of a rut using ⌘-Option-left arrow and -right arrow to leap from desktop to desktop, you can also combine ⌘-Option with the numerals 1–9 to leap to a particular desktop—that is, if you can remember which desktop is 1 and which 4. If you're a mouser, simply mouse your way off the left or right edge of one desktop onto the other. You'll want to spend a little time experimenting with the sensitivity (Preferences... → Active Edges → "Delay before switching") to get things just where you want them; otherwise, you'll find it all just a little too fiddly.

While you can't drag an application or window from one desktop to another, you can send it there by selecting its name from Current Desktop in the Desktop Manager menu and choosing another desktop to which to move it. In Figure 1-21, I'm moving this hack's Microsoft Word document to my Write desktop.

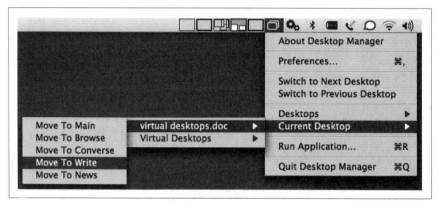

Figure 1-21. Moving a window to another desktop

Desktop Manager is incredibly configurable, thanks to a comprehensive yet intuitive Preferences panel, which you'll find by clicking the Desktop Manager menu bar icon (the center icon in Figure 1-20). Any time you feel you need a tad more room, add another desktop in the Desktops Preferences pane, shown in Figure 1-22.

While you're there, try out a few of the switch transitions for some mind-boggling Quartzian transforms between desktops.

 Don't forget to turn off the effects, or you may just end up unfairly disliking Desktop Manager.

The most interesting feature I found is that upon quitting Desktop Manager (I know, why would you?) you can choose to gather all your various belongings into the current single desktop or leave them where they are. If you gather them, they all slowly fade onto the screen before your eyes and you're back to your comparatively puny screen real estate. If you leave them where they are, you won't be able to get to them until you fire up Desktop Manager again, at which time they will all appear where you left them, as if by magic. (Just why you'd want to do this is, quite frankly, beyond me, but it's rather nifty anyway.)

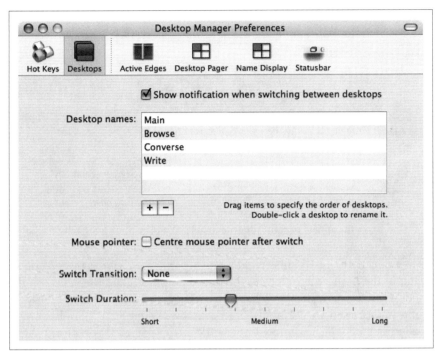

Figure 1-22. Configuring desktops and selecting a switch transition

Desktop Manager is by far the best virtual desktop application for the money (or lack of it). About the only oddity I found was having to hunt down iChat windows I'd left on another desktop before the person trying to reach me gave up and wandered off. CodeTek VirtualDesktop solves this problem with its stickiness settings.

CodeTek VirtualDesktop

The CodeTek VirtualDesktop (*http://www.codetek.com/ctvd*: $20 for Lite; $40 for Pro; trial available), or CTVD, is much like Desktop Manager in both base feature set and operation. Switch desktops using keyboard shortcuts, with your mouse, or by selecting one from the menu bar. Keep track of where you are with the pager and/or menu bar icon.

CTVD really shines by fully embracing the illusion that you're working in a large space where only your current view is restricted by the size of your monitor. Flipping from desktop to desktop is more like moving your window on a larger world than visiting another space entirely. You can drag applications between desktops, either by picking them up and doing so manually or by pushing their iconographic representations around in the pager, as shown in Figure 1-23. You can even end up with a window that spans two desktops, completing the illusion.

Figure 1-23. Dragging windows between desktops in the pager

You can *skin* (change the appearance of) the pager to match your desktop background or your purse. Create your own or download one from CodeTek's site (*http://www.codetek.com/ ctvd/virtual_skins.php*). While I've never quite understood the appeal of skins, they never fail to impress the young folk.

Switch directly to a particular window on a particular desktop by clicking its avatar in the pager; there's no need to switch desktops and then click on the window you're interested in. When you click an application icon in the Dock, you're transported to the app's front window, wherever it may be. Or, if you're not sure which window on which desktop you're looking for, browse for it and select it from the CTVD menu bar icon, as shown in Figure 1-24.

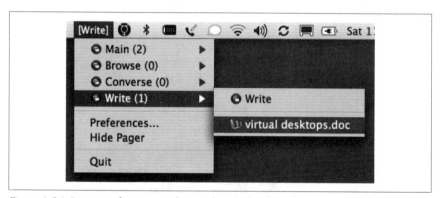

Figure 1-24. Browsing for a particular window in the menu bar

CodeTek VirtualDesktop is ultraconfigurable. Pin particular applications down so that they appear on every desktop, as shown in Figure 1-25; I do this with iChat so that I don't have to roam my desktops in search of an active chat window every time I hear the distant "pop" of a buddy popping by.

Both Desktop Manager and CodeTek Virtual Desktop work miraculously well; they both support even the Quartz goodness of Exposé. If you're short

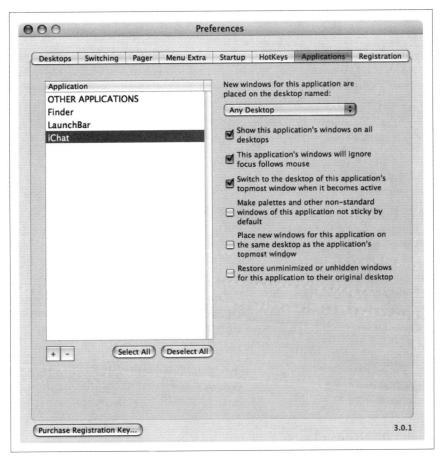

Figure 1-25. Tweaking CTVD's veritable cornucopia of preferences

on cash, Desktop Manager is a steal. If you're looking for something a little more polished that sports some nice extras, CodeTek VirtualDesktop is a must-have for the multitasking geek in you. Be sure to compare the features (*http://www.codetek.com/ctvd/virtual_features.php*) of the Lite and Pro versions before you buy. Since I'm not that fond of mousing between windows and don't care much for the extra visual bells and whistles (e.g., custom wallpapers for each desktop), about the only reason I could find to pony up for the Pro version was the focus-follows-mouse feature (i.e., raise windows simply by mousing over them, without ever having to click), but that feature might just be worth the extra $20 in and of itself.

Space.app

Space.app (*http://sourceforge.net/projects/space*; GPL open source license, free for personal and commercial use) is a rather limited virtual desktop app, especially considering it is about the same price (a donation) as the amazing Desktop Manager.

Rather than create actual virtual screens, Space.app operates by remembering which application is shown or hidden in each *view* (aka screen). You cannot, for instance, have two windows from the same application open in two different spaces; it's the entire app or nothing at all. The refresh when switching from screen to screen is also a little jerky, because applications are hidden and shown before your very eyes.

The project appears to have stalled, but both the application and its source are available for you to experiment with.

Keyboard and Mouse Shortcuts

Go beyond the menu, keep your hands on the keyboard at all times, and work faster than before.

The Mac was the computer that brought the mouse and point-and-click computing to the masses. But even as powerful as the mouse is, the use of keyboard shortcuts is an important part of the modern computing experience. Let's face it, hitting ⌘-S is a heck of a lot faster than taking your hand off the keyboard, finding the mouse, and then using the File → Save menu.

But using the mouse and keyboard is not an either/or situation. There are actually a few ways in which you can use the keyboard and mouse *together* to perform actions quickly.

Modifying Keyboard Shortcuts

Most applications provide a fairly reasonable set of keyboard shortcuts for menu items, but not all do. And even those that do don't always provide the most reasonable set of shortcuts. You were once stuck with whatever the maker of an application decided to provide, but no longer. In Panther, you can now set the keyboard shortcut for any menu of any application.

To access this feature, launch System Preferences and navigate to the Keyboard & Mouse Preferences panel, as shown in Figure 1-26.

Being able to tweak and add to this list of shortcuts is pretty nifty. However, we've found one neat way to hack this panel that makes using our Macs much better. How many times have you opened a batch of windows or tabs in Safari for later research and then accidentally hit ⌘-Q instead of ⌘-W and lost all of your reading in progress? Well, we've done this—along with the accompanying slap to the forehead—more times that we can count.

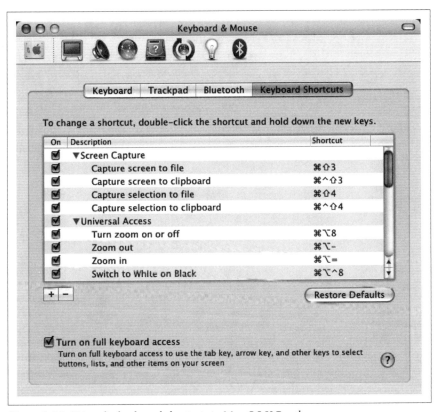

Figure 1-26. Using the keyboard shortcuts in Mac OS X Panther

As soon as we found the ability to remap keys in the System Preferences, we solved our problem by remapping File → Quit Safari from ⌘-Q to ⌘-Option-Q. Simply click the + button and then define the fields as shown in Figure 1-27.

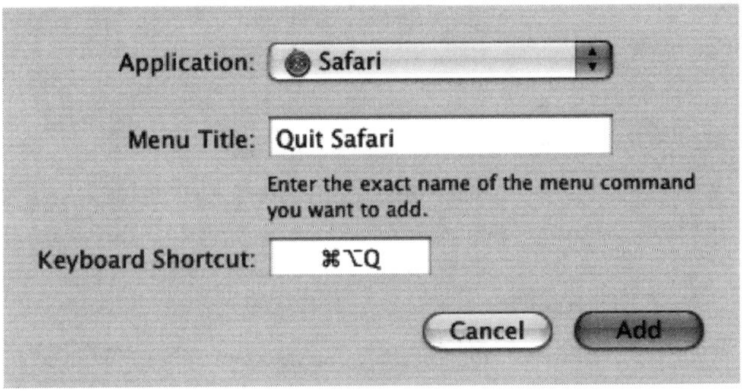

Figure 1-27. Remapping an existing shortcut

Menu Master

If the Keyboard & Mouse Preferences pane doesn't give you enough control over your keyboard shortcuts, you'll want to look into Menu Master. Menu Master (*http://www.unsanity.com/haxies/menumaster*; $10, trial version available) is a *haxie* (a termed coined by Unsanity to mean "hack") that allows you to customize the shortcuts on your application menus.

To show how Menu Master works, we're going to look at TextEdit. As shown in Figure 1-28, TextEdit's Window → Zoom menu item does not have a shortcut key assigned.

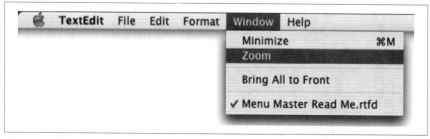

Figure 1-28. TextEdit's Window → Zoom menu without a shortcut

To assign a shortcut key to the menu item, simply select it and then press the key combination you want—for example, Option-⌘-Z. The shortcut will then be assigned to the menu item, as shown in Figure 1-29.

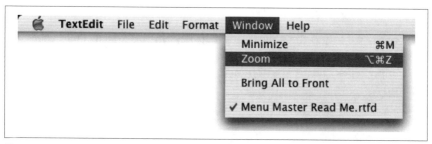

Figure 1-29. Using Menu Master to assign a shortcut

If you assign a key combination that has already been assigned (for example, ⌘-C), your latest key assignment will take precedent. So, before you assign a shortcut, be sure to check that the key combination has not been used before.

> Menu Master really comes into its own when you want to assign keyboard shortcuts to items in the AppleScript menu—something that the Keyboard & Mouse Preferences pane can't do.

Reclaiming Your Laptop's F Keys

On PowerBooks and iBooks, various function keys have been used to control screen brightness, audio volume, and the number lock. The latest PowerBooks have taken over even more of the function keys with controls for the backlighting of the keyboard. To access the normal functions of these keys, you must push the Fn key at the bottom-left of the keyboard. Over the years, quite a few people have wished that this behavior was reversed (i.e., that you had to push the Fn key to access the screen brightness controls).

A silent update in 10.3.3 grants this wish. In the Keyboard & Mouse Preferences panel, a checkbox now allows you to use the function keys for custom actions, as shown in Figure 1-30.

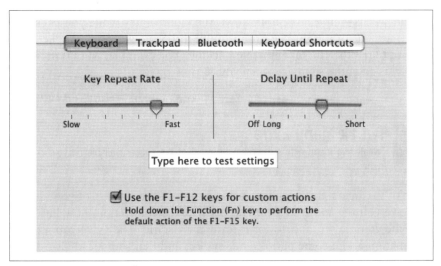

Figure 1-30. Reclaiming the F1 to F12 function keys

Using the Keyboard and Mouse to Switch Apps

No doubt you've played with Exposé [Hack #1] to switch between open windows. But if you use the mouse and keyboard together, you can switch windows even more gracefully. For example, if you've left the Exposé keyboard mappings with their default settings, press and hold down the F9 key. While all your open windows are spread out across the screen, mouse over the window you want to pop to the foreground. There's no need to click on the window; just release the F9 key and the window you selected will pop to the top.

We also found, much to our surprise, that this trick works when switching applications with Alt-Tab. Try it. Press and hold down the Alt and Tab keys.

Now, instead of hitting Tab → Tab → Tab to move the highlight between applications, scrub across the applications with your mouse. When you've highlighted the application you want, release the Alt and Tab keys. Voilà! The application you selected will pop to the top of your screen.

Don't Forget the Click Modifier Keys

Over the years, Apple has received quite a bit of criticism for shipping a one-button mouse. That criticism has only increased since the release of Mac OS X, because all the Unix and Windows switchers that have picked up the platform are used to mice with a plethora of buttons.

Of course, you can plug in a multibutton mouse, but what if you don't always have that option? Say you're on an airplane with your PowerBook. The answer is simple. Just hold down the Control key while you click; it's the equivalent of a right click on a multibutton mouse. Some applications also support other modifiers while clicking. For example, Microsoft Word highlights an entire sentence when you ⌘-click on it.

—*Wei Meng Lee and James Duncan Davidson*

Tweak Menu Extras
HACK #7
Tweak two menu extras to make the most of the space available on your menu bar.

Most of the menu extras—those icons sitting in the top-left of your screen that give you the status of your AirPort wireless connection, how loud you have the volume set, and so forth—are fairly static. They give you a bit of information about some part of your system and that's about it. Two menu items, however, by default take up quite a bit of space and might not be giving you the information you need—or not enough information to justify taking up the gobs of space that they do. These are the clock and the fast user switching menus, as shown in Figure 1-31.

Figure 1-31. Default menu extras

But never fear; there's a way to tame these menu extras and reclaim some space on your menu bar.

Clock

The first way to tame the clock and modify how it appears is to open up the
Date & Time Preferences pane, as shown in Figure 1-32. Here, you can set
whether to show the day of the week, use a 12- or 24-hour clock, or display
the AM and PM labels. You can even reduce the clock to a simple analog
clock that is quite nice, though it's a bit small for some people to see well.

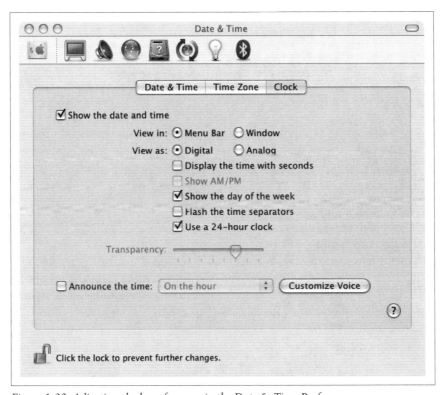

Figure 1-32. Adjusting clock preferences in the Date & Time Preferences pane

Unfortunately, the Date & Time Preferences pane doesn't give you a way to
put the date in the menu bar. However, a posting on the Mac OS X Hints
web site (*http://www.macosxhints.com*) tipped us off on how to do this. Basically, the clock reads a format string from your global preferences file. To
take a look at these format strings, enter the following command:

```
$ defaults read -g AppleICUTimeFormatStrings
{
    1 = "HH':'mm";
    2 = "HH':'mm':'ss";
    3 = "HH':'mm':'ss z";
    4 = "HH':'mm':'ss z";
}
```

The second key controls the clock format. For example, if you want to see the month and day along with the time of day, enter in the following command:

```
$ defaults write -g AppleICUTimeFormatStrings -dict-add 2 "MM'/'dd' 'HH':
'mm':'ss"
```

After executing this command, click and unclick one of the settings in the Date & Time Preferences pane and you'll see the date show up in the menu bar, as shown in Figure 1-33.

Figure 1-33. The date in the menu bar

If you want (or need) to return this setting to the default, enter in the following command:

```
$ defaults write -g AppleICUTimeFormatStrings -dict-add 2 "'HH':'mm':'ss"
```

Fast User Switching

Fast user switching is a great new feature in Panther. We really have only one issue with it and that's how much space your username can take up in the menu bar. Fortunately, Wincent Colaiuta has come to the rescue with WinSwitch (*http://winswitch.wincent.com*; donateware, 10–20 euros suggested). WinSwitch is a menu extra that gives you access to fast user switching through a menu that doesn't take up much real estate, as shown in Figure 1-34.

Figure 1-34. The WinSwitch menu extra

Not only can you have a generic icon show up in the menu bar, but WinSwitch also lets you show the current user image, the short username, and even the original behavior of the long username

HACK #8 Incorporate Services into Your Workflow

The Services menu is an integral part of the tricked-out Mac OS X environment.

The Services menu is perhaps the most overlooked built-in in all of Mac OS X, despite being a powerful part of the alpha geek's workflow. *Services* are snippets of functionality exported from Mac OS X itself and the apps you have in your Applications folder.

Think of services as context menu items (such as those you find after a ⌘- or right-click) that draw in external functionality and bring them to bear on what you're currently working with. Select the text of a reminder emailed by a friend into a sticky (Mail → Services → Make New Sticky Note) on your Desktop without having to launch Stickies (*Applications/Stickies*), copy, and paste. Highlight a technical term in any document and Google for it (Text-Edit → Services → Search With Google). Select a file anywhere in the Finder and send it via email (Finder → Services → Mail → Send File).

Perhaps the Services menu would be more widely used if it were indeed made available by ⌘- or right-click context menu.

It behooves you to give Services a whirl, working it into your daily work-flow. Even if you just end up using the odd service here or there, you'll find it grows on you in no time flat.

The default set of services in Mac OS X, shown in Figure 1-35, includes fold-ers for Finder (with Open, Reveal, and Show Info), the Grab screenshot app (with Screen, Selection, and Timed Selection), Mail (with Send Selection and Send To), Make New Sticky Note, Open URL (previously called *Net Ser-vices*), Script Editor, Search With Google, Send File To Bluetooth Device..., Speech (Start Speaking Text and Stop Speaking), Summarize, and TextEdit (New Window Containing Selection and Open Selected File).

These services are built into the system. Any additional services that might show up were either installed by other programs automatically or manu-ally by you; additional services should all be located in */Library/Services* or *~/Library/Services*, your own personal library of services in your home directory. Anytime you wish to install more services, you'll put them in one

Figure 1-35. Panther's default Services menu

of these two folders, depending on whether you want to make them available to all users on your machine or keep them to yourself.

One of the reasons most folks don't bother using the Services menu—assuming they even know of its existence—is that they find its inconsistency rather confounding. Not all services are available at all times, in all applications, and under all circumstances. If you navigate to your Services menu right now in the Finder without anything selected, several of the submenus (such as Grab's submenu, for instance) will remain entirely grayed out and unavailable to you. Many of the services that are available for use function properly only with something selected.

For example, if I choose Finder → Services → Speech → Start Speaking Text from the Finder without selecting anything first, rather than prompt me for a file or summarily ignoring me, my computer says "C. K. Sample's Desktop." Likewise, choosing Finder → Services → Mail → Send Selection from the Finder without selecting anything causes Mail to attempt to send the entire Desktop folder attached to an email message. However, if you first select a file that you do want to send to someone and then choose Finder → Services → Mail → Send Selection, Mail starts a new message with that file attached. It's all a matter of context; if you can get used to that—and it's well worth getting used to—then services make a whole lot of sense.

Screenshot Services

Although the Grab submenu is nonfunctional in the Finder (and Grab itself is not the best screenshot composer out there, since it produces PDFs of full-screen shots and the Grab menu is always visible), Grab can be useful from within iChat. Navigating to iChat → Services → Grab → Screen in mid conversation automatically launches Grab, takes a screenshot, and places that screenshot in your foremost iChat window, ready to send.

This is much quicker than launching my screen-capture program of choice, FreeSnap (*http://www.efritz.net/software.html*), taking the screenshot, and then locating the file and dragging it into the iChat window. This service can prove invaluable by quickly and visually instructing long-distance friends and family. Telling Dad that he can find Disk Utility in the Utilities folder in the Application folder inside his hard drive is one thing. Sending him a quick series of screenshots in iChat, showing him where exactly that is and how to get there, is entirely another.

Text Services

Some of the most powerful services, both built-ins and third-party, are text-based services. For example, say you are busy typing up a report for your boss. He calls you up and says that he's having an impromptu meeting in 15 minutes with his superiors and he wants to present a three-minute overview of the 10-page report you are in the process of writing. Rather than scramble to pull together a legible series of note cards that he can refer to in his meeting, you lean on the handy Summarize service.

> If you are working in Word (at least in Word X), you'll notice that Summarize, along with the rest of the Services menu, is not available to you. You'll need to get your text over to a services-enabled text editor. Select all your text (Edit → Select All or ⌘-A) and copy it (Edit → Copy or ⌘-C). Launch TextEdit and paste in (Edit → Paste or ⌘-V) the text from your Word document.

In TextEdit, select all the text (Edit → Select All or ⌘-A) and then choose TextEdit → Services → Summarize. Up comes the Summary service with a shortened form; the quality varies greatly, depending on the type, length, and variability of the writing. Figure 1-36 shows a summarized version of the opening paragraphs of Jane Austen's *Emma*.

You can specify the service to summarize sentences or paragraphs, sliding your way between shorter and longer versions. To open a new TextEdit document that contains the summarized version for fine-tuning, select

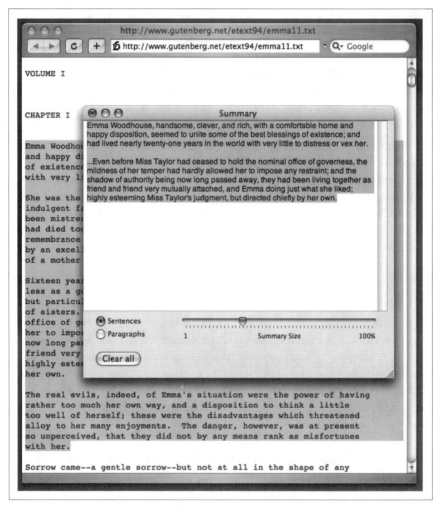

Figure 1-36. Summary service, mulling over Jane Austen's Emma

SummaryService → Services → TextEdit → New Window Containing Selection. If your Mac's algorithms put together a summary good enough for the purpose at hand, or if your boss called in the request from out of town, you can simply mail it to him right in his meeting by using SummaryService → Services → Mail → Send Selection.

You can also use this service from within Safari to post a summary of a long article online.

> If you are still using Internet Explorer, it's time to switch. IE does not, and probably will never, support services.

Devon Technologies is a purveyor of some rather nice third-party text services (*http://www.devon-technologies.com/freeware.php*; freeware). Anti-WordService enables any plain text–capable Cocoa application to open Microsoft Word documents; it makes use of the Unix command-line utility antiword. WordService provides 34 functions to convert, format, or speak selected text; insert data; show statistics on your selection; and more. CalcService calculates the result of a selected formula and either appends the result to the formula or replaces the formula with the result.

Lookup Services

Highlight text in any document, web page, or email message and type ⌘-Shift-L (or select Services → Search With Google from the current application's menu) to search Google for it.

Nisus Software offers a free Nisus Thesaurus (*http://www.nisus.com/Thesaurus*), complete with its own Services menu for us writers looking for that ~~right correct~~ precise wording.

And if you happen across an unfamiliar Klingon word on your favorite Trek-kie (or Trekker) newsgroup, use the MacSword Lookup service, which comes free with MacSword (*http://www.macsword.com*), to search for all appearances of that word in the *Klingon Language Version of the World English Bible*. There's something for everyone in the Services menu, I tell you!

Mail Services

To start a new email message with the selected text inserted or file or folder attached, highlight any text, file, or folder and select Services → Mail → Send Selection To from your current services-aware app. To compose mail to a specific person, highlight an email address (assuming it's not already hyper-linked to a *mailto:*, in which just clicking it will work) and select Services → Mail → Send To.

Bluetooth Services

Wondering just what mischief you can get up to with your Bluetooth-enabled PowerBook and Bluetooth-enabled cellphone or PDA? Send a copy of a public domain book from Project Gutenberg (*http://www.gutenberg.net*) over for e-book reading in the palm of your hand on the morning bus or train. Simply select the file on the Desktop, select Finder → Services → Send File To Bluetooth Device... (or ⌘-Shift-B), and Bluetooth it on over [Hack #86].

Devon Technologies' BlueService (*http://www.devon-technologies.com/freeware.php*) provides a select-and-send service for any plain or rich text from any Cocoa app (and certain Carbon apps that support the Services menu). All you need on the other end is a Bluetooth-capable device that supports OBEX Object Push or OBEX File Transfer, which your cellphone, PDA, and Mac/PC are bound to support. This is incredibly useful for sending short messages to yourself or nearby friends, MapQuest driving directions to your PDA, party details to a friend's phone, a shopping list to your spouse's handheld, and so forth. If you were feeling adventurous, you could script appointment reminders, breaking news, and other alerts to flow from your Mac to any mobile device currently in Bluetooth range, creating a broadcast network of information for your own personal area.

> Just such a thing has been done, albeit for Linux, by a clever hacker named Collin Mulliner (*http://www.mulliner.org/bluetooth*). His Bluetooth Joke of the Day sends the joke of the day to nearby devices, Bluetooth FileSystemMapping provides command-line access to Bluetooth devices as if they were local filesystems, and btChat is a Rendezvous-like chat app that uses Bluetooth.

Other Third-Party Services

Third-party standalone services and those advertised by third-party apps abound, as you can see in my tricked-out Services menu in Figure 1-37.

I'm a bit of a services junkie, I have to admit. Here are a few more I've accreted and found useful along the way.

Devon Technologies' DEVONthink personal database program and other similar programs, such as Chronos Software's StickyBrain (*http://www.chronosnet.com/&/products/sb_index.html*), use the Services menu to allow swift import of selected data into their databases.

If you want to grab a copy of a web page or entire web site for offline reading, WebGrabber (*http://www.epicware.com/webgrabber.html*) has a Grab URL service.

Search your mail archive in "Search Your Mail with ZOË" [Hack #38] or selected text via the ZOEService service. You'll find it in the *Zoe/Extra* folder; just drag it to your personal or systemwide *Library/Services* folder.

If you are a programmer, you'll enjoy the convenience of the Script Editor (*http://www.apple.com/applescript/scripteditor/11.html*), PerlPad (*http://perl-pad.sourceforge.net*), and ShellService (*http://www.apple.com/downloads/macosx/unix_open_source/shellservice.html*) services. ShellService adds an

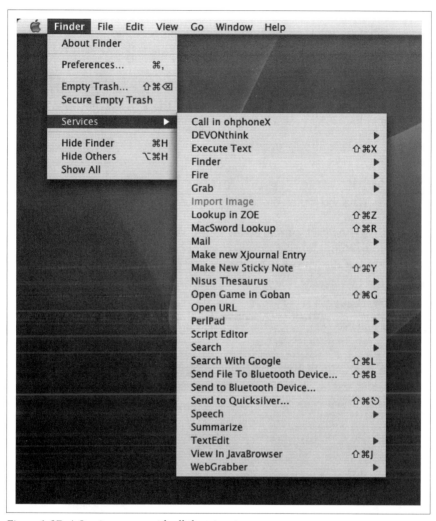

Figure 1-37. A Services menu with all the trimmings

Execute Text command that treats any highlighted text as fodder for the command line [Hack #91].

An Office Proviso

At the time of this writing, services don't work with Microsoft products, notably Office X, which greatly limits the applicability of this remarkable functionality at the office. However, according to word on the street, the next major release of Microsoft Office for OS X (Office 2004) will at least partially support the Services menu. For many users, this little bit of compatibility will serve as the missing link in making the Services menu an indispensable part of their daily workflow.

Final Thoughts

Office aside, the moment you start using Mac OS X's services—particularly if you assign keyboard shortcuts [Hack #6] to the services you use consistently—you'll wonder how you ever got along without them.

—*C. K. Sample III*

Autocomplete Your Words
Use old-school hacker word completion in modern GUI applications.

If you've used the *bash* or *tcsh* shells in the Terminal [Hack #91] for any length of time, you've no doubt become accustomed to being able to complete filenames by using the Tab key. Just in case you haven't discovered this, we're talking about typing the following into a shell:

```
$ cd ~/Si[tab]
```

The shell replies:

```
$ cd ~/Sites/
```

This is a hallmark feature of Unix applications that many hackers have grown to love over the years. Several people we know won't ever stop using the Emacs text editor because of its ability to complete words. Wouldn't it be cool if you could do something similar in all of your applications? Well, many applications on the system actually do support word completion, including TextEdit, Safari, and Xcode.

To activate this feature, type the beginning of a word and then press Option-Esc. A box shows you the choices of words to complete, as shown in Figure 1-38.

In TextEdit, the list of words to complete are sourced from your spell-checking dictionary. The same is true in Safari, where you can use Option-Esc in the Google search box, as shown in Figure 1-39.

To add words to the dictionary used by the spell checker, and therefore by the autocomplete functionality, open the Spelling dialog box in a Cocoa application (such as TextEdit), type the word into the text field, and click the Learn button.

In Xcode, the autocompletion functionality works a bit differently. Instead of using the spell-checking dictionary, Xcode uses a list of words specific to

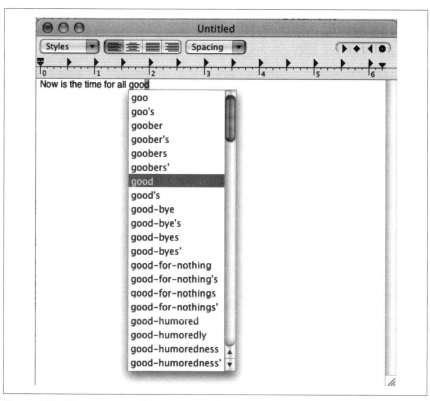

Figure 1-38. Using autocompletion in TextEdit

Figure 1-39. Using autocompletion in Safari

the language and project in which you are working. For example, if you are editing an Objective-C source file, Xcode presents a list of autocomplete possibilities that makes sense for that file, as shown in Figure 1-40.

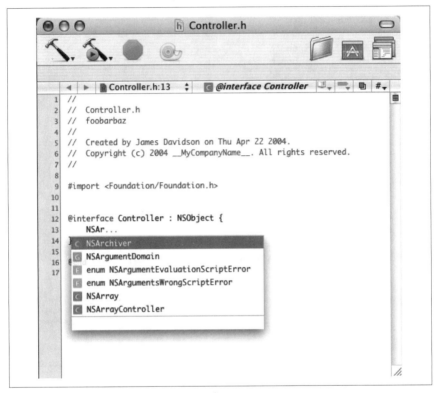

Figure 1-40. Using auto completion in Xcode

If you fool around a bit in other applications, you're sure to find other places where you can use text-completion to your advantage.

—*Wei Meng Lee and James Duncan Davidson*

HACK #10   Get Sidetracked

SideTrack makes your tired trackpad go to 11, adding scroll areas, extra buttons, keystroke equivalents, and more.

Trackpads have always struck me as less than optimal devices. For one thing, they're always in the way. As I type away on a laptop, my thumbs appear to have a life of their own, tapping and moving the mouse about at will. And even when I do intend to use the trackpad, my accuracy is nowhere near what it is with a mouse. Moving a mouse has become second nature to me; the trackpad still has me fumbling about, concentrating on controlling my fingers more than the mouse pointer.

So, when I got a laptop, I started dragging a mouse around with it. There are a number of reasons this doesn't always work, though. The mouse takes up room in an already-overloaded bag, requires a flat surface, and either adds to an already tangled web of cables around my workspace or chews through batteries if I go wireless. It's all but useless on those teensy airplane tray tables, worse when you're trying to work while sitting on the ground, and an unmitigated disaster in the car—even when I'm not the one driving.

At some point, the convenience of the trackpad won out over the mouse, but not by much. Often, I ended up carrying a mouse around "just in case."

My trackpad all but transformed into a different input device when I installed SideTrack (*http://www.ragingmenace.com/software/sidetrack*; freeware) from Raging Menace Software. SideTrack is a mouse driver that radically changes the way you think about and use that little rectangle of traction. No longer just for moving the mouse pointer about, SideTrack allows you to remap portions of your trackpad into a scroll bar, additional buttons, or even virtual keystrokes.

Currently, I have the right side of my trackpad set up for vertical scrolling, the bottom for horizontal scrolling, the trackpad off entirely while I'm typing, and the keypad tap emulating a right mouse-click. Figure 1-41 shows my settings in SideTrack's System Preferences pane (Apple Menu → System Preferences → SideTrack).

SideTrack is a download, double-click, and install application, but it does require a restart for the drivers to be recognized and take effect. Upon first visiting the Preferences pane, SideTrack has you calibrate its understanding of the size and proportions of your trackpad by moving your fingers around the active edges in a clockwise direction until it's satisfied it knows quite enough.

The SideTrack pane sports four tabs: Trackpad, Scrolling, Corners, and Advanced. Tracking contains your standard trackpad options, such as tracking and double-click speed, as well as not-so-standard options, such as setting your button click, trackpad tap, and whether your trackpad is active during typing.

Scrolling sets the location and size of vertical and horizontal trackpad scrolling areas, if you want them, along with scrolling speed. Scrolling areas are just like a mouse's scroll wheel—just very flat.

Corners lets you create corner buttons, allowing you to emulate the left mouse button (mouse button 1), the right mouse button (mouse button 2),

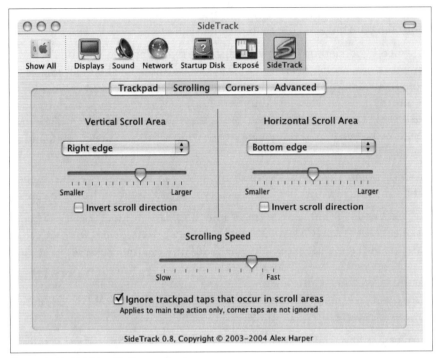

Figure 1-41. SideTrack's System Preferences pane

mouse buttons 3–6, or a keystroke with the tap of a finger. The mouse buttons 3–6 struck me as overkill—that is, until I read through SideTrack's FAQ, which mentioned that you can set buttons 3, 4, and 5 as keys for controlling Exposé [Hack #6] from your trackpad. Do give this a whirl; it's rather a lot of fun.

Finally, the Advanced tab allows you to recalibrate the trackpad (or, conversely, reset it to its defaults) and use different acceleration algorithms. Switching acceleration types modifies how the mouse speeds up over time when it detects continuing motion in a single direction. Each of the types has its own feel, and they're all different. The Mac OS X trackpad acceleration is slow and doesn't change much, but it is more accurate. The Redmond switcher acceleration is much faster than the other two options; it's great for zooming across the screen but harder to hit a point accurately. Mac OS X mouse acceleration is somewhere in the middle. Try each in turn until you find one you like, or just pretend you can tell the difference.

The plethora of option combinations can provide hours of titillation, and you look furiously busy to boot. Input devices are so personal that any specific recommendations are bound to fall flat.

It's worth the time and effort to find just the right settings for you. For me, it was like finding the trackpad for the first time. Sit down with your laptop, go about your usual tracking, clicking, and scrolling, and pay some level of attention to just how you tend to use the trackpad and when it doesn't provide what you're after. Do you use the edges, or does your finger stay pretty well dead-center? Do you use the entire width of the trackpad or repeatedly pick up and move your finger? Throw a switch here, press a button there, and try out your tweaked settings for a little while. Even if you think you'll hate a particular function, give it a whirl anyway. I had suspected the vertical scroll would be something I'd repeatedly trip over, but it turns out I can't use it enough.

SideTrack author Alex Harper suggests a few more usage ideas:

- Map the bottom-left and -right corners to ⌘-[(previous page) and ⌘-] (next page) for trackpad web browsing.

- Map the top- and bottom-right buttons to the Page Up and Page Down keys, respectively, for skimming long documents.

- Map a corner tap to your preferred launcher, such as LaunchBar or Quicksilver [Hack #4].

- Switch virtual desktops [Hack #5] with a tap in one of four invisibly mapped quadrants.

About the only complaint I have is that the corner buttons are hard to click. Even when I turn them up to their largest size, I still have to tap a number of times to find the corner. Having found the spot, I find it hard to do so consistently. Really, the spot needs to be a lot bigger at its largest setting.

Also, sometimes the trackpad seems to stick a little when using the smaller default settings, particularly when you start moving your finger across an item set aside for scrolling. Move out of the scrolling areas and try again, and it should work just fine.

HACK #11 eMac, Meet eBook

Turn your Mac into a big, beautiful e-book reader, thanks to the wonders of Preview.

It likely comes as no big news to you that you can open PDFs and images of various other flavors in Preview (Applications → Preview). But it never fails to surprise people that they've somehow managed to overlook the fact that you can hop into full-screen mode (View → Full Screen) to view these images and pages without all the clutter of anything else you happen to have open to distract you from their stunning Quartz-rendered visage.

eMac, Meet eBook

Just as iDVD's full-screen mode transforms your Mac into a little movie theater, so too does Preview's full-screen view turn your 23" Apple Cinema Display (or, more likely, your iBook's 12" screen) into a rather nice e-book, as shown in Figure 1-42.

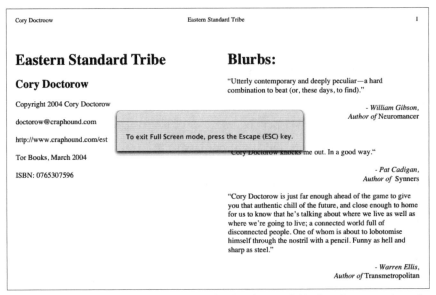

Figure 1-42. Cory Doctorow's Eastern Standard Tribe (available from http://craphound. com/est/ under a Creative Commons License), viewed in Preview's full-screen mode

Flip forward page by page with a click of your mouse or rap on your spacebar. The Page Up, Page Down, and arrow keys move you forward and backward, while Home takes you to the first page and End (surprise!) to the end of the document.

Exposé [Hack #1] continues to work, so you can temporarily switch to another program using the F9 key, a defined hot Exposé corner, or by using the basic Application Switcher (⌘-Tab). Switch back to Preview, and you're right back in full-screen mode. Hit the Esc key to return to normal, fully cluttered view.

And it gets even better for iBook and PowerBook owners. This newfound ability to use your Mac as an electronic book means being able to tote about the Library of Alexandria—or at least what's available in Project Gutenberg (*http://www.gutenberg.net*)—without adding an ounce to your load.

If your PDF is formatted in standard page layout (as most are), rotate it left or right (View → Rotate Left or View → Rotate Right) just before going full-screen and hold your laptop on its side as if it were actually a book—a book with a keyboard, admittedly. Sit back, take a sip of tea, and catch up with Ms. Austen and life at Mansfield Park.

Be sure to keep tabs on where you are in your reading, because Preview doesn't (not yet anyway—we're keeping our fingers crossed) have any sort of bookmark functionality. I suggest using a sticky (Applications → Stickies) with a Current Reads list of PDFs and associated page numbers.

Hacking the Hack

No PDF e-books on your virtual shelf? Pick one up at the amazing Project Gutenberg (*http://www.gutenberg.net*) site, a repository of more than 10,000 e-books, the lion's share of which are in the public domain.

They're usually in plain-text format, but there's a quick fix for that. Open the file in Safari, TextEdit, or any number of other apps that read plain text. Then, print the entire contents to PDF (Print... → Save as PDF...).

Similarly, about anything you have lying about your Documents folder or on your Desktop can be added to your growing virtual library.

Build Your Own Konfabulator Widget

Build a Konfabulator widget (which we will call HAWG) and display a window with the top three processor hogs on your system.

Konfabulator [Hack #2] is a fabulous piece of widget machinery developed by Arlo Rose and Perry Clarke. Who knew that behind each of those cool little Desktop widgets (clocks, iTunes remote controls, weather forecasters, news tickers, etc.) lies a swatch of JavaScript wrapped in XML packaging?

It's true. The Konfabulator engine does the lion's share of the work of running, displaying, allowing interaction with, and otherwise dealing with the widgets. The rest is up to the individual widget maker. And there are tons of widgets available in the gallery (*http://www.widgetgallery.com*)—610 at the time of this writing.

This hack walks you through the process of creating your very own Konfabulator widget, even if you know little to nothing about XML and JavaScript.

The Project

We'll build a widget based on the command-line tool top to display the three largest processor hogs on your system at any given moment (to find out more about top, type man top in the Terminal [Hack #91]).

To do this with top alone, type the following on the command line:

```
$ top -1 2 -ocpu -F -n3
```

The –1 2 (that's a lowercase *L* before the 2) flag limits the results to two checks (otherwise, Konfabulator will get bogged down in an attempt to redraw the live statistics continually). I chose two checks instead of one, because the first poll returned via top always lists CPU usage percentages at 0. The -ocpu tag orders the results by CPU usage, –F eliminates shared libraries/frameworks from the calculated polls (this decreases the amount of processor time that top itself takes), and -n3 limits the results displayed to the top three only. To siphon these results into a simple Konfabulator widget to float over the Desktop, we'll wrap the top -1 2 -ocpu -F -n3 command in some XML.

Let's dub the widget *HAWG*, as in processor *hog*, but with a slight misspelling as an homage to my Southern roots.

A Visit to the Workshop and Gallery

Assuming that we know virtually nothing about building Konfabulator widgets, we're going to start out by visiting the Konfabulator Widget Workshop (*http://www.konfabulator.com/workshop*). Here, we'll find a Konfabulator reference manual in PDF form, a Photoshop-compatible template for designing the widget's icon, and a link to O'Reilly's *JavaScript: The Definitive Guide*, should we want to learn more advanced JavaScript.

Download the "Widget XML & JavaScript Reference" (*http://www. konfabulator.com/workshop/Konfabulator_Ref_1.5.1.pdf*) and nose through it for some idea of the commands that Konfabulator understands.

Next, we'll visit the Konfabulator Gallery (*http://www.widgetgallery.com*) to find some other widgets to download, dissect, and learn (read: borrow some code) from. This is the norm, mind you; a good percentage of the widgets available for download from the gallery are based on the code of some other widget or widgets in the gallery. This type of borrowing and giving credit where it's due is all part of the cooperative Konfabulator community and one of its greatest strengths. If somebody has written widget *X* that covers everything you want in a widget except for one feature, you can simply download it, hack away the bits you don't need, hack in the bits you do, and turn it into a brand-new widget that you can either keep for your own use or share with the Konfabulator community.

A quick search through the gallery reveals that there are several widgets already in existence that work in a way similar to how we want HAWG to work, using top to report other parts of system performance. I chose Zen

Monitor (*http://www.widgetgallery.com/view.php?widget=25839*) by Cap'n
Hector as my starting point. After downloading Zen Monitor to your computer, Control- or right-click it and select Show Package Contents from the
context menu (shown in Figure 1-43) to get at its innards.

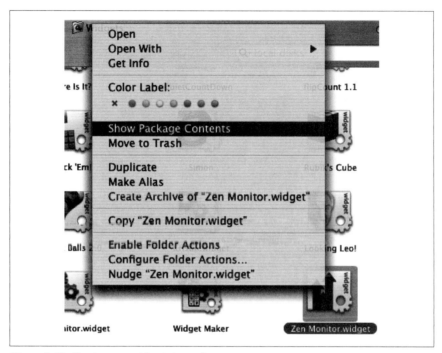

Figure 1-43. Getting at a widget's innards

Inside, you'll find a Contents folder that contains all the files that make the
widget what it is. The most useful of these is the *.kon* file, the actual code
that makes the widget run.

Building the Widget

With a cheat-sheet (in the form of another widget) in hand, let's get down to
building our own. Find a nice place somewhere on your hard drive; the Desktop's as good a place as any for now. Create a new folder (File → New Folder
or ⌘-Shift-N) and name it *Contents*. Create another folder and drag your Contents folder into it. Select and rename the outer folder *HAWG.widget*. A warning dialog box will confirm that you want to append the extension *.widget* to
your folder name; click the Add button to do so, and watch your plain old
folder transform itself right before your very eyes into a Konfabulator widget
(that is, at least the framework for one).

Build Your Own Konfabulator Widget

This little bit of folder renaming has tricked the Finder into thinking that *HAWG.widget* is a Konfabulator widget. However, if you double-click the widget, Konfabulator will give you an error, because as yet there are no apples inside that pie shell—no *.kon* code file inside the Contents folder.

Go back to Zen Monitor's Contents folder. Option-drag a copy of the *Zen Monitor.kon* file into the Contents folder of your *HAWG.widget* (as shown in Figure 1-44) and rename it *HAWG.kon*.

Figure 1-44. Copying Zen Monitor.kon into HAWG.widget/Contents as a code bootstrap

Open *HAWG.kon* in your text editor of choice (anything from pico to BBedit; I'm using SubEthaEdit [Hack #62]). The beginning of the code looks like this:

```
<?xml version="1.0" encoding="UTF-8"?>

<widget version="1.0" debug="off">

    <!--
    HAWG 1.0
    by Me
    Based on Cap'n Hector's Zen Monitor

    It's not pretty, but it works! ;-)
    -->
```

You'll notice in the comments that Zen Monitor borrows code from three other widgets and invites further hacking. And that's just what we are going to do.

Leave the first line, the XML declaration, as is. In the second line of code, replace off with on to turn on debugging.

 Since Konfabulator has a powerful XML parser, capable of handling either style of tag notation, you can alternately turn on debugging with <debug>on</debug>. Either style works, and you can feel free to mix and match according to your preference.

Replace everything between <!-- and --> with your own declaration about the HAWG widget—something like this:

```
<!--
    HAWG 1.0
    by Me, based on Cap'n Hector's Zen Monitor

    Hack it!
-->
```

This is just commentary and doesn't actually affect the workings of the widget itself.

Now, take some time and look through the remainder of the code for Zen Monitor and see if you can follow what some of the parts are doing. The general hierarchy of a widget starts with the declaration, which we just rewrote, and goes on to window settings and the text and images associated with the window. Up next are actions for the widget to perform, followed by preference settings. According to the Konfabulator manual, the general hierarchy should be as follows: <widget>, <about-box/>, <action/>, <hotkey/>, <image/>, <preference/>, <text/>, <textarea/>, <window/>, </widget>.

The bit we're after in particular is the updateCPU function:

```
function updateCPU( ) {
    cpuBackground.data = "CPU: " + runCommand("./cpucheck.pl")+"%";
    cpu.data = cpuBackground.data;
}
```

This bit of code defines a function that the widget will run within its set of actions. What is interesting here is the runCommand call out to an external command—in this case, a Perl script (found in Zen Monitor's Contents folder). If you open this Perl script, you will find that it grabs the percentage of CPU currently in use from top. We can avoid calling out to a separate script and simply run our top instructions within this runCommand command itself.

After you've looked around for a bit and familiarized yourself with the general hierarchy of the script, go ahead and delete everything between our initial `<!-- -->` declaration and the closing `</widget>` tag. We're going to code a basic, no-frills widget based loosely on what we've done thus far.

The Code

For the purposes of this hack, I am keeping the code for *HAWG.widget* as bare-bones as possible, forgoing an About box and other optional bits, which you can add if you prefer. It won't be particularly pretty, but it'll work:

```
<?xml version="1.0" encoding="UTF-8"?>
<widget version="1.0" debug="on">

    <!--
    HAWG 1.0
    by Me
    Based on Cap'n Hector's Zen Monitor

    It's not pretty, but it works! ;-)
    -->

<window title="HAWG" name="main_window" width="500" height="500"
alignment="left" visible="true" />

 <textarea>
  <name>HAWGS</name>
  <size>12</size>
  <columns>100</columns>
  <lines>25</lines>
  <bgColor>#FFFFFF</bgColor>
  <bgOpacity>250</bgOpacity>
  <editable>false</editable>
 </textarea>

 <action trigger="onLoad">
  function updateHAWGS() {
   HAWGS.data = "HAWGS: " + runCommand("top -l 2 -ocpu -F -n3")
  }
  updateHAWGS();
  main_window.visible = true;
 </action>

 <action trigger="onTimer" interval="10">
  updateHAWGS();
 </action>
```

```
<action trigger="OnMouseDown">
 closeWidget();
</action>

</widget>
```

The first part of the code is simply the XML declaration, followed by a bit of metadata about the program. The real programming begins with the window declaration that defines how large our widget's main window is going to be. Currently, *HAWG* is a screen hog and takes up a large chunk of space. This 500 by 500 window spread is invisible, however, until we stick something into it. I coded all the windows definitions in one line, but notice that for defining the text area, I switched to the other style of XML input that Konfabulator understands. I created a textarea named HAWGS (this is the handle by which I can refer to this textarea later in the program), defined its size so that it will actually hold all of the top output without scrolling, and made it white (in order for bgColor to work in textareas, you must also define opacity using bgOpacity) and noneditable. I did not include any data, so without anything else, this will simply display a white rectangle on the screen. We're relying on top to provide the text that will be displayed in the box, and for that we need to set up an action and define a function for that action.

I've set up three different actions. The first, onLoad, launches (as the name suggests) when you launch *HAWG.widget* in Konfabulator. I've defined a function called updateHAWGS( ), which drops a HAWGS textarea into place with "HAWGS: ", followed by the results of our runCommand. Right after defining this function, we invoke it, make sure the window is visible, and come to the end of the onLoad action.

The second action simply automates the updateHAWGS( ) function on a regular interval (every 15 seconds) using the built-in onTimer trigger.

Because there is no static text field defined in our widget, it is nearly impossible to Control-click on the *HAWG.widget* window (there's nothing to grab hold of) to navigate to Konfabulator's contextual menu. This makes the widget hard to close, so I've included a third action that invokes closeWidget( ) when you click (OnMouseDown) anywhere on the *HAWG.widget* window.

Running the Code

Once you've typed the code into your *HAWG.kon* file, go ahead and save it. Now, you can simply double-click on the *HAWG.widget* file on your Desktop to launch it (and Konfabulator itself, if it's not already running). A largish window should appear, along with Konfabulator's debugger (we left debugging on) that looks something like Figure 1-45.

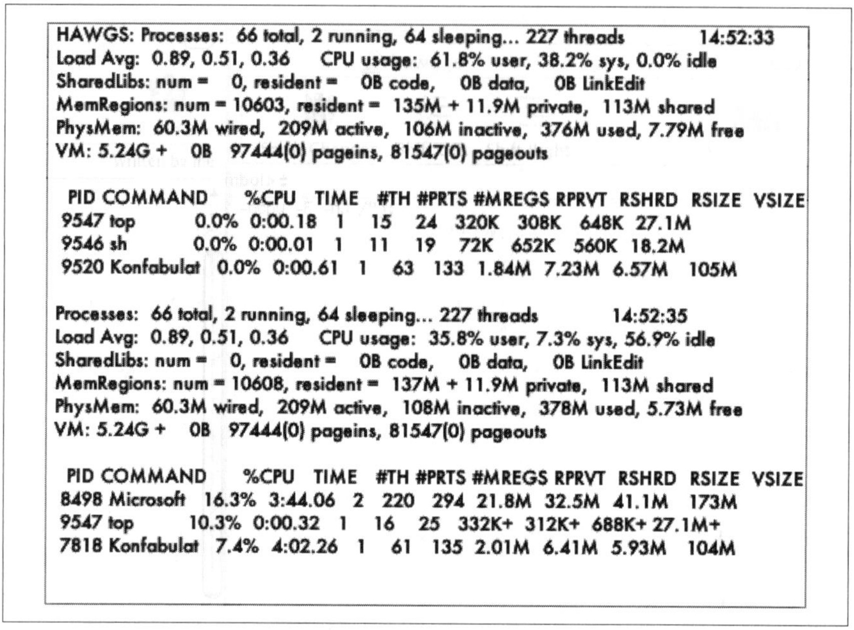

```
HAWGS: Processes: 66 total, 2 running, 64 sleeping... 227 threads        14:52:33
Load Avg: 0.89, 0.51, 0.36    CPU usage: 61.8% user, 38.2% sys, 0.0% idle
SharedLibs: num =   0, resident =   0B code,   0B data,   0B LinkEdit
MemRegions: num = 10603, resident = 135M + 11.9M private, 113M shared
PhysMem: 60.3M wired, 209M active, 106M inactive, 376M used, 7.79M free
VM: 5.24G +   0B  97444(0) pageins, 81547(0) pageouts

 PID COMMAND      %CPU  TIME   #TH #PRTS #MREGS RPRVT RSHRD  RSIZE VSIZE
9547 top          0.0% 0:00.18  1   15   24   320K  308K  648K  27.1M
9546 sh           0.0% 0:00.01  1   11   19    72K  652K  560K  18.2M
9520 Konfabulat   0.0% 0:00.61  1   63  133  1.84M 7.23M 6.57M  105M

Processes: 66 total, 2 running, 64 sleeping... 227 threads        14:52:35
Load Avg: 0.89, 0.51, 0.36    CPU usage: 35.8% user, 7.3% sys, 56.9% idle
SharedLibs: num =   0, resident =   0B code,   0B data,   0B LinkEdit
MemRegions: num = 10608, resident = 137M + 11.9M private, 113M shared
PhysMem: 60.3M wired, 209M active, 108M inactive, 378M used, 5.73M free
VM: 5.24G +   0B  97444(0) pageins, 81547(0) pageouts

 PID COMMAND      %CPU  TIME   #TH #PRTS #MREGS RPRVT RSHRD  RSIZE VSIZE
8498 Microsoft   16.3% 3:44.06  2  220  294  21.8M 32.5M 41.1M  173M
9547 top         10.3% 0:00.32  1   16   25  332K+ 312K+ 688K+ 27.1M+
7818 Konfabulat   7.4% 4:02.26  1   61  135  2.01M 6.41M 5.93M  104M
```

Figure 1-45. Running HAWG.widget

It has a look and feel only a programmer could love, but our little HAWG that could delivers the information we wanted in the second reporting, where we find that the top three processor hogs are currently Microsoft, top itself, and Konfabulator.

Hacking the Hack

How about adding some pizzazz to our little HAWG to make it your own?

Revisit the Konfabulator gallery, find widgets that intrigue you, crack them open, and try to figure out how you can apply what they've done to make HAWG more interesting and prettier.

Use a picture of an actual hog as the backdrop to your text area, and leave out the bgColor and opacity tags so that the text area itself will be invisible.

Perhaps add some actual preferences, such as one button to launch the preferences and another to quit.

Remove the OnTimer interval trigger and replace it with OnMouseDown, so that HAWG refreshes itself only when you click on it.

Also, if you like the idea of making your own widgets, but you don't really like typing all the XML bits by hand, you should check out Widget Maker (*http://www.widgetgallery.com/view.php?widget=35942*) by Harry Whitfield.

This handy little widget builds the *.kon* file for you, based on information you provide in each of its fields (see Figure 1-46).

Figure 1-16. The Widget Maker widget

Bet you never knew building a Desktop widget could be quite that simple.

—*C. K. Sample III*

CHAPTER TWO

Scripting
Hacks 13–26

Since the home-brew days of the Apple I, the little computer that could has always been the darling of the citizen engineer. Peeking and poking were *de rigueur*. Machine code was soon replaced by Basic in the Apple II, flinging open the doors to end-user scripting and tweaking.

With the appearance of the Mac, things got prettier and, eventually, a lot more colorful, but a lot harder to hack. The new operating system required some pretty in-depth knowledge of real programming: Pascal, C, and some Assembly thrown in for deep hacking. Basic made an appearance but was always a bit limited.

With the Pro version of System 7 came a little something called Apple-Script, an easy-to-use scripting language (it read almost, but not quite, like English) for fiddling with the Finder and automating any apps that cared to expose an AppleScript interface.

Today, Mac OS X brings together AppleScript and the world of Unix scripting. By interweaving AppleScript with hacker heavyweights Perl, Python, and Ruby, the Mac of today is getting more scriptable all the time.

This chapter introduces the Unix side of the family to the wonders of Apple-Script, including some of the more tenuous bits, such as GUI scripting. We also provide a taste of just what's possible on the Mac when you bubble the full power of Unix scripting up to the GUI and application level.

 HACK #13 A Hacker's Introduction to AppleScript
Bootstrap your AppleScript with this introduction by Matt Neuburg, author of AppleScript: The Definitive Guide.

In the late 1980s, Apple undertook a massive rewrite of the Macintosh operating system, dubbed System 7, which was ultimately released in mid-1991.

It was the first Mac system to enable true cooperative multitasking at the system level (rather than simulate it through ingenious hacks like Switcher and MultiFinder). Under this revision, the Finder became, for the first time, essentially just an application like any other, so a new means of communication had to be established between the Finder, where users could launch applications and open documents, and the applications themselves, which needed to be informed of the users' wishes.

In farsighted fashion, Apple generalized this means of communication into a powerful system-level messaging architecture, whereby any application could send a message to any other and get a reply. These messages, called *Apple Events*, had a pseudogrammatical structure of quite astonishing complexity. For example, a single Apple Event can say to an email application, "Look in the incoming mailbox, find the first message with a subject that starts with the word *applescript*, and move it into the *AppleScript* mailbox."

But Apple went even further. They wanted ordinary users to be able to construct and send Apple Events. Since an Apple Event is meant to be parseable by a computer and appears to a human being as a largely illegible data structure, this required a way of mapping between an Apple Event and something that human beings can read and write easily. In short, it required a programming language. That language was AppleScript, which first appeared as part of System 7 Pro in late 1993. Apple also provided the Script Editor application, where users could create, edit, and execute AppleScript programs.

The AppleScript language is a curious hybrid. It is small and simple, in some ways almost crude, partly because computer RAM capacities in 1993 were so low, so that AppleScript had to run in a tiny memory space. At the same time, it borrows some remarkably sophisticated elements from LISP (e.g., heavy use of lists and the ability to generate closures) and even incorporates some object-based features.

AppleScript's most salient aspects are its use of English-like terminology, its target-messaging model, and its ability to be extended in real time. These three points are intimately related. Recall that the point of AppleScript is to allow us to communicate with a running application by means of Apple Events. But there are no a priori rules regarding *which* Apple Events can be sent to an application; each scriptable application defines internally, and differently from all other applications, whatever Apple Events its developers have decided users should be able to send to it. Therefore, in order to expose itself to AppleScript as a potential target for Apple Event messages, a scriptable application must include a *dictionary* resource that describes the Apple Events it is prepared to receive. This means that the AppleScript language itself changes depending on which application is being addressed—not, to be sure, its grammar and syntax, but the nouns and verbs (or commands) that can be used.

AppleScript thus depends upon a mechanism of dynamic target-messaging and shifting terminology. Linguistically, the key to this, and indeed the most characteristic feature of the AppleScript language, is the *tell block*. Take, for example, the Finder. The Finder is scriptable, which means that we can send Apple Events to it by way of AppleScript. To do so, we use a structure like this:

```
tell application "Finder"
    get name of every folder of disk 1
end tell
```

The `tell` construct here does two things. It dictates that commands within it should be sent to the Finder, and it requires that these commands should be in a language that the Finder can understand. For example, the words `folder` and `disk` are not part of AppleScript itself. They are terms that the Finder defines. And that's a good thing, because the Finder is all about things like folders and disks; thus, it is natural that the user should want to be able to send it an Apple Event that discusses things like folders and disks.

In order for you to execute that little program, AppleScript first compiles it, at which point AppleScript checks with the Finder to make sure that words like `folder` and `disk` are okay with it (because they are *not* okay with AppleScript itself). It performs this check by consulting the Finder's dictionary. It must also translate the English-like phrase get name of every folder of disk 1 into an Apple Event. Then, as the program runs, AppleScript actually sends this Apple Event to the Finder, which parses it, obeys the instruction that it represents, and returns a reply:

```
{"Applications", "Developer", "Library", "System", "Users"}
```

But when we talk to a different application, we are in a completely different world. For example, here is a short program that addresses iTunes:

```
tell application "iTunes"
    get name of every track of current playlist
end tell
```

Words like `track` and `playlist` are proper to iTunes but meaningless to the Finder, just as `folder` and `disk` would be meaningless to iTunes.

A thing to notice in both these examples is the chain of ofs used to specify the desired object. In the Finder, a disk has folders and a folder has a name, so we can talk about the name of a certain folder of a certain disk. In iTunes, a playlist has tracks and a track has a name, so we can talk about the name of a certain track of a certain playlist. In effect, there is a hierarchy of objects and their attributes, which are unique to each target application; this is called the application's *object model*.

The previous examples emphasized nouns, but the same point should be made with respect to verbs (commands). AppleScript has a few built-in commands, of which get and set are the most commonly used, but otherwise it is up to the target application to extend the language by means of any required verbs. For example:

```
tell application "iTunes"
    play track 1 of current playlist
end tell
tell application "Finder"
    reveal folder 1 of disk 1
end tell
```

Here, play is not a command one could give to the Finder, and reveal is not a command one could give to iTunes (and neither is built into AppleScript itself).

The primary challenge for the AppleScript programmer is to discover what is permissible to say to any particular application. The application's dictionary, which is legible to a human being as well as to AppleScript, helps with this task; it is particularly useful for discovering the application's terminology (nouns and verbs that are proper to it) and the object model. But it does not provide complete information (for example, it doesn't say which commands can be applied to which objects), so sometimes an outside source, an example script, or trial-and-error is necessary.

Apart from the matter of targeting particular applications, AppleScript is fairly straightforward. It is a line-based language, and control structures are expressed with an opening and closing line, such as the tell and end tell lines in the previous examples. Here's an artificial script to illustrate some control structures:

```
set i to 6
repeat with j from 1 to 3
    set i to i - 1
    if i = j then
        display dialog "They are the same!"
    end if
end repeat
```

Observe that, unlike most other programming languages, a simple equals sign (=) is not used for assignment; it denotes comparison only. Assignment requires the more English-like set...to syntax. Also, variables do not have to be declared (though they can be, and doing so makes scoping behave more predictably), and they do not have a fixed data type.

Data types are much as one would expect: boolean, integer and real, string, and date, along with some system-oriented types such as file, alias, and application. A particularly important type is the list, which is an ordered collection of any values; AppleScript uses lists heavily and has some special syntax for manipulating them. Here, for example, is another way to acquire the names of all top-level folders on your computer:

```
tell application "Finder"
    set L to (get every folder of disk 1)
    -- L is a list
    set L2 to {}
    -- L2 is an empty list
    repeat with aFolder in L
        set end of L2 to name of aFolder
    end repeat
end tell
return L2
```

> You'll notice that lines beginning with -- appear even more like English than others—that's because they are. Any line beginning with a -- is a comment inserted for the reader's edification and is summarily ignored by the AppleScript engine.

That example also shows that a comment begins with two hyphens. Some built-in coercions from one data type to another are permitted, and some are performed implicitly. Operators are generally as one would expect, but note that the ampersand (&) is the string concatenation operator:

```
3 + "4" -- 7, with implicit coercion of string to number
"3" & 4 -- "34", with implicit coercion of number to string
4 as string -- "4", an explicit coercion
```

A user-defined subroutine (called a *handler*) is defined with the keyword on and is called by using its name. The syntax comes in some rather elaborate variations, but here's a simple example using parentheses:

```
on getTheName(whatever)
    return (get name of whatever)
end getTheName
tell application "Finder"
    set L to (get every folder of disk 1) as list
    set L2 to {}
    repeat with aFolder in L
        set end of L2 to my getTheName(aFolder)
    end repeat
end tell
return L2
```

The keyword my informs AppleScript that even though we are in the context of a tell block directed at the Finder, the call to getTheName( ) should be directed to this script, not to the Finder.

There is rather more to the language than this, but the foregoing should suffice to enable you to read the AppleScript hacks in this book with a fair degree of understanding. For the complete story in all its gory details, consult my book, *AppleScript: The Definitive Guide*.

A word now about AppleScript's place within Mac OS X. It is remarkable that AppleScript, only slightly changed from its 1993 original, has even survived the transition to Mac OS X. But not only has it survived, it thrives. Many applications are scriptable by means of AppleScript, so it deserves to be a part of every hacker's arsenal. And it can be used to achieve some remarkable effects. The application to be targeted can even be on a remote machine (this requires that Remote Apple Events be turned on in the Sharing panel of the target machine's System Preferences).

And AppleScript can be integrated easily with other scripting hacker's tools. For example, AppleScript can call into the Unix command line by means of the do shell script command, so you can run any Unix tool (including Perl, Python, and Ruby) from within AppleScript:

```
on convert(val, unit1, unit2)
    set text item delimiters to " "
    set conv to do shell script ({"units", unit1, unit2} as string)
    return val * (word 1 of paragraph 1 of conv as real)
end convert
return convert(4, "feet", "meters")
```

And, the other way round, Unix can call AppleScript by means of the osascript tool. Here's a silly example intended to be run in the Terminal:

```
#!/usr/bin/perl
$s = <<"END_S";
    tell application "Finder"
        count folders of disk 1
    end tell
END_S
chomp ($num = `osascript -ss -e '$s'`);
print "You have $num top-level folders.\n",
    "Which one would you like to know the name of?\n",
    "Type a number between 1 and $num: ";
$num = <>;
chomp $num;
$ss = <<"END_SS";
    tell application "Finder"
        get name of folder $num of disk 1
    end tell
END_SS
print `osascript -ss -e '$ss'`
```

Last, but certainly not least, Apple provides the free AppleScript Studio development environment (part of the Xcode Tools), which allows a Cocoa application to be written entirely in the AppleScript language. This would be particularly appropriate as a way of wrapping a Cocoa GUI around an existing AppleScript program.

—*Matt Neuburg*

AppleScript the GUI

#14   Expand your automation options by getting GUI with applications not otherwise readily AppleScript-able.

I was browsing with Safari not too long ago when I had a thought. "Self," I thought, "wouldn't it be cool if I could provide people with an OPML (*http://www.opml.org*) version of what I'm browsing at any particular time?" Just take a snapshot, so to speak, of what was open in the various tabs in my browser. From the OPML, I could further transform this moment in browsing time into RSS or HTML or anything I so desired.

"Why yes!" I agreed. "It would be!" And I launched Script Editor, prepared to execute this marvelous plan of mine using my friend and yours, Apple-Script. I checked Safari's scripting dictionary and my hopes popped like a balloon on a pin. Safari's tabs are not scriptable—at all. In fact, Safari supports only the same basic commands as most other applications (open, save, close, etc.) and a do JavaScript command. Not cool at all. Was my dream of a mini "What's Phil browsing?" blog to be dashed by a simple lack of scriptability?

Not at all, thanks to GUI Scripting (*http://www.apple.com/applescript/uiscripting*), also known as System Events, baked right into OS X Panther.

GUI Scripting was supported to some extent in a late release of Jaguar, but it has really come into its own in Panther. The syntax is getting easier to use (though it's still fairly arcane at times, all things considered), and many more elements of the Mac OS X user interface are now scriptable.

Turning on GUI Scripting

The first step in using GUI Scripting is to make sure that you can script the GUI in the first place. To throw the switch, launch System Preferences, visit the Universal Access pane, and make sure the "Enable access for assistive devices" checkbox is checked, as shown in Figure 2-1. Without this step, you'll get nowhere fast and your scripts will run into all sorts of errors.

UI Element Inspector

The next step is to figure out how to get at the various elements of Safari, the tabs in particular. I opened a Safari window and filled it with several tabs that held a nice array of sites (see Figure 2-2), so that I'd have something to work with. I figured five was a good number.

There are currently two apps available for exploring the GUI world and discovering where a certain UI element (tab, button, menu item, drawer, etc.) lie in the hierarchy of elements associated with any given window.

Figure 2-1. Enabling GUI Scripting in the Universal Access System Preferences pane

Figure 2-2. A few Safari tabs to get things going

The first of these is a free Apple utility called UI Element Inspector (*http://www.apple.com/applescript/uiscripting/02.html*). It's rather bare-bones, but what it does it does well. When you launch UI Element Inspector, a simple floating window appears, displaying a currently selected or active object's vital internal information, the object's place in the scheme of things (e.g., a button within a window within an application and so forth), and other interesting tidbits (e.g., its size, whether it is minimized, etc.). In Figure 2-3, the UI Element Inspector is looking at the window I'm using to type this hack.

If you nose about a bit, you'll see that the application's name is BBEdit and the active window is titled *Intro to GUI Scripting.html*, the working title of

Figure 2-3. The UI Element Inspector, examining the currently active BBEdit window

the hack you're currently reading. The window's *role* (read: what it is) is, of course, a window. It contains eight child objects: scrollbars, buttons, and other things contained inside a window. It's the main window (AXMain has a value of 1, meaning True). It's the object of current focus (AXFocused is 1). It isn't currently minimized (AXMinimized has a value of 0, meaning False). And it represents a document located at *file://localhost/Users/ulrichp/Desktop/ AppleScript Hacks/Intro to GUI Scripting/Intro to GUI Scripting.html*. Pretty nifty, eh?

UI Element Inspector displays info about any element that your mouse passes over. You can, however, lock the UI Element Inspector to the currently focused object by pressing ⌘-F10 (as noted at the bottom of Figure 2-3). This allows you to wander off, perhaps to do a little scripting in Script Editor, without losing track of the information you're after, while UI Element Inspector follows your mouse like a puppy.

The UI Element Inspector main window freezes (and its text turns red) and up pops a "Locked on <*object name*>" window (Figure 2-4), which you can use to inspect the attributes of the element that's been locked onto. You can even set some of the attributes, altering the object on the fly. Check the

Highlight box to highlight whatever you're locked onto; this is rather useful
for making sure you are indeed locked onto what you think you are.

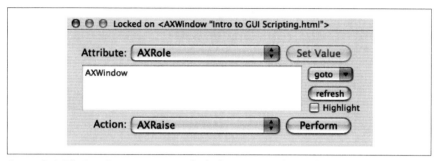

Figure 2-4. The UI Element Inspector, locked onto a BBEdit window

While all this is well and good, the one thing Apple's UI Element Inspector
won't do for you is write code. So, with these hints in hand, let's get to it.

I click the last tab in my five tabs (see Figure 2-2) and lock UI Element
Inspector to it. Here are that tab's details:

```
<AXApplication: "Safari">
 <AXWindow: "What is OPML?">
  <AXRadioButton: "What is OPML?">

Attributes:
 AXRole: "AXRadioButton"
 AXRoleDescription: "radio button"
 AXHelp: "What is OPML?"
 AXValue: "1"
 AXEnabled: "1"
 AXFocused (W): "0"
 AXParent: "<AXWindow: "What is OPML?">"
 AXWindow: "<AXWindow: "What is OPML?">"
 AXPosition: "x=766 y=95"
 AXSize: "w=179 h=22"
 AXTitle: "What is OPML?"

Actions:
 AXPress - press
```

> It seems, oddly enough, that a Safari tab is considered a radio
> button (a user interface element of role/type AXRadioButton)
> inside of a window (AXWindow), which is in turn inside the
> Safari application (AXApplication). Oh, and a tab has one
> available action, AXPress, which means it can be clicked.

Back to my original stated purpose, I wanted a script that would meander
my tabs and gather information on the pages they hold. Let's start with a

simple script to select each tab in turn, wait five seconds, and then move on to the next:

```
-- System Events is the app that really controls GUI scripting
tell application "System Events"
 tell process "Safari"
 -- Let's move Safari to the front so we can see this
 set frontmost to true
 get radio button in window 1
 repeat with i from 1 to number of items in the result
 click radio button i in window 1
 delay 5
 end repeat
 end tell
end tell
```

When you run this script, Safari should pop to the front and slowly cycle through each of the tabs in the front window.

The hard part for beginning GUI scripters is that the code is not easy to write. These elements were easy to get at, but what if you wanted, say, to script something as simple as a message's subject in Mail's message list? Here's the hierarchy for one of mine:

```
<AXApplication: "Mail">
<AXWindow: "In – phil@interalia.org">
<AXGroup>
<AXSplitGroup>
<AXScrollArea>
<AXTable>
<AXRow>
<AXTextField>
```

To access that single speck of information, I would have to write all of this code:

```
set a_subject to value of text field 1 of row 1 of table 1 of scroll area 1
of splitter group 1 of group 1 of window 1
```

Not exactly intuitive, is it? And Apple's UI Element Inspector shows you only the hierarchy; it's entirely up to you to figure out the actual name of each UI element and just how to script it.

Case in point: notice that an AXSplitGroup is actually referred to as a splitter group in AppleScript.

So, what's a scripter to do? After all, the purpose of AppleScript is to make things easier, not ridiculously frustrating.

Prefab UI Browser

Thank heavens for Prefab Software's UI Browser (*http://www.prefab.com/ uibrowser*; shareware, $55), a third-party software gem. UI Browser bills itself as "the ultimate assistant for GUI Scripting," and it's right. Here are a few of the things UI Browser can do that UI Element Inspector can't:

- Browse any application's user interface without actually having to switch to the app itself

- View an element's path as an AppleScript reference, then copy-and-paste it right into your script

- Float on top (like UI Element Inspector) or hide in the background without losing element focus

- Inspect and set attributes through a far more intuitive drawer-based interface

- Generate AppleScript code for you, whether just a reference to or an action against (e.g., click) an element

In Figure 2-5, I'm using UI Browser to generate code to select Safari's Location bar.

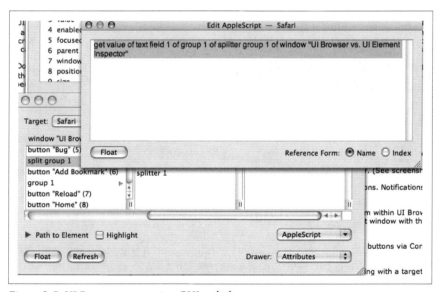

Figure 2-5. UI Browser, generating GUI code for me

With the candy-coated GUI shell cracked, I'm just a few lines of AppleScript away from generating that OPML version of my current tab list.

Combining that tab-roaming script from just a moment ago with some code generated by UI Browser, I end up with this:

```
--Turn Tabs into OPML

set opml_header to "
<?xml version=\"1.0\" encoding=\"UTF-8\"?>
<opml version=\"1.0\">
 <head>
 <title>What Was I Browsing?</title>
 </head>
 <body>

 "

set opml_body to ""

set opml_footer to "
 </body>
</opml>"

tell application "System Events"
 tell process "Safari"
  set frontmost to true
  get radio button in window 1
  repeat with i from 1 to number of items in the result
    click radio button i in window 1
    set opml_element to "<outline text=\"" & title of radio button i of ¬
window 1 & "\""
    set opml_element to opml_element & " htmlUrl=\"" & value of text field ¬
1 of group 1 of splitter group 1 of window 1 & "\" />
    "
    set opml_body to opml_body & opml_element
    delay 2
  end repeat
 end tell
end tell

set opml_document to opml_header & opml_body & opml_footer
set filepath to (POSIX path of (path to desktop)) & "SafariSnapshot.opml"
do shell script "echo " & quoted form of opml_document & " > " & quoted ¬
form of filepath
```

Run this script on a tab-filled Safari window, watch it go to town, and look on your Desktop for *SafariSnapshot.opml*, an OPML representation of the web pages loaded into those tabs. Here's what I ended up with:

```
<opml version="1.0">
 <head>
 <title>What Was I Browsing?</title>
 </head>
 <body>

 <outline text="The Idea Salon: Home" htmlUrl="http://ideasalon.org/" />
```

```
<outline text="raelity bytes" htmlUrl="http://raelity.org/" />
<outline text="eclecticism" htmlUrl="http://www.michaelhanscom.com/" />
<outline text="Slashdot: News for nerds, stuff that matters" htmlUrl="http:
//slashdot.org/" />
<outline text="What is OPML?" htmlUrl="http://www.opml.org/" />

</body>
</opml>
```

Caveat Scripter

Things are not always quite this easy, however. Even with tools like UI Browser and UI Element Inspector, there are some applications (particularly, Carbonized versions of Classic apps—Microsoft Word, for instance) that are resistant to having themselves scripted, even on the GUI level. This can be quite a stumbling block for creativity. If, for example, you wanted to script MSN Messenger to change your displayed screen name whenever iTunes changes songs, you're out of luck, the custom Carbon GUI element that Microsoft uses for display-name editing just isn't accessible through either regular AppleScript or GUI scripting.

Many apps, especially those written in Cocoa or made of Carbon but that don't make heavy use of custom UI elements, are GUI-scriptable. With GUI scripting in your toolbox, you'll find new vistas of automation open to you.

—*Phil Ulrich*

HACK #15 Fulfill Wishes with Address Book

This hack will find anyone in your Address Book that has an Amazon Wish List, but it's up to you buy them something!

The Macintosh operating system has always been a rather scriptable environment. Many applications support scriptable events that let you automate tasks or integrate separate programs. With Mac OS X, there are even more opportunities for scripting, now that the ultimate scriptable environment, Unix, is under the hood. But why limit yourself to the Desktop? The Mac's script-friendly environment can integrate your Desktop application with web applications such as Amazon.

This hack is a quick example that loosely integrates the Mac Address Book with Amazon. Using AppleScript and an underlying Unix tool called curl, this script finds people in your Address Book that also have an Amazon Wish List. This script might help you find a gift for someone you know, or it might just give you a different perspective on someone by finding what they're interested in. Most importantly, though, it shows how Desktop applications can become smarter by integrating with web applications.

The Code

Open the Script Editor (Applications → AppleScript), enter the following code, and save the script with a suitably snappy name, like *Get Wish Lists*:

```
(*
Find Wish Lists in Address Book

The script loops through people in your Address Book, checking Amazon
to see if they have a Wish List. If their Wish List is found, you
have the option to view it in your default browser.

by Paul Bausch
*)

-- set some variables for the curl command

set userAgent to "Mozilla/5.0 (Macintosh; U; PPC Mac OSX; en-us)"
set curlCommand to "curl -i -b -A -L \"" & userAgent & "\" "

-- open Address Book and loop through people

tell application "Address Book"
  repeat with thisPerson in the people
    set thisName to name of thisPerson
    repeat with thisAddress in email of thisPerson
      set thisEmail to value of thisAddress

      -- build the URL that will search for the Wish List

      set baseURL to "http://www.amazon.com/gp/registry/search.html"
      set thisURL to baseURL & "/?type=wishlist\\&field-name=" & thisEmail

      -- use curl to fetch the search page

      set thisWishPage to do shell script curlCommand & thisURL

      -- if the search returns what appears to be a match, prompt the user

      if thisWishPage contains "&id=" then
        set theAction to display dialog thisName & ¬
" has an Amazon wishlist." buttons {"View", "Ignore"}
          if button returned of theAction is "View" then

            -- Find the ID on the page

            set beginID to (offset of "&id=" in thisWishPage) + 4
            set endID to (offset of "'s Wish List" in thisWishPage) - 1
            set thisWishID to get text beginID thru endID of thisWishPage

            if thisWishPage contains "&id=" thenset beginID to 1
              set endID to (offset of "\">" in thisWishID) - 1
            set thisWishID to get text beginID thru endID of thisWishID
```

```
            -- Open the default browser to the Wishlist page

            tell me to open location "http://www.amazon.com/o/registry/" ¬
    & thisWishID
        end if
      end if
    end repeat
  end repeat
end tell
```

The script starts by setting some variables for curl that will be used later.

> If you'd like learn more about curl and what these settings
> mean, open a Terminal window (Applications → Utilities →
> Terminal) and type man curl. You'll get the complete docu-
> mentation that explains what all of these command switches
> do. Or, you can read "Downloading Files from the Com-
> mand Line" [Mac OS X Hacks, Hack #61].

Then, the script loops through all of the entries in the Address Book, looking for email addresses. It uses each individual email address to build a URL
that queries Amazon for a Wish List associated with that address. This is
where the script needs to step out of its AppleScript confines to the larger
world of Unix commands. With the do shell script command, curl contacts Amazon to see if this person has a Wish List.

If a Wish List is found, the display dialog command brings up a window
like the one in Figure 2-6, with two options: View or Ignore.

Figure 2-6. Script prompt

Clicking View tells the script to open the Wish List with the default browser.
Because this command takes place within the tell application "Address
Book" block, the context-switching tell me command needs to precede
AppleScript's open location function.

Running the Code

You can run the code directly from the Script Editor by clicking the Run
button.

To always have it a click away from your Address Book, move the script to the *Library/Scripts/Address Book Scripts* folder. This way, it'll be available from your Address Book's Scripts menu. Run the script at any time by selecting Script Menu → Get Wish Lists from the Address Book application's menu bar.

—Paul Bausch

 ## HACK #16 Fetch the Paper, AppleScript Style

Download web pages to your laptop or iPod for morning reading on the bus, train, plane, or ferry.

Each morning, I have a set of web sites I check in on to bootstrap my day's noodling. In most cases, I simply sic NetNewsWire on the task, gathering a virtual armload of syndicated content [Hack #30] for en-route reading. But some sites (hard to believe, I know) don't provide RSS feeds and so require a manual visit in my browser, a process that just doesn't fly on those days I'm dashing for the door.

What I needed was an automated way to grab copies of particular home pages, stashing them on my PowerBook for later perusal. I call my solution, appropriately enough, Morning News.

This smidge of AppleScript downloads web pages by way of the curl (as in "copy URL") command-line tool and drops them into a folder of your choosing.

The Code

There are two versions of this script. One is designed to run interactively, prompting you for a folder in which to store the downloaded pages. The other is designed to run automatically at a particular time (30 minutes or so before you dash out the door, let's say) and drops the pages into a specified location.

First, here's the interactive version:

```
-- Morning News
-- Slurps down a number of predefined URLs to a chosen folder as HTML files.
-- Author: Phil Ulrich

(* A list of URLs to be downloaded , along with their associated site
names*)
set interalia_dot_org to {name:"Among Other Things", URL:"http://interalia.
org"}
set raelity_dot_org to {name:"Raelity Bytes", URL:"http://raelity.org"}
set ideasalon to {name:"Idea Salon", URL:"http://ideasalon.org"}
set macslash to {name:"Macslash", URL:"http://macslash.org"}
```

```
set macintouch to {name:"Macintouch", URL:"http://macintouch.com/"}
set slashdot to {name:"Slashdot", URL:"http://slashdot.org/"}

(* Build a list of these URLs *)
set download_urls to {interalia_dot_org, raelity_dot_org, ideasalon,
macslash, macintouch, slashdot}

(* Prompt for a download folder *)
set download_folder to POSIX path of (choose folder with prompt "To which
folder should I save downloaded pages?") as string

(* Get 'em all using curl *)
repeat with this_url in download_urls
  set output_path to quoted form of (download_folder & (name of this_url))
  do shell script "curl " & URL of this_url & " -o " & output_path & " -m 90"
end repeat
```

When this script runs, it pops open a dialog box that asks for a preferred download folder; pick a folder and it'll get to work, stepping through the list of URLs and downloading them. The second-to-last line is where most of the heavy lifting is done. AppleScript calls curl, passing it a URL (e.g., curl http://interalia.org) and folder to which to save the contents (e.g., -o /Users/ulrichp/Desktop/MorningNews/Among Other Things). The -m 90 bit at the end tells it to give up if it can't get to the site after 90 seconds.

The noninteractive version is just about identical to the interactive one, except that it hardcodes the download folder rather than prompt for it (you won't be around to answer the prompt, will you?). Changes are called out in bold:

```
-- Morning News (Crontab Edition)
-- Slurps down a number of predefined URLs to a chosen folder as HTML files.
-- Author: Phil Ulrich

(* A list of URLs to be downloaded , along with their associated site
names*)
set interalia_dot_org to {name:"Among Other Things", URL:"http://interalia.
org"}
set raelity_dot_org to {name:"Raelity Bytes", URL:"http://raelity.org"}
set ideasalon to {name:"Idea Salon", URL:"http://ideasalon.org"}
set macslash to {name:"Macslash", URL:"http://macslash.org"}
set macintouch to {name:"Macintouch", URL:"http://macintouch.com/"}
set slashdot to {name:"Slashdot", URL:"http://slashdot.org/"}

(* Build a list of these URLs *)
set download_urls to {interalia_dot_org, raelity_dot_org, ideasalon,
macslash, macintouch, slashdot}

(* Hard code, rather than prompt for, the name of a download folder.
If the folder doesn't exist,go ahead and create it.*)
```

```
set notes_folder to "/Users/ulrichp/Desktop/MorningNews/"
try
    do shell script "mkdir " & notes_folder
end try

(* Get 'em all using curl *)
repeat with this_url in download_urls
  set output_path to quoted form of (notes_folder & (name of this_url))
  do shell script "curl " & URL of this_url & " -o " & output_path & " -m 90"
end repeat
```

Running the Code

Save either version of the script as *Morning News.scpt*. Run either by double-clicking its icon in the Finder; it obviously makes more sense to run the interactive one interactively.

To have the noninteractive script run automatically involves putting it somewhere readily accessible (in other words, somewhere you'll be able to find it again) and setting up a cron job [Hack #98] to have it run at a particular time.

Let's say I go to work at 10 a.m. (which I do) and I like my news downloaded at 9:30 so that I can drop it onto my iPod on my way out. I have the script in a Scripts folder within my Documents folder, so its path is */Users/ulrichp/ Documents/Scripts/Morning News.scpt*. I add this to my crontab [Hack #98]:

```
30 9 * * * /usr/bin/osascript /Users/ulrichp/Documents/Scripts/¬
Morning News.scpt &
```

Every morning at 9:30, osascript—a shell utility to run AppleScripts from the command line [Mac OS X Hacks, Hack #64]—calls the *Morning News. scpt* script quietly in the background and downloads my day's reading.

Hacking the Hack

My choice of morning reading probably doesn't tickle your taste buds, but that's easily fixed by editing the list of sites at the top of the script. Each site is represented as a pair (site name and URL) of key/value settings.

For example, if you want to add the front page of MobileWhack to the list, simply add the following line after Slashdot:

```
set mobilewhack to {name:"MobileWhack", URL:"http://www.mobilewhack.com"}
```

You also need to add it to the array of download URLs a couple of lines lower (change shown in bold):

```
(* Build a list of these URLs *)
set download_urls to {interalia_dot_org, raelity_dot_org, ideasalon,
macslash, macintouch, slashdot, mobilewhack}
```

In the noninteractive version, you can also change the location to which downloaded files should be saved. Simply change the path in the following line at the top of the script:

```
set notes_folder to "/Users/ulrichp/Desktop/MorningNews/"
```

Be sure to use the full path (*not* just something like /Desktop/Morning News/), and don't forget to include a trailing slash (the / in Morning News/").

Also, whenever possible, choose the most complete and lightest version possible of the page in which you're interested. Many sites have a text-only (or near text-only) version of their home page and printer-friendly versions of all their pages. These tend to include more or all of the full text on one page (rather than spread it over several) and typically go a little lighter on the advertising-to-content ratio.

For the full news-on-the-run effect, run the interactive version of the script and choose your iPod's Notes folder to have your morning news available to you right on your iPod's crisp little screen.

Realize that you have limited space for each note on your iPod, so it's even more important to find the lightest versions available of your Morning News sites.

—Phil Ulrich

 ## Batch-Convert Screenshots to JPEGs

#17 Drag PDFs into a folder and make use of Apple's Image Events and Folder Actions to automatically convert them into JPEGs.

As an indie software developer, I wind up taking a lot of screenshots—showing projects-in-progress for my blog, showing off features on a product's page, and so on. I tend to use Apple's built-in screenshot functions.

⌘-Shift-3 grabs the whole screen. ⌘-Shift-4 turns the mouse into a crosshair pointer, allowing you to click-and-drag to select a particular rectangular portion of the screen. Or, tap the spacebar after a ⌘-Shift-4 and move your mouse over any window or dialog box to capture it alone (I use this one a lot). Press Esc to cancel the screenshot altogether.

No matter which method you use, the screenshots are placed on the Desktop as PDF files with serial filenames: Picture 1, Picture 2, Picture 3, and so on. If you think about it, PDF makes sense; after all, PDF is the underlying technology behind Mac OS X's stunningly beautiful graphics. But it's not all that convenient for those of us who put screenshots up on the Web, where JPEG and PNG rule the roost.

Now you can always open any PDF screenshot in the Preview application (*Applications/Preview*) and File → Export... it in any number of formats [Mac OS X Hacks, Hack #21]. But opening each image in turn, dealing with export options, and saving each file again is quite time-consuming. Imagine doing so with 25 shots on a regular basis!

> You can save a step by using ⌘-Control-Shift-3 or -4. The addition of Control- saves the screenshot to the clipboard. Open Preview and select File → New From Clipboard (⌘-N) and File → Export... in any format you prefer. However, all this does is avoid the intermediary PDF file on your Desktop; in other words, it's not much of a time-saver.

AppleScript and Folder Actions to the rescue!

Folder Actions will be familiar to any Mac veteran who used an OS prior to OS X (OS 9, I believe they called it). Gone in OS X 10 through 10.2, they've thankfully resurfaced as a fully supported technology in Panther. Folder Actions essentially consist of a script or scripts attached to a folder that are triggered when opening or closing a folder, dropping files into or taking files out of a folder, and so forth.

What if I had a Folder Action that converted any number of PDFs named something in the format of *Picture 1.pdf* to JPEGs?

The Code

This hack shows off not only the Image Events technology used to script the manipulation of images, but also the return of Folder Actions, AppleScripts triggered by touching a particular folder:

```
-- PDF to JPEG Auto-Converter
-- Author: Phil Ulrich
-- Purpose: Convert any number of PDFs dropped in a folder into JPGs

on adding folder items to this_folder after receiving filelist
    tell application "System Events"
        set these_files to (every file in this_folder whose name starts ¬
with "Picture" and (file type is "PDF " or name extension is "pdf"))
    end tell
    repeat with i from 1 to the count of these_files
        set this_file to POSIX path of (item i of these_files as alias)
        tell application "Image Events"
            launch
            set this_image to open file this_file
            save this_image as JPEG in (this_file & ".jpg") with icon
```

```
            close this_image
        end tell
    end repeat
end adding folder items to
```

Drop any files into the folder to which this script is attached and it goes about making a list of files that begin with *Picture* and end with *pdf* (or that have the file type of PDF).

Anything matching this pattern is opened in another new Panther built-in tool, Image Events (*http://www.apple.com/applescript/imageevents*). Image Events exposes the built-in Scriptable Image Processing Server (SIPS) and allow you to automate image manipulation in AppleScript. Here, we're converting each PDF file to JPEG, adding a preview of the image to the icon, and closing it. The original PDF is left untouched.

Running the Code

Save the script as *PDF2JPEG.scpt*. Create a folder on your Desktop (or anywhere else, for that matter) and attach the script as a Folder Action. Right- or Control-click the folder and select Enable Folder Actions to enable Folder Actions globally (if you instead see a Disable Folder Actions option, Folder Actions are already enabled). Now to add a Folder Action to this folder in particular. Again, right- or Control-click the folder, this time selecting Attach a Folder Action..., as shown in Figure 2-7. Navigate to and select your *PDF2JPEG.scpt* script, and click the Choose button to attach it to the folder.

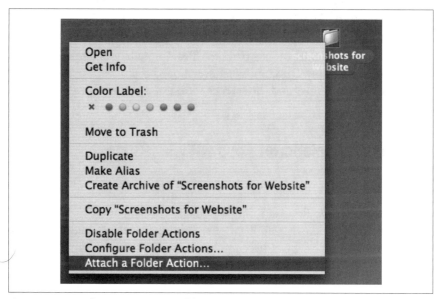

Figure 2-7. Attaching a script as a Folder Action

Examine all currently active Folder Actions on your system by right- or Control-clicking any folder and selecting Configure Folder Actions.... In *Figure 2-8*, the *PDF2JPEG.scpt* script is attached to my *Screenshots for Website* folder.

Figure 2-8. Examining all folders with attached Folder Actions

I should point out a couple of caveats. When I wrote this script, I had originally hoped to attach it to the Desktop, so that any screenshot would automatically be converted whenever I took one. In some ways, this works; if I drag a screenshot that matches the *Picture #.pdf* profile to the Desktop, it works as expected. Apparently, however, taking a screenshot does not qualify as adding a file to the Desktop folder, so ⌘-Shift-3 or -4 won't, in themselves, trigger conversion. Oddly, the script will also activate when you remove a file from the folder.

That said, this script works fantastically if you want to convert some screenshots, either individually or as a batch of files. I now have such a folder permanently living on my Desktop; whenever I need to convert a screenshot, I just drop it in that folder and the screenshot is good to go on my site.

—Phil Ulrich

HACK #18 Build AppleScript Apps with FaceSpan

FaceSpan is a self-contained program-building environment that leverages the power of AppleScript to build standalone Cocoa applications.

AppleScript is primarily a scripting language; it is intended to let the user communicate with existing applications. Still, having developed a scripting solution with AppleScript, a user might naturally want to wrap a standard application interface around it. So, how can a user take advantage of Apple-Script to write a standalone application?

FaceSpan 4.0 is a small (7MB) Cocoa application in which you can use AppleScript as a programming language to build a Cocoa application. You draw your interface in a window editor, adding interface elements to a window and specifying some of their physical behavior in an info panel (the palette labeled *window* in the lower right of Figure 2-9). Then, you write AppleScript code to dictate what should happen when the user interacts with those interface elements to generate an event (starting up the application, choosing a menu item, pressing a button, and so forth).

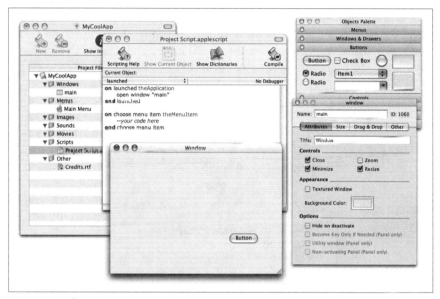

Figure 2-9. The FaceSpan development environment

FaceSpan uses the same underlying dictionary as AppleScript Studio (the AppleScriptKit dictionary) for referring to and communicating with the parts of the interface. Indeed, working in FaceSpan is much like working in AppleScript Studio, except that you are spared having to operate in two different applications. In AppleScript Studio, you draw your application's interface in Interface Builder and you write and test your code in Xcode, but FaceSpan is completely self-contained.

I'll note further differences between the two environments as we go along. The biggest difference, of course, is that AppleScript Studio is free, whereas FaceSpan costs $200 (or $90 for a limited version that builds applications that require the presence of FaceSpan itself in order to run). The question of whether FaceSpan possesses a sufficient superiority over AppleScript Studio to justify this pricing is a matter for the free market to decide; in other words, only time will tell.

This hack is intended to provide a taste of what's possible with FaceSpan. The AppleScript code is rather advanced and draws extensively from my book *AppleScript: The Definitive Guide* (O'Reilly).

Disk Lister Example

Let's start with a Disk Lister example, intended simply to illustrate Apple-Script driving an external application (the Finder) from within a standalone application. Our application merely displays the names of all mounted drives (or partitions) in a table view within a window. My book shows how to do this using AppleScript Studio, REALbasic, and Cocoa/Objective-C; now, we'll add FaceSpan to our box of tools.

Start up FaceSpan and ask for a New Project; call it *Disk Lister*, and use the default template. In a moment, the Project Window appears, as shown in Figure 2-10.

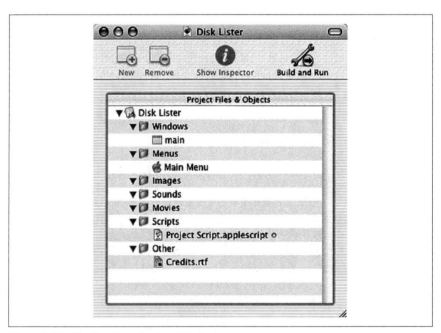

Figure 2-10. The FaceSpan Project Window

Double-click the *main* window listing to open it so that we can design our window. Show the Objects Palette if it isn't showing already, open the Tables section, and drag a table view into the main window, as shown in Figure 2-11.

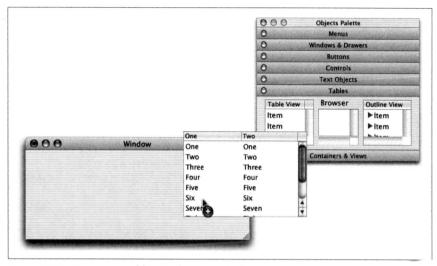

Figure 2-11. Dragging a table into the main window

Show the Info Panel if it isn't showing already, and double-click the table view in the *main* window so that the Info Panel is talking about the table view, not the scroll view that contains it. Set the number of columns to 1, and select the column header so that the Info Panel is now talking about the table column. Title that column Your Disks and give it an identifier of *disks*, as shown in Figure 2-12.

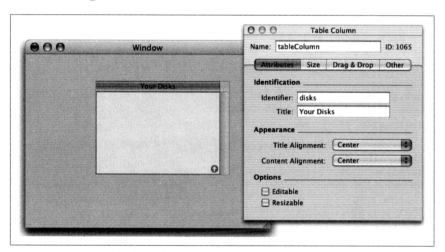

Figure 2-12. Giving the table column a name and identifier

Ajust the size of the window and the table view to your preference. So much for designing the interface.

Now, we'll write the code. In the Project Window, open the script provided for you, *Project Script.applescript*. You'll find that there is already a launched handler:

```
on launched theApplication
  open window "main"
end launched
```

Modify the script by adding the following code:

```
on launched theApplication
open window "main"
tell application "Finder" to set L to (name of every disk)
set ds to make new data source at end of data sources
set tv to table view 1 of scroll view 1 of window 1
set col to make new data column at end of data columns of ds ¬
with properties {name:"disks"}
repeat with aName in L
set aRow to make new data row at end of data rows of ds
set contents of data cell "disks" of aRow to aName
end repeat
set data source of tv to ds
end launched
```

That's it. Press ⌘-R to save the project and run the built application. After a moment's delay, the Disk Lister application appears and displays its window, shown in Figure 2-13.

Figure 2-13. The Disk Lister application

A nice feature of FaceSpan is the Object Browser (see Figure 2-14) that appears in the Scripting Help drawer attached to script windows. It lists objects in the application's interface, and you can double-click a listing to insert a reference to that object in your code. For example, if we didn't know that we can access our table view as "table view 1 of scroll view 1 of window 1," the Object Browser would tell us how to do it (using names instead of index numbers).

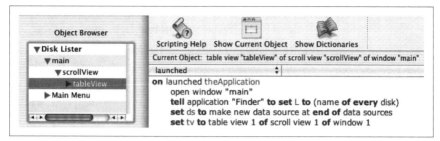

Figure 2-14. The FaceSpan Object Browser

If you were writing this application and you didn't know how to use table views and data sources, you'd read the FaceSpan manual. You would also consult the dictionary, which is displayed in a window (Figure 2-15) that looks a little different than how the Script Editor or Xcode presents it.

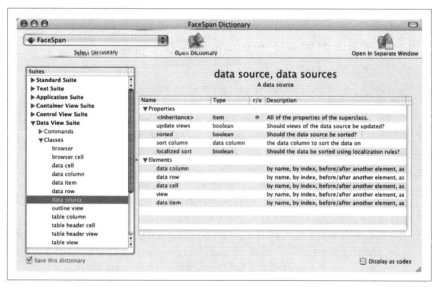

Figure 2-15. The FaceSpan Dictionary

Search TidBITS Interface

Let's move on to something rather more elaborate, involving interactive interface elements, multiple windows, and an embedded Perl script. The purpose of the application is to act as a frontend to the TidBITS archive server. The user enters text in some search fields and presses a button. The application constructs an HTTP POST request and uses curl to submit it to the TidBITS server. When the response comes back as an HTML page, the application uses Perl to parse the HTML, extracting the titles and URLs of the found articles, and presents the list of titles to the user. The user can then double-click on a title to open the corresponding URL in a browser.

To create the Search TidBITS example, start up FaceSpan and create a new project called *Search TidBITS*. In the Project Window, select Other and use the contextual menu's Add Files item to copy the following *parseHTML.pl* Perl script into the project; this ensures that the Perl script will appear in the built application's package, within its Contents/Resources directory, where we will be able to access it from our running code. Here is the Perl script:

```perl
$s = "";
while (<>) {
  $s .= $_;
}
$s =~ m{search results (.*)$}si;
$1 =~ m{<table(.*?)</table>}si;
@rows = ($1 =~ m{<tr(.*?)</tr>}sig);
for ($i=0;$i<$#rows;$i++) {
  ($links[$i], $titles[$i]) =
  ($rows[$i+1] =~ m{<a href="(.*?)">(.*?)</a>}i);
}
print join "\n", @links, @titles;
```

In the Project Window, select Windows and use the contextual menu's New Window item to create the second window. Now you can design the interface. First, design the windows; the idea here is similar to the design in the AppleScript Studio implementation, except that FaceSpan has no NSForm control, so I just use separate text fields to make up the Search window, as shown in Figure 2-16.

Now, we'll design the menu. We provide two menu items of our own, New and Close, as shown in Figure 2-17.

If you want a menu item to be active and to send an event when it is chosen, you must select it and choose the "execute script" action in the Info Panel. So, this must be done now for the New and Close menu items.

Next, we assign names to those interface elements that need them, by selecting each element and typing into the Info Panel. I've called the two windows *main* and *results*; in the *main* window, the three editable text fields have been named textField, titleField, and authorField. Other interface elements can be identified easily enough by index number or in some other way, so there's no need to assign any further names.

Search TidBITS Code

Next, we'll write our application's code. There are two big differences between writing code in AppleScript Studio and writing it in FaceSpan. First, in AppleScript Studio, you must use the Info Window to declare

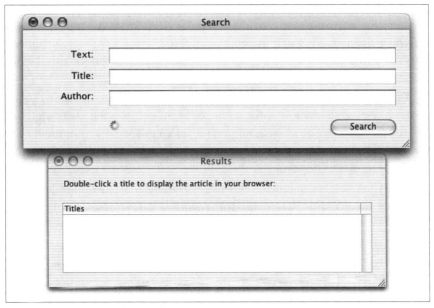

Figure 2-16. Designing the interface

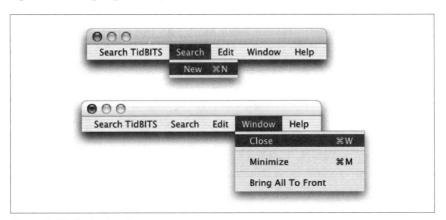

Figure 2-17. Designing the menu

explicitly which events sent by each interface item you want to handle. In FaceSpan, there is no need for this; if you want to handle an event, you just write a handler for it.

Second, FaceSpan permits you to organize your code according to a container script inheritance hierarchy. The idea is that different interface elements can have scripts of their own. Behind the scenes, these scripts are related using script inheritance. Therefore, a script can see handlers and globals in the script of the interface element's container. When an interface element generates a user event, the event propagates up the container hierarchy, starting with the script of the interface element itself, until it finds a matching handler. This permits an object-based style of code organization. This code organization, while purely optional, can be considerably neater than what you have to do in AppleScript Studio.

To illustrate, we're going to make three more scripts, each attached to a particular interface element: one for the push button within the *main* window, one for the *main* window itself, and one for the table view within the *results* window. Thus, counting the *Project Script.applescript* script that comes with the project, we will end up with four scripts.

These scripts will automatically form a hierarchy that corresponds to the container hierarchy (I have put the *results* window script in brackets, because we're not going to bother creating it):

```
Project Script.applescript
  "main" window script
  push button script
  ["results" window script]
  table view script
```

A script at a lower level of the hierarchy can call a handler or (using the keyword my) access a property in a script at a higher level above it. Furthermore, propagation of a user event will start with the script of the interface element that generated the event.

For example, both a push button and a table view will generate a clicked event when the user clicks on them. In AppleScript Studio, you might have just one on clicked handler where both these events would arrive; that handler would then have to distinguish which interface element generated the event, in order to decide what to do. But there is no need for this in FaceSpan. We can put an on clicked handler in the push-button script, and it will be called *only* when this push button is clicked.

To create a script associated with an interface element, select it in its window editor and use the contextual menu to choose Edit Script. After you've created a script for an interface element, FaceSpan displays a little script icon in the lower right of that element, as shown in Figure 2-18.

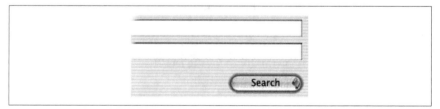

Figure 2-18. A script associated with an interface element

Having created our three additional scripts, we can organize our code. There
are many ways to do this, so I'll just make some arbitrary decisions. The
top-level *Project Script.applescript* holds only the properties and handlers
that reasonably should go at the top level of our code structure:

```
property perlScriptPath : ""
property L1 : {}
property L2 : {}

on launched theApplication
 local f
 open window "main"
 set f to resource path of main bundle
 set perlScriptPath to POSIX path of ¬
 POSIX file (f & "/parseHTML.pl")
 set perlScriptPath to quoted form of perlScriptPath
end launched

on choose menu item theMenuItem
 local theTitle
 set theTitle to (get title of theMenuItem)
 if theTitle is "New" then
 show window "main"
 hide window "results"
 tell window "main"
 set string value of text field "textField" to ""
 set string value of text field "titleField" to ""
 set string value of text field "authorField" to ""
 end tell
 else if theTitle is "Close" then
 hide window 1
 end if
end choose menu item

on displayResults()
 local ds, tv, col, aName, aRow
 set ds to make new data source at end of data sources
 set tv to table view 1 of scroll view 1 of window "results"
 set col to make new data column at end of data columns of ds ¬
 with properties {name:"titles"}
 repeat with aName in L2
 set aRow to make new data row at end of data rows of ds
 set contents of data cell "titles" of aRow to aName
 end repeat
 set data source of tv to ds
 show window "results"
end displayResults
```

Unfortunately, the on choose menu item handler is called
when the user chooses either of our two menu items, just as
in AppleScript Studio. FaceSpan provides no way to give a
menu item its own script.

The push-button script simply receives the clicked event and calls a handler in the *main* window script:

```
on clicked theObject
  startNewSearch( )
end clicked
```

The *main* window script does all the work after the user clicks the push button:

```
property textSought : ""
property titleSought : ""
property authorSought : ""

on startNewSearch( )
 tell window "main"
 set textSought to
 (get string value of text field "textField")
 set titleSought to
 (get string value of text field "titleField")
 set authorSought to
 (get string value of text field "authorField")
 end tell
 urlEncodeStuff( )
 doTheSearch( )
end startNewSearch

on urlEncodeStuff( )
 set textSought to urlEncode(textSought)
 set titleSought to urlEncode(titleSought)
 set authorSought to urlEncode(authorSought)
end urlEncodeStuff

on urlEncode(what)
 set AppleScript's text item delimiters to "+"
 return (words of what) as string
end urlEncode

on feedbackBusy(yn)
 tell window "main"
 if yn then
 set enabled of button 1 to false
 start progress indicator 1
 else
 set enabled of button 1 to true
 stop progress indicator 1
 end if
 end tell
end feedbackBusy

on doTheSearch( )
 local d, u, f, r, L, half
```

```
set d to "'-response=TBSearch.lasso&-token.srch=TBAdv"
set d to d & "&Article+HTML=" & textSought
set d to d & "&Article+Author=" & authorSought
set d to d & "&Article+Title=" & titleSought
set d to d & "&-operator"
set d to d & "=eq&RawIssueNum=&-operator=equals&ArticleDate"
set d to d & "=&-sortField=ArticleDate&-sortOrder=descending"
set d to d & "&-maxRecords=2000&-nothing=MSExplorerHack&-nothing"
set d to d & "=Start+Search' "
set u to "http://db.tidbits.com/TBSrchAdv.lasso"
set f to "/tmp/tempTidBITS"
feedbackBusy(true)
try
do shell script ¬
"curl -s --connect-timeout 15 -m 120 -d " ¬
& d & " -o " & f & " " & u
set r to do shell script ¬
("perl " & my perlScriptPath & " " & f)
feedbackBusy(false)
set L to paragraphs of r
set half to (count L) / 2
set my L1 to items 1 thru half of L
set my L2 to items (half + 1) thru -1 of L
displayResults()
on error
feedbackBusy(false)
beep
end try
end doTheSearch
```

Here is the code for the table-view script:

```
on double clicked theObject
set r to clicked row of theObject
if r is less than or equal to (count my L1) then
open location (item r of my L1)
end if
end double clicked
```

The code itself is just like the AppleScript Studio code in *AppleScript: The Definitive Guide*. The difference here is simply in its organization. And note that this is not the only way to organize the code! For example, in the *main window* script, I call the displayResults handler. That handler, for purposes of this example, is located in the top-level *Project Script.applescript* script, but it doesn't have to be there. It could just as well be in *main window* script, or even in the push-button script! The point is that FaceSpan can help you use whatever style of organization feels natural to you as you develop and maintain your code.

Final Thoughts

In its earlier incarnations, FaceSpan had an enthusiastic base of users, who have naturally been clamoring for a Mac OS X update. Now, such an update exists, and it promises to be an easy and enjoyable way to develop standalone applications with AppleScript. It will be interesting to see how further development of FaceSpan pans out. If FaceSpan 4.0 had existed when I was writing *AppleScript: The Definitive Guide*, I certainly would have included some discussion of it. So, now that it does exist, I'm glad to have been able to offer this little addendum to my book.

—Matt Neuburg

HACK #19   Mac::Glue Your Perl

Mac::Glue makes the Mac sticky enough to entice even this wiley Perl hacker.

Thanks to the popularity of Mac OS X, the new iBook, and the PowerBook G4, it's no longer uncool among Perl hackers to talk about owning an Apple. Longtime Mac devotees have now been joined by longtime Unix devotees and pretty much anyone who wants computers to be shiny, and speakers at conferences are beginning to get used to looking down over a sea of Apple laptops.

One of the great features of Apple's Mac OS is its support for flexible Inter-Process Communication (IPC), which Apple calls Inter-Application Communication (IAC). One of the components of IAC, *Apple Events*, allows applications to command each other to perform various tasks. On top of the raw Apple Events layer, Apple has developed the Open Scripting Architecture (OSA) for scripting languages such as Apple's own AppleScript.

But the last thing the wily Perl hacker wants to do is fiddle about with AppleScript. The Mac::Glue (*http://search.cpan.org/~cnandor/Mac-Glue*) module provides OSA compatibility and allows us to talk to Mac applications with Perl code. Let's take a look at how to script Mac tools at a high level in Perl.

The Prehistory of Mac::Glue

In the beginning, there was Mac::AppleEvents (*http://search.cpan.org/~cnandor/Mac-Carbon-0.66*). This module wrapped the raw Apple Events API, with its cryptic four-character codes to describe applications and their capabilities, and its collection of awkward constants. You had to find out the four-character identifiers yourself and you had to manage and dispose of memory yourself, but at least it got you talking Apple Events. Here's some Mac::AppleEvents code to open your System Folder in the Finder:

```
use Mac::AppleEvents;

my $evt = AEBuildAppleEvent('aevt', 'odoc', typeApplSignature,
 'MACS', kAutoGenerateReturnID, kAnyTransactionID,
 "'----': obj{want:type(prop), from:'null'()," .
 "form:prop, seld:type(macs)}"
);

my $rep = AESend($evt, kAEWaitReply);

AEDisposeDesc($evt);
AEDisposeDesc($rep);
```

Obviously this isn't putting the computer to its full use. In a high-level language such as Perl, we shouldn't have to concern ourselves with clearing up descriptors when they're no longer in use or mucking with providing low-level flags. We just want to send the message to the Finder. So, along came Mac::AppleEvents::Simple (*http://search.cpan.org/~chandor/Mac-AppleEvents-Simple/*), which does more of the work:

```
use Mac::AppleEvents::Simple;
do_event(qw(aevt odoc MACS),
 "'----': obj{want:type(prop), from:'null'()," .
 "form:prop, seld:type(macs)}"
);
```

This is a bit better. At least we're just talking the IAC language now, instead of having to emulate the raw API. But there are still those troublesome identifiers: aevt for the Finder, odoc to open a document, and MACS for the System Folder.

Maybe we'd be better off in AppleScript after all. The AppleScript code for the same operation looks like this:

```
tell application "Finder" to open folder "System Folder"
```

And before Mac::Glue came to Mac OS X, this is effectively what we had to do:

```
use Mac::AppleScript qw(RunAppleScript);
RunAppleScript('tell application "Finder" to open folder "System Folder"');
```

This is considerably easier to understand, but it's just not Perl. Mac::Glue uses the same magic that allows AppleScript to use names instead of identifiers, but wraps it in Perl syntax:

```
use Mac::Glue;
my $finder = Mac::Glue->new('Finder');
$finder->open( $finder->prop('System Folder') );
```

Setting Up and Creating Glues

On Mac OS 9, MacPerl comes with Mac::Glue. However, OS X users need to install it themselves. Mac::Glue requires several other CPAN modules to be installed, including the Mac-Carbon distribution.

Because Mac-Carbon in turn requires some Carbon headers, you need to install Apple Developer Tools. Download them from the Apple Developer Connection site (*https://connect.apple.com/*).

With the correct headers installed, the best way to get Mac::Glue up and running is by using (what else?) a Perl module. On the command line, type:

```
% perl -MCPAN -e 'install "Mac::Glue"'
```

This command downloads all the prerequisites from the Comprehensive Perl Archive Network (CPAN) and installs them; it then downloads and installs the Mac::Glue module itself.

When Mac::Glue installs itself, it also creates *glue files* for the core applications: Finder, the System Events library, and so on. A glue file is used to describe the resources available to an application and what can be done to the properties that it has.

If you try to use Mac::Glue to control an application for which it doesn't currently have a glue file, it will say something like this:

```
No application glue for 'JEDict' found in
'/Library/Perl/5.8.1/Mac/Glue/glues' at -e line 1
```

To create glues for additional applications that are not installed by default, you can drop them onto the Mac OS 9 *macglue* droplet. On Mac OS X, run the gluemac command.

What's a Property?

Once you have all your glues set up, you can start scripting Mac applications in Perl. It helps if you already have some knowledge of how AppleScript works before doing this, because sometimes Mac::Glue doesn't behave the way you expect it to.

For instance, say we want to grab a list of all the active To Do items from iCal. To Do items are associated with calendars, so first we need a list of all the calendars:

```
use Mac::Glue;
my $ical = new Mac::Glue("iCal");

my @cals = $ical->prop("calendars");
```

The problem we face immediately is that $ical->prop("calendars") doesn't give us the calendars. Instead, it provides us with a way to talk about the calendars' property. The property is an object; to get the value of that property, we call its get method:

```
my @cals = $ical->prop("calendars")->get;
```

This returns a list of objects that allow us to talk about individual calendars. We can get their titles like so:

```
for my $cal (@cals) {
  my $name = $cal->prop("title")->get;
```

Now we want to get the To Do items in each calendar that haven't yet been completed or have no completion date:

```
my @todos = grep { !$_->prop("completion_date")->get }
$cal->prop("todos")->get;
```

Then, we can store the summary for each of the To Do items in a hash keyed by the calendar name:

```
$todos{$name} = [ map { $_ >prop("summary")->get } @todos ] ¬
if @todos;
}
```

This allows us to print the summary of all the outstanding To Do items in each calendar:

```
for my $cal(keys %todo) {
  print "$cal:\n";
  print "\t$_\n" for @{$todo{$cal}};
}
```

Putting it all together, the code looks like this:

```
use Mac::Glue;
my $ical = new Mac::Glue("iCal");

my @cals = $ical->prop("calendars")->get;
for my $cal (@cals) {
  my $name = $cal->prop("title")->get;
  my @todos = map {$_->prop("summary")->get }
  grep { !$_->prop("completion_date")->get }
  $cal->prop("todos")->get;
  $todo{$name} = \@todos if @todos;
}

for my $cal(keys %todo) {
  print "$cal:\n";
  print "\t$_\n" for @{$todo{$cal}};
}
```

The question is, where did we get the property names (such as summary and completion_date) from? How did we know that calendars have *titles* while To Do items have *summaries*?

There are two answers to this. The first is to use the documentation created when the glue is installed. Type gluedoc iCal on the Mac OS X command line for a list of the verbs, properties, and objects the application supports. For instance, under the calendar class, you should see this:

```
This class represents a calendar

Properties:

    description (wr12/utxt): This is the calendar
    description. (read-only)
    inheritance (c@#^/item): All of the properties of the
    superclass. (read-only)
    key (wr03/utxt): An unique calendar key (read-only)
    tint (wr04/utxt): The calendar color (read-only)
    title (wr02/utxt): This is the calendar title.
    writable (wr05/bool): If this calendar is writable
    (read-only)

Elements:

    event, todo
```

From this, we can tell that a calendar can be asked for its title property, as well as the events and todos contained within it. Similarly, when we get the events back, we can look up the event class in the documentation and see which properties are available on it.

The second, and perhaps easier, way to find out what you can do with an application is to open the AppleScript Script Editor application (Applications → AppleScript → Script Editor), select Open Dictionary from the File menu, and choose the application you want to script. From there, you can browse a list of the classes and commands associated with the application, as shown in Figure 2-19.

When you need to know how to translate those classes and commands back into Perl, you can then consult the glue documentation. It takes a few attempts to get used to the way Mac::Glue works, but once you've done that, you'll find that you can translate between the AppleScript documentation and a Mac::Glue equivalent in your head.

For a taste of just the sorts of shenanigans you can get up to once you have the basics of Mac::Glue down, dive into a more extensive, real-life example [Hack #20].

—*Simon Cozens and Chris Nandor*

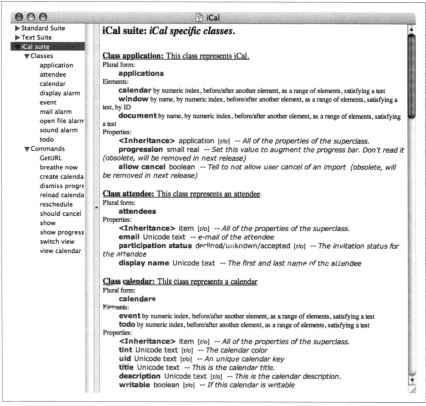

Figure 2-19. Browsing the iCal AppleScript dictionary for available classes and commands

Update iChat Status with Mac::Glue

Keep your many committed fans apprised of what you're doing at just this moment in time, as reflected in your iChat status.

For some reason, many people like to let other people know what they're doing. In the long tradition of JenniCam (*http://www.google.com/ search?q=jennicam*) and now the blogging phenomenon, some people on the Internet like to update their web pages or instant messaging status with what they are doing, watching, listening to, or thinking about at any particular moment in time.

When iChat was first released, there was no easy way to update your status automatically; you had to do so manually. One intrepid programmer found a way to do automate this process via iChat's private framework; the result was iChatStatus [Hack #31], which included various AppleScripts people could use to display their currently playing iTunes track, frontmost application, the document they're currently editing, and more.

But later versions of iChat support Apple Events for setting the status, and that's where this hack comes in.

The Code

This Perl script uses Mac::Glue [Hack #19] to get the current track information from iTunes, find the frontmost application, and tell iChat to update its status to reflect your current activity.

You'll need to have the Mac::Glue Perl module installed before this script will work.

Save the script as *happening.pl*, wherever you please:

```perl
#!/usr/bin/perl
# what's happening!

# you need to create glues for all apps you will script, of course:
# % sudo gluemac /Applications/iTunes.app
# % sudo gluemac /Applications/iChat.app

use strict;
use warnings;
no warnings 'utf8', 'uninitialized';

use Encode 'from_to';
use File::Spec::Functions;
use Mac::Apps::Launch;
use Mac::Glue 1.15;
use Mac::Glue ':all';
use Mac::Files;

my($app, $state, $track, %props, $status, $message, %apps);

my $tmp = FindFolder(kUserDomain, kTemporaryFolderType, kCreateFolder);
my $file = catfile($tmp, 'mystatus');

my $sleep = 10;
my $timeout = 5;

while (1) {
    my $output = itunes();
    my $front = frontmost();

    if ($output) {
        $output = $front . '; ' . $output
            unless $front =~ /^.?iTunes$/;
```

```
    } else {
        $output = $front;
    }

    ichat($output);

    sleep $sleep;
}

sub itunes {
    my $itunes = get_app('iTunes') or return;

    $state ||= $itunes->prop('player state');
    return unless $state->get eq 'playing';

    $track ||= $itunes->prop('current track');
    %props = map { $_ => $track->prop($_) } qw(name artist)
        unless keys %props;

    my %info;
    for my $prop (keys %props) {
        $info{$prop} = $props{$prop}->get;
    }

    my $str = $info{artist}
        ? "$info{artist} - $info{name}"
        : "$info{name}";
    from_to($str, "MacRoman", "iso-8859-9");
    return $str = "\x{266C}$str";
}

sub ichat {
    my($output) = @_;

    my $ichat = get_app('iChat') or return;

    $status ||= $ichat->prop('status');
    return unless $status->get eq 'available';

    $message ||= $ichat->prop('status message');
    $message->set(to => $output);
}

sub frontmost {
    my $system = get_app('System Events') or return;
    $app ||= $system->prop(name => item => 1,
        application_process => whose(frontmost => equals => 1)
    );

    my $front = $app->get or return;

    my $output = "\x{261B}" . $front;
    return $output;
}
```

```
    }

    sub get_app {
        my($app) = @_;
        if (!$apps{$app}) {
            eval { $apps{$app} = new Mac::Glue $app };
            if ($@) {
                $apps{$app} = 'NA'; # cache the failure
            }
            # set timeout for failure
            $apps{$app}->TIMEOUT($timeout);
        }

        # tried and failed
        if ($apps{$app} ne 'NA' && IsRunning($apps{$app}->{ID})) {
            return $apps{$app};
        } else {
            return;
        }
    }

    __END__
```

The script runs in a loop. The itunes( ) function checks to see whether iTunes is running and playing anything; if so, the script retrieves the name and artist of the current track and converts it into a string. A musical note ("\x{266C}" in Unicode) is added to the beginning of the string for giggles.

The frontmost application is discovered similarly; the frontmost( ) routine causes the background application System Events to return the name of the frontmost application, prepending it with a Unicode pointing hand ("\x{261B}").

Back in the main loop, the frontmost application name and current track (if any) are concatenated into one string, which in turn is sent to ichat( ), where it is set as the value of the status message.

The main loop then sleeps for 10 seconds before starting all over again.

A larger version of this hack, with a lot more features (including setting your user icon in iChat to the album cover of the song you're listening to in iTunes), is available at *http://dev.macperl.org/files/scripts/happening*.

Running the Code

Before the script will run as expected, you'll need to create glues for all the applications you plan to talk to from Perl. In this hack, you'll use iTunes and iChat, so type the following on the command line (you'll be prompted for your password after the first command):

```
% sudo gluemac /Applications/iTunes.app
% sudo gluemac /Applications/iChat.app
```

Run the script from the command line [Hack #91], like so:

```
% perl happening.pl &
```

The script launches iChat and iTunes, if they aren't already running, and runs in the background (that's what the & bit at the end does). Your status will be updated periodically and will be both reflected in your own iChat buddy list (Figure 2-20) and associated with your name in the buddy lists of your friends and admirers.

Figure 2-20. Your automagically updated buddy list status

Hacking the Hack

The nice thing about this script is that it is so easily modifiable to suit your needs. You could query Safari to get the title or hostname of the web page you are looking at, query the Finder to get the name of the window you're currently occupying, or query iChat to retrieve the name of the buddy you're chatting with. If you're geeky enough, you could run and use the output from uptime.

 For more information on uptime, type man uptime on the command line [Hack #91].

Or, use LWP and a little web services magic get the latest weather report. Any of these things can be stuffed, space permitting, into your status message. The only hitch is that you have only about 50 or so characters to play with, and that's assuming the people on the other end have their windows set wide enough to see all of it.

 Holding your mouse over a buddy's name in iChat reveals the rest of a long status message.

—*Chris Nandor*

Hack Your Address Book with Perl

#21 Perl, with a little glue, can interact directly with Mac's built-in applications' databases.

Most tools for importing and exporting data from one address book to another are flawed in some way, either because they simply don't work or because they don't quite fit your needs. Perl has always been a great tool for extracting and massaging data into the right format, but it can also be used to feed databases directly.

In the case of Address Book in Mac OS X, you can feed the data via Apple Events with Mac::Glue [Hack #19]. This hack presents a simple example that pokes about and adds entries to your Address Book.

The Code

Through the wonders of Perl and the Mac::Glue module, this script adds an entry for Stevie Wonder to your Address Book.

> You'll need to have the Mac::Glue Perl module installed before this script will work. For more on Mac::Glue, read "Mac::Glue Your Perl" [Hack #19].

Save the script as *addressbook.pl*, wherever you please:

```perl
#!/usr/bin/perl
use strict;
use warnings;

use Mac::Glue ':all';

my $ab = new Mac::Glue 'Address Book';

my $person = $ab->make(new => 'person',
  with_properties => {
    first_name => 'Stevie',
    last_name => 'Wonder',
  }
);

$ab->make(new => 'email', at => location(end => $person->prop('emails')),
  with_properties => {
    value => 'swonder@example.com',
    label => 'work',
  }
);

$ab->make(new => 'phone', at => location(end => $person->prop('phones')),
```

```
  with_properties => {
    value => '555-123-4567',
    label => 'work',
  }
);

$ab->make(new => 'phone', at => location(end => $person->prop('phones')),
  with_properties => {
    value => '555-890-1234',
    label => 'home',
  }
);

$ab->make(new => 'address', at => location(end => $person->
prop('addresses')),
  with_properties => {
    street => '123 Main St.',
    city => 'New York',
    state => 'NY',
    label => 'home',
  }
);

  __END__
```

The general method is to call the $ab->make( ) function to create a new person. You can set the various properties of that person after the fact with statements like this:

```
$person->prop('job_title')->set(to => 'Musician');
```

However, it is easier to add the initial property values with the with_ properties parameter, as shown in the first few lines of the script:

```
my $person = $ab->make(new => 'person',
  with_properties => {
    first_name => 'Stevie',
    last_name => 'Wonder',
  }
);
```

While you could guess some of the properties of the person class, you'll find a consummate list in the Address Book glue manpage by typing gluedoc "Address Book" on the command line [Hack #91]—assuming, of course, you have Mac::Glue installed.

For elements of a person (also listed in the Address Book glue manpage), there may be multiple values: multiple addresses, email addresses, phone numbers, and so on. To create elements of this sort in the person's address record, use $ab->make( ) again, similar to how we used it to create a person:

```
$ab->make(new => 'phone', at => location(end => $person->prop('phones')),
  with_properties => {
```

```
            value => '555-123-4567',
            label => 'work',
        }
    );
```

Note the addition of the location this time; this says to add the new element to the end of the person's existing list of phone numbers. The label property states which type of element (e.g., work, fax, home, cell) you're creating.

Running the Code

Before the script will run as expected, you'll need to create a glue for the Address Book, so that Perl can talk to it. Type the following on the command line (you'll be prompted for your password):

```
% sudo gluemac /Applications/AddressBook.app
```

Run the script from the command line, like so:

```
% perl addressbook.pl
```

Now, check your Address Book (Figure 2-21).

Figure 2-21. A new Address Book entry created with a little Perl glue

Lo and behold, you should find an entry for the apple of everyone's eye, Mr. Stevie Wonder.

Hacking the Hack

Here's an example of that Address Book glue put to real work. Perl hacker David Wheeler wondered (*http://use.perl.org/~Theory/journal/18860*) if there were a simple way to prepend a +1 on to any phone number in the Address Book without a +International Code—i.e., all those presumed to be U.S. numbers. Indeed there is:

```perl
#!/usr/bin/perl

# Add +1 to any Address Book phone numbers without a + International code

# By Chris Nandor and David Wheeler

# you need to create a glue for Address Book, of course:
# % sudo gluemac /Applications/AddressBook.app

use Mac::Glue;

my $ab = new Mac::Glue 'Address Book';

my $people = $ab->obj('people');
for my $person ($people->get) {
    for my $phone ($person->prop('phone')->get) {
        my $value  = $phone->prop('value');
        my $number = $value->get;
        next if $number =~ /^41-/ || $number =~ /^0/;
        next unless length $number > 9 && $number !~ /^\+/;
        if ($number =~ /(†{3})[.-\s](†{3})[.-\s](†{4})(.*)/) {
            $number = "+1 ($1) $2-$3$4";
        } else {
            $number = "+1 $number";
        }
        print "$number\n";
        $value->set(to => $number);
    }
}
```

Save the script as *plusone.pl* or the like. If you've not already done so, create a glue for the Address Book as described in this hack's "Running the Code" section. Then, run the script on the command line like so:

```
% perl plusone.pl
```

—Chris Nandor

Manipulate Images on the Command Line

#22   Tap into the power of Quartz to poke, prod, and manipulate images from the command line.

The Quartz imaging layer of Mac OS X, responsible for providing much of the image-processing magic of the Aqua user interface, provides a rich set of graphics-processing APIs. Unfortunately, most of this power is available only to programmers who know how to interact with the Quartz system at a low level. With the release of Panther, however, Apple has provided the Scriptable Image Processing Server (SIPS), which provides access to basic image-manipulation functionality. Better yet, this functionality can be accessed from the command using the /usr/bin/sips tool.

SIPS isn't Photoshop by any stretch of the imagination, but it provides the ability to automate some common image operations, such as resizing, rotation, converting between formats, cropping, and working with ICC profiles. And since it provides a command-line tool, you can easily integrate these functions into whatever kind of workflow you want.

Unfortunately, the /usr/bin/sips tool doesn't come with a manpage. However, we've done a bit of research, scoured the Web, and used the help that is available with the sips -h command to come up with the instructions for some common operations.

Obtain Information About an Image

There's quite a bit of information about an image, such as how big it is and when it was captured, just waiting to be used. To get a listing of all the properties associated with an image, you can call SIPS with the following syntax:

```
sips --getProperty [all|propertyname] filename
```

For example, to look at the properties of an image from a digital camera, use the following command:

```
$ sips --getProperty all IMG_8790.jpg
/Users/duncan/Desktop/images/IMG_8790.jpg
  pixelWidth: 2272
  pixelHeight: 1704
  format: jpeg
  formatOptions: default
  dpiWidth: 180.000
  dpiHeight: 180.000
  samplesPerPixel: 3
  bitsPerSample: 8
  space: RGB
  creation: 2004:04:17 22:34:12
  make: Canon
```

```
model: Canon PowerShot S45
software: QuickTime 6.5
```

You can also get just the value for a particular property of an image. For example, if you had a script that organized images by the date on which they were created, you could use the following:

```
$ sips --getProperty creation IMG_8790.jpg
/Users/duncan/Desktop/images/IMG_8790.jpg
  creation: 2004:04:17 22:34:12
```

 To get a complete list of property names that SIPS supports, execute sips -H.

Convert from One Format to Another

SIPS can read and write a variety of image formats, including JPEG, JPEG2, MS Windows bitmap (BMP), Photoshop (PSD), PDF, PICT, PNG, and QuickTime images. It can also read GIF, SGI, and Targa (TGA) files, though it can't write to these formats. Because of the wide variety of formats that SIPS can read and write, it's a great tool for converting files from one format to another.

To perform a conversion, you'll need to use a command of the following form:

```
sips --setProperty format [jpeg|tiff|png|jp2|pict|bmp|qtif|psd] filename
--out filename|dirname
```

For example, to convert a Photoshop file to a TIFF for use in an application that can't read Photoshop files, use the following command:

```
$ sips --setProperty format tiff goldengatebridge.psd --out
goldengatebridge.tif
/Users/duncan/Desktop/images/goldengatebridge.psd
 /Users/duncan/Desktop/images/goldengatebridge.tif
```

SIPS responds with a couple of lines of output, telling you that it read the Photoshop file and output the TIFF file. You can check its work by opening the TIFF file:

```
$ open goldengatebridge.tiff
```

To convert multiple image files—for example, a number of JPEG files from a digital camera—you could use the following command:

```
$ sips --setProperty format tiff *.jpg --out .
/Users/duncan/Desktop/images/IMG_8790.jpg
Warning: Output file suffix changed to .tif
 /Users/duncan/Desktop/images/IMG_8790.tif
```

```
/Users/duncan/Desktop/images/IMG_8791.jpg
Warning: Output file suffix changed to .tif
  /Users/duncan/Desktop/images/IMG_8791.tif
```

SIPS responds with a few lines of output for each file, letting you know which file is being processed and its new filename.

Rotate Images

Rotation is another common task that needs to be performed on images, especially images from digital cameras. Here's the command to rotate an image:

```
sips --rotate angle filename
```

The angle to rotate an image is specified in degrees clockwise. For example, the following command rotates an image 90 degrees clockwise:

```
$ sips --rotate 90 IMG_8790.jpg
/Users/duncan/Desktop/images/IMG_8790.jpg
  /Users/duncan/Desktop/images/IMG_8790.jpg
```

When executed this way, SIPS replaces the original image with the rotated one. If you would like to keep your original image, you can do the following:

```
$ sips --rotate 90 IMG_8791.jpg --out IMG_8791_rotated.jpg
/Users/duncan/Desktop/images/IMG_8791.jpg
  /Users/duncan/Desktop/images/IMG_8791_rotated.jpg
```

Resizing Images

Resizing images is yet another common task, usually to provide a thumbnail-sized image for quick viewing. There are few ways to resize an image. The first is to provide width and height arguments to SIPS:

```
sips --resampleHeightWidth height width filename
```

The second way to resize an image is to specify only a width or a height argument and let SIPS figure out the other dimension:

```
sips --resampleHeight height filename
sips --resampleWidth width filename
```

The third and most useful way to resize images is to create a slew of thumbnails:

```
sips --resampleHeightWidthMax value filename [filename...]
```

For example, the following command creates thumbnails of a directory of JPEG files and places them into a subdirectory:

```
$ sips --resampleHeightWidthMax 100 *.jpg --out thumbs/
/Users/duncan/Desktop/images/IMG_8790.jpg
  /Users/duncan/Desktop/images/thumbs/IMG_8790.jpg
```

```
/Users/duncan/Desktop/images/IMG_8791.jpg
 /Users/duncan/Desktop/images/thumbs/IMG_8791.jpg
/Users/duncan/Desktop/images/IMG_8796.jpg
 /Users/duncan/Desktop/images/thumbs/IMG_8796.jpg
```

HACK #23 Script CoreGraphics with Python

Use Python 2.3 and its interface to the CoreGraphics library to rescale and decorate images for publication on the Web.

Mac OS X Panther includes many updated Developer Tools. Among them is an enhanced Version 2.3 of the Python programming language (*http://www.python.org*), with its own SWIG-based bindings to the CoreGraphics library. Creating PDFs, JPEGs, and documents in other graphical formats just became a lot easier.

Simplified Wrapper and Interface Generator (SWIG) exposes an interface to portions of a language such as Objective-C to a scripting language such as Python. In this way, Python can gain access to and work with some of the core Objective-C frameworks that underlie Mac OS X, such as CoreGraphics.

This hack provides a taste of the capabilities in the Python CoreGraphics module and shows how to use Panther's CoreGraphics to rescale and decorate images for publication to the Web.

Getting Started

This hack assumes you know a little something about Python programming. That said, Python is an approachable, easy-to-read language; some call it "English that actually manages to run." Even if you've never done a lick of programming or have only dabbled a little in AppleScript or even Basic in some previous lifetime, you should be able to follow along and get the gist of just how far Panther and a little Python scripting can go.

To dive into Python proper, you might want to pick up a copy of *Learning Python* by Mark Lutz and David Ascher (O'Reilly).

You can use Python's CoreGraphics bindings right out of the box. However, it's a good idea to install the Developer Tools (*http://www.apple.com/macosx/developertools*) that ship with Panther, because the */Developer/Examples/Quartz/Python* folder contains the main source of documentation for the CoreGraphics module.

The *API-Summary* file in that directory shows how comprehensive the bindings are. They include functions for loading GIF images and saving graphics in JPEG, PDF, PNG, and TIFF formats. The bindings also let you create new grayscale, RGB, and CMYK bitmap graphics contexts, as well as PDF contexts. Context instances offer a full set of Bezier path construction methods, and they support affine coordinate transformations. You can even control the rendering of shadows.

The CoreGraphics wrapper exposes much of the Quartz 2D graphics library to Python, but some pieces are still missing. For example, the bindings include a CGContext.drawShading( ) method, which should fill a path with a gradient from one color to another. But the bindings provide no way to create the CGShadingRef instance, which drawShading( ) requires as an argument.

Despite the rough edges, the bindings are useful. In fact, as the contents of */usr/libexec/fax* show, Panther itself uses Python and CoreGraphics to handle incoming faxes and to generate cover sheets for outgoing faxes.

> Panther also cleverly generates cover sheets by formatting the pages as HTML, then using CoreGraphics to rerender the HTML to PDF format.

Apple's own reliance on using Python with the CoreGraphics module is reason to hope that it will continue to be improved in future releases of Mac OS X.

Putting CoreGraphics to Work

Now let's use CoreGraphics to prepare images for the Web. First, we'll walk through a Python class, ImageDecorator, which reads an existing image from disk, rescales it to fit within size parameters you specify, adds a white image border with a thin image outline and a drop shadow, and saves the results to a new image file. Figure 2-22 shows the picture before and after.

> The full source code for the ImageDecorator class is available at *http://www.macdevcenter.com/mac/2004/03/19/examples/ ImageDecorator.py*.

ImageDecorator.py uses a wildcard import of the CoreGraphics module. Wildcard imports are discouraged in Python, because they tend to pollute the namespace of the importing module and increase the chance of namespace collisions. But all public attribute names in CoreGraphics have a CG prefix, which reduces the risk of namespace collisions, and qualified name references would make the source code in this hack harder to read.

Figure 2-22. An image file, before (left) and after (right)

The __init__ method for ImageDecorator isn't presented here, but you can find it in *ImageDecorator.py*. It simply records settings for all of the image-decoration parameters. In addition to setting the dimensions of the image and its decorations, the __init__ parameters include settings for the image's background color and rescaling quality. We'll discuss these parameters in more detail later in this hack.

Loading an image. To load an image from disk using CoreGraphics, we just have to create an image data provider and pass it to CGImageImport:

```
def _loadImage(self, pathname):
    return CGImageImport(CGDataProviderCreateWithFilename(pathname))
```

Computing the new image's dimensions. We'll need to reserve room for the new image's border and the other decorations, while ensuring that the image fits within the specified maximum size. At the same time, we'll need to preserve the aspect ratio of the original image. Two methods, _findInsideSize( ) and _findRescaledSize( ), satisfy these constraints.

The _findInsideSize( ) method computes the size of the region inside the decorated image, where the rescaled source image will be rendered. It ensures that the new *inside* dimensions have the same aspect ratio as the original image:

```
def _getInsideSize(self, img, margin):
    width = img.getWidth( )
    height = img.getHeight( )
```

```
aspect = float(width) / height
if aspect > 1.0:
  internalWidth = (self._maxWidth - margin)
  internalHeight = (internalWidth / aspect)
else:
  internalHeight = (self._maxHeight - margin)
  internalWidth = (internalHeight * aspect)
return (internalWidth, internalHeight)
```

The _findRescaledSize() method adds the decoration margins to the size computed by _findInsideSize(). Then, it stores the new image dimensions as instance attributes, for later reference:

```
def _findRescaledSize(self, img):
  margin = (self._borderWidth + self._margin)
  (insideWidth, insideHeight) = self._findInsideSize(img, margin)
  self._newWidth = insideWidth + margin
  self._newHeight = insideHeight + margin
```

Creating the graphics context. Given the size of the output image, we can create a graphics context into which to render the image. We'll define another method, _getGraphicsContext(), to do the job.

CoreGraphics provides several functions for creating bitmap graphics contexts. Assuming the source image contains color, we'll want to render to a color graphics context. So, we'll use CGBitmapContextCreateWithColor.

CGBitmapContextCreateWithColor creates a graphics context with the given pixel dimensions, colorspace, and background color. In this case, we'll use an RGB colorspace. We'll also use the background color that was specified in the __init__ method:

```
def _getGraphicsContext(self):
  self._gc = CGBitmapContextCreateWithColor(
    self._newWidth, self._newHeight,
    CGColorSpaceCreateDeviceRGB(),self._bgColor)
```

The background color argument to CGBitmapContextCreateWithColor() is a sequence of color-component intensities. It has one value for each component in the provided colorspace, plus an extra value for the alpha (or, *transparency*) component. Each value should be in the range of 0.0 (lowest intensity) to 1.0 (highest intensity). For example, in the RGB colorspace, a solid white background is represented as (1.0, 1.0, 1.0, 1.0).

Ready to draw. Once the graphics context is initialized, we can start drawing the image decorations. We'll define another method, _drawShadowedBorder(), to render the bordered rectangle and the image shadow. To mimic the appearance of a bordered photographic print, we'll render the rectangle in white:

```
def _drawShadowedBorder(self):
  shadowedRect = CGRectMake(
    0, self._margin,
    self._newWidth - self._margin,
    self._newHeight - self._margin)
  self._gc.addRect(shadowedRect)
  self._gc.setShadow(
    CGSizeMake(self._shadowOffset, -self._shadowOffset),
    self._shadowBlur)
  self._gc.setRGBFillColor(1, 1, 1, 1)
  self._gc.fillPath()
  # Remove the shadow:
  self._gc.setShadow(CGSizeMake(0, 0), 0)
```

shadowedRect defines the extent of the image's white border. Here, we've offset the rectangle upward by the size of the shadow margin, self._margin. This leaves room for the shadow below and to the right of the image.

The addRect() call simply adds the rectangle to the current drawing path.

setShadow() takes two arguments: one specifies the width and height by which to offset the shadow relative to its source graphic, and the other specifies how *sharp* the shadow should appear (the distance over which it should fade out). Once more, we're using settings specified in the __init__ method.

The context's fillPath() method fills the current drawing path with the current fill color. Since our graphics context uses the RGB colorspace, we've set the color using setRGBFillColor(). Other methods are available for use with other colorspaces.

After drawing the image border, we need to remove the shadow from the graphics context. Otherwise, every subsequent drawing operation would be rendered with its own separate shadow.

Adding the outline. The last bit of decoration on our image is a thin gray line around the image border. This outline will make it easier to distinguish the unshaded sides of the image's border from the image's background color:

```
def _drawOutline(self):
  self._gc.setRGBStrokeColor(0.5, 0.5, 0.5, 0.5)
  self._gc.setLineWidth(0.5)
  margin = self._margin
  outlineRect = CGRectMake(0, margin + 0.5,
    self._newWidth - margin - 0.5,
    self._newHeight - margin - 1)
  self._gc.addRect(outlineRect)
  self._gc.strokePath()
```

Whereas setRGBFillColor() controls the color used to fill a path, setRGBStrokeColor() sets the color used to draw the path itself. In this case, we're drawing a thin gray line that is a half-pixel wide. The goal is to create an outline that is visible but doesn't look like it was rendered with a felt-tip pen. The path along which we're drawing has slightly different dimensions than the filled image border, in order to compensate for the line width.

Drawing the source image. With the shadowed image border in place, we're almost ready to render the rescaled source image. First, we need to specify the rectangular region into which it will be drawn:

```
def _getBorderedRect(self):
  w = self._newWidth
  h = self._newHeight
  margin = self._margin
  border = self._borderWidth
  return CGRectMake(border, border + margin,
    w - margin - 2 * border, h - margin - 2 * border)
```

Then, we need to set the interpolation quality to use when rescaling the source image and, at last, draw the image:

```
def _renderSrcImage(self, img):
  r = self._getBorderedRect()
  self._gc.setInterpolationQuality(self._quality)
  self._gc.drawImage(r, img)
```

If we could hardwire the output format, saving an image would be even simpler than loading one. As it is, the ImageDecorator class lets clients save in any bitmap image format that CoreGraphics supports.

```
def _saveAs(self, pathname):
  extToFormat = {
    ".png": kCGImageFormatPNG,
    ".jpg": kCGImageFormatJPEG,
    ".tif": kCGImageFormatTIFF,
    }
  extension = os.path.splitext(pathname)[1]
  try:
    imgFormat = extToFormat[extension.lower()]
    self._gc.writeToFile(pathname, imgFormat)
  except KeyError:
    raise ValueError("Can't save image as %r -- "
      "unknown format %s" % (pathname, extension))
```

extToFormat is a Python dictionary that maps filename extensions to Core-Graphics format constants. The _saveAs() method extracts the filename extension from the provided output pathname and then uses it to look up the image format to use.

The lower() string method gets the extension in all-lower-case letters before performing the dictionary lookup.

If it can determine the format, _saveAs( ) uses the context's writeToFile( ) method to save the image data. Otherwise, it reports the unrecognized filename extension by raising a Python ValueError.

Putting it all together. The method names we've defined so far have all had leading underscores. That's a hint to other Python programmers that they should treat these as protected methods and invoke them only from within the ImageDecorator class or derived subclasses.

For other clients, we'll make ImageDecorator easy to use. Aside from its constructor, it will provide just one public method, decorate( ):

```
def decorate(self, srcPathname, destPathname):
    img = self._loadImage(srcPathname)
    self._findRescaledSize(img)
    self._getGraphicsContext( )
    self._drawShadowedBorder( )
    self._drawOutline( )
    self._renderSrcImage(img)
    self._saveAs(destPathname)
```

Using ImageDecorator

Here's an example of how to use ImageDecorator to process a directory full of images:

```
from ImageDecorator import ImageDecorator
import os, glob

decorator = ImageDecorator(bgColor=(1, 1, 1, 1))
images = glob.glob("test/*.jpg")

for srcname in images:
    basename = os.path.basename(srcname)
    dirname = os.path.dirname(srcname)

    destname = os.path.join(dirname, "decorated_%s" % basename)

    decorator.decorate(srcname, destname)
    os.system("open %r %r" % (srcname, destname))
```

This example uses Python's glob module to find all JPEG images in the *test* subdirectory of the current working directory. A decorated copy of each image is created with the same filename as the original, but with a prefix of *decorated_*.

The os.system( ) call at the bottom of the loop takes advantage of the OS X open command to display the original and decorated images side by side. On my system, both images are displayed using the Preview application.

Image Format Trade-Offs

In the previous example, each decorated image was saved in JPEG format. Since JPEG doesn't support transparency, the example placed the decorated image on a solid white background. Obviously, if we'd wanted to include such an image in a web page, we would have had to choose a background color that didn't clash with the background color of the web page.

A better solution might be to store the image in a format that does allow transparency, such as PNG or GIF. Unfortunately, each of these formats has drawbacks with respect to the CoreGraphics bindings. As noted earlier, CoreGraphics doesn't support saving images in GIF format. It actually does let you create GIF image files, but in every test I performed, the resulting files were zero bytes in size.

Almost as if to compensate, images saved in PNG format are huge. They are often 5 to 10 times as large as the corresponding JPEG images.

Interpolation Quality

In `ImageDecorator`'s `__init__` method, we used a default quality of `kCGInterpolationHigh`. In CoreGraphics, image interpolation quality controls how a source image's pixels are sampled when computing destination-pixel intensities.

In addition to `kCGInterpolationHigh`, you can use two other settings: `kCGInterpolationNone` or `kCGInterpolationLow`. These settings produce results that are often hard to distinguish from one another, but they are significantly different from the results of `kCGInterpolationHigh`.

The easiest way to demonstrate these differences is to compare their effects side by side. The following code sample uses `ImageDecorator` to produce three images, one with each interpolation quality setting. It also generates an HTML page in which to display the images. Once the page is generated, the script uses the `os.system("open ...")` technique to display the results; on my system, the page appears in a new Safari window.

Let's start by defining a couple of HTML page templates. First, we'll define the template for the web page as a whole. It includes a placeholder, `%(comparisonCells)s`, into which we'll format a sequence of HTML table cells:

```
_template = '''<html>
<head>
<title>Image Interpolation Qualities</title>
</head>
<body>
<table>
```

```
<tr>
%(comparisonCells)s
</tr>
</table>
</body>
</html>'''
```

Next, we need to define a template string for the content of each data cell in
comparisonCells. The content consists of an img whose URL is specified by
%(imagePathname)s, followed by a caption that describes the quality
%(settingName)s used to generate the image:

```
_imageRowTemplate = '''
<td><img src="%(imagePathname)s"><br>
Quality: %(settingName)s</td>
'''
```

The main function in this example loops through the supported image quality settings, creating a separate copy of the source image for each setting.
Each generated image is stored as a new entry in comparisonCells:

```
def main():
    comparisonCells = []
    sourceImage = "../images/image_1.jpg"
    for settingName, quality in [
    ["None", kCGInterpolationNone], ["Low", kCGInterpolationLow],
        ["High", kCGInterpolationHigh]]:
        imagePathname = ("image_1_%s.jpg" % settingName)
        decorator = ImageDecorator(maxWidth=200, maxHeight=200, quality=quality)
        decorator.decorate(sourceImage,imagePathname)
        comparisonCells.append(_imageRowTemplate % locals())
    comparisonCells = "\n".join(comparisonCells)
    htmlFilename = "quality_comparison.html"
    outf = open(htmlFilename, "w")
    outf.write(_template % locals())
    outf.close()
    os.system("open %s" % htmlFilename)
```

comparisonCells begins life as a Python list of _imageRowTemplate strings.
Once all the images have been generated, comparisonCells is turned into a
single string that joins its list elements together with newline characters:

```
comparisonCells = "\n".join(comparisonCells)
```

Finally, main() generates and displays the comparison HTML page:

```
htmlFilename = "quality_comparison.html"
outf = open(htmlFilename, "w")
outf.write(_template % locals())
outf.close()
os.system("open %s" % htmlFilename)
```

After running the script, you can see the effects of the different interpolation
quality settings, as shown in Figure 2-23.

Figure 2-23. The effects of different interpolation quality settings (from left to right)—
none, low, and high

Final Thoughts

This hack has shown how Python and Panther's CoreGraphics module can
simplify some image-processing tasks. I hope it has piqued your curiosity;
there's much more to the CoreGraphics module than could be presented
here. I encourage you to check out the documentation and code examples in
/Developer/Examples/Quartz/Python, scan through /usr/libexec/fax/, and
experiment with CoreGraphics on your own.

—Mitch Chapman

HACK   Tap RSS with Shell Scripts
#24
A little shell scripting can go a long way. It can get you the latest Slashdot
news at your fingertips whenever you drop down to the Mac OS X Terminal.

If you're like me, you want to keep up with the latest news and information.
Shell scripts help me do just that. In this hack, I'll show you how I wrote a
shell script that watches the news at Slashdot (http://www.slashdot.org) and
automatically shows me the latest story headlines every time I launch a Terminal application.

First Things First

Before any work with shell scripts begins, the first step is to figure out the
URL of the RSS page on Slashdot.

> Really Simple Syndication (RSS) is an XML-format data
> stream that's much more easily parsed and tracked than
> HTML pages, at least programmatically.

The Slashdot home page doesn't make it particularly easy to find, but the rightmost link on the last line is *rss*, and the URL behind that link is *http://slashdot.org/index.rss*.

To look at the feed from within the Terminal, I'm going to use the powerful curl application and pipe the output to head to ensure that I'm not drowned in output:

```
$ curl --silent 'http://slashdot.org/index.rss' | head
<?xml version="1.0" encoding="ISO-8859-1"?>

<rdf:RDF
  xmlns:rdf="http://www.w3.org/1999/02/22-rdf-syntax-ns#"
  xmlns="http://purl.org/rss/1.0/"
  xmlns:dc="http://purl.org/dc/elements/1.1/"
  xmlns:slash="http://purl.org/rss/1.0/modules/slash/"
  xmlns:taxo="http://purl.org/rss/1.0/modules/taxonomy/"
  xmlns:admin="http://webns.net/mvcb/"
  xmlns:syn="http://purl.org/rss/1.0/modules/syndication/"
```

Yes, this looks fairly scary as output goes, I admit, but with a little help from the grep utility, this can quickly become a lot more user-friendly. In this case, let's just pull out the lines that are tagged as either the <title> or the <description>:

```
$ curl --silent 'http://slashdot.org/index.rss' | grep -E '(title|
description>)' | head
<title>Slashdot</title>
<description>News for nerds, stuff that matters</description>
<title>Slashdot</title>
<title>Yahoo To Charge For Search Listings</title>
<description>ibi writes "Yahoo will start taking payments
to "tilt the playing field" for companies that want their
listings given more prominence by Yahoo's search engine. ...</description>
<title>Infinium Labs Threatens HardOCP Again</title>
<description>XBox4Evr writes "In a follow-up from two weeks ago,
Infinium Labs is again threatening the tech web site HardOCP
with legal action. This in itself, is no big ...</description>
<title>SCO Postpones Lawsuit, Now Threatening Two</title>
<description>zzxc writes "In a surprise turn of events, SCO says
that they need more time to prepare an announcement of who
they are going to sue. According to SCO, the ...</description>
<title>Gyroscopic Wireless Mouse</title>
```

Not bad. In fact, that's really almost all we need. So, let's turn this into a shell script.

Getting Headlines Only

Turning this command line into a shell script is a breeze: just open your favorite Terminal command-line editor.

I use vi, but I've been trapped in Unix since 1980, so it's already subverted my neural pathways. You might prefer pico or even BBEdit or similar editor.

Whichever you choose, type in the following, a standard shell script preamble:

```
#!/bin/sh
```

This tells the operating system that when this particular file is executed, it should be given to the shell (sh) to be run. Then, let's create a variable that contains the URL:

```
url="http://slashdot.org/index.rss"
```

Now, we can reference $url, and the entire script has become more portable and easily modified. The next line is the entire command:

```
curl --silent "$url" | grep -E '(title>|description>)'
```

If you get a "command not found" error with curl, you might need to specify a full path. In standard installations of Panther, the curl command can be found at /usr/bin/curl.

This script produces the output we've already seen, so let's make two tweaks to make it more useful. First, the first three lines of output (the Slashdot title and description) never change, so it would be just as easy to strip them out of the output. This can be done a variety of ways, but I'm going to turn to the sed command, which has many hidden powers. One of these hidden powers is that, by default, if you specify the -n flag, it won't output any of its input. What's the value of this? Then we can specify a pattern of some sort and output only those lines that match the pattern, like this:

```
curl --silent "$url" | grep -E '(title>|description>)' | \
  sed -n '4,$p'
```

Notice the trailing backslash here; rather than have our command pipe stretch longer and longer, the backslash (which must be the last character on the line) lets me wrap the command to multiple lines and make it generally more readable.

We're getting close to trying the script. The only other tweak worth making is to strip out the <title>, </title>, <description>, and </description> tags themselves. This too can be done with sed, in typical Unix fashion:

```
curl --silent "$url" | grep -E '(title>|description>)' | \
  sed -n '4,$p' | \
  sed -e 's/<title>//' -e 's/<\/title>//' -e 's/<description>/ /' \
  -e 's/<\/description>//'
```

The XML tags are effectively stripped out, except the <description> tag is replaced by two spaces, just for formatting. Here's the result, assuming you've saved the script as *slash-rss.sh*:

```
$ sh slash-rss.sh | head -4
Yahoo To Charge For Search Listings
  ibi writes "Yahoo will start taking payments to "tilt the
  playing field" for companies that want their listings given more
  prominence by Yahoo's search engine. ...
Infinium Labs Threatens HardOCP Again
  XBox4Evr writes "In a follow up from two weeks ago, Infinium Labs
  is again threatening the tech web site HardOCP with legal action. This in
  itself, is no big ...
```

This output shows the top two stories (two titles and two descriptions in four lines). Not bad. Not beautiful, but certainly functional for a first script.

I always spend way too much time fine-tuning scripts to get just the output I want, so let's continue working on this to ensure that the output is more readable, shall we? It's so easy, you'll be amazed:

```
curl --silent "$url" | grep -E '(title>|description>)' | \
sed -n '4,$p' | \
sed -e 's/<title>//' -e 's/<\/title>//' -e 's/<description>/ /' \
-e 's/<\/description>//' | \
fmt
```

Here are the results, again piped through head:

```
$ sh slash-rss.sh | head
Yahoo To Charge For Search Listings
  ibi writes "Yahoo will start taking payments to "tilt the playing
  field" for companies that want their listings given more prominence
  by Yahoo's search engine. ...
Infinium Labs Threatens HardOCP Again
  XBox4Evr writes "In a follow up from two weeks ago, Infinium
  Labs is again threatening the tech web site HardOCP with legal
  action. This in itself, is no big ...
SCO Postpones Lawsuit, Now Threatening Two
  zzxc writes "In a surprise turn of events, SCO says that they
```

The problem now is that head needs to be between the sed invocations and the fmt command, because we have no way of knowing how many lines each description is going to produce when fed through fmt. The solution is to build the next generation of this script!

Getting as Many Headlines as You Want

The obvious solution is to add a command flag that lets you specify how many headlines you want. Multiply the number of headlines by two to obtain the value to feed head within the script. Here's how that looks as part of a shell script ($# is the number of arguments and $1 is the first argument):

```
#!/bin/sh

url="http://slashdot.org/index.rss"

if [ $# -eq 1 ] ; then
 headarg=$(( $1 * 2 )) # $(( )) specifies that you're using an equation
else
 headarg="-8" # default is four headlines
fi

curl --silent "$url" | grep -E '(title>|description>)' | \
 sed -n '4,$p' | \
 sed -e 's/<title>//' -e 's/<\/title>//' -e 's/<description>/ /' \
 -e 's/<\/description>//' | \
 head $headarg | fmt
```

Now, I can specify that I want only the top headline, the newest entry on the Slashdot site, by simply specifying -1 when I invoke the script:

```
$ sh slash-rss.sh -1
Yahoo To Charge For Search Listings
 ibi writes "Yahoo will start taking payments to "tilt the playing
 field" for companies that want their listings given more prominence
 by Yahoo's search engine. ...
```

That's pretty cool, I think. I could tweak it forever, but let's stop here and see how to turn this into a Unix command, just like ls and cd.

> You can download this shell script in finished form at *http:// www.intuitive.com/articles/slash-rss.sh.shtml.*

Turning the Script into a Command

There are two ways to turn a shell script into a command: create an alias or make the script executable and ensure it's in your PATH. If you're using Bash, you can create an alias like this:

```
alias slashdot="sh slash-rss.sh"
```

Then you can see the headlines by just typing slashdot on your command line.

To make the shell script itself executable, first make sure you've saved it in a directory that's in your PATH by typing this command:

```
$ echo $PATH
/bin:/sbin:/usr/bin:/usr/sbin:/sw/bin:/usr/X11R6/bin:
/usr/local/bin:/Users/dt/bin:/sw/bin
```

You can see that my PATH includes /Users/dt/bin; that's where I save this script and others like it. Once the script is saved in the right place, you'll need to make it executable by using the chmod command:

```
$ chmod +x slash-rss.sh
```

Optionally, you could of course rename the script to be a bit more friendly.

Automatically Executing upon Terminal Launch

If you're running the Bash shell, which you probably are if you're in Panther, then it's easy to make the script execute automatically upon launching the Terminal. Move to your home directory and append an invocation of the script to your *.bash_login* file:

```
$ cd
$ echo "sh slash-rss.sh -2" >> .bash_login
```

 Make sure you use two angle brackets (>>), not one, on that last command! Also, if you are using the *tcsh* shell, you'll want to add this command to your *.login* file instead of *.bash_login*.

Now, the next time you start up a Terminal application window, you'll see this:

```
Last login: Tue Mar 2 23:09:36 on ttyp3
Welcome to Darwin!
Yahoo To Charge For Search Listings
  ibi writes "Yahoo will start taking payments to "tilt the playing
  field" for companies that want their listings given more prominence
  by Yahoo's search engine. ...
Infinium Labs Threatens HardOCP Again
  XBox4Evr writes "In a follow up from two weeks ago, Infinium
  Labs is again threatening the tech web site HardOCP with legal
  action. This in itself, is no big ...
$
```

Hacking the Hack

You should be able to pull in just about any RSS feed in the same manner. Just change the URL in this line:

```
url="http://slashdot.org/index.rss"
```

While RSS should be pretty much the same from feed to feed, feeds can indeed differ in minor ways that require a little more tweaking to parse.

It's also worth noting that this use of shell scripts to parse and format XML has other applications. For example, go to *http://www.casino-bookstore.com* and take a close look at the Latest Casino Gambling News box. It uses almost an identical script to keep track of the Casino Gambling News XML feed from About.com (*http://www.about.com*). Need another example? Go to *http://www.healthy-bookstore.com* and look at the MedicineNet (*http://www.medicinenet.com*) news feed. Again, it uses curl and sed to turn the XML data into HTML data.

—Dave Taylor

HACK #25 Add a Dab of GUI to Unix Scripts

Build a graphical dialog front-end to your Unix scripts with just a snippet of Perl or Python glue code.

When it comes to combining Unix scripting and GUI, more often than not, a little dab will do. Such was the case with the Mac OS X Installer I was building for Blosxom (*http://www.blosxom.com*), my designed-for-Mac-yet-runs-anywhere weblog [Hack #30] application.

I'd built a nice Mac OS X package (*http://developer.apple.com/documentation/DeveloperTools/Conceptual/SoftwareDistribution*), which turned my otherwise rather Unix-y application into a double-clickable install. However, I still needed to set a configuration setting or three and didn't want to require my users to resort to editing Perl scripts by hand. So, I set about divining an elaborate—and not a little bit grotty—scheme involving one part shell scripting, two parts Perl, and a pinch of AppleScript.

The Grotty Way

As part of its standard procedure, the Mac OS X Installer runs any *postflight* shell script it finds in a package at the end of the installation process—thus the name *postflight* (*http://developer.apple.com/documentation/DeveloperTools/Conceptual/SoftwareDistribution/Concepts/sd_pre_post_processing.html#//apple_ref/doc/uid/20001945/TPXREF19*). This gives the package maker a chance to perform any last-minute reshuffling, fix permissions, run additional scripts, and generally do anything you can do on and from the command line. I slipped a call to a Perl script, *configure.pl*, into Blosxom's *postflight* script like so:

```
echo Running perl/applescript configuration scripts...

sudo /usr/bin/perl "$PACKAGE_PATH/Contents/Resources/configure.pl"
```

The output generated by echo in the preceding shell snippet and print in the following Perl snippet are never seen by the user; they're silently recorded in the installer's log. To watch the log as a package is installed, select Show Log from the Installer's File menu.

One of the things this *configure.pl* Perl script does is call an AppleScript script, *configure.scpt*, to prompt the user through a series of dialog boxes for the answers to various configuration questions and retrieve the responses as a string of key/value pairs (stored in $options), later to be applied automagically to the Blosxom application itself. Calling the AppleScript script itself is just a matter of passing the script to the osascript command-line utility that takes care of actually running it for me:

```
print "... prompting for answers to configuration questions\n";

my $options = `/usr/bin/osascript $PACKAGE_PATH/Contents/Resources/
configure.scpt 2>&1`;

...

# Do something magical with the contents of $options

...
```

Finally we come to the GUI bit itself. The *configure.scpt* AppleScript consists of nothing more than a series of display dialog statements, each prompting for a single configuration setting and saving the user's responses:

```
tell application "Finder"

activate

    display dialog "You're mere moments away from your very own blog." & return
    & return & "Before letting you get on with it, however, let's get a few last
    settings taken care of for you." & return & return & "To skip this step,
    click Cancel." & return with icon 1
1   display dialog "What would you like to call your blog?" default answer
    "blosxom"
2   set blog_title to (text returned of result)
    display dialog "How would you describe your blog (keep it short)?" default
    answer "yet another blosxom blog"
    set blog_description to (text returned of result)
    display dialog "What language code would you like to associate with your
    blog (e.g. en=English, fr=French, de=German)?" default answer "en"
    set blog_language to (text returned of result)
    display dialog "How many entries would you like displayed on your blog's
    home page?" default answer "40"
    set blog_num_entries to (text returned of result)
    display dialog "What URL should be used for your blog (leave blank to have
    Blosxom figure this out for itself)?" default answer ""
    set blog_url to (text returned of result)

3   set result to ("$$$blog_title=" & blog_title & "$$$blog_description=" &
    blog_description & "$$$blog_language=" & blog_language & "$$$num_entries=" &
    blog_num_entries & "$$$url=" & blog_url)

end tell
```

For instance, line 1 displays prompts for a blog name, as shown in Figure 2-24, while line 2 saves the result to the AppleScript variable blog_title.

Figure 2-24. One of a series of AppleScript dialogs

Line 3 strings all the various responses together to be returned to the calling *configure.pl* Perl script.

While this actually does work remarkably well, it is overly involved (albeit not particularly complex) for the rather simple requirements it has to meet. Also, it has quite a staccato feel to it from the user's point of view, with dialog boxes bouncing up and down one after another. Unfortunately, there was just no way, without doing quite a bit more programming, that I could get around sending the user (very possibly a newbie) to the command line—a no-no in my book.

The Nifty Way

Thankfully, I stumbled upon Carsten Blüm's Pashua (*http://www.bluem.net/ downloads/pashua_en*; donateware), a rather nifty tool for creating simple, native Aqua GUIs from Perl, Python, PHP, Tcl, Rexx, and AppleScript. Pashua's capabilities are limited to dialog windows, but it does provide a nice collection of widgets: labels, tool tips, text fields, password fields, checkboxes, radio buttons, pop-up and combo boxes, file selectors, and buttons.

I can now replace that staccato series of dialog boxes with a single dialog box that sports all the configuration questions I need—at least one window's worth.

Installation

Installing Pashua is just a matter of downloading the disk image and copying the contents across to your hard drive. To have the *Pashua.app* itself readily accessible from anywhere you care to use it, you might consider dropping it into your Applications folder. You'll also want to make sure that the associated Perl or Python module (*Pashua.pm* and *Pashua.py*, respectively) you'll be using in your code is somewhere Perl or Python will expect to find it.

My preference is to keep all of the Pashua bits together, simply creating a Pashua folder in my *Documents/Code* directory (where I do all of my coding).

You just need to be sure that the *Pashua.app* application and appropriate *Pashua.pm* or *Pashua.py* module is available to your script. The simplest way to do this is to copy these into the same folder as your script and distribute the entire folder to anyone who'll be using your software.

The Basics

Pasha scripts are simply wrappers around a configuration string that's fed to the Pashua application. This string defines the dialog window itself and the various GUI widgets you'd like Pashua to display.

While I'll not delve into every widget in turn, each definition looks a little something like this:

```
title_type=textfield
title_label=What do you want to call your blog?
title_width=200
title_default=My Blosxom
title_tooltip=Keep it simple.
```

title is the name I've given to this particular widget; I could have used any string of letters or numbers (e.g., title1, thingy, or wotsit22). Each widget is described by using attributes, prefixed with an underscore (_) and appended to the widget's name. Most widgets take four attributes: type (textfield, button, checkbox, etc.), label (what appears alongside the checkbox or on the button), width (in pixels), and a default (which radio button is initially selected, the initial value of a textfield, etc.). So, this widget is a 200-pixel-wide textfield named title, labeled What do you want to call your blog?, and with an initial value of My Blosxom.

 It's all much like designing an HTML form, except that attributes are listed as name_attribute, one per line, rather than in an HTML tag. The just-described textfield might look something like this in an HTML form:

```
What do you want to call your blog?
<input type="text" name="title" size="200"
value="My blosxom" />
```

Here's another:

```
future_type=radiobutton
future_label=Should I show entries from the future?
```

```
future_option=No
future_option=Yes
future_default=No
```

This one is a radiobutton group named future, labeled Should I show entries from the future?, with No and Yes options, the former selected by default.

As for the dialog window itself, there's not much to fiddle with:

```
# Set window title
windowtitle=Blosxom Configuration Wizard
# Set transparency: 0 is transparent, 1 is opaque
transparency=0.95
# Set the window to brushed metal; the default is regular Aqua
appearance=metal
```

This window is titled Blosxom Configuration Wizard and sports a 95% opaque (5% transparent) brushed-metal look.

You'll find complete documentation for these directives in the Pasha package itself (*Pashua/Documentation/documentation.html*) and various hints in the code and comments of the examples used in this hack.

Simple Example

Let's start out with a simple example, one that displays a single dialog window with some number of GUI widgets representing the minimal configuration settings Blosxom requires.

The code. While I could have chosen any of the supported languages, I thought I'd stick to Perl, because that's what Blosxom is written in and I can write Perl in my sleep (although, admittedly, I'm more of a Python devotee at heart).

To a folder named Simple (*Documents/Code/Pashua/Simple*), I copied *Pashua.app* and *Pashua.pm*. I then wrote the following script, borrowing the basic framework from the example code (*Pashua/Examples/example.pl*) found in the Pashua distribution. I saved the file as *Simple.pl*:

```
1   # !/usr/bin/perl -w
2
3   # Simple.pl
4   # A simple Pashua example
5
6   # Add the local directory to the queue of places to look for Pashua.pm
7   BEGIN {
8       use File::Basename;
9       unshift @INC, dirname($0);
10  }
11  use strict;
```

```
12  use Pashua;
13
14  # Define what the dialog should be like
15  # Take a look at Pashua's Readme file for more info on the syntax
16  my $conf = <<EOCONF;
17  # Lines starting with a hash character are
18  # comments, empty lines are ignored
19
20  # Set transparency: 0 is transparent, 1 is opaque
21  transparency=0.95
22
23  # Set window title
24  windowtitle=Blosxom Configuration Wizard
25
26  txt_type=text
27  txt_text=Welcome to Blosxom.[return][return]You're mere moments away from
    your very own blog.[return][return]This wizard will take you through some
    last minute configuration settings.  If you're in need of some details, take
    a gander at the gory details on the Blosxom Configuration page at http://
    www.blosxom.com/documentation/users/configure/.
28
29  title_type=textfield
30  title_label=What do you want to call your blog?
31  title_width=200
32  title_default=My Blosxom
33
34  description_type=textfield
35  description_label=How would you describe your blog?
36  description_width=400
37  description_default=Yet another blosxom blog.
38
39  language_type=textfield
40  language_label=What will be your primary written language? (e.g. en=English)
41  language_width=25
42  language_default=en
43
44  future_type=radiobutton
45  future_label=Should I show entries from the future (i.e. post-dated
    entries)?
46  future_option=No
47  future_option=Yes
48  future_default=No
49
50  # Add a cancel button - if you like, you can set the
51  # button label by uncommenting the second line below
52  cncl_type=cancelbutton
53  #cncl_label=If you click here, no values will be returned
54
55  # A default button is added automatically - if you want to
56  # change the button title, you should uncomment the next
57  # two lines to override the "built-in" default button
58  #default_type=defaultbutton
```

```
59  #default_label=Click here to return the values
60  EOCONF
61
62  # Pass the configuration string to the Pashua module
63  my %result = Pashua::run($conf);
64
65  if (%result) {
66      print " Pashua returned the following hash keys and values:\n";
67      while (my($k, $v) = each(%result)) {
68          print "    $k = $v\n";
69      }
70  }
71  else {
72      print " No result returned. Looks like the 'Cancel' button has been
    pressed.\n";
73  }
```

Lines 7–12 make the *Pashua.pm* Perl module in the current folder available
to the script.

The heart of the script is a long configuration string that defines the various
aspects of the dialog window itself (lines 20–24) and component GUI widgets (lines 26–59) stashed in a $conf variable.

Line 63 is where the actual work gets done: the $conf configuration string is
passed to the Pashua::run( ) method of the *Pashua.pm* Perl module, which,
in turn, asks the *Pashua.app* application to display a dialog box that contains the various described widgets.

Lines 65–73 print the results to the Terminal window, although you'll most
likely want to do something far more useful with them in any application
you're building with Pashua.

Running the code. Run the Perl script on the command line, like so:

```
$ perl Simple.pl
```

You'll see the Pashua application bounce into being in your Dock and your
dialog pop up on the screen, as shown in Figure 2-25.

Click the OK button or just hit the Return key on your keyboard to send the
values of the various dialog widgets to the Terminal:

```
$ perl Simple.pl
  Pashua returned the following hash keys and values:
    cncl = 0
    title = My Blosxom
    future = No
    description = Yet another blosxom blog.
    language = en
```

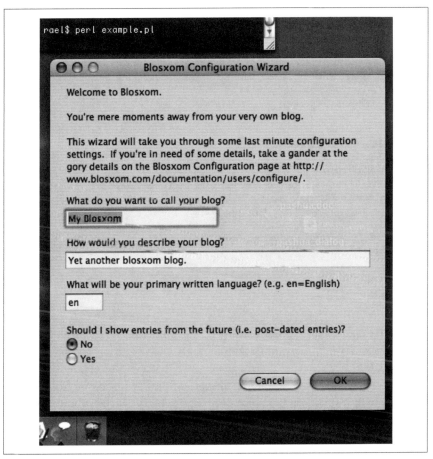

Figure 2-25. A simple Pashua-generated dialog

Hacking the hack. Since the lion's share of your script is Pashua configuration, the process is just about identical regardless of the language you choose. Here's the same thing (the configuration is abbreviated) in Python:

```
#!/usr/bin/env python

import Pashua

conf = """
# Lines starting with a hash character are
# comments, empty lines are ignored

# Set transparency: 0 is transparent, 1 is opaque
transparency=0.95
```

```
# Set window title
windowtitle=Blosxom Configuration Wizard

...

# two lines to override the "built-in" default button
# default_type=defaultbutton
# default_label=Click here to return the values
"""

Result = Pashua.run(conf)

if Result['cncl'] is 'o':
  print "  Pashua returned the following dictionary keys and values:"
  for Key in Result.keys():
    print "    %s = %s" % (Key, Result[Key])
else:
  print "  No result returned. Looks like the 'Cancel' button has been
pressed.";

print
```

Wizard Example

I created a new folder named Wizard (*Documents/Code/Pashua/Wizard*) and
again copied *Pashua.app* and *Pashua.pm* into it.

The code. The following script, *Wizard.pl*, defines two separate dialog window configurations, $general and $configurestatic, each to be fed serially
to the Pashua engine (additions and alterations from the code in the preceding "Simple Example" section—mostly the addition of a second screen configuration—are called out in bold):

```
1  #!/usr/bin/perl -w
2
3  # Wizard.pl
4  # A multi-screen Pashua Wizard example
5
6  BEGIN {
7      use File::Basename;
8      unshift @INC, dirname($0);
9  }
10 use strict;
11 use Pashua;
12
13 # Define the Wizard's first screen
14 my $general = <<GENERAL;
15 # Lines starting with a hash character are
16 # comments, empty lines are ignored
17
18 # Set transparency: 0 is transparent, 1 is opaque
```

```
19  transparency=0.95
20
21  # Set window title
22  windowtitle=Blosxom Configuration Wizard: General
23
24  txt_type=text
25  txt_text=Welcome to Blosxom.[return][return]You're mere moments away from
    your very own blog.[return][return]This wizard will take you through some
    last minute configuration settings.  If you're in need of some details, take
    a gander at the gory details on the Blosxom Configuration page at http://
    www.blosxom.com/documentation/users/configure/.
26
27  title_type=textfield
28  title_label=What do you want to call your blog?
29  title_width=200
30  title_default=My Blosxom
31
32  description_type=textfield
33  description_label=How would you describe your blog?
34  description_width=400
35  description_default=Yet another blosxom blog.
36
37  language_type=textfield
38  language_label=What will be your primary written language? (e.g. en=English)
39  language_width=25
40  language_default=en
41
42  future_type=radiobutton
43  future_label=Should I show entries from the future (i.e. post-dated
    entries)?
44  future_option=No
45  future_option=Yes
46  future_default=No
47
48  cncl_type=cancelbutton
49
50  # A default button is added automatically - if you want to
51  # change the button title, you should uncomment the next
52  # two lines to override the "built-in" default button
53  default_type=defaultbutton
54  default_label=Next
55  GENERAL
56
57  # Define the Wizard's second screen
58  my $configurestatic = <<CONFIGURESTATIC;
59  windowtitle=Blosxom Configuration Wizard: Static Settings
60
61  staticdir_type=openbrowser
62  staticdir_label=Where would you like the static version of you blog to live?
63  staticdir_width=400
64  staticdir_default=/Library/WebServer/Documents
65
66  staticpwd_label=What would you like to use as your static rendering  password?
```

```
67  staticpwd_type=password
68  staticpwd_width=200
69  staticpwd_default=
70
71  staticentries_type=radiobutton
72  staticentries_label=Would you like to statically render individual entries?
73  staticentries_option=No
74  staticentries_option=Yes
75  staticentries_default=No
76
77  editor_type=popup
78  editor_label=When would you like static rendering to run?
79  editor_width=200
80  editor_option=Manually
81  editor_option=Every 1/2 Hour
82  editor_option=Every 1 Hour
83  editor_option=Every 2 Hours
84  editor_option=Every 3 Hours
85  editor_option=Every 4 Hours
86  editor_option=Every 5 Hours
87  editor_option=Every 6 Hours
88  editor_option=Every 12 Hours
89  editor_option=Every 24 Hours
90  editor_default=Manually
91
92  cncl_type=cancelbutton
93  cncl_label=Cancel
94  default_type=defaultbutton
95  default_label=Next
96  CONFIGURESTATIC
97
98  # Define the rest of the wizard's screens
99  # ...
100
101 # Pass each configuration string in turn to the Pashua module to create
102 # a Wizard-like screen-by-screen interface and gather the results along
103 # the way
104 my %result = Pashua::run($general));
105 %result = (%result, Pashua::run($configurestatic));
106 # All the rest of the screens go here in the same manner
107 # %result = (%result, Pashua::run($shareware));
108
109 if (%result) {
110     print "  Pashua returned the following hash keys and values:\n";
111     while (my($k, $v) = each(%result)) {
112         print "    $k = $v\n";
113     }
114 }
115 else {
116     print "  No result returned. Looks like the 'Cancel' button has been
    pressed.\n";
117 }
```

Line 104 runs Pashua::run( ), feeding it the first screen configuration held in the $general variable. Line 181 calls Pashua::run( ) again, this time feeding it the second screen, as described in $configurestatic.

Running the code. Run the Perl script on the command line, like so:

```
$ perl Wizard.pl
```

Up comes the first screen of your wizard. Click the Next button to move on to the next screen, shown in Figure 2-26.

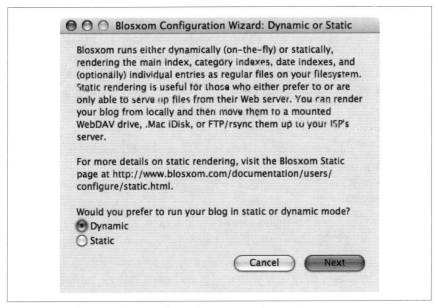

Figure 2-26. The second screen of a Pashua-generated wizard

Click the Next button again (in your final wizard, a Finish button is probably more appropriate for the last screen) or just hit the Return key on your keyboard to send the values of the various dialog widgets across all the wizard's screens to the Terminal:

```
$ perl Wizard.pl
Pashua returned the following hash keys and values:
    title = My Blosxom
    default = 1
    description = Yet another blosxom blog.
    future = No
    staticdir = /Library/WebServer/Documents
    staticentries = No
    staticpwd = s33kr1t
    cncl = 0
    editor = Manually
    language = en
```

Be sure to choose diffrent names for your various variables across wizard screens, because all the key/value pairs are stored in a single hash (at least in this example) and a second widget of the same name on another screen will overwrite the value of the first.

And this gets me to right where I wanted to be: a multiscreen configuration wizard that's capable of being called as a script by the Mac OS X Installer.

But if you try this yourself, you'll notice something slightly irritating: for each screen, the Pashua app is brought to life and killed off, over and over. While not quite as staccato as the grotty way I started out with and far more feature-filled and flexible, it still feels a mite bit rough around the edges. And what if the user wanted to rerun it? She'd have to visit the command line and invoke it from there—still a no-no.

Double-Clickable Example

Wouldn't it be nice to make a self-contained, double-clickable application of this, turning your simple Unix script into a GUI wizard that's virtually indistinguishable (except for the more limited form-driven-only functionality) from a first-class application?

The Pashua distribution includes just such a thing in the form of *Doubleclickable Example (Pashua/Examples/Doubleclickable Example.app)*.

Option-drag a copy of *Doubleclickable Example* somewhere for editing (leaving the original as it is, in case you need it again as a starting point); my copy is *Documents/Code/Pashua/Doubleclickable Example*.

Control- or right-click the application and select Show Package Contents from the context menu, as shown in Figure 2-27. Browse through the app until you get to *Doubleclickable Example/Contents/MacOS*. Notice that both the *Pashua* app and *Pashua.pm* Perl module are baked right into the application's contents so that they're readily available to the core script. The script itself has the same name as the outer application, *Doubleclickable Example*.

Otherwise, open the script in your favorite plain text editor [Hack #78] and edit to your heart's content.

The code. Here's what is essentially the same code as appeared in the preceding "Wizard Example" section. I've added in a few more screens and put in some basic logic for which screens to show, given the input provided on the previous screen and so forth:

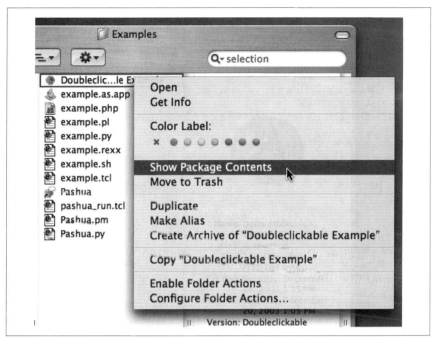

Figure 2-27. Show Package Contents

```perl
#!/usr/bin/perl -w

# Doubleclickable Example
# A double-clickable Pashua Wizard example

BEGIN {
    use File::Basename;
    unshift @INC, dirname($0);
}
use strict;
use Pashua;
#!/usr/bin/perl -w

use strict;
use Pashua;

my $general = <<GENERAL;
windowtitle=Blosxom Configuration Wizard: General Settings

txt_type=text
txt_text=Welcome to Blosxom.[return][return]You're mere moments away from
your very own blog.[return][return]This wizard will take you through some
last minute configuration settings.  If you're in need of some details, take
a gander at the gory details on the Blosxom Configuration page at http://
www.blosxom.com/documentation/users/configure/.
```

```
title_type=textfield
title_label=What do you want to call your blog?
title_width=200
title_default=My Blosxom

description_type=textfield
description_label=How would you describe your blog?
description_width=400
description_default=Yet another blosxom blog.

language_type=textfield
language_label=What will be your primary written language? (e.g. en=English)
language_width=25
language_default=en

future_type=radiobutton
future_label=Should I show entries from the future (i.e. post-dated
entries)?
future_option=No
future_option=Yes
future_default=No

cncl_type=cancelbutton
cncl_label=Cancel
default_type=defaultbutton
default_label=Next
GENERAL

my $staticordynamic = <<STATICORDYNAMIC;
windowtitle=Blosxom Configuration Wizard: Dynamic or Static

txt_type=text
txt_text=Blosxom runs either dynamically (on-the-fly) or statically,
rendering the main index, category indexes, date indexes, and (optionally)
individual entries as regular files on your filesystem. Static rendering is
useful for those who either prefer to or are only able to serve up files
from their Web server. You can render your blog from locally and then move
them to a mounted WebDAV drive, .Mac iDisk, or FTP/rsync them up to your
ISP's server.[return][return]For more details on static rendering, visit the
Blosxom Static page at http://www.blosxom.com/documentation/users/configure/
static.html.

staticdynamic_type=radiobutton
staticdynamic_label=Would you prefer to run your blog in static or dynamic
mode?
staticdynamic_option=Dynamic
staticdynamic_option=Static
staticdynamic_default=Dynamic

cncl_type=cancelbutton
cncl_label=Cancel
default_type=defaultbutton
default_label=Next
```

```
STATICORDYNAMIC

my $configurestatic = <<CONFIGURESTATIC;
windowtitle=Blosxom Configuration Wizard: Static Settings

staticdir_type=openbrowser
staticdir_label=Where would you like the static version of you blog to live?
staticdir_width=400
staticdir_default=/Library/WebServer/Documents

staticpwd_label=What would you like to use as your static rendering
password?
staticpwd_type=password
staticpwd_width=200
staticpwd_default=

staticentries_type=radiobutton
staticentries_label=Would you like to statically render individual entries?
staticentries_option=No
staticentries_option=Yes
staticentries_default=No

editor_type=popup
editor_label=When would you like static rendering to run?
editor_width=200
editor_option=Manually
editor_option=Every 1/2 Hour
editor_option=Every 1 Hour
editor_option=Every 2 Hours
editor_option=Every 3 Hours
editor_option=Every 4 Hours
editor_option=Every 5 Hours
editor_option=Every 6 Hours
editor_option=Every 12 Hours
editor_option=Every 24 Hours
editor_default=Manually

cncl_type=cancelbutton
cncl_label=Cancel
default_type=defaultbutton
default_label=Next
CONFIGURESTATIC
my $shareware = <<SHAREWARE;
windowtitle=Blosxom Configuration Wizard: Shareware

txt_type=text
txt_text=Blosxom is free for the taking and sharing.  That said, it does
take a considerable amount of not-so-free time and loving care.  This
Blosxom Installer for Mac OS X is shareware; when you've yourself situated
and have a moment, please do pay the one-time $15 shareware fee at:
[return][return]http://www.amazon.com/paypage/P13LC7VUIVYON .

cncl_type=cancelbutton
```

```
        cncl_label=Cancel
        default_type=defaultbutton
        default_label=Next
        SHAREWARE

        my $finish = <<FINISH;
        windowtitle=Blosxom Configuration Wizard: Finishing Up

        txt_type=text
        txt_text=That's all there is to it.  Click the Finish button, let the
        installer finish up, and you'll be whisked away to your brand new blog.

        cncl_type=cancelbutton
        cncl_label=Cancel
        default_type=defaultbutton
2       default_label=Finish
        FINISH

3   my %result;
4   %result = Pashua::run($general);
5   $result{cncl} and exit;
6   %result = (%result, Pashua::run($staticordynamic));
7   $result{cncl} and exit;
8   $result{staticdynamic} eq 'Static' and %result =
        (%result, Pashua::run($configurestatic));
9   $result{cncl} and exit;
10  %result = (%result, Pashua::run($shareware));
11  $result{cncl} and exit;
12  %result = (%result, Pashua::run($finish));

        # Do something useful with the results (or just save them
        # somewhere for now)
        open OUT, "> /tmp/pashua.out";
        print OUT "  Pashua returned the following hash keys and values:\n";
        while (my($k, $v) = each(%result)) {
            print OUT "    $k = $v\n";
        }
        close OUT;
```

There are some slight changes—aside from the whole thing running as a first-class, double-clickable application, that is—worth pointing out here.

Line 2 is a cosmetic change, replacing the Next button of the previous screens with a more appropriate Finish button.

Lines 3 through 12 call the Pashua::run( ) method for each screen and store the results in a %result hash. I have added some logic to check after each screen that the user isn't trying to get out of the wizard by hitting the Cancel button (Lines 5, 7, 9, and 11). If so, we terminate the script on the spot.

Now, of course, we could simply have dropped all the screen names into a loop and iterated over them one by one, like so:

```
my %result;
foreach my $screen ( ($general, $staticordynamic, $configurestatic,
  $shareware, $finish) ) {
    %result = (%result, Pashua::run($screen));
    $result{cncl} and exit;
}
```

Line 8 (requiring an exception) is why I chose to do things manually. We offer the user a choice of configuring Blosxom for dynamic or static rendering. Since only the latter requires any kind of additional configuration, the $configurestatic screen is called only if the user selects the Static radio button in Line 1.

The last few lines of the script do something useful with the results—or, in this example, simply stash them somewhere for now. You can't just print the values out to the Terminal (as in the case in the Simple or Wizard examples), because this script runs as a double-clickable app and doesn't involve a visit to the Terminal at all.

Running the code. Double-click the *Doubleclickable Example* application icon in the Finder to open your dialog window. Click the Next button to jump from screen to screen. Be sure to select Static mode on the Dynamic or Static screen; otherwise, you'll never get to see the Static Settings (as well you shouldn't) shown in Figure 2-28. At the end, click the Finish button to finish up. You can quit the app at any time by clicking the Cancel button or hitting the Esc key on your keyboard.

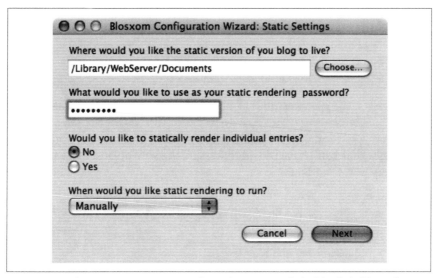

Figure 2-28. The Static Settings screen of a Pashua-powered, double-clickable application

Notice that the Pashua app no longer ebbs and flows between each screen, making for a nice, smooth experience for the end user.

If you're interested in what shows up in the temporary output file, open a Terminal window and type the following command:

```
$ less /tmp/pashua.out

    Pashua returned the following hash keys and values:
       description = Yet another blosxom blog.
       editor = Every 1 Hour
       staticpwd =
       language = en
       cncl = 0
       title = My Blosxom
       staticdir = /Library/WebServer/Documents
       future = No
       staticentries = No
       staticdynamic = Static
       default = 1
/tmp/pashua.out (END)
```

Hacking the hack. While the documentation says that to change the name of the app you need to change both the name of the outer application, *Doubleclickable Example.app*, and inner *Doubleclickable Example* Perl script, I found that changing the name of the outer without touching the inner worked like a charm; indeed, changing the inner script's name caused the app not to run at all.

Automatically Dim Your Laptop Screen

#26 Those of us with laptops are always trying to maximize the amount of time we can run on battery power. One of the most important ways to minimize power consumption is to dim your screen.

An LCD's backlight takes quite a bit of juice to operate, especially at full brightness. Unfortunately, it's easy to forget to turn down the screen brightness when you unplug. Several times, I've realized an hour and a half into a plane flight that I still have the brightness all the way up and I've used up all my battery power an hour too early.

The good news, though, is that you can set up your PowerBook or iBook to automatically dim the screen when you go on battery power and then raise the brightness again when you plug in.

This hack requires three major steps:

1. Figure out how to adjust screen brightness automatically.

2. Write a script that queries the status of the power supply and adjusts the screen brightness to match.

3. Arrange for the system to call that script when the status changes.

Programmatic Brightness Control

Changing the screen brightness from a program is surprisingly difficult. It's clearly possible, though, because the Displays panel in System Preferences does it! However, it appears to do so by using undocumented system interfaces. I'm sure it's possible to reverse-engineer those interfaces, but I chose not to go down that path. Instead, I chose a simpler (and somewhat more intrusive) technique: AppleScript. And since System Preferences has only limited scripting support, I had to use UI scripting, driving the user interface widgets directly.

UI scripting works through the accessibility interfaces provided by Cocoa and Carbon. The first step is to enable those interfaces. In System Preferences, choose the Universal Access panel and check the box at the bottom of the panel labeled "Enable access for assistive devices," as shown in Figure 2-29.

The following AppleScript sets the screen brightness to the dimmest setting.

You don't need to go type this into Script Editor right now. For reasons I'll explain, this won't be a standalone Apple-Script. I present it here, alone, only for ease of explanation.

```
tell application "System Preferences"
  activate
  set current pane to pane "com.apple.preference.displays"
end tell

tell application "System Events"
  tell process "System Preferences"
    tell tab group 1 of window "Color LCD"
      click radio button "Display"
      tell group 2 to set value of slider 1 to 0.0625
    end tell
  end tell
end tell

ignoring application responses
  tell application "System Preferences" to quit
end ignoring
```

Automatically Dim Your Laptop Screen

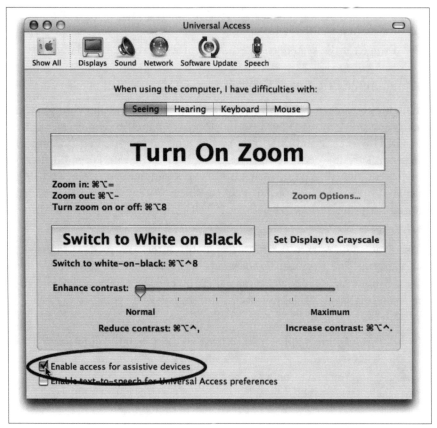

Figure 2-29. Enabling UI scripting

The first block simply activates System Preferences and chooses the Displays panel. That's about all we can do before we have to start scripting the UI directly.

UI scripting commands are addressed through the System Events application. In the second block, I choose the Color LCD window.

> If you have multiple monitors attached, you will see more than one Preferences window at this point, but at least with Apple displays there's no confusion; the built-in screen is the only one called Color LCD.

Next, I ensure that the Display tab is selected and then adjust the brightness slider.

The brightness slider doesn't have a name, so I just have to refer to it by its position within the UI structure. If later releases of OS X rearrange this panel significantly, this script will break.

Finally, in the third block, I direct System Preferences to quit.

The reason we can't set this up as a standalone AppleScript is simple, but frustrating: AppleScripts cannot take parameters. We need to use this script to set the brightness to a low value (when we go on battery power) and also to a high value (when we plug into a power supply again), so we need to be able to pass in the desired brightness value. The best option—with apologies to the AppleScript diehards out there—is to embed the AppleScript in a more powerful language.

The powerChange Script

Now that we can set the screen brightness, we need to decide when to do so and what brightness level to set it to. That's the job of the powerChange script.

How powerChange gets invoked is the subject of the final section of this hack.

I wrote powerChange in Ruby, for three reasons:

- It's my programming language of choice these days.
- Ruby programs are usually readable even by those who don't know the language.
- I can, because Ruby is bundled with Panther!

The script is a little long, but all will be explained:

```ruby
#!/usr/bin/ruby

def get_source
  IO.popen("scutil", "r+") { |pipe|
    pipe.puts %{
      open
      get State:/IOKit/PowerSources/InternalBattery-0
      d.show
      close
    }
    pipe.close_write
    while line = pipe.gets
      if line =~ /Power Source State : (.+)\s*$/
```

```
                return $1
          end
      end
   }
end

def set_brightness (level)
  level = [0, level].max
  level = [16, level].min
  IO.popen("osascript", "w") { |pipe|
    pipe.puts %{
      tell application "System Preferences"
          activate
          set current pane to pane "com.apple.preference.displays"
      end tell

      tell application "System Events"
          tell process "System Preferences"
              tell tab group 1 of window "Color LCD"
                  click radio button "Display"
                  tell group 2 to set value of slider 1 to #{level*0.0625}
              end tell
          end tell
      end tell

      ignoring application responses
          tell application "System Preferences" to quit
      end ignoring
    }
  }
end

POWERCHANGE_FLAG  = "/tmp/powerChange_flag"
BATTERY_FLAG = "/tmp/battery_power_flag"

exit if test(?e, POWERCHANGE_FLAG)
system("touch #{POWERCHANGE_FLAG}")

if get_source == "Battery Power"
  if !test(?e, BATTERY_FLAG)
    system("touch #{BATTERY_FLAG}")
    set_brightness 1
  end
else
  if test(?e, BATTERY_FLAG)
    system("rm #{BATTERY_FLAG}")
    set_brightness 16
  end
end

system("rm #{POWERCHANGE_FLAG} ")
```

The first method, get_source, uses the scutil program to find out what the current power supply is. scutil doesn't have very powerful command-line parameters, so I have to open a pipe to it, push a string of commands, and then search through the output to find the power source.

Using scutil By Hand

In case you're curious, here's what the command interaction looks like when you type it in manually:

```
oblivion:~ glv$ scutil
> open
> get State:/IOKit/PowerSources/InternalBattery-0
> d.show
<dictionary> {
Current Capacity : 68
Name : InternalBattery-0
Max Capacity : 100
Transport Type : Internal
Time to Full Charge : 0
Power Source State : Battery Power
Time to Empty : 106
Is Present : TRUE
Is Charging : FALSE
}
> close
```

This sequence of commands queries the status of the system configuration setting State:/IOKit/PowerSources/InternalBattery-0. (We'll see that setting again in the next section.) When your laptop is running on batteries, the Power Source State line will read Battery Power; otherwise, it will say AC Power.

The second method, set_brightness, embeds the AppleScript from the previous section. It accepts a number between 0 (backlight turned off) and 16 (full brightness), corresponding to the 16 brightness settings accessible via the brightness keys on the keyboard. After interpolating the desired brightness setting into the AppleScript, the osascript command invokes the AppleScript and adjusts the brightness.

After the two methods, powerChange concludes with a short bit of code that decides whether the circumstances warrant a change in screen brightness. Two files in /tmp are used as flags to help powerChange avoid taking action when it shouldn't. Existence of the *powerChange_flag* file indicates that powerChange is already running, so this invocation should exit, to avoid interfering with the first one.

 It's easy to cause the script to be invoked while it's already running. For example, you can unplug your laptop and plug it in again after just two or three seconds.

The existence of the second file, *battery_power_flag*, is used to determine whether the state of the power supply has actually changed, because the script can get called in other situations as well. We don't want screen brightness to change just because, for example, the system decides to update the "time to empty" status in the menu bar.

You can change the two calls to set_brightness near the end if you prefer different default brightness levels. The current values are 16 (for maximum brightness when using AC power) and 1 (for minimum brightness when running on battery power).

Put this script in a file called *powerChange* and drop it where you usually store scripts. I have a directory under my home directory that I use for that purpose: *~/bin*. Then, you'll need to make the script executable by using this command:

```
$ chmod +x powerChange
```

At this point, before you arrange for powerChange to be invoked automatically, it's a good idea to test it. Unplug and then execute powerChange from the Terminal to see if the screen dims properly. (You will see System Preferences start up while this happens.) Run it again to make sure that nothing happens if there's been no change in the status of the power supply. Then, plug back in and run it a third time; this time, the screen should brighten. If powerChange is working properly, it's time to move to the final step.

Watching Power-Supply Events

The powerChange script, when invoked, can decide whether a change in brightness is required, and it can use AppleScript to adjust the brightness. There's just one missing piece: arranging for powerChange to be invoked automatically when the power supply changes.

Edit the *Kicker.xml* file, found at */System/Library/SystemConfiguration/ Kicker.bundle/Contents/Resources/Kicker.xml*. If you have the Developer Tools installed, you can do this with Property List Editor, but you must either do it as root or copy the file off to the side, edit it, and then copy it back to the right spot using sudo cp.

Figure 2-30 shows what the changes look like using Property List Editor, but I think it's easier simply to edit the file with a text editor (after making a backup copy, of course).

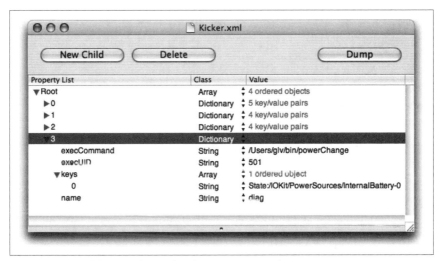

Figure 2-30. Modifying Kicker.xml with Property List Editor

Here's what I did:

```
$ cd /System/Library/SystemConfiguration/Kicker.bundle/Contents/Resources
$ sudo cp Kicker.xml Kicker.xml.backup
$ sudo vi Kicker.xml
```

Near the top of the file, you should see an <array> element, which contains a list of several-line <dict> elements. That array of <dict> elements is the bulk of the file; the closing </array> tag should be near the end of the file. You need to add a new <dict> to that array (I added it at the end of the array):

```
<dict>
<key>execCommand</key>
<string>/Users/glv/bin/powerChange</string>
<key>execUID</key>
<string>501</string>
<key>keys</key>
<array>
<string>State:/IOKit/PowerSources/InternalBattery-0</string>
</array>
<key>name</key>
<string>powerChange</string>
</dict>
```

This tells configd, the system configuration daemon, to invoke the powerChange script whenever the state of the internal battery changes. You'll need to modify the highlighted lines. The line following the execCommand key should be the path where you stored the powerChange script. The line following the execUID key should be your uid number, so that powerChange will be invoked with your identity.

 You can discover your uid number by typing id in the Terminal.

When you've successfully modified that file, you must prompt configd to reload it. It will read its configuration settings at boot time, but you can prompt it to reload the settings with this command:

```
$ sudo kill -HUP `cat /var/run/configd.pid`
```

Trying It Out

Finally, all the pieces should be in place. You have a script, powerChange, that (when invoked) can determine if the power supply has changed and use AppleScript to adjust the brightness appropriately. You've also told configd that it should invoke powerChange when the status of the power supply changes in any way.

Now you can try it out: unplug your laptop (or, if you've been doing this from the recliner, head for your desk and plug it in). It worked right away for me, but at least two friends who have tested this for me had to reboot at this point to get configd to change its behavior. If it doesn't work right away, try a restart.

There are quite a few questions you might be asking at this point. What if you unplug while nobody's logged in? (The auto-dim happens anyway, which is a strange thing to watch.) What if you unplug while another user is logged into your Mac? (The auto dim happens then, too, which might not be what the current user wants. And, if they're fast and sneaky, it could be a security risk, because System Preferences will be running with your privileges.) What if you disable UI scripting at this point? (Our AppleScript will give up, leaving System Preferences open, but nothing serious will happen.)

Enjoy! And if you'd like to learn more about scutil and configd, *Mac OS X Panther for Unix Geeks*, by Brian Jepson et al (O'Reilly), is a good resource.

—*Glenn Vanderburg*

Web, Chat, and Mail

Hacks 27–40

There have never been quite so many ways to interact with peers, family, friends, and virtual buddies than exist today on the Mac. With the built-in industrial-strength Mail client, state-of-the-art Safari web browser, and AV-enhanced iChat instant messaging, how could things possibly get any better?

Web, chat, and email are, unsurprisingly, three of the most interesting areas of third-party hacks, plug-ins, and applications. They're augmenting and informing just how things should and will be to the degree that it's not uncommon to find Apple learning as much from the hackers as from their own programmers and designers. This chapter shows off some of the must-use bits of communication that are either already present or just a download away.

Hack Safari

#27

Squeeze all you can out of Safari, the venerable Mac web browser. Combine keyboard shortcuts, alternatives to Google, debugging features, and live dictionaries for browsing to the nth degree.

Safari seems to be the web-browsing choice of a new generation, leaving the good-for-its-time Internet Explorer far behind and relegating Mozilla and derivatives to experimental use. But are you getting the most out of Safari or just using the bare minimum (and what a bare minimum that is) of its features?

Bits and Bobs

You always assume everyone knows the same accumulated *bits and bobs*—helpful shortcuts and neat menu items—that you do. And you're often wrong. In case you're not in the know about all of these yet, here are some of my favorite Safari tips and tricks.

Activity (aka Context). Open Safari's Activity window (Window → Activity or ⌘-Option-A), select all (⌘-A), and copy (⌘-C). You now have the URLs of all open tabs in the clipboard. Paste them into a sticky (*Applications/Stickies*) for safekeeping, in case Safari crashes (as it sometimes does, taking hours' worth of context with it). Paste them into iChat to share your context with a friend or colleague.

Downloads. The same thing is true of Safari's Downloads window (Window → Downloads or ⌘-Option-L), where copy and paste nets you the source URLs for your recent crop of downloads. Save them to a *download_log.txt* file somewhere for a record of what you've downloaded (and possibly installed). Copy a single download URL by Control- or right-clicking any item in the Downloads window and selecting Copy Address from the contextual menu.

Tabs. At the bottom of each bookmark folder, there is an option to Open in Tabs. Click it to open all the bookmarks in that folder in a set of tabs in a single window. This is useful for setting up your day's context first thing in the morning or keeping an eye on sites you track on a regular basis (but which don't syndicate their content [Hack #30]).

With tabbed browsing enabled in Safari's Preferences pane (Safari → Preferences → Tabs → Enable Tabbed Browsing), ⌘-click opens a link in a new tab, ⌘-Shift-click opens it in a new tab and brings that tab to the fore, ⌘-Option-click opens a link in a new window behind the current one, and ⌘-Option-Shift-click opens a link in a new window and brings it to the fore.

Links. Click, hold, and drag on links or images to drag them from Safari. You can place them on the Desktop or in any other folder or drive, into the text bar of an iChat window, or into just about any document. You can also drag an image from Safari over your icon in the iChat buddy list to use it as your icon or drag it over the chat area to set it as the background for your conversation.

Keyboard Shortcuts

Safari provides a local file listing the majority of its keyboard shortcuts (*file://
/Applications/Safari.app/Contents/Resources/Shortcuts.html*); bookmark it in Safari for quick reference.

 You'll also find it under Keyboard and Mouse Shortcuts in the Debug menu. See the next section of this hack, "The Debug Menu."

You should also bookmark Dori Smith's extended list of shortcuts (*http://www.dori.com/safariShortcuts.html*), which vastly improves upon Apple's default list.

Dori further notes that you can add keyboard shortcuts to your favorite bookmarks. Quit Safari, open the Terminal (*Applications/Utilities/Terminal*), and type the following command on the command line:

```
% defaults write com.apple.Safari NSUserKeyEquivalents '{"bookmark
name"="keyboard shortcut";}'
```

Replace *bookmark name* with the name of the bookmark and *keyboard shortcut* with one or more of the following: @ for ⌘, $ for Shift, ~ for Option, or ^ for Control. Follow the special key or keys with another regular keystroke. For example, I might set Control-Shift-M to call up Mobile-Whack (*http://www.mobilewhack.com*), like so:

```
% defaults write com.apple.Safari NSUserKeyEquivalents
'{"MobileWhack"="^$m";}'
```

Launch Safari and give it a go.

The Debug Menu

The hidden Debug menu gives you a glimpse of what's going on underneath Safari's hood and also provides some nice additional functionality.

Close Safari, launch the Terminal (*/Applications/Utilities/Terminal*), and type the following on the command line:

```
% defaults write com.apple.Safari IncludeDebugMenu 1
```

When you relaunch Safari, you'll see a Debug menu to the right of the Help menu in Safari's menu bar.

Perhaps the most useful feature in the Debug menu is the ability to import bookmarks (Debug → Import Bookmarks... or Debug → Import IE/NS/Mozilla Bookmarks) from other browsers or from a file. You can also export your Safari bookmarks (Debug → Export Bookmarks...) to a web page that can be imported into another browser, opened within your browser, or uploaded to your web site to share your favorite links with the world.

If you're trying to gain access to some site that doesn't appear to (or outright claims not to) support Safari (this is often just the result of bad browser-detection code), you can emulate another browser by altering your User Agent string (what you use to identify the browser you're using to view a site). Choose an alternate browser from the Debug → User Agent menu (Figure 3-1) and visit the site. This emulation is applied on a window-by-window or tab-by-tab basis, so you'll want to have a window or tab open

and selected before applying the change. When you close the window or
tab, you're back to being Safari again.

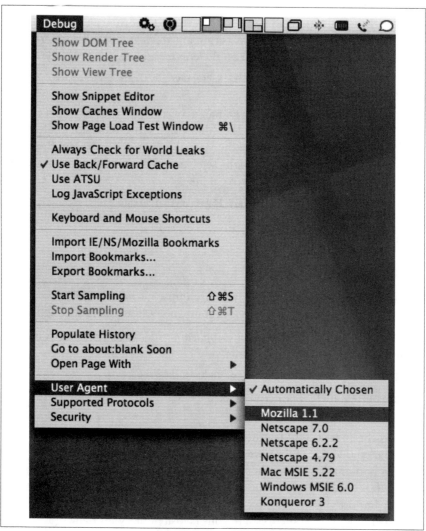

Figure 3-1. Masquerading as another browser through the Debug → User Agent menu

This is just the tip of the iceberg. Explore at will; you can always uncheck or
change back any setting you twiddle—or just close and relaunch Safari.

If you don't like the Debug menu and want to get rid of it, launch the Terminal again and type this:

```
% defaults write com.apple.Safari IncludeDebugMenu 0
```

If you don't like playing around in the Terminal, several of the Safari helper programs mentioned in the following sections include an option to turn on the Debug menu for you.

Enhancing Safari

Safari Enhancer (*http://www.lordofthecows.com/safari_enhancer.php*; donate-ware) by Gordon Byrnes is a nice little freeware program that provides the functionality of the Debug menu through a simple interface (Figure 3-2).

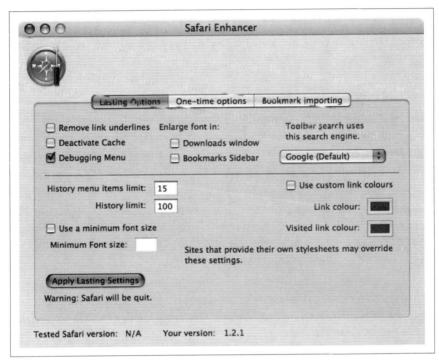

Figure 3-2. The Safari Enhancer interface

Gordon also throws in a few added features, such as the ability to strip Safari's metallic look and customize the search bar to work with a search engine other than Google.

Speed Up Safari

This little hack is courtesy of macOSXhints.com (*http://www.macosxhints.com/article.php?story=20040516220739506*) and boy oh boy does it work well! The hack comes out of an interesting discussion piece written by the Safari developer David Hyatt on the adding of timers to browsers (*http://weblogs.mozillazine.org/hyatt/archives/2004_05.html#005496*). In order to avoid a flashing effect when a web page loads—due to the client getting data of various sorts from any number of sources: stylesheets, images, JavaScript includes, etc.—web browsers are programmed with a little delay. The delay is, appropriately, conservative. By adjusting a variable in the Safari preference file you can speed up Safari's delay time.

Quit Safari and, on the command line [Hack #91], type:

```
defaults write com.apple.Safari WebKitInitialTimedLayoutDelay 0.25
```

The default delay is 1.0; you've now changed that to 0.25. Now go ahead and relaunch Safari. Notice a difference? I sure did! As someone commented on macoxhints.com, it was like getting a new machine. I wouldn't go that far, but it certainly feels like Safari has been administered a double shot of espresso.

Enabling Alternative Search

SafariKeywords (*http://safarikeywords.sourceforge.net*; freeware) is an open source project that adds a SafariKeywords System Preference to Panther, allowing you to teach Safari where to search for any words you type into the search bar instead of always defaulting to Google.

For example, if you want to search for an iBook on eBay, you can type ebay iBook in the search bar to comb through eBay (as shown in Figure 3-3) rather than search Google. SafariKeywords comes with a large set of Google alternatives and also offers you the ability to link your own custom keywords to your favorite specialized search engines.

If you'd rather do away with the search bar altogether, you should check out Sogudi (*http://www.atamadison.com/w/kitzkikz.php?page=Sogudi*; donateware), which provides practically the same functionality as SafariKeywords inside the location bar instead.

Avoiding the Ads

PithHelmet [Hack #29] blocks unwanted ads, which improves readability and speeds up page loading. You can customize PithHelmet to filter out any unwanted content from sites (e.g., images, Flash-based content, and MIDI files) and choose which content to block on a site-by-site basis. You can also toggle the Debug menu from within PithHelmet.

For much more on PithHelmet and related ad-blocking tools, be sure to read "Avoid the Ads" [Hack #29].

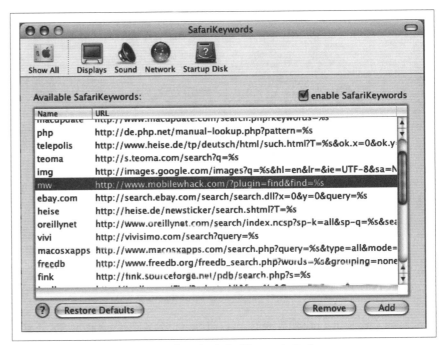

Figure 3-3. Adding a custom search to the SafariKeywords Preferences pane

Viewing PDFs

Rather than download every PDF file to then open in either Preview or Adobe Acrobat Reader, consider using Schubert-it's PDF Browser Plugin (*http://www.schubert-it.com/pluginpdf*; free for personal and nonprofit use; $69 for a site license) to automatically open any PDFs you come across within Safari and fully integrate PDFs into your web-browsing experience. After installation, PDFs launch within Safari, just like any web page. There's an additional menu bar at the top, which you can use to save, print, or open the PDF in another program, such as Acrobat Reader or Preview.

Consulting the Dictionary

LiveDictionary (*http://www.mikeash.com/software/livedictionary*; $25 shareware) is a Safari extension that overlays quick and convenient dictionary lookup on your web browsing, as shown in Figure 3-4.

LiveDictionary appears as a Safari menu item and supports multiple dictionaries. Just hold your mouse over a word you want defined for a few moments; a translucent window pops up with the definition, floating above

Figure 3-4. LiveDictionary's definitions, laid over a web page

the web page. Move the mouse to make the window disappear again. If you prefer, you can add a modifier key so that simply loitering over a word won't needlessly throw definitions in your face.

Hacking the Hack

If, even with all these add-ons, hints, and tweaks, Safari still isn't quite doing it for you, you might try "browsing different" with Firefox [Hack #28].

Or, if you're feeling *exceedingly adventurous*, you can always launch Xcode and roll your own browser (*http://www.macdevcenter.com/pub/a/mac/2004/01/23/webkit.html*).

—*C. K. Sample III and Hadley Stern*

Browse Different

#28

If you are still using Internet Explorer on Panther, I have good news for you: your turtle of a web browser that slowly loads the Internet like the prehistoric pre-Panther piece of abandoned bloatware that it is is about to be replaced by a fast speedy little fox: Firefox.

Chances are, you're well and truly settled in to Apple's Safari web browser, having jumped ship from the now-stalled Internet Explorer (IE) for Mac you found so impressive back in OS 9. IE was good for its time—in many ways, even better than its Windows kin. But Safari, with its simple candy-coated shell and tabbed windows, is now the undisputed champion of the Mac browsing world.

Lest you forget that there are actually some rather nice alternatives out there, we present one of our favorite contenders: a little something called Firefox (*http://www.mozilla.org/products/firefox*). Firefox is a member of the Mozilla clan (*http://www.mozilla.org*), the open source offspring of Netscape. These browsers' names provide a not-so-subtle hint as to their relative strengths. Mozilla (think Godzilla) is a powerful monster of a web browser, replete with integrated email client, IRC chat client [Hack #36], HTML editor, and just about anything else you need to stomp through the Internet, knocking over anything that gets in your way. It's all a little too heavy, quite honestly. Firefox, on the other hand, is Mozilla's faster and sleeker cousin, free of all the extras and focused on doing just one thing well: browsing the web.

Why Bother?

The obvious question no doubt already forming in your mind is "Why bother, when we Mac users have Safari?" Glad you asked.

Firefox isn't just a stripped down, standalone Mozilla. It can be served with all the trimmings, buffet style. There are spoonfuls of themes, a good helping of extensions, and a dollop of standalones to go along with it—most notably Thunderbird (*http://mozilla.org/products/thunderbird*), the powerful, flexible mail client stripped out of Mozilla.

There are things you can do with Firefox that you just can't do with the one-browser-fits-all Safari, even if you just want to see how your site might look to non-Mac, non-Safari users or visit sites that aren't Safari-friendly (e.g., Weight Watchers).

 You can actually get Safari to masquerade as other browsers, but that doesn't mean you truly get to see through the eyes of another browser. See "The Debug Menu" in "Hack Safari" [Hack #27] for more information.

Also, if you're a cross-platform user, spending time in some combination of the Mac, Windows, and Unix worlds, you'll appreciate being able to take your browser—look and feel, functionality, shortcuts, bookmarks, and all—with you. Safari, quite frankly, just isn't that much better than Firefox to make all the bustling between Safari on Mac, IE on Windows, and Mozilla on Unix worthwhile.

At this point, I've either convinced you to give Firefox a look-see or to never leave your beloved Mac and Safari browser behind. I do hope it's the former.

Switching Gears

After downloading and installing Firefox, the first thing you are going to want to do is launch Safari. I know this sounds odd, but bear with me. From Jaguar to Panther, the place to set your default web browser moved from an Internet Preferences pane (now vanished) to Safari's Preferences. Select Safari → Preferences → General and, under Default Web Browser, select Firefox from the drop-down menu, as shown in Figure 3-5.

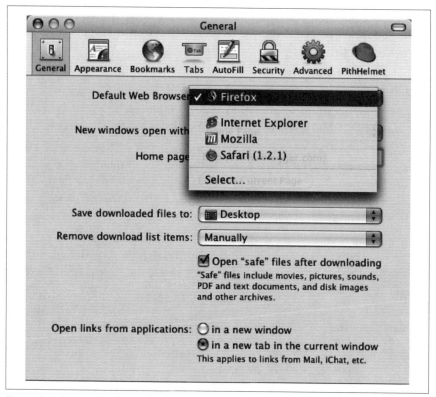

Figure 3-5. Setting Firefox as the default browser in Safari's Preferences

   If it isn't listed, choose Select... and navigate to Firefox in your Applications folder.

If you don't take this step, links from Mail, iChat, and the like will keep opening in Safari. To give a new browser a whirl, you really do want to get the full effect rather than browse some here, some there.

If Safari is currently your browser of choice, you will also want to export all your bookmarks so that you can have them available to you in Firefox and not just start out flying blind. To do so, you will first need to enable Safari's debug menu [Hack #27].

> In short, close Safari, launch the Terminal, type `defaults write com.apple.Safari IncludeDebugMenu 1` on the command line, and relaunch Safari.

From Safari's Debug menu, select Export Bookmarks... and save the bookmarks to your Desktop. Close Safari and launch Firefox. Select Bookmarks → Manage Bookmarks to open the Bookmark Manager, choose File → Import, browse to the exported bookmarks on your Desktop, and import them.

> Firefox imports IE Favorites and Mozilla/Netscape bookmarks by default, so you should find them already in folders in the Bookmark Manager. You will also find all the Safari bookmarks you just imported at the bottom of the list.

After you've finished organizing your bookmarks the way you'd like them, close the Bookmark Manager and visit Firefox → Preferences (Figure 3 6).

For now, just click through and familiarize yourself with the various settings available. Most of them will be familiar to you from other browsers you've used in the past. Under Web Features, you'll find that pop-up windows are blocked by default. Themes is a list of installed skins for customizing the appearance of Firefox; there's also a Get New Themes link to a site where you can find more (58, in fact, as I write this). You'll also notice an Extensions tab; we'll get to those beauties in just a moment.

Taming the Fox

With everything good to go, navigate to one of your favorite sites and notice just how fast Firefox runs; it's comparable to Safari and oh so much faster than IE. Speed is Firefox's number-one claim to fame.

Firefox's second claim to fame—at least in the usability nightmare of open source interfaces (to our Mac eyes, that is)—is its clean, simple interface. It's

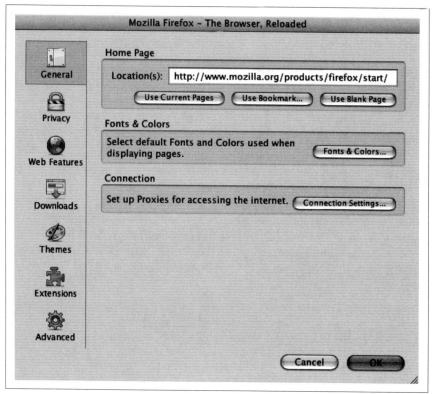

Figure 3-6. Firefox Preferences

almost Mac-like, whether you're running Mac, Windows, or Unix under the hood.

Firefox, like Safari, integrates tabbed browsing, allowing you to exchange a proliferation of windows with multiple tabs within a single window (or multiple windows, if you insist). If you've enabled the "Open links in the background" feature under Firefox → Preferences → Advanced → Browsing, while you continue reading, you can ⌘-click links and have them load in a new tab in the background for later; this makes for a smoother reading experience. You can also select Open in Tabs from any one of your bookmark folders to have the entire folder open in an array of tabs, as shown in Figure 3-7.

Search Different

Though Firefox's single search box looks just like Safari's, there's more to Firefox searching than meets the eye. While the search box is set to search Google by default, you can customize it to search as many different search

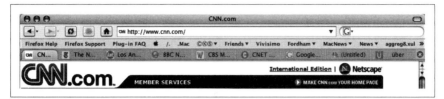

Figure 3-7. A selection of sites in Firefox's tabbed window

engines as you please. Click the little arrow next to the Google icon to open a drop-down menu of available engines and an option to "Add engines...," as shown in Figure 3-8.

Figure 3-8. Choosing another search engine to use with Firefox's search box

Select "Add engines..." to visit a page (*http://mycroft.mozdev.org/ download.html*) that's chock-full of pluggable search-engine modules, from online dictionaries to news to file-sharing.

There's a "Find in this Page" option in the search box's drop-down menu, which behaves much like Safari's Find (⌘-F). However, Firefox has a groovy feature that you'd never think to ask for but, after just a few minutes, you can never do without. With any page loaded, just start typing; the page starts scrolling and highlights matches to what you're typing as you go. If you type something that matches a hyperlinked word or phrase, hit the Return key when the word is highlighted to follow the link—no mouse or excessive taps of the Tab key necessary (as were required to move between links in IE). If you instead press ⌘-Return, the link will open in a new tab.

Navigate Different

For those of you who loathe to overuse your mouse or trackpad, this opens up an entire new world of keyboard browsing. Scroll up and down with the arrow keys, jump a whole page at a time with Page Up and Page Down keys, and type your way from link to link, pressing Return to leap.

Option-left arrow goes back a page, and Option-right moves you forward. ⌘-K highlights the search box, wherein the up and down arrows scroll through search history. ⌘-F pulls up Find in This Page, and Esc dismisses it. ⌘-G finds the most recent text search again. Control-Tab cycles forward through open tabs; Control-Shift-Tab cycles backwards. Tab bounces between text boxes in the web page. ⌘-L takes you back to the location/address bar, ready to enter a new URL.

Type dict and *word* in the location bar for a visit to Dictionary.com (*http://www.dictionary.com*). Hit ⌘-E to view the Downloads Manager, ⌘-B to visit your Bookmarks, and ⌘-Shift-H to open your History. (Tab through any of the History links and hit Return to open them, or tab on over to the search box to find the page you're after.)

Phew! And that's just the beginning; visit *http://www.texturizer.net/firefox/keyboard.html* for the consummate list of Firefox keyboard shortcuts.

> Since the keyboard shortcut page is geared to Windows and Linux users, be sure to substitute ⌘ for all the Control keys listed.

Then, of course there are mouse gestures (*http://texturizer.net/firefox/extensions/#mousegest*), but we leave you to experience that mind-blowing adventure on your own.

Embrace and Extend

One of the most attractive features of Firefox is its expandability, which is available through user-contributed extensions. From Firefox → Preferences, choose the Extensions tab, as shown in Figure 3-9.

Click the Get New Extensions link at the bottom-left of the Extensions Preferences pane to browse the library of extensions (168 at the time of this writing). Installation of each extension is just a matter of clicking its download link and then clicking through a couple of dialog boxes. Extensions require a restart of Firefox before they'll take effect; you can install a few at once, though, and restart the browser only once when you have a good batch onboard.

Some highlights of the available extensions include a nice Java port of the only Windows app I have ever loved, Minesweeper; mozedit, an advanced text editor available under the Tools menu; Tabwarning, which warns you if you are about to close a window with more than one tab (Safari tab users will recognize the value of this); Mouse Gestures, which allow you to navigate the Web with certain predefined mouse movements (a must-have for

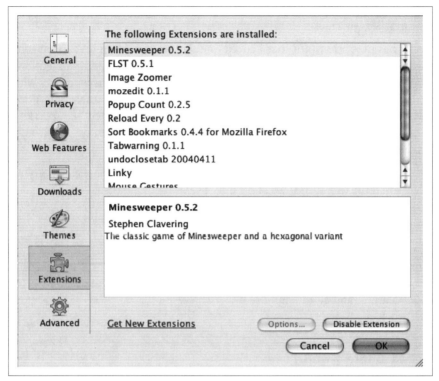

Figure 3-9. The Firefox Extensions Preferences pane

the keyboard-weary); RSS Reader Panel, which allows you to read syndicated content [Hack #30] right in your browser; and...really, I should stop now.

 When you start loading lots of Extensions in Firefox, there is a good chance you'll run into extension conflicts similar to those that haunted the Macintosh OS back in the pre–OS X days.

The Catch

While you have to do quite a bit of hacking to make Safari do some of what Firefox does right out of the box, there are a few reasons why I still use the latter only as my secondary browser:

- It does not support the Services menu [Hack #8]. I love services and use them all the time; not having them available within my default browser has serious repercussions for my workflow.

- It doesn't spellcheck as you type. I work on my blog quite a bit from my browser, and while Firefox supports more default Blogger GUI goodness than Safari, it doesn't offer squiggly underlining of misspelled words in its text-entry box.

- It has no option (not that I could find, anyway) to open links from other programs in a new tab in the current window. At the end of a NetNews-Wire session, I suddenly find myself with 15 or so open windows when I'd prefer to find one nicely organized window with 15 tabs. Safari does this rather nicely (enable it from Safari → Preferences → General → "Open links from applications in a new tab in the current window").

- Firefox is still in beta and it has a few bugs.

- Most of the online documentation and several of the extensions are geared toward Windows and Linux users.

Hacking the Hack

Firefox has rather extensive customization options available. Check out the Tips & Tricks page (*http://texturizer.net/firefox/tips.html*) for a multitude of ways to hack Firefox: block ads, turn on kiosk mode, tweak the "find as you type" feature, and so much more.

—C. K. Sample III

Avoid the Ads

HACK #29

Speed up and tone down the Web by filtering out annoying banner ads, pop-ups, and unwanted Flash and MIDI files.

Much of the Internet is to some degree supported by advertising. This is good for the advertisers and sites that are able to hold their own on the Web through advertising, but for people like myself, who are prone never to click on any of these advertisements, banner ads, or pop-ups, all that extra content adds unnecessary lag and serves only to annoy. TiVo helps people like me fast-forward through television commercials; I want that "badoop-badoop-badoop-badoop" fast-forward feature for the Web. This hack discusses several of the options out there to help you realize a faster Internet experience on your Mac, unobstructed by unwanted in-your-face advertisements.

Safari

Unlike the applications I'll talk about in a moment, Apple's Safari browser doesn't sport any of the fancy ad blockers. It does, however, allow you to optionally block *pop-ups*: those annoying windows that appear out of nowhere when you visit various sites, from your bank to those unmentionable sites you meander through late at night. From the Safari menu, select Block Pop-Up Windows (as shown later in Figure 3-10) to turn on pop-up blocking (the menu item should be checked when blocking is active). This doesn't affect windows you pop up by clicking links; it affects only those that pop up automagically (and annoyingly), without your asking them to.

PithHelmet

If your browser of choice is Safari, you're in luck; the most powerful and easily customizable Mac-based content filter for the Internet, PithHelmet (*http://culater.net/software/PithHelmet/PithHelmet.php*; free/donateware), is right up your alley. In the unlikely event you're using another browser, Pith-Helmet may well persuade you to switch. If not, alternative solutions are to be found, although, in my experience, none of them work quite as well.

After installing PithHelmet, you'll notice several slight changes in Safari, as shown in Figure 3-10. Under the Safari menu, there's an option to Block Filtered Content, which toggles PithHelmet on and off. There's also a page-by-page override, Reload Page Unfiltered, under the View menu; as the name suggests, this temporarily turns off filtering in the current page after reloading it.

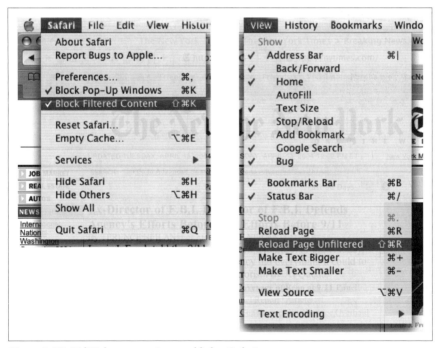

Figure 3-10. PithHelmet menu items added to Safari

PithHelmet sports its own Safari Preferences pane (Figure 3-11) for customizing the plug-in to suit your needs. PithHelmet comes preset with rules that should be powerful enough to filter most unwanted content for most users.

Figure 3-11. The PithHelmet Preferences pane, available under Safari Preferences

If you like, you can set up additional rules that are specific to particular sites or generalized to all sites or, on the contrary, you can mark certain sites for exclusion from these rules. For example, if you would rather not see stunning Shockwave or flashy Flash-based content in most of the sites you visit, you can set up a rule to not load Flash.

Say, on the other hand, you like to play Flash-based games or watch Flash-based movies at Shockwave.com (*http://www.shockwave.com*). Simply set up an exemption rule for Shockwave.com. Expand the Exempt Sites list and click on the plus sign (+) on the upper-right corner of the window. Type Shockwave.com, as shown in Figure 3-12, to exclude this site from being blocked by PithHelmet.

You can test any of the rules you set up by clicking on the Test Rules button in the bottom-left corner of the PithHelmet Preferences pane (Figure 3-13).

Alternately, you can set up exclusion rules on the fly via the contextual menu in Safari. Control-click any image in the current page to summon a

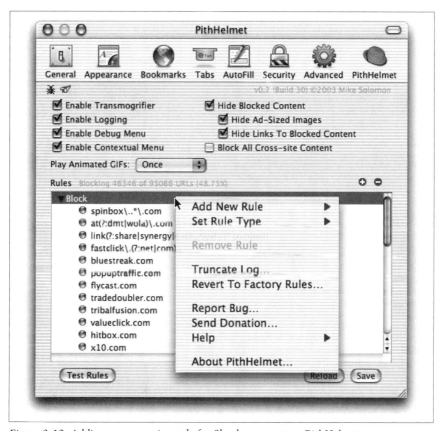

Figure 3-12. Adding an exemption rule for Shockwave.com to PithHelmet

contextual menu with the option to Block Images from or, conversely, Never Block Content from the current site (Figure 3-14).

If you find PithHelmet as useful as I expect you will, please consider making a donation to Mike Solomon, the developer, at the PithHelmet web site.

Privoxy

If you use a browser other than Safari and want to stay in the no-cost arena of ad blocking, check out Privoxy (*http://www.privoxy.org*).

A Mac OS X installer for Privoxy is available at Privoxy's SourceForge page (*http://sourceforge.net/project/showfiles. php?group_id=11118&package_id=29783*).

Privoxy is a *web proxy* (i.e., it sits between the Web and your browser rather than being embedded into your browser itself) with advanced filtering for

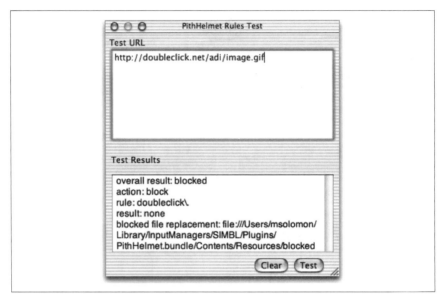

Figure 3-13. Testing new PithHelmet rules

Figure 3-14. Creating exclusion rules from the Safari contextual menu

protecting your privacy by bypassing click-tracking scripts, filtering web-page content, managing cookies, and removing ads and pop-ups.

After running the installer, you will need to either restart your system to activate Privoxy, or launch the Terminal (Applications → Utilities → Terminal) and type the following at the command line:

```
/Library/Privoxy/StartPrivoxy.command
```

You will be prompted for your administrator password, because the program is located in the root */Library* directory on your machine. After installing Privoxy, it automatically loads whenever you start up your computer. To uninstall it, revisit the Terminal and type the following at the command line:

```
/Library/Privoxy/uninstall.command
```

After installing Privoxy, point your web browser to *file:///Library/Privoxy/ index.html*. Bookmark this page; it will become invaluable for navigating through all of Privoxy's extensive documentation for more specific configuration according to your needs. For starters, you can get by with default filtering settings.

To tell your browser to use Privoxy as an HTTP and HTTPS (SSL) proxy, you will need to set the proxy configuration to 127.0.0.1, port 8118. To do so in Netscape and Mozilla, visit Preferences → Advanced → Proxies → HTTP Proxy. Though Firefox is a derivative of Mozilla, its proxy settings are under Firefox → General → Connection Settings.... In Internet Explorer, you'll find these settings in Preferences → Network → Proxies. In any case, check the Use Proxy checkbox and fill in the appropriate information.

> Your browser's disk and memory caches might still hold copies of ads you've run across before. These should eventually fade from memory, but you can force the browser to forget instantly by clearing your cache. In Mozilla, for instance, use Mozilla → Preferences → Advanced → Cache → Clear Cache.

Point your browser at a site that's usually filled with ads, and bask in the glow of commercial-free browsing.

ADGate

If for some reason you don't tend to trust software you can't pay for, you might want to check out ADGate (*http://haoli.dnsalias.com/ADGate/index.html*; two-week free trial; $15 per user or $100 for a site license thereafter).

All of ADGate's settings are nicely presented by the ADGate application (as shown in Figure 3-15), which you install by dragging a downloaded disk image to your Applications folder.

ADGate must run as root to do its thing, so you will be prompted for your administrator password on first launch. ADGate works through a combination of HTML and domain-name filtering. For URL blocking (effectively blocking any content that originates from certain URLs), it uses HTML filtering, removing any links to blocked sites. For advertisement blocking, it first examines DNS-lookup results and substitutes the location of images that match your predefined settings with HTML pointing to the local host via the built-in Apache server.

For example, if you've decided to block all ads coming from site X, ADGate will scan the page for matching results and redirect all links to site X and all images from site X to locations on your local Mac's internal Apache server. The result is an empty 2×2–pixel GIF where each banner ad or other advertising image would usually appear.

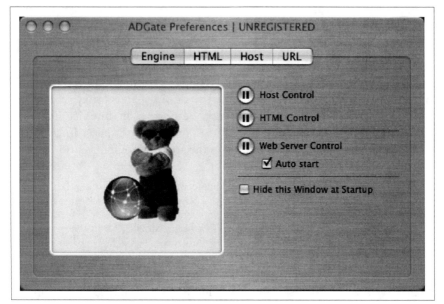

Figure 3-15. AdGate's settings

Hacking the Hack

If you really want to experience fast, no-frills web surfing, or if you just want to impress your friends with how 1337 (that's pronounced "leet" as in "elite") you can be, you might consider using one of the open source text-based browsers that run inside the Terminal. The two text-based browsers I use on a regular basis are Links (*http://links.sourceforge.net*) and Lynx (*http://www.osxgnu.org/software/Networking/lynx*), both of which have OS X versions.

Neither of these programs actually filter out ads, but since they present you with the Web only as text (see Figure 3-16) and the majority of the advertisements are images, they won't take any time loading, you won't be bombarded with pop-up windows, and you will quickly learn to ignore the irrelevant *advert.jpg*, *advert.gif*, and *advert.png* links sprinkled throughout your pages.

Text-based browsing isn't for everyone, but as Rael once mentioned to me in iChat, the six of us OS X users who do use text-based browsers really enjoy it!

—*C. K. Sample III*

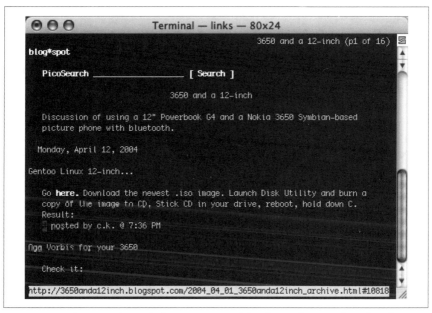

Figure 3-16. The text-only Links browser—a world without ads or Technicolor of any kind

Read Syndicated Online Content

The syndicated news reader is to syndicated content from weblogs, web sites, and online magazines as newsreaders are to Usenet news of old.

If you have been surfing the Web in the last couple months, you undoubtedly have come across sites known as *weblogs* (also commonly referred to as *blogs*). Simply put, weblogs are like diaries of the thoughts and wanderings of a person or group of people, pointing at and annotating things of interest on the Web. On the surface, a weblog looks no different than a conventional web page, but one salient feature of a weblog is that its content is usually exposed, in addition to the default web-page view, as an XML document (RSS, to be precise) for syndication.

In fact, an inordinate number of traditional content sites, from News.com to *The New York Times*, are now RSS-enabled, syndicating stories either in one massive feed or by section or category.

As this book was being written, a new syndication formation known as Atom was undergoing development. Even though they are different dialects of XML, for the purposes of this hack, RSS and Atom feeds perform the same kind of duties.

News Aggregators

News aggregators are applications that collect all these RSS documents at regular intervals. The advantage of using news aggregators is that you need not visit each individual site in order to know about the latest happenings. You can simply aggregate the news into one central location and selectively view the sites in which you are interested. Nowadays, a great number of online news sites and magazines have caught the syndication bug and are distributing news via RSS, which makes it all the more convenient for you to travel the world from the comfort of your Mac.

NetNewsWire

Ranchero's NetNewsWire (*http://ranchero.com/software/netnewswire*; Pro version is $39.95 per user, $29.95 per user for two or more users; 30-day demo available; the Lite version is freeware/donateware) rules the RSS reading roost for Macintosh.

The default interface (shown in Figure 3-17) is not unlike those of Usenet newsreaders of the past.

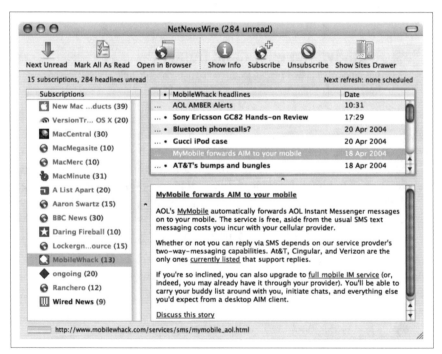

Figure 3-17. NetNewsWire's default interface

The left pane contains a list of news, web sites, and weblogs to which you are subscribed. NetNewsWire comes presubscribed to a list of popular and Mac-slanted blogs, news sites, and online magazines. The top-right pane shows the list of headlines from the site selected on the left. Select a headline to display an abstract of the content in the bottom-right pane. Want to read the story in its entirety and native web form? Double-click the headline to have your default web browser fetch and display it for you.

Subscribing to feeds. Of course, with the proliferation of syndicated online content, the list of presubscribed feeds provides only a starting point. NetNewsWire comes with a list of well-known feeds, in addition to those in the default subscription list. Click Show Sites Drawer or press ⌘-L to display the feeds in the Sites Drawer, as shown in Figure 3-18.

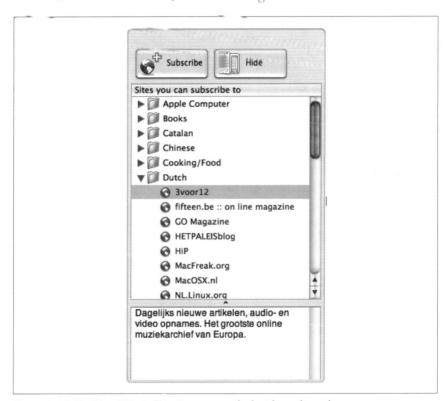

Figure 3-18. NetNewsWire's Sites Drawer, packed with syndicated sources

Feeds in the Sites Drawer are grouped nicely into categories for your convenience. Control-click on a feed's name and you're presented with three choices: subscribe to the feed, open it in your browser for a quick taste of what it has to offer, or open the RSS feed itself in your default browser.

Another way of subscribing to sites is to supply the RSS URL yourself; perhaps you've copied it from a web page of interest. Select Subscriptions → Subscribe... or press ⌘-Shift-S. Type or paste in the RSS feed's URL and click OK to subscribe. You'll notice the feed appear and update itself in the bottom-left of the screen.

> Many weblogs have a link to their RSS feeds right from the home page. These links usually appear as easily recognizable orange XML buttons. Other sites have an embedded tag in their home page that points to their RSS feeds; NetNews-Wire will notice and follow this link if you simply provide the site's home page URL in the Subscribe... dialog box.

Housekeeping. If you have a long subscription list, it makes sense to organize feeds into groups—akin to keeping similar folders together on your hard drive. Control- or right-click anywhere in the Subscriptions pane and select New Group to do so. Create as many groups as you like: one for Tech, another for Sports, and so on. Drag feeds into the groups, organizing things any way you wish. You can even nest groups to keep your baseball news and basketball news separate, yet both in the Sports group.

A different view. Under the View menu, you'll find options galore for sorting and otherwise changing the way NetNewsWire lays out its content and, indeed, itself. If you prefer to read your syndicated content in one long stream rather than click through headline after headline, use Combined View (View → Use Combined View), as shown in Figure 3-19. Collapse or expand a headline by clicking the associated disclosure triangle or pressing ⌘-left arrow or ⌘-right arrow, respectively.

If you have one of those newfangled widescreen PowerBooks or Cinema Displays, you'll love NetNewsWire's Widescreen View (View → Use Widescreen View), which moves the content frame from the bottom-right to right alongside the Headlines list, as shown in Figure 3-20.

Useful settings. You might want to configure the rate at which subscriptions are refreshed and new stories are dropped into your reader. The default refresh is manual. If you are pretty much always on the network, you're better off setting it to refresh at regular time intervals so that you're always reading the latest headlines.

NetNewsWire's Preferences (NetNewsWire → Preferences... or ⌘-,) has no shortage of settings. A few you should tweak right away have to do with how the application deals with the links.

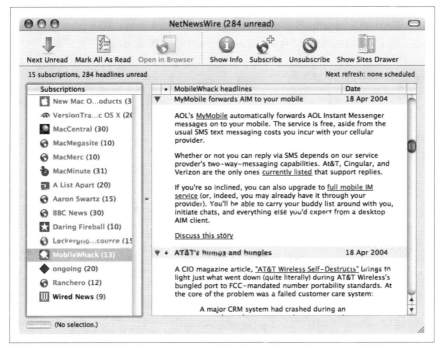

Figure 3-19. NetNewsWire's Combined View

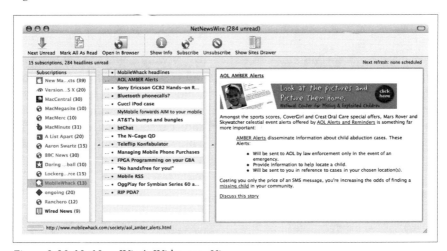

Figure 3-20. NetNewsWire's Widescreen View

Extras. On top of being a fantastic syndicated content reader, NetNews-Wire also incorporates some features that enable you to write some syndicated content of your own. A fully equipped onboard Weblog Editor (Figure 3-21) posts to Blogger, Movable Type, Radio Userland, Blosxom, and various other weblog engines—without ever leaving the comfort of Net-NewsWire. Write something from scratch or comment on another story by selecting it and choosing New → Post to Weblog (⌘-Shift-P).

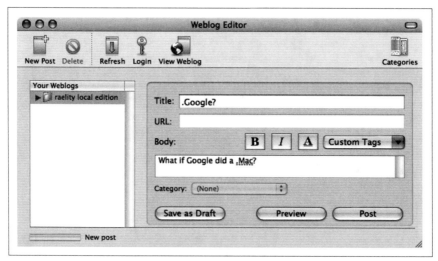

Figure 3-21. NetNewsWire's Weblog Editor

There's even a built-in Notepad for fleshing out thoughts on the day's news in outline form, whether for your own edification or for posting later to your weblog.

Final thoughts. Brent Simmons of Ranchero Software has done an amazing job of creating and maintaining a reading and writing tool for the Net generation. NetNewsWire evolves constantly (if you're lucky, this hack will be completely out of date by the time you read this and download a copy of NetNewsWire 2.0 to try out), usually in direct response to user feedback. Consequently, NetNewsWire feels more like a community than a user base—just like the home-brew days of old.

Shrook

Challenging NetNewsWire's one-newsreader-to-rule-them-all lead is Shrook (*http://www.fondantfancies.com/shrook*; $19.95) by Graham Parks. Shrook takes advantage the latest developments from Apple and the news-aggregation world and uses them to build a handy news aggregator with some rather interesting features.

Schrook's layout reflects NetNewsWire's Widescreen View and the Finder's Column View; it's a multiple-column view that displays the subscribed RSS feeds on the left, the list of RSS headlines in the middle, and the full RSS feed item on the far right. As base functionality goes, Shrook and NetNews-Wire have a great deal in common: they both read RSS feeds and present them in a clean, multiple-pane interface.

While the similarities between Shrook and NetNewsWire might appear to make differentiation difficult, they cater to different end users and each program's features reflect those end users' needs. While NetNewsWire is perfect for people who run weblogs (you won't find a weblog editor in Shrook), Shrook's features lean toward mobile end users and users with multiple computers.

A different view. Like the Finder's Column View, Shrook's interface is a window with four panes. From left to right, they are the Source pane, the Channel pane, the Item pane, and the Details pane, as shown in Figure 3-22. Clicking on an item in one pane opens it in the pane to its right, as with the Finder's Column View.

Figure 3-22. Shrook's interface

Looking to the far-left pane, you start out with four lists in the Sources column: Library, Channel Guide, Mac Sites and Marked Items, as shown in Figure 3-23. Library is exactly like the iTunes Library: a list of all of the feeds to which you are currently subscribed. Channel Guide is similar to the iTunes Radio list; in this case, though, it's a list of RSS feeds to get you started. Mac Sites and Marked Items are both premade *Smart Lists*: lists of items in the Library that fit the criteria you select.

Figure 3-23. Shrook's Source pane

If you click on Library, you'll see that it contains nothing when you start; instead, click on Channel Guide to bring up a set of feed categories in the next pane on the right. Click on any category to display a list of channels in the third pane. Selecting one of these channels causes a fourth pane to describe the RSS feed and let you add it to your library.

Select a channel and add it to your Library. If you look next to the *Library* label, you'll notice a gold star with a number. That's the number of news articles you haven't read yet. A blue circle indicates that you have unread items but have looked at the channel.

Now that you've added an item to your Library, click on Library. You'll see a list of channels, plus an All Channel listing that lists everything in the Library. Select any one of your channels to bring up the stories from that feed in the Item pane. If you select a story, the Details panel will show a text version of the item itself.

Filling in the features. So far, Shrook is similar to NetNewsWire. Both read news features and display them. However, Shrook contains quite a few features that NetNewsWire doesn't.

For one, Shrook features built-in web browsing; you won't need to use Safari to see the web site for the news story. To use Shrook's internal web browser, click the little Safari-like compass icon on the bottom-right of the window; the text version of the item you've selected is replaced by the web page to which the item links (*permalinks*), as shown in Figure 3-24.

The web browser comes courtesy of Apple's WebKit technology, which Safari itself uses. That said, Shrook isn't intended as a general web browser; clicking on any of the links inside of Details pane brings up your default browser.

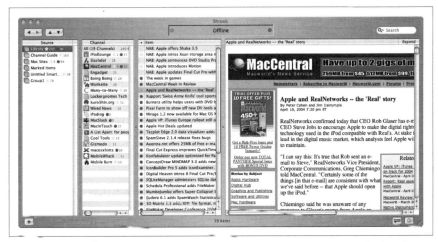

Figure 3-24. Reading a story in its native web-page environment, right inside Shrook

It's unlikely that most web pages will fit into the relatively small area provided by the Details pane. To get a better view of the web page, try clicking the Expand button in the upper-right corner of the Details pane (View → Expand Item Pane or ⌘-D) to expand the view so that only the Item and Details columns show.

If you're missing NetNewsWire's Combined View, try Shrook's Show Previews option (View → Show Previews). This view shows the first line of the story immediately under the headline in the Item pane.

Shrook also sports Smart Groups, similar in idea to the Smart Playlists of iTunes: select File → New Smart Group (or click the plus button at the bottom of Shrook's window) and select Smart Group. Shrook will ask you for criteria for this group; you can use any of the details about an RSS feed to include or exclude feeds from this group.

One interesting feature is the ability to mark items (click next to the item in the Item pane), similar to flagging a message in Mail. By creating a Smart Group that contains only elements that have been marked, you can work through a large list quickly, marking those you want to come back to later. Marked items are indicated by a red slash.

Shrook on the go. Shrook's main strength over NetNewsWire is that it caters to those lucky souls with multiple computers. You can synchronize your subscriptions and read/unread status with Shrook.com (*http://www.shrook.com*), keeping your home computer's subscriptions in sync with those on your laptop. Once you've set up an account, visit Shrook → Preferences → shrook. com and fill in your Shrook.com account information.

If you're on the go, you can take your Shrook-fed stories with you on your iPod. Select File → Export to iPod (⌘-T) to export the latest news to your little bundle of music joy.

On the down side. Using Shrook after having used NetNewsWire, I found I missed a few things.

I use newsreaders primarily to find things to post to my weblog. Shrook is just not designed to be a writer's tool. It has no weblog editor, and its internal web browser doesn't have bookmarks, so bookmarklets are out. To be fair, though, this isn't Shrook's intent.

Shrook isn't AppleScriptable like NetNewsWire is. While most people would consider this a minor point, being able to draw information from a newsreader has always struck me as important.

Finally, Shrook doesn't allow you to drag and drop URLs. When I find a site with an RSS feed, NetNewsWire allows me to drag and drop the URL onto its Subscriptions pane. With Shrook, I have to copy the URL and then add it manually to subscribe. It's a minor point, but one I bump into all the time.

That said, as syndicated content readers go, Shrook is an excellent program for multiple-computer users, mobile travelers, iPod users, and leading-edge technologists. Shrook's few liabilities are minor compared with the innovative features that Graham Parks has come up with.

See Also

Syndicated content readers are proliferating at a remarkable rate. While we've highlighted the two front-runners (at least at the time of this writing), there are a few others you might want to check out:

- PulpFiction (*http://www.freshlysqueezedsoftware.com/products/pulpfiction*) by Freshly Squeezed Software takes its organization cues from Mail, allowing you to treat RSS feeds somewhat like mailing lists.
- NewsMonster (*http://www.newsmonster.org*) is a Mozilla **[Hack #28]** add-in with collaborative reading capabilities.
- Amphetadesk (*http://www.disobey.com/amphetadesk*) is a locally running web-based reader.
- ZOË **[Hack #38]** has a built-in RSS reader of sorts.

—Ted Stevko, Rael Dornfest, and Wei Meng Lee

HACK #31 Breathe Life into Your Staid Buddy List

Why settle for a boring old "Available" message and equally staid iChat buddy icon when you can stream your mug and status live to your loyal fans?

The one downside to all this working remotely business is that it's a rather quiet affair: no real-world buddies popping their heads into your cube to say "Hey," no tapping of the keyboard or tunes wafting in from the office next door. (Okay, so this can be a blessing too.)

iChat and email keep you in touch with your peers, friends, and family, but it can be just a little too virtual to be satisfying. Surely there's some way to inject a little color and motion into the rather bland "Available" and "Busy" status messages in your Buddy List.

Why, yes there is, thanks to a couple of nifty iChat sidekicks.

iChat Streaming Icon

At first, I thought I was imagining it. Perhaps it was just the slightly different icon I was noticing. No, come to think of it, my buddy was actually moving—looking this way and that, stretching, talking to someone in the background. At least his iChat icon was.

iChat Streaming Icon (*http://ichat.twosailors.com*; $5 shareware) streams your mug via iSight or the like as your iChat icon, live to anyone who has the (mis)fortune of having you in their buddy list.

I've always kept my buddy list visible, right there on the right side of my Desktop. Being virtual, it provides a sense of folks being around—virtual cube-mates, if you will. Now, thanks to the technical know-how of Andreas Pardeike, I can watch them type and pace, see what they're having for lunch, or just watch them bobbling and jiggling about on my Desktop like so many Tamagotchis (those oval, plastic virtual pets that were all the rage in the 90s). All I do is talk to them once a day, send them a file or three every other evening, and respond quickly to their "mornin's".

Your iSight or any other FireWire or USB webcam [Hack #34] that works with your Mac and iChat AV will work with iChat Streaming Icon. Plug in the camera, launch iChat AV, and then launch iChat Streaming Icon.

iChat Streaming Icon will begin capturing images every two seconds (you can vary this from every 0.5 seconds to every 5 minutes) and continually replace your iChat AV icon with the latest image. The new image appears not only on *your* computer, but also on the computers of all the people with whom you are chatting—whether they're using Windows, Linux, or Mac— as long as their chat client supports icons, as most do. The resulting effect is a live, animated you, in both buddy lists and chat windows, as shown in Figure 3-25.

Figure 3-25. A live, animated you in every buddy list

If you don't have an iSight or webcam, you can still have a little fun with iChat Streaming Icon by animating a short series of icons or even showing a QuickTime movie as your icon.

> The only downside is that iChat Streaming Icon tends to slow down both your machine and the machine of the person with whom you're chatting. A handy cache-cleaner script (*http://ichat.twosailors.com/ClearIconCache.tgz*) can erase the large cache file for the image icon that will inevitably develop over time. It's not a great solution, but hey.

iChatStatus

To accompany your streaming iChat icon—or instead of, if you're more textual than visual—there's iChatStatus (*http://ittpoi.com/?type=frameset&product=com.ittpoi.ichatstatus*; donateware). This System Preferences pane updates your iChat status message automatically every few seconds (5 to 300, with 20 as the default). Out of the box, iChatStatus lets the world know what you're listening to in iTunes, as shown in Figure 3-26, by displaying a music note followed by the artist name and song title of the currently playing track.

Figure 3-26. iChatStatus, sharing your currently playing iTunes track

But that's just one option. iChatStatus comes with a whole slew of alternate scripts to display everything from your foremost app to free memory, local temperature, and the page loaded up in Safari, as shown in Figure 3-27.

Figure 3-27. Showing what application is in the foreground

You'll want to be careful about sharing some things—where you're browsing in Safari, for instance—so as not to surprise your buddies with anything either out of character or just plain off-color.

Install the iChatStatus Preferences pane (Figure 3-28) into your System Preferences by double-clicking it; you'll be asked whether you prefer iChatStatus to be available to all users on your machine or just you. Depending on your choice, it'll drop the pane into either the systemwide */Library/PreferencePanes* folder or your personal *~/Library/PreferencePanes* folder. You'll want make the sample scripts available to iChatStatus by clicking the Open Scripts Folder button and dragging the contents of the Example Scripts folder there from the mounted image.

Because all the plug-in scripts are swatches of AppleScript, you can write your own quite easily. Here's a slight variation on the Safari script

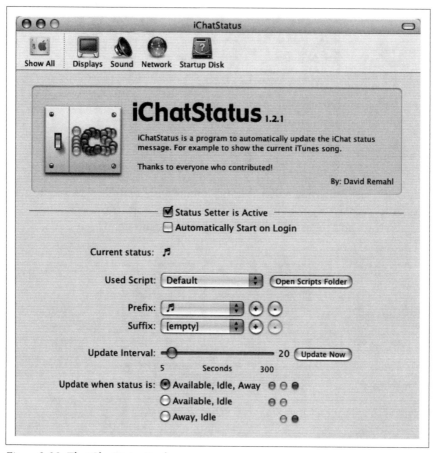

Figure 3-28. The iChatStatus Preferences pane

(alterations are shown in bold) that displays the URL rather than name of the web page in the forefront:

```
tell application "System Events"
 if ((application processes whose (name is equal to "Safari")) count) is
greater than 0 then
 tell application "Safari"
 if (count of windows) is greater than 0 then
 return "Safari: " & URL of document 1 of front window
 else
 return ""
 end if
 end tell
 else
 return "Off"
 end if
end tell
```

Save your script to the iChatStatus scripts folder (~/*Library/Application Support/iChatStatus*) and give it a descriptive name—in this case, *Safari URL.scpt*. You'll have to quit System Preferences and relaunch it to have any new scripts show up in iChatStatus's drop-down menu.

While technically unsupported, iChatStatus runs rather nicely and does just what it is supposed to do.

Hacking the Hack

Combine iChat Streaming Icon and iChatStatus into a little Mystery Science Theater 3000 (*http://www.mst3kinfo.com*) fun. Use a small QuickTime clip from your favorite movie or some other media as your iChat Streaming Icon. Write an AppleScript addition for iChatStatus that automatically generates subtitles for the streaming movie in your iChat status bar.

See Also

- "Update iChat Status with Mac::Glue" [Hack #20] performs about the same feats as iChatStatus, but in Perl.

—C. K. Sample III

Better iChat Transcripts HACK #32

Browse and search your iChat conversations and even export them as plain text or, with a little AppleScript magic, web pages.

iChat is generally regarded as vastly more pleasing to use and in some ways more feature-packed than the official AOL Instant Messenger (AIM) client (*http://www.aim.com/get_aim/mac/latest_macosx.adp*). iChat's one Achilles heel—at least for those of us who do about as much business in chat as in mail—is its lack of usable transcripts. Mail has folders, both for sent and received messages. There's nothing quite analogous in iChat. That's not quite fair; iChat is indeed able to log conversations. But it insists upon storing them in rather horrid binary form and provides no decent interface to browse and search earlier chat sessions. AIM, on the other hand, can save your tête-à-têtes as HTML, so they're viewable in any web browser.

Let's see what we can do about that, shall we?

iChat Logs

Unless you've chanced upon them in your Documents directory, you probably don't know that iChat keeps logs of every conversation you have. You'll find them all in ~/Documents/iChats, listed by buddy (full name or buddy handle) and number, starting with 1 (e.g., *Steve Jobs #7.chat*).

iChat keeps logs only if you ask it to; do so by checking the "Automatically save chat transcripts" preference in iChat → Preferences... → Messages, as shown in Figure 3-29.

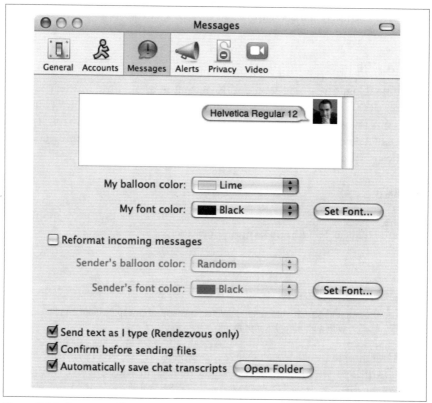

Figure 3-29. Automatically saving iChat transcripts

Don't bother trying to read the transcripts in a text editor; they're serialized objects (*noise* to you and me) that are viewable only programmatically or from within iChat. Open an old chat by selecting File → Open... (⌘-O) and selecting it from the list, as shown in Figure 3-30.

Up comes an exact replica of an earlier chat, replete with buddy icons and smileys. Of course, you can remove old logs at any time by simply deleting them from ~/Documents/iChats. They're only files, after all.

The built-in functionality to read over old conversations is great if you know precisely who you were talking to and when; in other words, it's far from useful.

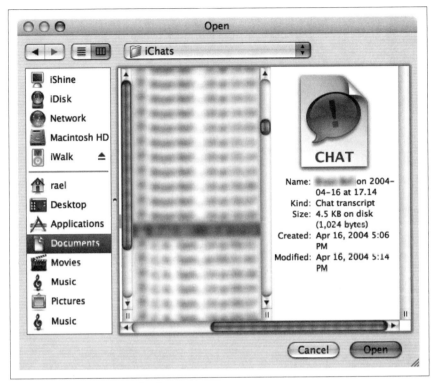

Figure 3-30. Opening an iChat log entry

Logorrhea

> n. pathologically excessive talking
>
> *—spiny.com/logorrhea*

Logorrhea (*http://spiny.com/logorrhea*; donateware) is a marvelous tool that picks up where iChat's logs leave off. According to the home page, "It pulps, it purees, it locates incriminating past conversations with incredible speed!"

Browse earlier discussions by buddy and date in a nice, speedy, three-pane interface, as shown in Figure 3-31, which is much easier than opening and closing chat after chat in iChat.

Search across all your archived conversations by keyword, as shown in Figure 3-32. You'll often find some conversations you'd forgotten you had.

> One oddity I found (at least in the current incarnation) is the lack of a Stop Searching button. The only way, it seems, to stop a Logorrhea search is to close the application (⌘-Q). It appears that Logorrhea has a bad case of searchorrhea. ;-)

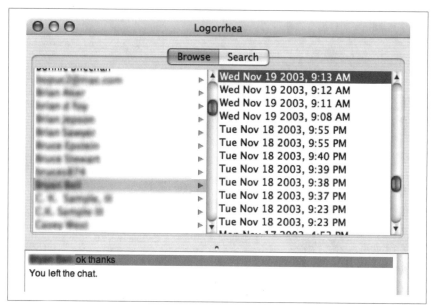

Figure 3-31. Browsing old chats by buddy and date

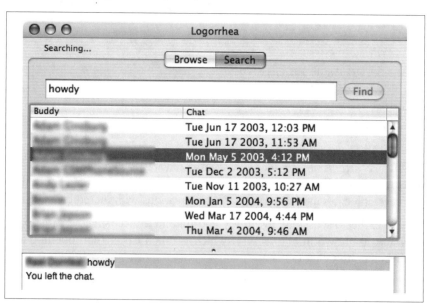

Figure 3-32. Searching prior conversations by keyword

But we were after some way of exporting chats to HTML or plain text, weren't we?

Logorrhea does have an export (File → Export Chats) feature that'll dump every single chat with every single buddy as a nice big hunk of tab-delimited text. For each sentence sent over the wire, you'll find a line in the exported file containing buddy name, speaker, date and time, and what was said. Here's a typical—albeit uninteresting—entry:

```
Cousin Adam myself 06/03/2003 22:12:15 205 you betcha!
```

While usable, it's still not quite the friendly HTML output AIM produces.

The Code

With a little bit of GUI AppleScripting [Hack #14], combined with a touch of Perl and a smattering of Unix grep goodness, you can have Logorrhea generate its logs and then turn them into nicely formatted HTML pages, one per buddy:

```
-- Transcripts Away
-- Purpose: Uses GUI scripting to script Logorrhea to export iChat
   logs out to HTML files.
-- Author: Phil Ulrich

set peopleNames to {}

(* Part 1: Get the names of people we've iChatted with *)
tell application "Logorrhea" to activate
tell application "System Events"
  tell process "Logorrhea"
    get static text in radio group 1 of scroll area 1 of scroll area 1 of
browser 1 of tab group 1 of splitter group 1 of window
    repeat with i in the result
      copy the value of i to the end of peopleNames
    end repeat
  end tell
end tell

(* Part 2: Find out which names we need *)
tell application "Logorrhea"
  set chosen_ones to choose from list peopleNames with prompt "Whose chats ¬
would you like to export?" OK button name "Export" cancel button name ¬
"Cancel" with multiple selections allowed without empty selection allowed
end tell

(* Part 3: Export, export, export! *)
tell application "System Events"
  tell process "Logorrhea"
    tell menu bar 1
      tell menu bar item "File"
        tell menu "File"
          click menu item "Export Chats..."
```

```
          end tell
        end tell
      end tell

    keystroke "D" using command down
    set value of text field 1 of sheet 1 of window 1 to "ChatTranscripts"
    click button "Save" of sheet 1 of window 1

    try
      delay 2
      click button "Replace" of window 1 -- account for possibility that the
file exists already
    end try
  end tell
end tell

(* Part 4: Done with Logorrhea. Begin parsing. *)
set infile to "~/Desktop/ChatTranscripts.txt"
do shell script "perl -pi -e 's/\\x0d/\\x0a/g' " & infile
repeat with a_name in chosen_ones
  set output_string to "<html><head><title>" & a_name & "</title></head>¬
<body><table border=\"1\">"
  set outfile to quoted form of ((POSIX path of (path to desktop)) & ¬
a_name & ".html")

  try
    set result_lines to do shell script "grep ^\"" & a_name & "\" " & ¬
infile without altering line endings
    set old_delims to AppleScript's text item delimiters
    set AppleScript's text item delimiters to "
"
    set alternating_lines to text items of result_lines

    repeat with j from 1 to number of items in alternating_lines
      set top_line to item j of alternating_lines
      set AppleScript's text item delimiters to " "
      set top_line_parts to text items of top_line
      set output_string to output_string & "<tr>"
      set item_count to the number of items in top_line_parts

      repeat with i from 2 to the item_count
        set part to item i of top_line_parts
        if i is item_count then
          if part is "" then
            set output_string to output_string & "</tr></table><p /><hr />¬
<p /><table border=\"1\"><tr>"
          else
            set output_string to output_string & "</tr><tr><td colspan=\"5¬
\">" & part & "</td></tr>"
          end if
        else
```

```
            set output_string to output_string & "<td>" & part & "</td>"
        end if
    end repeat

    end repeat

    set AppleScript's text item delimiters to old_delims
    set output_string to output_string & "</table></body></html>"
    do shell script "echo \"" & output_string & "\" | cat - > " & outfile
    do shell script "rm " & infile
    end try

    end repeat
```

Here's how it works. AppleScript activates Logorrhea, pulls out the name of everyone for whom an iChat log exists (using GUI scripting), and pushes the name on to an array. The script then pops up a dialog that asks you which buddies' chats you want to export; it creates a separate HTML page for each buddy.

Again using GUI Scripting, the script calls Logorrhea's File → Export Chats... menu item to create that single whopping great text file of all available chats. If there is an existing file on the Desktop called *ChatTranscripts.txt* (the default filename), you'll notice a Replace or Cancel dialog pop up. Just wait; the script will "click" Replace for you automatically. (Alternately, you can click it yourself if you're just that impatient.)

AppleScript then calls out to the Unix shell (do shell script) for a quick spot of Perl [Hack #19] and grep [Hack #91] to convert Mac line endings to Unix and scan for lines that match the buddies you chose to build transcripts for, respectively.

> If any of your buddies' aliases contain characters that grep considers special, such as [] or ( ), the script might fail silently. It would be helpful if there were an option in Apple-Script for *escaped form*, to go along with *quoted form*.

Finally, the script parses the matching lines by using AppleScript's text-parsing abilities and pipes them out to a file via Unix's echo and cat.

Running the Code

Save the script from Script Editor as *logorrhea2html.scpt* or the like and run it by double-clicking its icon in the Finder. Be patient, because it might take quite a bit of time to meander through your possibly massive collection of chat sessions.

Final Thoughts

This script is a great example of how several of Apple's core technologies can be tied together by AppleScript—the great Aqua GUI via GUI scripting [Hack #14] and underlying Unix tools such as Perl and grep by way of shell scripting—to make something that would've been hard (if not impossible) to accomplish otherwise.

—Phil Ulrich

HACK #33   Gather Ye Buddies While Ye May

Keep those Rendezvous buddies, even when you're not on the same local network.

Sitting with Doc Searls (*http://doc.weblogs.com*) at a recent conference, we were noticing just how many people were running Macintoshes, witnessed by the multitudes showing up in our collective iChat Rendezvous list.

What if you could use the opportunity of being in close proximity to such a collection of smart people (not only smart enough to buy Apple, mind you) to gather a few buddies you've always meant to add to your personal Buddy List?

"Can't I just drag someone from here to here?" whispered Doc, his mouse pointer hovering over a rather desirable buddy-to-be.

"Not that I know of," I answered in a rather distracted surely-I'd-have-noticed kind of way.

But Doc, charmingly naïve tinkerer that he is (and I mean that in only the best way), wasn't to be dissuaded by my dismissive response and gave it a shot. And, sure enough, it worked. The two of us then spent the better part of the conference session gathering buddies by the armload—only people we knew but had yet to add, I assure you. ;-)

It turns out that, by default, your AIM or .Mac name is shared as part of iChat's Rendezvousing. Using this information, iChat allows you to add these names to your Buddy List with a simple drag and drop between the two windows, as shown in Figure 3-33.

You can optionally keep this information off the Rendezvous network, rendering yourself ungatherable, by flipping the "Block Rendezvous users from seeing my email and AIM addresses" switch (check the checkbox) on the iChat → Preferences... Privacy tab, as shown in Figure 3-34.

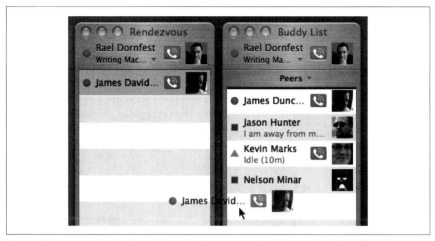

Figure 3-33. Dragging and dropping Rendezvous buddies to a personal Buddy List

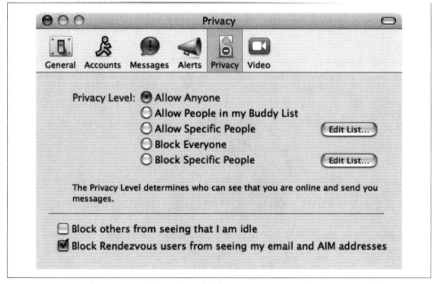

Figure 3-34. Rendering myself ungatherable by preventing Rendezvous users from seeing my AIM address

By *email address*, iChat refers to your email address as it appears in your own Address Book card.

> Title of this hack inspired by "To the Virgins, to
> Make Much of Time," by Robert Herrick

HACK #34   USB Videoconferencing

Coax iChat into treating your old USB webcam as a legitimate video input source.

If you're one of those lucky chaps who can afford to buy a FireWire video camera or the snazzy new Apple iSight (*http://www.apple.com/isight/*) and iChat AV, you then have full-fledged videoconferencing at your fingertips. If you don't quite have the budget for either of these two beauties, the next-best solution is to get a cheap USB webcam or repurpose one you already have.

Unfortunately, Apple has not paid much attention to supporting USB webcam users. Short of waiting for Apple to do something about it (see the online petition at *http://www.petitiononline.com/iChatUSB/petition.html*), your options involve fiddling about with some of the workarounds that have surfaced for getting iChat to work with USB webcams.

In this hack, I'll show you how to do just that. This research was driven by my own desperation to press back into service a Logitech USB QuickCam (see Figure 3-35). In Jaguar, the solution wasn't too difficult (there are drivers that allow your webcam to work in Mac OS X). However, the release of Panther complicated the matter, because it broke the existing drivers.

Figure 3-35. The Logitech USB QuickCam

So, to make a long story short, here are the steps to get your webcam to work with iChat in Panther:

1. Find and install a Mac OS X driver for your webcam.
2. Install the Application Enhancer utility.
3. Install the iChatUSBCam module.

Installing a Driver for Your Webcam

The first thing you need to do is install a driver for your webcam so that Panther can recognize it. You have two options:

- Get a free driver from Macam (*http://webcam-osx.sourceforge.net/*).
- Buy a driver from IOXperts (*http://ioxperts.com/usbwebcam.html*).

For this hack, I'll use the free driver from Macam. There are some problems with installing Macam on Panther, so you'll need to download a fix (from *http://www.multi-cam.net/camera_downloads.html* under the header "Macam driver for Panther fix!"). Be sure to copy the *macam.component* folder to the */Library/QuickTime* folder.

Testing Your Webcam

Once the Macam driver is installed, it is useful to test your webcam to see if it is working properly (and also to preserve your sanity when troubleshooting all the problems later on). You can use the Video Viewer (*http://www.schubert-it.com/videoviewer/*) to test your webcam, as shown in Figure 3-36.

Figure 3-36. Using Video Viewer to test your webcam

Installing Application Enhancer

If you do not have Application Enhancer already installed on your Mac, you should now download and install Application Enhancer 1.4.1 from Unsanity (*http://www.unsanity.com/haxies/ape/*). The iChatUSBCam module that we will install in the next section is an Application Enhancer module; hence, we need to install Application Enhancer now.

To check whether you have Application Enhancer installed, look in your System Preferences window and locate the APE Manager icon (see Figure 3-37).

Figure 3-37. Locating the APE Manager icon

Installing the iChatUSBCam

To ensure that iChat recognizes your USB webcam, you need an Application Enhancer module known as iChatUSBCam (*http://www.ecamm.com/mac/ichatusbcam/*).

Download a demo version of the iChatUSBCam module or purchase the full version for $9.95. Once iChatUSBCam is downloaded, the APE Manager will show iChat as an application that is enhanced by the iChatUSBCam module, as shown in Figure 3-38 (look in your System Preferences, under the APE Manager icon).

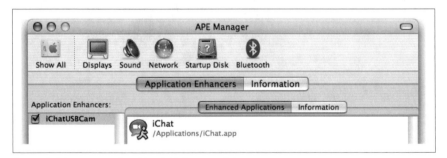

Figure 3-38. Viewing the iChatUSBCam module

Now, launch iChat. If everything is installed correctly, you should be able to see the green video icon next to your name. Click on the video icon to see a preview of yourself, as shown in Figure 3-39.

Figure 3-39. Previewing myself through iChat

To initiate a videoconference with another user, simply click on the video icon of the other user (see Figure 3-40). If the other user does not have video-conferencing capability, you can also initiate a one-way video conversation.

Hacking the Hack

In the process of preparing for this hack, I encountered several errors that I think are useful to share with you:.

- Be sure to install the fix for the Macam driver before you begin. If you don't, your webcam might not work properly. Worse, you might have problems booting up your Mac after a restart.

- If you have problems booting up your Mac, make sure you unplug the USB webcam from your Mac. In my experience, this will remove the problem and let your computer boot up properly.

- Restart iChat (or your Mac) if your webcam cannot be detected.

—Wei-Meng Lee

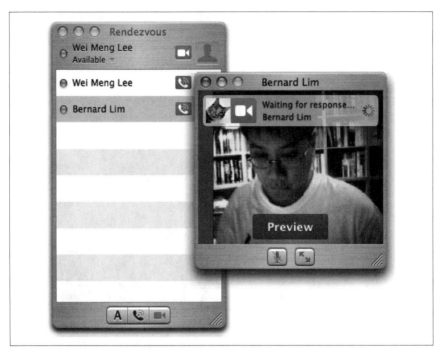

Figure 3-40. Initiating a video conference with another user

Provide Remote Support

As any tech support person can tell you, the hardest part of helping somebody with her computer remotely is getting the person on the other side to give you the right information. Thankfully, there are a few tools at your disposal to help.

As a Mac power user, you are honor bound to help anybody who considers you a friend with their Mac problems. At least it feels like that sometimes. And most of the time you're probably happy to help. But the problem is that, quite often, these calls for help come over the phone or iChat, and it's hard to have enough information to solve the problem.

Well, there are a few tools you can use to help your friends help you help them.

Capturing the Screen

While writing this book and the many other books that we've worked on, we have clicked off dozens, if not hundreds, of screenshots. As authors, the ability to use Mac OS X's built-in screen-grabbing functionality is invaluable for creating illustrations to explain what we are writing about. But the usefulness of grabbing the screen and sending it to somebody isn't limited to just book writers. It can be useful to anybody trying to explain how to do something on the Mac or trying to help a friend troubleshoot.

For example, imagine your friend has recently switched to the Mac and he finds you on iChat. And then you have the following conversation:

```
Him: Hey, my Mail application is messed up.
You: What's happening?
Him: Well, I can see my messages, but I can't actually see them.
You: I don't understand…
```

The irritating thing about these conversations is that if you were there, you could see what your friend meant and help him fix his problem immediately. Well, if you know the commands to take screen grabs, the rest of the conversation can go like this:

```
You: Ok, take a screen capture for me. Hit Command-Control-Shift-3.
You: That will copy your screen to the clipboard. Now, paste that into this
chat window.
Him: Ok, here you go.
```

Now that you can see his screen, shown in Figure 3-41, you can see what the problem is and help him restore his message viewer.

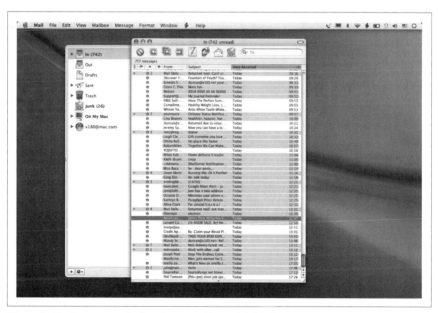

Figure 3-41. A screen grab showing a problem with Mail

Table 3-1 shows the keyboard commands to grab the entire screen or parts of the screen.

Table 3-1. Screen-grab keyboard shortcuts

Shortcut	Description
⌘-Shift-3	Capture screen to file. The file will appear on the Desktop as a PDF.
⌘-Control-Shift-3	Capture the screen to the clipboard.
⌘-Shift-4	Capture a region of the screen to a file. The file will appear on the Desktop as a PDF.
⌘-Control-Shift-4	Capture a region of the screen to the clipboard.

Going to Video

Sometimes, a screenshot isn't enough, especially if you need to show a sequence of events or help somebody with a hardware issue. For example, if you are trying to help your friend plug something into her Mac, it can be a bit tricky to help if she doesn't know the difference between a USB and a FireWire cable. If you and your friend have an iSight or a USB webcam that can work with iChat [Hack #34], then you have everything you need. Start up a video chat and then tell your friend to point the camera at the onscreen problem or hardware in question, as shown in Figure 3-42.

The only caveat to this hack is that you'll want to make sure that the person holding the camera can hold it still enough for the picture to settle down. You'll notice that the image will get quite chunky during quick transitions, but with a steady hand you can see enough to help anybody out of a jam quickly.

HACK #36 IRC: Chatrooms for Hackers

Leave the safety of your iChat buddy list and step out for an evening of conversation in the world of Inter-Relay Chat.

If you enjoy those daily tête-à-têtes with your iChat buddies and occasionally frequent an AOL chatroom or two, you might well be ready to spend some time in the geekier environs of Inter-Relay Chat (IRC).

IRC is more a series of caves and tunnels than the chat rooms; it consists of a worldwide network of subnetworks and servers. Instead of rooms named "Buffy" or "Collectible Cars," you have channels—reminiscent of the chatty CB radios of 70s past—named *#slash* and *#macusers*. Between the odd channel names—odd because they're abbreviated and start with a pound or hash (#) character—and plethora of different subnetworks and channels, seemingly without rhyme or reason, no one but the alpha geeks tends to find their way to IRC.

Also, until recently, IRC clients (read: applications) have been about as geeky and inelegant as you can get. A profusion of buttons and windows

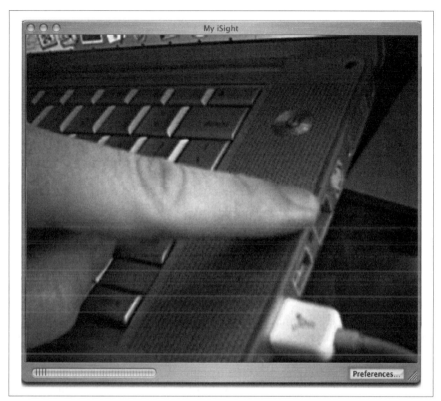

Figure 3-42. Helping troubleshoot with the aid of iSight and iChat

and dialog boxes, combined with a seemingly arcane Unix-like set of commands, have felt about as inviting as the Unix command line to most. But this is changing; today's IRC clients, while not ameliorating the basic confusion around just what IRC is and how to climb onboard, have come a long way. Conversation, just one of the many choices, looks and feels so much like iChat, you'll find yourself rather at home.

A Crash Course in IRC

IRC is not a place any more than the Web is. It is a network of networks of servers. Where it differs from the Web as a network is that, depending on where you come in (i.e., which server you log into), you'll find a completely different set of rooms (channels) and faces. Many hackers spend a lot of time on the Freenode IRC network (*http://www.freenode.net*), home to countless projects and groups that mix work with idle chatter. Undernet is home to (among its other myriad groups) the *#macusers* channel (*http://www.macusersirc.org*), a space to discuss all things Mac. Finding the right network and channel to join can be a trick and is often best accomplished by asking your friends where they hang out.

Once you decide on a network to join and connect to a server on that network, you're ready to start joining channels. IRC channels are analogous to chatrooms. You join a channel (or channels) by clicking your IRC client's Join button and supplying a channel name (usually *#something*—pronounced "pound something" or "hash something," depending on where you live—where *something* is the name of the channel). A few moments later, you'll find yourself among friends and strangers, all chatting away a mile a minute. When you type something, it is relayed through the network to everyone on that channel. You can also talk quietly to someone directly by using the Message button or equivalent in your client.

There is a whole host of commands you can issue, either instead of or to supplement what your client provides in GUI form (buttons and other things to click). The command /join #macusers, for instance, joins you to the *#macusers* channel. Typing /msg a_friend Howdy! sends a private "Howdy!" to someone on the IRC network with the moniker *a_friend.*

As with all group environments, there is also some etiquette. Some channels have a particular focus, be it cars or Objective-C programming; meander in and start talking about last night's Buffy episode and you're bound to be met with a hard (albeit virtual) stare or three. If you're responding to someone in particular in a channel, prefix your response with their moniker and a colon, like this: a_friend: yes, of course i have an ipod. Often, channels have an associated web page, where they spell out the focus and rules of the road.

Obviously, this has been nothing short of a crash course, and there's so much more to IRC that we could actually fill a book on the subject. Thankfully, though, there is just such a book, a peer of the one you're reading: *IRC Hacks* by Paul Mutton (O'Reilly).

Macintosh IRC Clients

There is no shortage of IRC clients for Macintosh users. Chatzilla (*http://www.mozilla.org/projects/rt-messaging/chatzilla*), the truly outstanding IRC client that's integrated into Mozilla, is popular among Mac users and can also be used on other operating systems. For non-Mozilla users, there are many alternatives. Some applications, such as Fire (*http://fire.sourceforge.net/*), combine IRC chat with ICQ, AIM, and JabberIM. Each client has its own pluses and minuses. Some are cheerful and user-friendly, others are powerful and not-so-user-friendly, and still others are both friendly and powerful enough. One of the friendliest and three of the more popular and more powerful IRC clients available for OS X are presented in this hack: Conversation, X-Chat Aqua, Snak, and IRCle.

Conversation

Conversation (*http://www.conversation.pwp.blueyonder.co.uk*) is about as close as you'll come to using iChat for IRC. As shown in Figure 3-43, it sports a rather iChat-like look and feel, with just about everything accessible through an intuitive set of buttons and switches and drag-and-drop support throughout. It has a Favorites list to hold your best buddies and preferred channels so that you can just log on and click your way to conversation. A Recent channels and users list helps you find that person you were chatting with yesterday or where you had that fabulous conversation last week. Or, just set things up so that you automatically log in and join your various discussion channels.

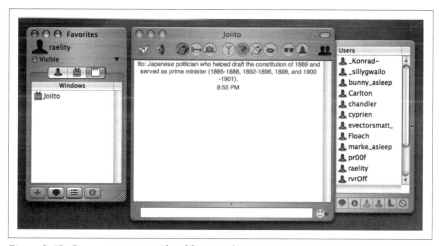

Figure 3-43. Conversation, an iChat-like IRC client

While you're best off comparing and contrasting Conversation's feature set with the other clients covered here, it's a good bet you'll find it an intuitive vehicle for your first foray into IRC.

X-Chat Aqua

X-Chat Aqua is an OS X version of the popular Unix IRC client XChat. It is freeware and can be downloaded from *http://xchataqua.sourceforge.net/*.

When X-Chat Aqua launches, it prompts you to enter nicknames and personal information and choose a server in the Server List window, as shown in Figure 3-44. A list of networks is provided by default, and you have the option to add to the list. Once nicknames and a server are selected, clicking Connect connects and opens a server window.

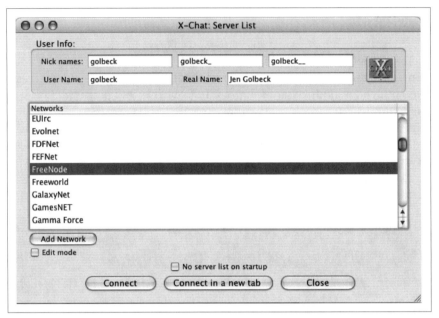

Figure 3-44. X-Chat Aqua's initial Server List pop-up

X-Chat Aqua can use a tab- or window-based view of channels and servers. The default setup puts each channel in a tab at the bottom of the window as you join the channel. Channels can be opened in new windows, instead of as tabs, by using File → New Channel Window.

Figure 3-45 shows a connection to the freenode IRC network (shown at the top of the window) and three channels (shown in tabs at the bottom of the window). Channel participants are displayed in the bar on the right. While this window is white on black, colors can be configured to your preferences.

The File menu also has options to connect directly to a new server in either a tab or a new window, or to use the Server List to establish a new connection. All commands and messages can be given in the input line at the bottom of each window, and some are also included as selectable options under the User menu.

Snak

The Snak IRC client (*http://www.snak.com*) is shareware that is free for 30 days. After that time, Snak will automatically quit after 30 minutes every time you use it, until you register it for $20.

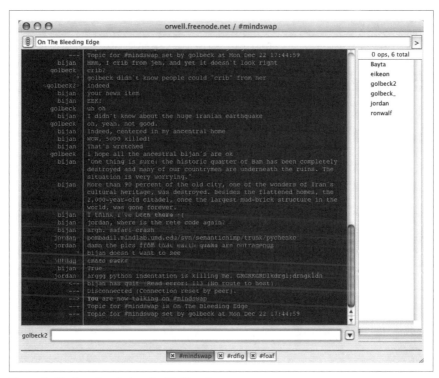

Figure 3-45. A main window for X-Chat Aqua

The Server List is the window in the lower-right corner (see Figure 3-46). Notice that the *#rdfig* and *#mindswap* channels have been grouped into one window, while the server, *irc.freenode.net*, is in a separate window in the upper right.

The first time Snak is launched, a wizard walks you through the process of creating a nickname and selecting a preferred channel. This information is stored in the Preferences. Connections to any server can be made through the Profile List. This window comes up by default and can also be found in the Windows menu. It lists all the stored IRC servers with your preferred nickname and startup commands. To connect to one of the servers, just locate it in the Server List and click Connect.

Docking is an interesting feature of Snak. Channels can be open in separate windows. Using the Dock command in the Windows menu, you can change the windows into tabs in other windows. This allows you to group multiple channels any way you like; they need not necessarily be docked with the server window. Channels can also be customized by appearance. Each channel window can have its own color scheme, which you can set by using Edit → Channel Settings.

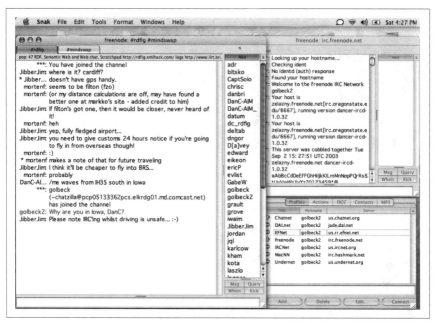

Figure 3-46. The main Snak window

Ircle

Ircle (*http://www.ircle.com*) is a Macintosh-only IRC client. It is available as shareware and free to try for 30 days, and all features are enabled during the trial. Registration is $20 and gets rid of the warning messages that appear when the application is launched.

When you run Ircle for the first time, you need to modify the Connections list. The Connections window should appear by default (as shown in Figure 3-47), but you can also find it in the Windows menu if it doesn't. There will be 10 default connections (the maximum number of server connections that IRCle supports), and they will all be configured to use the nickname *ircleuser*.

To change the default nickname, click on a connection and then click the Edit... button at the bottom of the window. This will bring up a dialog box (Figure 3-48) in which you can change your nickname, real name, exit message, and other properties.

To connect to an IRC server with this new nickname, select the connection in the Connections window and then click the Server... button. A window with a long list of servers comes up. You can choose from that list or click Add to add a new server. Once you have found the server you want in the list, click it, and then click Select. The connection is now configured to

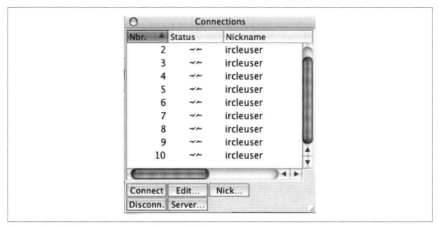

Figure 3-47. Connections window in Ircle

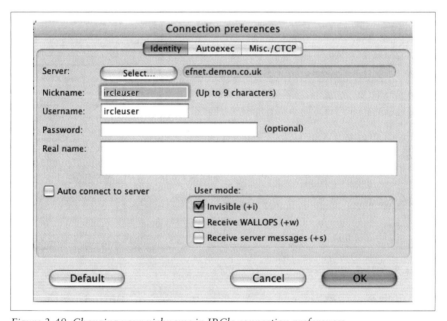

Figure 3-48. Changing your nickname in IRCle connection preferences

connect to the server. Click the Connect button in the Connections window to attach to the server.

The server messages appear in the Console window. The Inputline window is used to join channels, send commands, and type messages to a channel. Each channel appears in its own window. Depending on which window is in focus, the Userlist window changes to show the name and participants of the current channel. Private chats established using /query also get their own window. If someone else sends a private message to you without a separate window, the message will appear in the Console.

The multitude of windows in Ircle, as shown in Figure 3-49, can become overwhelming. A feature called the Channelbar is available to make them a bit more manageable. Found under the Window menu, the Channelbar puts a bar across the top of the window, with buttons for each channel, console, and chat window. Clicking a button brings the corresponding channel to the foreground. Option-clicking a button hides the selected channel window without disconnecting from it.

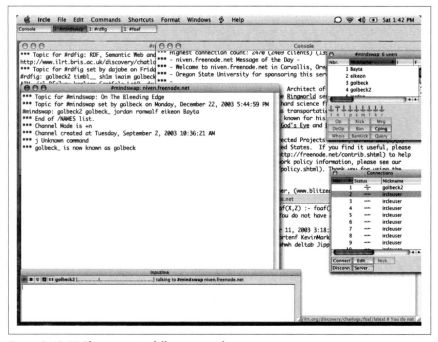

Figure 3-49. IRCle running in full-screen mode

With this many IRC clients for Macintosh, how can you resist giving it a whirl?

—Jennifer Golbeck and Rael Dornfest

Label Your Mail

Bring Eudora's colorful labels to your Mail messages, and learn a little something about the Scripts menu and keyboard shortcuts in the process.

One thing many switchers from Eudora to Mail miss is the ability to flag, identify, and categorize messages within a mailbox by using different colors and associated textual categories. In Eudora, a labeled message appears in its mailbox with its text colored and the name of the label entered in the Label column, as shown in Figure 3-50. This rather handy feature is unfortunately just not part of the Mail feature set.

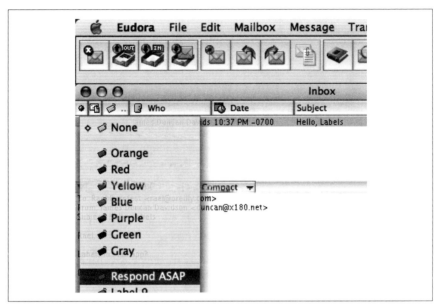

Figure 3-50. Using Eudora's colorful labels to identify and categorize messages within a mailbox

Using simple AppleScripts, it's possible to duplicate this colorization in Mail—except for the Label column. That is, this hack allows you to select one or more messages, perform a menu or key command, and have the message lines change color as they are listed in a mailbox window. (In Mail, the background of the message line, rather than the text itself, changes color.)

The Code

Even the newest of newbies should be able to take a quick gander at this rather simple bit of AppleScript and understand what it does. It acts on any messages currently selected in Mail and changes the background color of each in its turn to orange:

```
-- Colorize Mail.app messages

using terms from application "Mail"
 on perform mail action with messages msgs
 tell application "Mail"
 repeat with msg in msgs
```

```
        set background color of msg to orange
        end repeat
      end tell

      end perform mail action with messages

      on run
        tell application "Mail" to set selectedmsgs to selection
        tell me to perform mail action with messages selectedmsgs
      end run
    end using terms from
```

Now, here's the interesting part, and it's not limited to this hack alone.

Save the code to a file named *Respond ASAP – Orange___ctl-o.scpt*; that's three underscore characters (___), mind you. While you could call the script whatever you like (e.g., simply *ASAP*), there's magic in those last few characters. The ending characters (___*ctl-o*) assign the keyboard shortcut Control-O (that's the letter O) to the script so that simply selecting some messages and typing Control-O calls the script and colorizes the messages.

Save the script in your */Library/Scripts/Mail Scripts* folder. If the *Scripts* or *Mail Scripts* folders do not exist, go ahead and create them.

Create a similar script for any other of the available colors: blue, gray, green, orange, purple, red, and yellow. All you need to change in the script for each is the name of the color. So, making the following change (as indicated in bold) and saving the script as */Library/Scripts/Mail Scripts/Reply Some Day___ctl-g.scpt* provides a Control-G keystroke to turn messages gray:

```
        set background color of msg to gray
```

Be sure to create one with the color none for use in removing a color label.

Running the Code

Open Mail if it's not already open. From the Scripts menu (that little icon of a paper scroll between the Window and Help menus), select Update Scripts Menu to tell Mail to pay attention to the new scripts you've added.

When you next open the Scripts menu, you'll see the new Label items listed, along with their Control key shortcuts, as shown in Figure 3-51.

To label messages, just select them by clicking them as usual (⌘-click to pick more than one; ⌘-click a selected message to deselect it) and choose a label command from the Scripts menu or press the associated Control-key shortcut. Figure 3-52 shows a message with the orange Reply ASAP label applied.

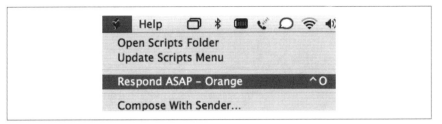

Figure 3-51. A mail-label script in Mail's Script menu

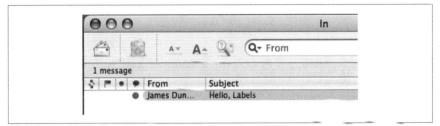

Figure 3-52. A message labeled "Reply ASAP" and colored orange

To strip the label, choose the None label script from the Scripts menu.

Once your messages are labeled, you can also sort them by color by using View → Sort By → Color.

—Chris Stone

HACK #38   Search Your Mail with ZOË

Google's Gmail service offers a gigabyte of email storage and full-text searching of all your messages since the dawn of time—at least since you started using Gmail. ZOË brings an analogue to your very Desktop.

ZOË (*http://zoe.nu*; free under a Creative Commons Attribution/Noncommercial license) is a web-based email application that lives on your Desktop and provides a Google-like interface to your email. Backed by the powerful Lucene full-text search engine (*http://jakarta.apache.org/lucene/docs/index.html*), it uses your regular POP or IMAP account to grab your incoming email silently, indexes it, and extracts salient bits, including contributors (i.e., the senders of the mail), recipients, URLs, and attachments.

While ZOË is hardly a stand-in for Mail, Entourage, or Eudora, it does serve as a useful sidekick, and I found it quickly made its way into my regular workflow.

First and foremost, it eliminates the need to manually (or create formal rules to) sort and categorize your email; ZOË automatically does this for you in the background. Unlike your run-of-the-mill email client, messages are linked together into a personal web of conversations and contexts. While some clients do keep similar emails together to some degree (Mail displays related email as threads), these links are tenuous at best and usually disappear the moment you file your message away. ZOË keeps an eye on these connections and provides a nice hyperlinked pathway through them.

And, as a nice side effect, ZOË creates a full-text backup of your mail, which you can later export to other computers or mail clients, should you ever like to do so.

Running ZOË

The only prerequisite to getting ZOË up and running is Java Runtime 1.4 or later; if you're running Panther or have been letting Software Update keep things up-to-date for you, you're in good shape.

Download and decompress the ZOË .tar file, leaving you with a Zoe folder on your Desktop. You can either leave the folder where it is (messy, but good enough for evaluating ZOË) or drop it in your Applications or any other folder (a little cleaner). Whatever you do, don't fiddle about with the folder's internal hierarchy; if you do, you risk confusing the application.

Launch ZOË by double-clicking the Zoe.jar file in the Zoe folder.

 There are various ways of starting and stopping ZOË. If you choose to install the items in the *Extra* folder, you can instead click the Play button in the ZOË Preferences pane or choose Start from ZOË's icon in the menu bar. If you're a Terminal user, navigate to the Zoe folder and type java -jar Zoe.jar.

ZOË should automatically launch your default web browser and open your local ZOË home page. If for some reason it doesn't do so, open your browser and point it to *http://127.0.0.1:10080*. Either way, you should bookmark the address so that you can quickly jump to ZOË whenever it is running.

Setting up Email Accounts

Now that you have ZOË up and running, you'll need to tell it all about your email account so that it can start grabbing your email and so that you can ask it to meander through your existing mailboxes for past messages.

Jump to ZOË's Preferences page (Figure 3-53) by clicking the ZOË link at the top left of ZOË's home page or by pointing your browser at *http:// 127.0.0.1:10080/preferences/accounts/*.

⁑ ACCOUNT
ZOË ▷ PREFERENCES ▷ ACCOUNTS ▷ NEW ACCOUNT

New Account
status: new

ACCOUNT	HOST	SMTP	
			(CANCEL)
TYPE	HOST NAME	SMTP HOST	
(IMAP ⬍)	mail.myemail.com	smtp.myemail.com	(DISCARD)
	eg mail.mac.com	eg smtp.mac.com	(SAVE)
EMAIL ADDRESS	USER NAME	SMTP USER	
me@myemail.com	me	me	
eg steve@mac.com	eg steve	eg steve	
NAME	PASSWORD	SMTP PASSWORD	
MY NAME	•••••	•••••	
eg steve smith			(IMPORT)
☑ Enable this account	☑ Leave messages on server	☐ Forward messages to server	
	☐ Use SSL	☐ Use SSL	

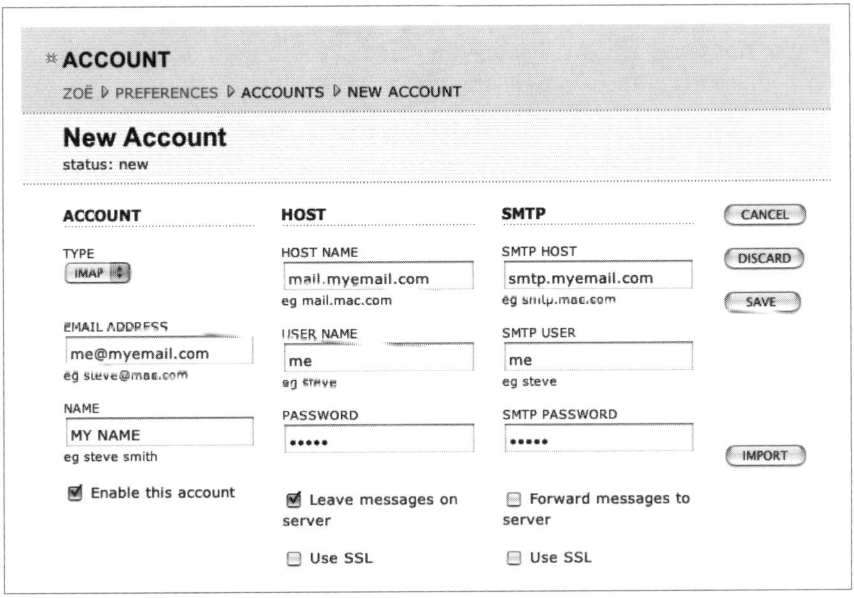

Figure 3-53. ZOË's Preferences page

Fill in the New Account form with your email settings. Take a gander at your Mail settings if there's anything you can't remember. When you're done, click Save.

> Set up as many accounts as you like by pointing your browser at the New Account page (*http://127.0.0.1:10080/ preferences/accounts/*) and filling in the form for each.

Importing Messages

You may choose to start clean and not have ZOË bother digging through ancient history. But the real power of ZOË is found in its ability to deal with all those old messages, so do consider importing them. To do so, visit the Preferences page and click the link associated with the account you'd like to scan. On that account's configuration page, click the IMPORT button.

ZOË will check your *~/Library/Mail* folder for any mailboxes and import them. It'll grind away for some time, becoming quite the processor hog while it sifts through your years' worth of correspondence. Go grab a cup of coffee until you hear that hard drive stop its clickety-clacking.

While ZOË's initial mail import can bring your system to a crawl, the rest of the time it's rather well behaved and you probably won't ever notice that it is even running.

If you're not using OS X's default Mail client, you'll need to use Mail as an intermediary to get those old mailboxes into ZOË.

The procedure goes a little something like this. Launch Mail and select File → Import Mailboxes. An Import wizard (Figure 3-54) will guide you through the rest of the process. Mail shunts mailboxes from Entourage, Outlook Express, Netscape, Eudora, and other email applications over to ZOË.

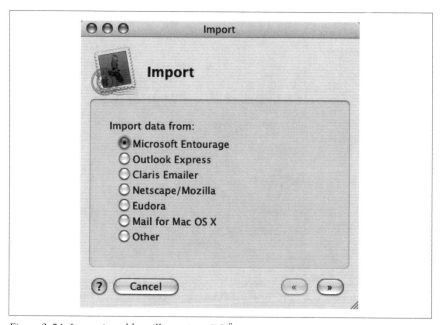

Figure 3-54. Importing old mailboxes into ZOË

You'll find a full backup of your mail (in ZOË's own organizational scheme) in the *Zoe/Library/SZ/Mails* folder.

Using ZOË

Enough with the preamble and setup; let's spend a little time with ZOË, shall we?

It all begins with the ZOË home page (*http://127.0.0.1:10080*). Figure 3-55 shows my email page for Today (April 13, 2004). Today's messages are listed in the left column, each with the message subject, sender, sender's domain, date and time, and a small snippet of message content. A paperclip icon indicates that a message has attachments. Googlish, isn't it?

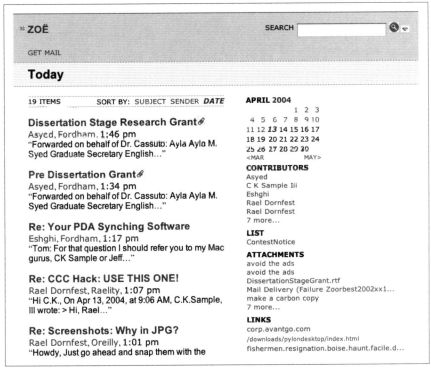

Figure 3-55. A typical ZOË home page

The right column sports relevant information extracted from these messages. *Contributors* are people who've sent me email. *Attachments* are any attachments that arrived in the mail. *Links* are any URLs ZOË noticed embedded in the bodies of my messages. A handy calendar at the top right jumps to another year, month, or day.

If you're ever wondering what ZOË's doing if it appears to be grinding away, check the info bar (immediately underneath the Today heading) for an update. As with any other web page, click your browser's Reload button to refresh this information.

Click the Get Mail link at any time to check for new mail. Since you have just set up your accounts, ZOË will most likely be up-to-date.

By default, ZOË checks for new email every three minutes. To change this setting, visit the Configuration page (*http:// 127.0.0.1:10080/preferences/assistants/configuration/*)   and change the value for the time interval. The time interval is expressed in milliseconds, so setting it to 10800000 causes ZOË to check for new mail once per hour.

Searching and Strolling ZOË

ZOË's true power lies in its searching, which provides a Google-like interface to your email, its contents, senders, receivers, and (if they are raw text files) attachments.

Start with the simplest of searches; Apple's a good one. Type it into ZOË's Search box and hit Return or click the magnifying glass. ZOË will return a result set of any email message in which you mentioned Apple, in which the sender or any of the recipients work for Apple (whether Apple Computer or Apple Music), or which included an attachment with *Apple* in its name. Even the attachment itself, if plain text, is subject to search by ZOË.

To further constrain any result set, type a new search into the search box and click the little yellow triangle—only present if you're already in the midst of a search—to search only within the current crop of results.

For the ins and outs of the flexible search syntax of the Lucene engine that powers ZOË's search functionality, read up on it at *http://jakarta.apache.org/ lucene/docs/index.html.*

If you click one of the results, you'll notice that your messages are *webified* with links to related email, people, files, and any URLs associated with the message.

Bookmark the search to create a virtual mail folder of sorts. There's no need to act as librarian for your correspondences, filing things away meticulously by project or person (or, heaven forbid, both). Forget all about setting up rules for filtering and sorting incoming mail. Just as Google all but made bookmarks moot, so too can ZOË mean an end to putting any mindshare into just how you sort your mail so you can find it later.

When you click an attachment, ZOË either downloads it to your selected download folder or (if it is plain text or another format supported by your browser) opens it in your browser. Click one of the Contributors for a list of every piece of email that person has ever sent you; Figure 3-56 shows some of my interactions with Rael during the writing of this book.

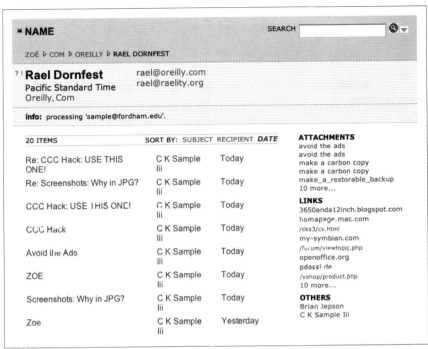

Figure 3-56. A typical ZOË Name page, showing correspondences with a particular person

If you use ZOË as your main email client's SMTP server, you'll also see any messages you've sent to that person.

The messages are presented in reverse-chronological order, much like a weblog. As on the main page, there is a list of Attachments and Links. The mysterious Others is a list of other people copied in any of this correspondence. If you look carefully, you'll notice all sorts of hidden extras: any email addresses ZOË believes are associated with Rael, his primary domain (*oreilly.com*), even his time zone—good to know when coordinating an iChat or phone conversation.

The page in Figure 3-56 (*http://127.0.0.1:10080/address/com/ oreilly/rael*), as with every other in ZOË, is bookmarkable for quick access later.

Click any message to open it. The lists in the right column change to show Links, Recipients, and Copy Recipients. Everything of any worth on the message page is a live link. Immediately above the body is a row of links, most of which are self-explanatory. The ampersand (@) opens ZOË's Compose page to compose a new email message right from your browser.

"Spam, spam, spam, spam…"

Spam flows into ZOË just like it does your regular email app. However, ZOË does filter messages tagged by well-known spam filters such as Spam Assassin. You can further specify message headers and their associated values that should be caught (and not imported) by ZOË. Edit the *SpamHeader.properties* configuration file found in *Zoe/Library/SZ/Configurations/Default/*. For details, visit *http://zoe.omara.ca/DealingWithSpam*.

Hacking the Hack

Despite its length and depth, this hack barely scratches ZOË's surface. Here's a little more grist for the ZOË mill:

- Want to archive all that old mail once and for all? Don't fret having to do all the organizing by hand; drop it all into one Mail folder and sic ZOË on it.

- Use ZOË's built-in SMTP server, loaded on an always-on Mac with a static address or your local laptop, and index all of your outgoing mail in the process.

- Subscribe ZOË to mailing lists using its own *zoe@yourdomain* email address to keep the clutter out of your inbox and build a searchable repository of things you're interested in.

- Set ZOË up on your company's intranet or (in a password-protected fashion) extranet and use it as a workgroup server. Copy a *zoe@yourcompany* email address with any messages of interest to the group. Even subscribe ZOË to your various aliases and let it keep track of the group on its own.

- Subscribe to your email just as you would any other syndicated content. Point your favorite RSS newsreader [Hack #30] to *http://127.0.0.1:10080/rss/*. This is particularly useful in the workgroup setting suggested earlier; keep up with what's new in your group, along with other goings-on in the world.

- Remember that full-text backup of your email that ZOË maintains for you? Anytime you switch computers or change email clients, forward the whole ZOË ball of wax via email or other means and run it there or import the messages into your new mailbox.

Take a gander at the ZOË Docs project (*http://zoe.omara.ca*) for further inspiration and the odd bit of help.

Encrypt and Sign Your Mail

Sign and seal your email with a personal certificate before sending it out into the wild and wooly Internet.

Email is one of the oldest Internet technologies, designed and put to use at a time when the Net was still a safe and friendly place. This is no longer the case, yet many email servers still allow anyone on the Internet to access their services to send spam email, and many of us still send our account passwords and email messages in clear text (think postcard versus envelope) over the wire.

The version of Mail that ships with Mac OS X 10.3 gained the ability to sign and encrypt email messages. This is great news, because it allows us to verify the identity of the sender of a received email message, verify that the message has not been tampered with in transit, and, finally, send encrypted email messages; in other words, it offers the ability to put our email messages in an envelope and seal them.

This hack provides a step-by-step guide for getting started with these new features in Mail. My aim is to make this all easy enough so that there's just no excuse for leaving your email open for all the world to read and unsigned for nobody to trust.

The Digital Certificate

In the real world, there are several trusted authorities that specifically validate a person's identity. These identifications can be documented in the form of a driver's license or a passport. In the digital world, there are similar authorities that issue *digital certificates*.

There are several types of digital certificates; this hack concerns *email certificates*. An email certificate is used to verify that the sender of an email message is indeed the owner of the email address that the message is sent from.

In other words, if you receive an email message from *John.Doe@mail.com*, the certificate doesn't tell you who the owner of that email address really is; rather, it tells you that the owner of that email address—whomever that person might be—is the person sending the message.

You need a digital certificate to take advantage of the new features in Mail. There are of course several Certification Authorities that issue digital certificates. This hack gets the certificate from Thawte, a South Africa–based company owned by VeriSign, which offers free email certificates.

You currently need to use either Safari 1.2 or Mozilla to request and download certificates. This hack shows you how to work with Safari only, because it makes the whole process much easier. Read the "FAQ" section later in this hack to find out if you would benefit from using Mozilla.

Please note that this is not idle talk; you actually do need to use one of these two web browsers, because the other browsers available for Mac OS X don't have the required support for certificates.

Head over to Thawte's Personal Cert System Enrollment page (*http:// www.thawte.com/html/COMMUNITY/personal/index.html*) and create an account by filling out the form provided after you hit the Join button.

Be sure to provide a secure password for the Thawte account. Use Mac OS X's Keychain Access (*Applications/ Utilities/Keychain Access*) application to store this password **[Hack #94]** and the *challenge/response* questions you provide as a Secure Note.

Once the account is created, go ahead and log into the Thawte member site (*https://www.thawte.com/cgi/personal/cert/enroll.exe*) and request a certificate by filling out the form provided when you hit the Request button.

Accept the default values on the four first pages of the form. On the fifth page, choose Accept Default Extensions. When moving past the sixth page, a key pair is generated and downloaded to your Keychain. If the Keychain is locked, Thawte prompts you to unlock it to allow the keys to be added. Accept the last page of the form to send the request to Thawte.

I expect that most of you will choose to take advantage of the ability to opt out from being contacted by Thawte and "Thawte holding companies, subsidiaries, business partners, or representatives" about anything not directly related to your certificates. You can opt out by submitting your email address to *http://www.thawte.com/compref*. You can peruse the Thawte privacy statement at *http://www.thawte.com/ html/CORPORATE/privacy.html*.

This is a good time to take a short break. Thawte is generating your new certificate, and that will take a few minutes. You can either wait for the email message they are supposed to send when done or monitor your certificate's progress on Thwate's Certificate Request Status page (*https://www.thawte.com/ cgi/personal/cert/status.exe*).

Initially, the status of your new certificate is "pending." When the process is finally complete, the certificate's status changes to "issued." When the certificate is issued, you can hit the link labeled Navigator to be redirected to a page where the details of your certificate are presented and where a Fetch button lets you download the certificate.

The Download panel opens and Safari downloads your new certificate. Once complete, Safari automatically launches Keychain Access to incorporate the certificate into its database, as shown in Figure 3-57.

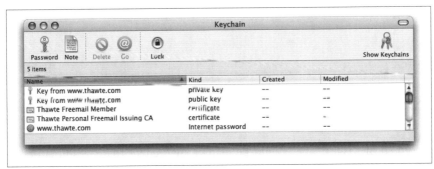

Figure 3-57. Keychain Access, incorporating a new Thawte certificate into its database

 You need a separate certificate for every email address you are using.

Return to Thawte to register additional email addresses and download certificates for each in turn, following the steps outlined in this section.

Signatures and Encryption in Mail

A signed message allows you to validate the integrity of the message (i.e., make sure it has not been tampered with since it was signed by the sender) and the identity of the sender. The message, however, is still delivered in clear text, unless it's also encrypted. An encrypted message protects the body of the message from prying eyes, but it is not signed unless you explicitly sign it.

To send a signed email message, simply click the Sign button in the new message window (Figure 3-58, right). Similarly, to send an encrypted message, click the Encrypt button (Figure 3-58, left).

You should always select both buttons if they're available, unless the recipient of the message has explicitly requested not to receive signed or

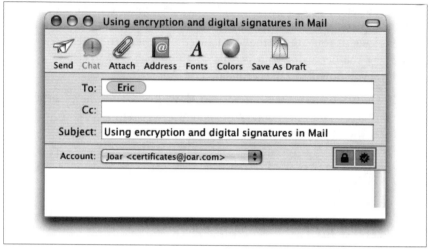

Figure 3-58. Encrypting and signing an outgoing message with the click of a button (or two)

encrypted messages. They might be using a mail client that doesn't support encryption and signatures—a PDA or smartphone, for instance.

If you have a certificate, you can send signed messages to anyone, but you can send encrypted messages only when both you and all recipients of the message have certificates.

Mail needs the certificates to encrypt the outgoing message. If Mail did not require that you, not only the recipients, need to have a certificate in order to be able to send encrypted email messages, you wouldn't be able to read your sent encrypted messages later.

The easiest way to let Mail know that a recipient has a certificate, and to give Mail access to that certificate, is to have that recipient first send you a signed message (not encrypted, just signed). Mail automatically stores the certificates it receives in the Keychain for future reference.

The Encrypt button is not visible when the recipient doesn't have a certificate or if she has one but you don't have a copy of the certificate stored in your Keychain.

Figure 3-59 shows what a signed and encrypted message looks like on the receiving end. The little badge with the checkmark is the seal that ensures that the identity of the sender is known to be correct and that the message has not been modified since it was signed by the sender.

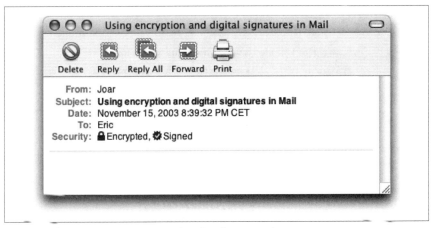

Figure 3-59. An incoming message, signed and encrypted

If Mail can't verify the message signature, such as when text has been added after the message was signed (as shown in Figure 3-60), Mail alerts you with a warning, as shown in Figure 3-61.

Figure 3-60. A message that has failed verification because it has been tampered with

FAQ

In case you run into any trouble, I've provided this FAQ, which should address any questions you might have.

Figure 3-61. A warning of unverifiable messages

Q: *The keychain will not import a certificate, because "The specified item already exists in the keychain."*

A: This is most likely because the certificate about to be added has the same email address as a certificate already in the Keychain. Inspect the imported certificates in the Keychain Access application to verify whether this is the case.

     If you have certificates for more than one email address, you might have requested or downloaded the same certificate more than once.

Q: *I have a certificate for my email address in my Keychain. Why doesn't Mail allow me to sign or encrypt email?*

A: Verify that the email address in the certificate and the one configured for the account in Mail are typed exactly the same—including case. Even though the two addresses *John.Doe@mail.com* and *john.doe@mail.com* would most often be delivered to the same email account, Mail still treats them as separate identities while trying to match a certificate to an account (in order to comply with section 2.4 of RFC 2821 for SMTP).

Q: *Why am I not able to create encrypted messages?*

A: Please reread the note in this hack about the requirements for sending encrypted messages. Basically, it comes down to the fact that Mail needs the certificate of the recipient of the message in order to be able to encrypt it.

Q: *You said that you can send an encrypted message only to someone that you have previously received a certificate from. Isn't this a catch-22?*

A: No. There is a difference between a *signed* message and, an *encrypted* message (see previous note that explains the difference). You can send a *signed* message to anyone, thus providing that person with your certificate, which allows the recipient an opportunity to create a reply with an *encrypted* message.

Q: *I need to use my certificate on another machine. How do I export my certificate from my Keychain?*

A: Unfortunately, the Keychain Access application currently (as of Mac OS X 10.3.2) doesn't know how to export a certificate into a portable format. The only workaround that I know of for this problem is to avoid downloading your certificates with Safari and instead use Mozilla. Mozilla can export certificates into a format that can be imported into the Keychain.

Final Thoughts

It is my hope that Apple will establish secure email as the norm, rather then the exception, just as they helped to establish USB, WiFi, and many other technologies over the years. This is probably impossible as long as the process of acquiring a certificate is as difficult as it is today. Apple could solve this problem by providing every .Mac member with an email certificate. In this way, the acquisition of email certificates could be made completely transparent to the end user.

See Also

- Apple's "How to Use a Secure Email Signing Certificate (Digital ID)" (*http://docs.info.apple.com/article.html?artnum=25555*)
- Thawte's "Overview of digital signatures and certificates" (*http://www.thawte.com/html/SUPPORT/crypto/certs.html*)
- RSA's "What is S/MIME?" (*http://www.rsasecurity.com/rsalabs/faq/5-1-1.html*)
- Mac DevCenter's "How to Set Up Encrypted Mail on Mac OS X" (*http://www.macdevcenter.com/pub/a/mac/2003/01/20/mail.html*)

—Joar Wingfors

HACK Interleave Mail and Pine
#40

Use Mac OS X's Mail and Terminal-based Pine email applications interchangeably as the mood strikes.

Mac OS X's built-in Mail application is a crisp, clean, powerful email client used by just about everyone who comes to OS X. It sports easy configuration, an intuitive interface, easy mail shuffling and filtering, and a terrific adaptive spam filter.

Pine is a lightweight, powerful, text-based email client that's just about as intuitive as you can get on the command line. Featuring configurability to the nth degree, an all-keystroke interface, and countless ways to sort, shuffle, and sift through your email, Pine is often the quickest way to deal with your morning's—or, indeed, vacation's—worth of email. It's also faster than using email remotely via Telnet or SSH over a slow, choppy modem connection, which is ill suited to remote-desktop Mail usage.

While Mail satisfies my sweet tooth, I often yearn for the no-nonsense interface to my email of Pine, my mailer of choice for a good many years. Then again, Pine has nothing on Mail when it comes to viewing HTML and oddly encoded messages and dealing with attachments. Wouldn't it be nice to use them interchangeably as the mood strikes?

Of course, IMAP is always an option that allows virtually seamless switching between almost any IMAP-enabled email client, Pine included. But I usually find myself wanting the raw sorting abilities of Pine when I'm blazing through old email on a plane flight and, without connectivity, I'm pretty well out of luck. A local IMAP install (in concert with fetchmail mail retrieval) does the trick and allows you to have your email on your laptop but still usable from about any email client. But this means dealing with some of the oddities, restrictions, and speed of IMAP, which sometimes differ from client to client.

There is a simpler and more efficient solution, at least when it comes to using the Mail and Pine email clients specifically. It turns out that both share the same semistandard *mbox* mailbox format. So, you can point Pine at one of your Mail mailboxes—whether an Inbox or arbitrary mail folder—and it'll read from and write to it like a champ. The inconvenience comes in not being able to simply point Pine at Mail's Mailboxes directory (*Home/Library/Mail/Mailboxes*), because Mail lays things out differently and makes use of some index and other files that would only clutter Pine's Folder List.

A typical Mail folder looks something like this:

```
House
 Home Repair.mbox
 Info.plist
```

```
mbox.SKindex
mbox.SKindex.isValid
table_of_contents
House.mbox
 Info.plist
 mbox.SKindex
 mbox.SKindex.isValid
 table_of_contents
```

Here, `House` is a folder that contains a Home Repair mailbox, but `House` is also, itself, a mailbox (notice `House.mbox`). So, you can drop messages into both the Home Repair mailbox and into the House folder that encloses it. Though this seems like a somewhat confusing dual-role when you look at it from the command-line point of view, it's perfectly understandable from within Mail.

Each mailbox (*.mbox*) contains several files, only one of which is useful for our purposes at hand: *mbox*. The *mbox* file contains the actual messages in a particular mailbox in plain text, which is readable by Pine. The *Info.plist* file contains internal user preferences for the mailbox at hand, and those *SKindex* and *table_of_contents* files are Mail's indexes for the mailbox, which are all useless to Pine.

The Code

Loosely based on an idea posted to Mac OS X Hints (*http://www. macosxhints.com*), the following script traverses your Mail mailboxes and creates a representative mailbox/folder hierarchy in Pine's preferred mail directory: *Home/mail*.

 Mac OS X Hints's version didn't quite suit my needs, because it didn't take into account mailboxes within folders within folders and so on. Also, this version is a self-contained script that takes care of Inboxes, mailboxes/folders, and Sent Items in one fell swoop.

Nested folders (e.g., House → Home Repair) are represented as nested folders/directories, and the mailboxes they contain are represented as `mailboxname.mbox` (e.g., `Home Repair.mbox`). The Inboxes associated with each of your Mail accounts and the Sent Messages folder associated with the first account the script finds are also symlinked, so that your sent messages are also archived in a Mail-accessible location:

```
#!/usr/bin/perl

# Mail2Pine
# Author: Rael Dornfest <rael@oreilly.com>
```

```
# Version: 2003-04-14

# Creates symbolic links between Mac OS X's Mail.app inboxes and
# mailboxes and Pine's mail directory (~/mail) allowing you to interleave
# Mail.app and Pine usage as the mood strikes.

my $user = $ENV{USER};
my $account_dir = "/Users/$user/Library/Mail/";
my $mailbox_dir = "/Users/$user/Library/Mail/Mailboxes";
my $mail_dir = "/Users/$user/mail";

use File::Find;

# Make a pine mail directory
-d $mail_dir or mkdir $mail_dir, 0700;

# Find and symlink Mail.app's account inboxes to ~/mail
find(\&accounts, $account_dir);

sub accounts {
 $File::Find::name =~ m!(POP-[^\/]+)/INBOX.mbox/mbox$! or return 0;

 # Symlink the INBOX
 -e "$mail_dir/INBOX-$1"
 or symlink($File::Find::name, "$mail_dir/INBOX-$1");

 # Symlink the Sent Messages mailbox if first account found
 -e "$mail_dir/sent-mail"
 or `ln -s "$account_dir/$1/Sent Messages.mbox/mbox" "$mail_dir/sent-mail"`;
}

# Find and symlink Mail.app's mailboxes to ~/mail
find(\&mailboxes, $mailbox_dir);

sub mailboxes {
 $File::Find::name =~ /SKindex/ and return 0;

 my($path, $mbox) = $File::Find::name =~
 m!^$mailbox_dir/(.*/)?([^\/]+)\.mbox/mbox!;

 $mbox or return 0;

 # Perform a little cleanup on paths and mbox filenames
 $path =~ s!^/|/$!!g;
 $path =~ s/[^\w\/]/_/g;
 $mbox =~ s!^/|/$!!g;
 $mbox =~ s/\W/_/g;

 $File::Find::name =~ s! !\\ !g;

 # Uncomment this line if you want to see what's going on along the way
 #print "$File::Find::name ~/mail/$path/$mbox\n";
```

```
`mkdir -p $mail_dir/$path`;
-e "$mail_dir/$path/$mbox"
or `ln -s $File::Find::name $mail_dir/$path/$mbox.mbox`;
}
```

Running the Code

Copy and paste the script into TextEdit or similar text editor and save it as a text file—*mail2pine.pl*, for example—on your Desktop. Fire up the Terminal application (Applications → Utilities → Terminal) and run it like so:

```
$ cd ~/Desktop
$ perl mail2pine.pl
```

That's all there is to it. Your Pine mail directory (Home → mail) hierarchy should look something like this:

```
sent-mail
Drafts.mbox
Family.mbox
Friends.mbox
House
 Home Repair.mbox
House.mbox
INBOX-POP-rael@oreilly.com
INBOX-POP-raelity@raelity.org
...
```

Of course, your accounts and folders will be different than mine. Notice how the script keeps the mailboxes proper as .mbox to distinguish them from folders of the same name (e.g., House versus House.mbox).

Using Pine

Let's take a gander at those new accounts, folders, and mailboxes in Pine, shall we? Launch Pine by typing pine on your Terminal command line. Select Pine's Folder List by typing L . Your list should look something like this:

```
 PINE 4.53 FOLDER LIST Folder: INBOX-POP-rael@localhost 5 Messages

INBOX sent-mail
Drafts.mbox Family.mbox
Friends.mbox House
INBOX-POP-rael@oreilly.com INBOX-POP-raelity@raelity.org
...

 [ALL of folder list]
? Help < Main Menu P PrevFldr - PrevPage A Add R Rename
O OTHER CMDS > [View Fldr] N NextFldr Spc NextPage D Delete W WhereIs
```

Of course, your accounts and folders will be different than mine. I have two accounts, represented by the two *INBOX-POP* files; you probably have only one. The *sent-mail* file is a symbolic link to Mail's Sent Items folder associated with the first account the *mail2pine.pl* script found: *INBOX-POP-rael@oreilly.com*. Notice the couple of mailboxes, Family.mbox and Friends. mbox, along with our House folder mentioned earlier.

To visit an account's Inbox, select the appropriate *INBOX-POP-account_name* by using the arrow keys and hit Return to select it. Here's my *rael@oreilly.com* Inbox, doctored more than slightly for illustrative purposes:

```
PINE 4.53 MESSAGE INDEX Folder: BOX-POP-rael@oreilly.com Message 5 of 5 NEW

1 Apr 9 Silly Sammy Slick (2144) mail2pine is nifty!
N 2 Apr 14 JJJ Schmidt (6269) you gotta love that...
...


? Help < FldrList P PrevMsg - PrevPage D Delete R Reply
O OTHER CMDS > [ViewMsg] N NextMsg Spc NextPage U Undelete F Forward
```

When I visit my House folder, either from the Folder List or from the Message window by typing G (as in *Go*), then typing House, hitting the Tab key, and selecting the House/ folder, I find that it contains, as expected, a Home Repair mailbox:

```
PINE 4.53 FOLDER LIST Folder: -POP-rael@rael@oreilly.com 22 Messages

Local folders in mail/
Dir: House/
-------------------------------------------------------------------------

Home_Repair.mbox
...
```

Fetching Mail

You'll still want Mail to fetch your mail for your various accounts from their associated mail servers and filter and junk according to your rules and Mail's Junk Mail filter. Just leave it running, hiding it from the Desktop if you so wish; it is less confusing than having both it and Pine running on your Desktop at the same time.

## CHAPTER FOUR

Multimedia
Hacks 41–49

Mac OS X is an unequivocal multimedia powerhouse. Professionals have long enjoyed the media capabilities of the Mac. Now, iLife brings this power to everyone and joins together the disparate components of your digital life with a suite of simple, powerful applications: iPhoto, your digital shoebox; iTunes and iPod, your personal audio jukebox, both at home and on the go; iMovie and iDVD for the budding independent filmmaker; iCal and Address Book to keep track of where you're supposed to be next and who you know when you get there; and iSync to keep it all together.

This chapter finds some nonobvious uses for the iApps and throws a few third-party applications into the mix.

HACK #41 Build a Household MP3 Server

Turn just about any Mac into an iTunes-powered jukebox and bring your home alive with the sound of streaming music.

Rather than shuffle music from Mac to Mac, I have a single repository for all of my music sitting in my basement and feeding, via Rendezvous music sharing, iTunes running on all the other machines. This makes it easier to find things, doesn't unnecessarily fill up my laptop's hard drive, and makes for easier music backups [Hack #84].

Choosing Your Server

Now for the big question: which machine to use. You'll need an always-on machine with a good amount of storage and hardwired network connectivity (wireless is slower). As for power, it's rather tempting to want to use the most powerful machine at your disposal as your household music server. But the truth is that, while using a lovely silver G5 for such a purpose might provide some emotional satisfaction, there's no real reason to throw anything but the most basic of machines at the job.

In fact, that shiny new G5's otherwise stunning form factor is significantly disadvantaged in that it is harder to add hard drives and you're limited to just two. You can purchase an after-market kit (*http://www.wiebetech.com/ pricing/WebPricing.htm#G5Jam*) that lets you pop up to four hard drives inside, but if you have a G4 or an even older G3 lying about, why not use it instead? If it's fast enough to run OS X and iTunes and physically capable of holding more storage, it's just right for an MP3 server.

For this hack, I used an old blue-and-white Power Mac G3 I have lying around. In the past, I installed four additional drives (bringing the total to five) in an old beige G3 and used that as my home MP3 server. However, Panther won't run without using a third-party utility such as Xpostfacto (*http://eshop. macsales.com/OSXCenter/XPostFacto/Framework.cfm?page=XPostFacto.html*) and it's just a tad too slow on the draw.

Adding Drives and Capacity

The first thing you need to do is get ahold of some large, cheap hard drives. When the Mac lineup moved over to IDE hard drives from SCSI, Mac users suddenly had access to the same cheap drives that PC users use. This means you can go down to your local brick-and-mortar retailer or find a good online e-tailer and buy the hard drives they have on special. You should be able to find hard drives (at the time of this writing) for between 50 cents and a dollar per gigabyte. This means you can get four 200GB drives for around $400 to $800 dollars. Assuming 20 albums per gigabyte, this means you can hold approximately 16,000 albums in AAC format. Now that's a music server!

> While this shouldn't be a problem, if you want to be absolutely sure the drive in your hand will work with you Mac, check the manufacturer's web site before you unwrap the shrink-wrap. The box often won't say, but the web site usually will. While it is tempting to believe some slip of paper inside the box itself will tell you all you need to know, this is most likely a pipe-dream that'll cost you the ability to exchange the drive (at least not without a "restocking" fee).

If your choice of Mac doesn't have a built-in IDE controller, you'll also need a PCI IDE/ATA card to control the hard drives. There are a number of options available to you, including Sonnet Tech's line (*http://www.sonnettech.com*). Install the PCI card and hard drives. While this can take some doing if you've never done it before, there are only a couple of gotchas. Make sure you have the correct master/slave settings for the hard drives. Make sure you seat all the connections firmly, without being too rough; you don't want to break anything!

If you've never dinked about with hardware, you might want to ask a more experienced friend for help. While it's all rather straightforward, things can get a bit fiddly and a set of steady helping hands can mean the difference between music and frustration.

After installing the hard drives and PCI card, it is now time to boot up. The hard drives may or may not show up right away on your Desktop. Either way, open Apple's Disk Utility (*Applications/Utilities/Disk Utility*). Select the Erase tab and erase each drive in turn. There are a number of options when you erase a hard drive, including the ability to slice it into various partitions. Since you are going to use these drives to store music files, you can skip partitioning.

If your drives don't show up in Disk Utility, something is wrong either with the master/slave settings on one or more of the drives or in how the drives and/or PCI card are physically installed. Shut down your machine, open it up again, and make sure all the various bits are tightly seated. Close it up, reboot, and see if the drives show up. If they still don't appear, chances are, your master/slave settings aren't correct. Shut down again, check the jumpers (comparing them to manufacturer's instructions), and reboot.

Pour in Your Digital Music Library

With the hardware in place, you now have an incredible digital jukebox at your very fingertips. Now's the time to transfer all that digital music onto your new machine.

But before you run off and do so, there's one more bit to twiddle. You'll want to make sure that "Copy files to iTunes Music folder when adding to library" is unchecked on the iTunes → Preferences... → Importing tab, as shown in Figure 4-1.

If you leave "Copy files to iTunes Music folder when adding to library" checked, you'll end up with two copies: one in the original location on one of your many new hard drives and the other in your *Music/iTunes Music* folder.

In the past, you may have kept all your music in your personal Music folder. But with all this additional disk space, you'll want to keep your music wherever it makes the most sense to you. I keep my music organized by folder, one for each letter (Talking Heads go in *T*, Alanis Morissette goes in *A* or *M*, and so on). The order and organization, on one drive or many, doesn't matter to iTunes. When you import the music into your library, iTunes keeps

Figure 4-1. Turning off "Copy files to iTunes Music folder when adding to library"

track of where everything is and maintains its own internal order by reading the ID3 tags embedded in each file/song.

Copy all the MP3 and AAC files to your new drive or drives. When you're done, launch iTunes and import all the tunes into your library. Do so either by selecting File → Import... from within iTunes itself or by dragging folders of music and dropping them on the iTunes window.

You can also take the opportunity to finally rip all those CDs you still have lying around. Pop them in, rip and listen, and file them away through the course of your day's work or play.

Share and Stream

You now have a machine that's capable of holding an immense amount of music. Using just what's built into iTunes, you can stream this music throughout your house to any other networked (wired or unwired) Mac or PC running iTunes 4.0 or later. You'll need to share your music explicitly; select iTunes → Preferences..., visit the Sharing tab, and check "Share my music," as shown in Figure 4-2.

Give your shared music a name; I chose Household Music. If you prefer, you can share only specific playlists. This is a great feature if you want to stream

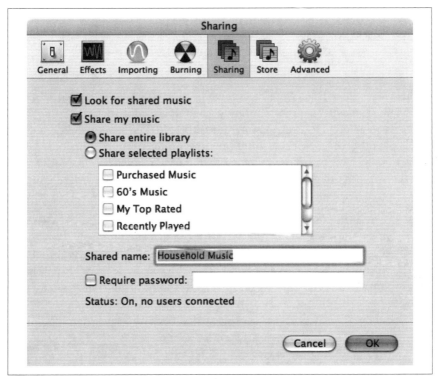

Figure 4-2. Sharing your tunes with any PC or Mac (running iTunes 4.0 or later) on your network

children's music to your kid's room but want to pass on that Snoop Dogg album. As an extra measure of protection, you can also password-protect your collection; or, you can just leave it open and share with the neighbors.

Your music is now available to anyone on your home network.

> If you are using iTunes at work and have sharing turned on, do be aware that anyone within a subnet of your computer can see and stream your music. While this is a nice thing to do in your local WiFi-enabled coffee shop, you might want to password-protect your tunes or turn off sharing entirely around your peers and supervisors.

Building a digital jukebox is surprisingly easy and affordable. Mix in iTunes's ability to stream music using Rendezvous, and your house is alive with the sound of music. (I just couldn't resist!)

—*Hadley Stern*

HACK
#42

Clutter Your Desktop with Music

Neatness sometimes just doesn't count, particularly when it comes to artistic expression. Clutter your Desktop with click-to-play album covers from your iTunes library.

Remember when disks weren't compact? I'm talking about *albums*, those lovely black plastic platters cluttering shelf space and spinning away with the occasional crackle and pop on your turntable. If you've made the switch to all digital yet still wax nostalgic for thumbing through your old record collection—each record lovingly tended, all but scratch-free, and gently placed within its sleeve—and find iTunes a little too sterile, you're going to love Clutter (*http://www.sprote.com/clutter*; freeware).

This groovy little app from Sprote Rsrch. gives all the MP3s and AACs in your iTunes 4 Library the tactile feel of those stacks and stacks of records, eight tracks, cassettes, and CDs you have left behind in your frenzy to join the 21st century. Set aside any tendencies toward neatness you may have, toss album covers on your Desktop like so many throw pillows, and just enjoy the colorful clutter, as shown in Figure 4-3.

Figure 4-3. Embracing the clutter and enjoying the color

When you first launch Clutter, a small Not Playing window appears (Figure 4-4, left). Launch iTunes, start playing any song in your library, minimize or hide iTunes, and bring Clutter to the front. Clutter's Now Playing window now sports the album cover (if available) in the formerly empty square (Figure 4-4, right). You have a nice set of Play/Pause, FF, and Rew buttons, overlaid (in music-video style) with the name of the artist, song, and album (if defined in iTunes).

Figure 4-4. Clutter's Not Playing (left) startup and Now Playing (right) windows

If no artwork appears and the album name is defined, select File → Find Cover On Amazon (⌘-F) to search for and download the associated album cover, as shown in Figure 4-5. If Amazon.com turns up nothing, you can also Google for something appropriate by using File → Search Google (⌘-G).

Figure 4-5. Finding cover art on Amazon

If you have an image on hand, simply drag it into the window. With your preferred cover art showing, you can by use Clutter's File → Copy Cover to iTunes to copy it over to iTunes if you like.

There are several other programs available—not to mention a handful of Konfabulator widgets [Hack #2]—that display album covers. But what separates Clutter from all those other programs is the ability to clutter your Desktop with these works of art. That's right, throw them anywhere you like. Click and drag the album cover from the Now Playing window onto your Desktop.

> It took me just a few minutes to clutter my Desktop with a rich assortment of colorful album covers. The only glitch I encountered was when Clutter gave a song from Guns N' Roses' *Greatest Hits* album the artwork from Fleetwood Mac's *Greatest Hits*, even though the cover art was already defined in iTunes and both songs came from the iTunes Music Store. A quick Amazon.com search-and-replace corrected the problem.

Each of these covers are independent; move them around, stack them on top of one another, or organize them neatly in rows (if you really have to). Browse your Desktop for something you want to hear, double-click the album cover, and it'll start playing in iTunes. If you can't find a particular cover in all the mess you've made on your Desktop, you can cheat by Control- or right-clicking Clutter's Dock icon and selecting it from a list. Just try that with your physical album collection spread across your floor or real desktop!

Not sure what album a piece of artwork belongs to? Simply Control- or right-click it to bring up a contextual menu with all available information on the album. Artist and album name, along with all the songs from the album, are all available right there from the menu. Just choose your favorite song to jump right ahead to it.

If you switch back over to iTunes, you'll see that Clutter has its own playlist that contains the currently playing album.

Before Panther and Exposé, I hated windows cluttering my Desktop, and as a result, I never really got into Clutter. Now, however, I can easily shuffle through all of my albums, or push them all out of the way with a mouse gesture or a keystroke whenever I want, and any song I want is simply a couple clicks away without having to scroll through a long alphabetical list in iTunes.

I have my albums again!

Feed Streaming Audio to Your iPod

Capture an Internet audio stream to an MP3 file, save the file to your hard drive, and automatically upload those files to your iPod when it connects to your computer.

Before the Internet, the wonders of nonlocal radio were out of reach of most people; the fabulous BBC World Service broadcasts only on shortwave radio, or occasionally late-night radio. These days, eight BBC channels and World Service are streamed over the Internet 24 hours a day. You can hear not only World Service daily, but also old *Dr. Who* and *Goon Show* episodes that were nearly impossible to obtain in the U.S.

On the other hand, being next to a computer to listen isn't always practical. Sometimes, you need to get out just to get some sunshine. Wouldn't it be nice to have your favorite streams recorded and uploaded automatically to your iPod?

This hack shows how, with a few simple steps, you can put together a few programs to time-shift that BBC broadcast, or any streaming audio, onto your iPod. Here is what you'll need:

- Rogue Amoeba's Audio Hijack or Audio Hijack Pro (*http://www. rogueamoeba.com*)
- An iPod (natch)
- LittleAppFactory's iPodScripter (*http://www.thelittleappfactory.com/ download/iPodScripter.dmg*) or Zapptek's iPod Launcher (*http://www. zapptek.com/ipod-launcher/*)
- Apple's Script Editor

Getting the Audio

If you want to capture audio from an audio stream, the easiest way to do so is to get Rogue Amoeba's (*http://www.rogueamoeba.com*) Audio Hijack ($16) or Audio Hijack Pro ($30). Both programs are built to record any audio your computer plays, including streams of many different types, such as RealAudio, Windows Media Player, QuickTime, and MP3 streams. Depending on your needs and budget, each has its advantages. Audio Hijack, as of Version 2, can record a stream from a URL and is a little cheaper, but it can encode streams only as AIFF files. Audio Hijack Pro can record to MP3 directly and can use VST audio plug-ins to modify the stream, even multiple sources at the same time. Pro does cost a little more. Also, Pro must have a file to load from the program you want to record. For example, if you want to record a Real Audio stream, you have to have a file that's associated with RealPlayer that will open that stream. This does make it a tad more complex to get it up and running.

Audio Hijack. To record, Audio Hijack requires a URL, file, or AppleScript and the name of the program that the URL will open. Launch Audio Hijack and select File → New Preset, then File → Edit Preset. You'll arrive at a dialog for the new preset.

The Preset Settings window contains four tabs: Target, Timer, Recording, and Effects. In this hack, you need concern yourself with only the first three.

On the Target tab (Figure 4-6), you can name your preset, set the application for Audio Hijack to record, and set the URL that the application (or file or AppleScript) needs to open. Find a link to the stream itself: the link which, when clicked, starts streaming the stream. Right- or Control-click the link, copy its URL, and paste it into the Open URL/File/AppleScript text area.

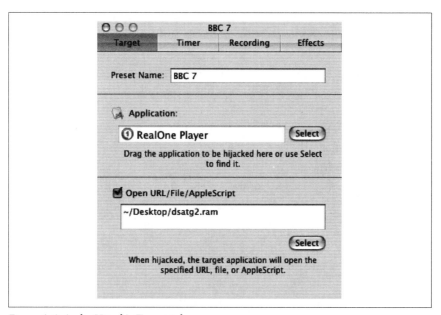

Figure 4-6. Audio Hijack's Target tab

Next, you need to select which application the audio will be coming from. If you're not sure which program the link will launch, just click it and see what pops up. It's most likely one of the big four: RealPlayer, Windows Media Player, iTunes, or Quicktime. But it could be nearly anything, even the browser itself. Whatever program is in the foreground and appears to be playing the stream after you click that link is the one to select from the Application field on the Target tab.

The Timer tab (Figure 4-7) is where you specify the date and time at which to record this stream. You also have the options to mute the program while recording and quit the program once you're done with it.

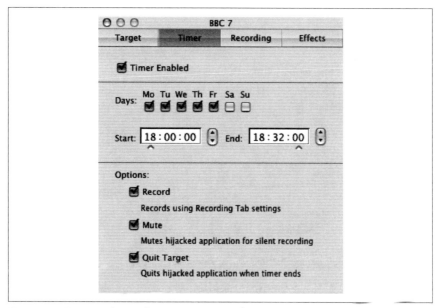

Figure 4-7. Setting a date and time to start recording.

To record a BBC stream from 6:00 p.m. to 6:30 p.m. local time, Monday through Friday, select each of the day checkboxes for Monday through Friday. Then, set a start time, using 24-hour time (add 12 to every hour after noon). I recommend you set the clock to start a little before and end a little after the time that you want, to allow for slight differences in clocks at your house and the BBC studios. Select Record as well; otherwise, this timer will kick off your stream but won't record it. Finally, select Mute if you're not interested in hearing the stream while it's recording, and select Quit Target if you want the application to shut off after it's done.

The Recording (Figure 4-8) tab provides options for where to save the recording and how large to make the files.

Save the recorded files to whatever location you wish, but note that location; you'll need it in a minute. I recommend picking someplace to record your files that is either obvious, such as a folder on your Desktop, or not on your main hard drive at all. It's easy to forget that you have Audio Hijack recording files on your computer. Mac OS X uses empty disk space on its main hard drive as swap space; filling swap space up can kill your hard drive. I put all my recordings on my Desktop and then go through them about once every couple of weeks to sort out the chaff.

As for file size, keep the setting at Make A New File Every at 2 GB. This value lets you set the point where Audio Hijack splits the recording into a new file. Audio Hijack saves the stream as an AIFF file, which gets quite

Figure 4-8. Specifying the size and location of recorded streams

large. If you leave it lower, it might cut up your program into multiple files and then have to stitch them together later. Either way, convert the AIFF file as soon as possible, and then delete it. Then, you have room for more audio.

You can optionally run an AppleScript after recording a file. Audio Hijack comes with a couple of prebuilt AppleScripts to run after recording. One of these AppleScripts, Encode To MP3 With iTunes, converts your newly recorded file to MP3 using iTunes. To run this script, double-click a preset and select Recording in the inspector window that pops up. In the section, marked When Finished Recording, select the drop-down menu to find this built-in AppleScript and others.

Before you run Encode To MP3 With iTunes, though, you'll want to set your iTunes conversion preferences (iTunes → Preferences → Importing → Setting) to Good Quality, High Quality, Higher Quality, or a custom set of values. Otherwise, iTunes will convert your file using its current settings, whatever they are at the time.

Audio Hijack Pro. Audio Hijack Pro's preset settings (Window → Show Presets) look quite different from the regular version, as shown in Figure 4-9. All the options are in one dialog window, but the options themselves are nevertheless similar.

Almost everything said of Audio Hijack still applies, with two major exceptions. First, Audio Hijack Pro automatically records MP3 files, so you won't need to convert the files afterward.

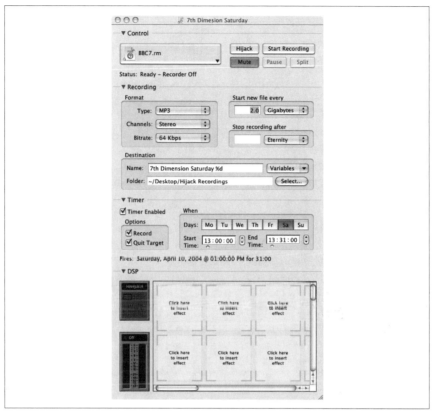

Figure 4-9. Audio Hijack Pro consolidates all of the settings into one Preset dialog box

Second, to open, Audio Hijack Pro needs a file from the program you want to record, not just a URL. To record from Safari, just click and drag the link to the Desktop. For applications like RealPlayer and Windows Media Player, the easiest way to get a file is to right-click on the link to your favorite audio stream, select Download Linked File As…, and save it to the Desktop with a memorable name. This *kickoff file* loads the stream into the right application, as long as that application is associated with that file type. Be sure to save these files in a location where they won't be accidentally removed; if they disappear, your stream won't get recorded.

Getting the Files into Your iPod

Unfortunately, there are no off-the-shelf products to shuffle audio files right from your Desktop to your iPod. However, quite a few products synchronize playlists created in iTunes. If you're looking for programs to synchronize all your music between your iPod and your Mac, try iTunes.iPod from

The Case of the Ever-Changing Stream URL

Some web sites that stream change their URLs daily or use JavaScripts to load the stream. You might think that these streams cannot be recorded; they can, although they might take a little effort. The key is to figure out *how* the link you're clicking tells the server which show to stream. By looking at a couple of URLs for a particular show, you can figure out how the URL changes and then play around with the URL to find out which URL will get you what you want. Most radio shows use either the date or the show number to archive the file, so the URL often uses the date or show number.

Web sites that use JavaScript to build this kind of URL can be a little tougher to crack, but doing so is by no means impossible. JavaScripts are embedded inside the web page that contains the link. If you look at the source of the HTML page, the JavaScript will be either directly in the HTML page or in a file that the HTML page loads. Once you have the script, you can then find out how the site is building the URL you want.

Either way, you can then build an AppleScript to open a program with a particular show and use Audio Hijack to kick off that AppleScript. If you want to record, say, NPR's *Wait Wait… Don't Tell Me*, which uses a date to archive its programs, opening today's URL might look something like this:

```
set today to (do shell script "date +%Y%m%d")
tell application "RealOne Player"
        GetURL "http://www.npr.org/dmg/dmg.php?mediaURL=/waitwait/" &
today & "_waitwait&mediaType=RM "
end tell
```

The do shell script command gets today's date in the form *YYYYMMDD* (e.g., 20040522 for May 22, 2004) and tacks it onto the URL for the show. This AppleScript opens the URL in RealOne Player, which in turn downloads a file and runs it.

crispSofties (*http://www.crispsofties.com*), iPodRip from LittleApplication-Factory (*http://www.thelittleappfactory.com/software/ipodrip.php*), or iPodit from Zaptekk (*http://www.zapptek.com/ipod-it*). iPodIt also synchronizes iCal, Address Book, Mail, Stickies, and even Entourage if you want. iPod-Rip is tuned for individualized manual syncing and specifically allows for importing and exporting files. iTunes.iPod synchronizes a little differently but has the added benefit of syncing AAC and Audible tracks as well.

Using any of these apps requires placing the audio in an iTunes playlist, which means you have to load them into iTunes. It is possible to do this automatically. The Audio Hijack post-recording script menu also lets you add the files to iTunes, but the script menu allows you to run only one script after you record a stream; if you use the post-recording script menu to put files into iTunes, you can't also convert your Audio Hijack files to MP3. To do so, you have to either deal with AIFF files (which take up a lot of space unnecessarily) or convert these AIFF files by hand. Neither of these options are exactly what I'm after.

When I connect my iPod, I want to have a script start up, read what's in my Audio Hijack recording folder, add anything that's in that folder to my iPod, put all of my files into a separate folder for discarding later, and remove anything on my iPod that I've listened to already or that is out of date.

If you're looking for a good resource for iTunes- and iPod-specific AppleScripts, Doug's AppleScripts for iTunes (*http://www.malcolmadams.com/itunes/index.php*) has an Apple-Script to move tracks from one iPod to another, another to copy your clipboard to the iPod contacts, and one that copies news to your iPod (NetNewsWire Subscription to iPod Contacts v1.0), to name but a few.

The Code

I really have two problems: I need a script that does what I want it to do and something needs to see the iPod is attached to my computer and run the script.

Choosing which language can be pretty important, especially when you're trying to connect multiple programs. Most of Apple's programs can work with shell scripting or Perl [Hack #19], and I prefer their speed and flexibility to other scripting languages. But Apple has built AppleScript into iTunes, the program I want, so it's a little easier to work with AppleScript for this task.

Here's the AppleScript I use to copy my files to my iPod:

```
property thePlaylist : "TestPlaylist"
property theiPod : "Professor Processor"
property theRecordingFolder : "Powerbook ¬
    G4:Users:stevko:Desktop:hijack"
property theStorageFolder : "Powerbook ¬
    G4:Users:stevko:Desktop:hijack:storage"
property tempPlaylist : "TempPlaylist"
property timeToKeepFilesInDays : 7

set fileList to (list folder theRecordingFolder)

tell application "iTunes"

    set onList to {}
    try
        set pod to source theiPod
    on error
        display dialog ¬
```

```
                "Could not find iPod " & theiPod buttons {"Cancel"}
        end try
        try
            set podPl to user playlist thePlaylist of pod
        on error
            display dialog ¬
                "Could not find playlist " & thePlaylist & " on iPod " &
    theiPod buttons {"Cancel"}
        end try

        if fileList is not {} then

            -- create temp playlist
            try
                set tempPl to (make new user playlist)
                set name of tempPl to tempPlaylist
            on error
                display dialog ¬
                    "Could not create playlist with name " ¬
                        & tempPlaylist buttons {"Cancel"}
            end try

            -- add files to temp playlist

            repeat with q from 1 to (count of fileList)
                set thisFile to item q of fileList
                if thisFile is not ".DS_Store" then
                    try
                        set pth to theRecordingFolder & ":" & thisFile
                        add file pth to tempPl
                    on error
                        -- ignore; if we can't get one,
                        -- we might be able to get more
                    end try
                end if
            end repeat


            -- find if any of the names of the temp playlist items
            -- are the same as the ones on the iPod playlist

            set deleteList to {}
            repeat with r from 1 to (count of tracks in tempPl)
                set temptrack to track r of tempPl

                repeat with s from 1 to (count of tracks in podPl)
                    set podtrack to track s of podPl
                    if name of podtrack is name of temptrack then
                        set n to name of temptrack
                        set deleteList to deleteList & n
                        exit repeat
                    end if
                end repeat
```

```
end repeat

repeat with y in deleteList
    try
        delete track y in tempPl
    on error
        -- again, ignore; it's nice to delete extras,
        -- but not necessary
    end try
end repeat

-- remove any from iPod that are more than a week old,
-- or that have already been heard.
-- THIS DOES DELETE FILES OFF OF YOUR IPOD WITHOUT A WARNING!!

-- (That's one of the points of this Applescript)

set delList2 to {}
repeat with p from 1 to (count of tracks in podPl)
    set ptt to track p of podPl
    if (played count of ptt is greater than 0) or ¬
        (played date of ptt is ((current date) ¬
            - (timeToKeepFilesInDays * days))) then
        set pptn to name of ptt
        set delList2 to delList2 & name of ptt
    end if
end repeat
repeat with y in delList2
    try
        delete track y in podPl
    on error
        -- again, ignore
    end try
end repeat

-- copy everything that's on playlist to the iPod
-- optionally, this will also convert the files
-- at the same time; uncomment the line below to do so.
repeat with m from 1 to (count of tracks in tempPl)
    set mt to track m of tempPl
    -- convert mt
    duplicate mt to podPl
end repeat

-- remove temp playlist

set delList3 to every track in tempPl
repeat with t in delList3
    delete track (name of t) in library playlist 1 ¬
        in source "Library"
end repeat
delete tempPl
```

```
        else
            display dialog ¬
                "Could not find any files in folder " ¬
                    & theRecordingFolder buttons {"Cancel"}
        end if
    end tell


    -- this moves the files from the recording folder to a storage folder
    -- if you use delete instead of move, you can trash the files instead.
    tell application "Finder"
        repeat with t in fileList
            try
                move file t in folder theRecordingFolder to
    theStorageFolder
            on error
                display dialog ¬
                    "Could not move file" & name of t & " from " ¬
                        & theRecordingFolder & " to " ¬
                        & theStorageFolder buttons {"Cancel"}
            end try
        end repeat
    end tell
```

This AppleScript has five major functions. The first is to find the iPod and the playlist on the iPod that we're going to use. If we can't find these, it errors out automatically. After all, there's no point in uploading to an iPod's playlist if you can't get to the iPod or the playlist.

Second, it creates a temporary playlist of all of the items inside our Audio Hijack recording folder and then sees if any of these new files are already on the iPod (no point in reloading files that are already there). The temporary playlist is necessary because we need to compare apples and apples, not apples and oranges—in this case, files and tracks. The files inside of the Hijack folder are just that, *files*, while the files on our iPod register only as *tracks* in iTunes. The name of a file is its filename, and the name of a track is the ID3 tag name; and those often don't match. The easiest way to compare the two sets of files is to make them the same type, and doing this through iTunes is a tad easier, especially since we want to build a playlist with these files anyway.

After determining which files aren't to be found on the iPod, the script then moves on to determine which files are on the iPod and need to be removed. The criteria for files to be removed includes items that have been played through once or files that are more than n days old. In this case, n in this case is the property timeToKeepFilesInDays; set it to suit your fancy. Once a file meets either of those criteria, the file is trashed; in theory, we don't want it anymore. The script also trashes these files because getting files off of an iPod is another hack altogether, and I want to stick to the topic.

After removing the unneeded iPod files, the script copies the files on the temporary playlist to the iPod. The temporary playlist should contain only the subset of files that were in the folder and were not already on the iPod when the script started. So, you should get a nice batch of new files on your machine and get rid of the old ones at the same time so that you don't fill up the iPod with old tracks.

Finally, the script performs a little cleanup. First, it gets rid of the tracks we added temporarily, by deleting them from the Library. When you add tracks, they automatically go into the library. Since you don't want them added permanently, kill them off. The script then kills off the temporary playlist, just to make things nice again. Finally, it moves the files from the recording folder to a storage folder in case it's needed later.

So, now you have an AppleScript that copies what you want to the iPod. To finish, we need something to kick off the AppleScript when the iPod connects. As mentioned, there are several applications that do just that. I like iPodScripter the best, because it's only a System Preferences panel installation. iPod Launcher, on the other hand, is a background application and preference panel that checks every specified number of minutes for the iPod. Both work equally well, and either will do.

Download either app and install it. The interfaces for the programs are similar: iPodScripter displays a list for applications and a second list for scripts (as shown in Figure 4-10), while iPod Launcher displays just one list for both. Just drag and drop the script on the appropriate list. The script runs whenever you dock your iPod.

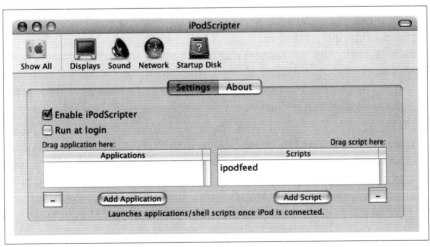

Figure 4-10. The iPodScripter user interface

Now that you're all set up, it's time to find some interesting shows, record them, and connect your iPod for a quick transfer. Enjoy the unlikely mix of sunshine and British broadcasting!

—*Ted Stevko*

HACK #44 Autofeed Text to your iPod

Place RSS and text files into your iPod automatically, or convert them to audio files.

At some point in every gadget lover's life, they come to a decision point: how many toys must I carry around on a regular basis? It's a tough one; lots of those beautiful gadgets are just made for taking out, and who knows when you'll need that GPS unit in a hurry? But if you start carrying around your PDA, cell phone, pager, iPod, laptop, and digital camera, all at the same time, you'll either look like Lou Ferrigno in the Incredible Hulk days, or you'll be writhing on the sidewalk, pinned down by your clothes.

So, when possible, I try to find ways to reuse the gadgets I have to make them do more with less. As an example, while sitting in meetings, I've often wanted an Internet connection so that I could read my favorite blogs on a PDA such as a Palm or a PocketPC. But, PDAs are expensive if you don't already own one and just another thing to carry if you do own one. So, I figured out how to put news onto my iPod.

iPod and Text

iPods are, first and foremost, music players. But even with the first generation of iPods, Apple provided a way to show some textual information as contacts from Apple's Address Book. These contacts are stored as vCard 3.0 files, which not only can contain the usual contact-specific information, but also have room for several fields that allow an unlimited amount of text. Hackers soon took advantage of these text fields to store text documents that could then be read using the Contacts menu item on the iPod.

Included in third-generation iPods, those using iPod Software 2.0, a Notes application allows text files to be displayed directly on an iPod. Notes offers some formatting options, such as titles, paragraphs, and link break, and allows links to other text files and music files on the iPod. It's not a perfect solution. For some reason, the program is limited to files of 4 KB (around 4,000 characters) and limits the total number of files to 1,000.

Because of this, many applications still use Contacts for their text files or allow you to choose between the Notes format and the Contacts format. Simply put, Contacts allows you to build bigger and continuous files, while

Notes has smaller files that can link to one another. Which you choose depends on your taste and file sizes. I prefer long e-books in Contacts and short text snippets in Notes.

If you're interested in building your own text files for the Notes application, Apple has kindly provided a PDF on how the Note file format works (*http:// developer.apple.com/hardware/ipod/ipodnotereader.pdf*). Also, RFC 2425 (*http://www.ietf.org/rfc/rfc2425.txt*) and RCF 2426 (*http://www.ietf.org/rfc/ rfc2426.txt*) detail the vCard file format used with Contacts.

Before hacking out your own solution, though, definitely take a look at pre-built solutions. There are tons of programs currently available that can create either Notes files or Contact files out of your text files. Even better, several programs also retrieve online content for you and create readable files on your iPod for you.

Downloading News as Text

One program stands out for me, because it does exactly what we're talking about (download news) and much more. Kainjow Software's Pod2Go (*http://www.kainjow.com/pod2go*), shown in Figure 4-11, downloads RSS feeds [Hack #30] to your iPod, as well as weather forecasts, stock reports, movie times, horoscopes, driving directions, and any arbitrary text files you want to take with you. It also syncs iCal, Address Book, Stickies, and Safari bookmarks with your iPod.

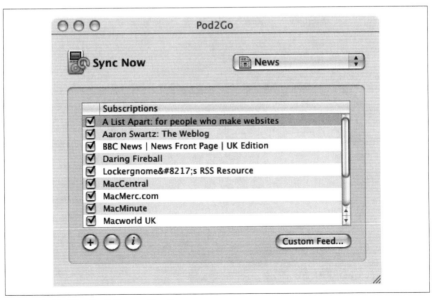

Figure 4-11. The Pod2Go application

When Pod2Go runs, a single window appears with a menu from which you can pick content to load onto your iPod. The News page contains an RSS reader that lets you load any RSS feed you want; it also comes with several hundred feeds. Adding feeds is as easy as either entering the RSS URL or dragging and dropping the URL from such programs as NetNewsWire. You can also download weather forecasts, by choosing a city or cities; movie times, by choosing a Zip Code and picking specific movie theaters; stock picks, by looking up stock ticker codes; and directions, by entering addresses and getting the route between them. Pod2Go parses and downloads any text files you want on your iPod.

Pod2Go also comes with a menu extra for your menu bar, which loads on startup and automatically syncs with the iPod every time you connect your iPod to your machine. This Menu Bar application also can launch applications when your iPod connects to it. Just add the applications by going to Menu Bar → Pod2Go → Configure. This is especially handy when you're loading AppleScripts that need to kick off when an iPod attaches to your computer.

It's not all sunshine, though. Often, people who are looking for news on their iPod already have an RSS newsreader, and maintaining two RSS lists is a pain. The easy way to solve this problem is to use your RSS reader's list to determine which RSS feeds to upload to your iPod. I created a quick AppleScript that grabs all the subscriptions in NetNewsWire and puts them into Pod2Go:

```
set listOfURLs to {}

tell application "NetNewsWire"
    activate
end tell

tell application "NetNewsWire"
    repeat with i from 1 to count of subscriptions
        set theSub to (get a reference to subscription i)
        set theRSSURL to RSS URL of theSub as text
        if theRSSURL is not equal to "" then
            set end of listOfURLs to theRSSURL
        end if
    end repeat
end tell

tell application "Pod2Go"
    activate
end tell

tell application "System Events"
    tell window "Pod2Go" of process "Pod2Go"
        click pop up button 1
        pick menu item "News" of menu ¬
```

```
                    "OtherViews" of pop up button 1
            delay 0.5
        end tell
    end tell


    repeat with i in listOfURLs
        try
            tell application "System Events"
                tell window "Pod2Go" of process "Pod2Go"
                    click button "Custom Feed..." of ¬
                        group 1 of group 1
                    tell sheet 1
                        set value of text field 1 to ¬
                            (contents of i as text)
                        delay 0.5
                        click pop up button 1
                        pick menu item "Other" of menu 1 ¬
                            of pop up button 1
                        set value of text field 2 to ¬
                            "Feed from NetNewsWire"
                        delay 0.5
                        click button "OK"
                    end tell

                end tell
            end tell
        end try
    end repeat
```

The script puts together a list of all of the RSS URLs for every subscription
in NetNewsWire [Hack #30]. If it doesn't find a URL for the RSS feed, it ignores
it. Then, it adds each URL to Pod2Go, by using AppleScript's GUI Apple-
Scripting feature to click and add the appropriate items to each. Be careful,
though: if any of your URLs turn out to be unreachable, Pod2Go pops up an
error message. Just click the OK button and move on.

Uploading Text as Audio

Now, much of my time during any given day is spent coding. Most often,
I'm listening to my iPod, not reading from it. Still, keeping up with the news
is handy. Instead of reading it, I can listen to it.

Again, there are a number of applications that build audio files from text files
by using Apple's built-in text-to-speech conversion program. Two programs
specifically seem to cater to iTunes and iPod use: ZappTek's iSpeak It (*http://
www.zapptek.com/ispeak-it*; $12.95; trial version available) and Alex Tow
and Adam King's ReadItToMe (*http://www.tow.com/software/read_it_to_me*;
Donateware, $5.00 suggested amount). Both of these programs use Apple's
text-to-speech software to convert text files to MP3 files for iTunes.

iSpeak It, shown in Figure 4-12, automatically downloads and builds audio files from Google's News page, a weather page, or any web page or text file that you wish to load. iSpeak It also creates the iTunes file with ID3 tags of your choice. Just go to iSpeak It → New and click on the iTunes icon in the upper-left corner. An ID3 tag editor then lets you specify, say, that the artist is *iSpeak It* and create a Smart Playlist in iTunes to hold those files.

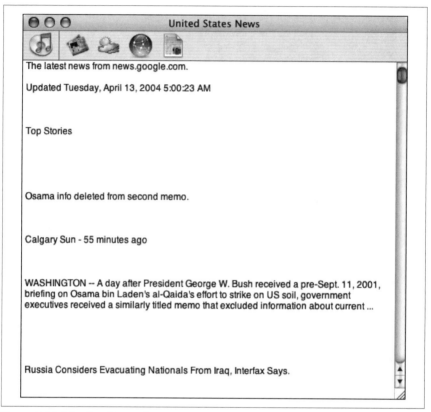

Figure 4-12. The iSpeak It application

One of the best features about this program is its ability to replace hard-to-speak phrases with clearer alternatives. Apple's speaking voices are much better in Panther than they've been in years, but they're still only so-so. By allowing you to switch out some of the worst phrases, you can get rid of the most jarring parts of any text-to-speech conversion.

Sadly, while iSpeak It has some great features, it falls down in two key areas: loading web pages other than news and weather and automatically loading files onto iTunes. If you're interested in pages other than Google's news page, it loads the page—the *whole* page, HTML and all. The same thing occurs with RSS feeds. So, while loading files automatically would be great, hearing "R-S-S version-two-dot-oh" a few hundred times rapidly wears out the best of us. And, without any AppleScript hooks into the program, it makes using the web page feature a little difficult.

There's also a few options you'll want to set until you are certain everything is set up correctly. In iSpeak It, look in the menu bar for iSpeak It → Preferences. The preferences contain an Automatic iTunes Transfer checkbox, a Load On Launch checkbox, and an Exit On Completion checkbox. It's not kidding; on launch, it automatically loads the files you check, transfers them to iTunes, and then exits without giving you a chance to stop the program to fix anything. Keep these settings unchecked until you *know* you have what you want, and be prepared to stop a few transfers in iTunes if you want to change things once you do turn it on.

The goals of ReadItToMe, shown in Figure 4-13, are considerably different. It does one thing: create an audio file for each unread RSS news feed at Net-NewsWire. It then puts that audio file into iTunes—no frills, no extras. It does one thing, and it does it well.

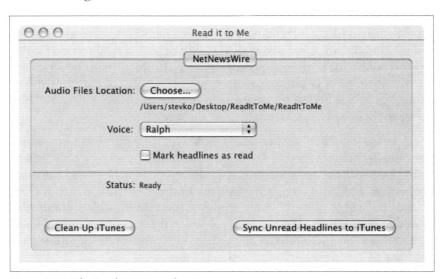

Figure 4-13. The ReadItToMe application

There are a number of benefits of this approach. You have to maintain only one RSS list. That means you have only one list of news either to read with NetNewsWire or to listen to on your iPod. ReadItToMe automatically cleans up the RSS audio files that it creates, if you want it to. Each RSS feed item is created in its own separate file, so you don't have to search through long audio files to find where you left off.

On the negative side, you need a copy of NetNewsWire for ReadItToMe to work. You can't use the free NetNewsWire Lite. Also, ReadItToMe can read RSS files only, and there's no built-in text correction as there is in iSpeak It.

Each of these solutions creates files that can be gathered with Smart Playlists and then set up to sync with your iPod. To sync a playlist with your iPod, first connect your iPod to your Mac. Then, when your iPod shows up inside iTunes, right-click or Option-click your iPod and select iPod Options.... This lets you select particular playlists to sync with your iPod—including Smart Playlists that contain nothing but the latest RSS feeds.

—Ted Stevko

HACK #45   Automate a Web Photo Gallery with iPhoto and Perl

If iPhoto is working nicely as your digital shoebox, but you want to automate the process of creating web galleries for your own server, here's a nifty setup using sendmail, MySQL, and Perl.

My wife, Rhonda, recently started needing to send up to several thousand images from iPhoto directly to a MySQL database on a remote server on an ongoing basis. She is an avid photographer and volunteers to take pictures for our city. One of her photos recently made the cover of the city's annual report, which got her more interested in putting up a web gallery and perhaps even offering pictures for sale along the way.

She's been using iPhoto on her iMac G4/800 for a couple years to manage a few thousand photos using two different digital cameras. Since she has so many images, there was really no choice but to build a database to manage the pictures and use a web gallery to present them. What I wanted was for Rhonda to be able to work within iPhoto as much as possible and not have to worry about the actual publishing process to the web server. Since I travel a bit, it had to be a setup that didn't require me to mount disks, format photos, build SQL commands, or process email messages.

I've been running an iMac G3 as a colocated web server for small businesses for a couple years, which is perfectly adequate for her site needs. So, we started building her site, knowing that I could take full advantage of Macs from both ends. What I needed was a way to get several thousand photos from iPhoto to a MySQL database on our web server in as few steps as possible. I specialize in task automation, making computers and networks do all the work and eliminating as much human error as possible, and it was nice to be able to apply some of my knowledge to our home life.

After looking at several different ways to set this up, I settled on a path that makes the most use of iPhoto, includes Apple Mail, sendmail on the server, MySQL, and plenty of Perl to hook it all together.

In iPhoto, photos are selected based on category and formatted using iPhoto's email capabilities. iPhoto then uses Apple Mail to build an email message that includes the photos and emails it away to an address on the server. As the message arrives at the server, a Perl program intercepts it, picks out the various pieces and accompanying photos, applies some basic ImageMagick, then drops it all into a MySQL database on the server. When folks visit her site, based on what they select, a couple different applications access the MySQL database to present the photos from our server.

iPhoto

There are no real procedures for working with iPhoto to make this setup work. iPhoto has enough bells and whistles and allows good management and basic editing of an ever-growing photo library. With a little discipline and some cooperation from your digital camera, iPhoto has everything you need to manage your collection.

If the camera you're using stores images as a unique sequence, that's perfect. Rhonda uses a Kodak DX6490 (four megapixels and 10X zoom are the main features), which stores photos as a sequence: *100_1219.JPG, 100_1220.JPG, 100_1221.JPG*, and so on. An older Sony Mavica that she used until this year also stores files in a sequence: *MVC-660X.JPG, MVC-661X.JPG, MVC-662X.JPG*, and so on. When the images are imported into iPhoto, these become unique titles for the images.

My wife has made a habit of entering comments for her pictures after she imports them. This was a great asset to her collection for a variety of reasons, particularly in this project. The iPhoto comments are used as captions when the photos are displayed in the web gallery, as shown in Figure 4-14, in which Size, Titles, and Comments boxes are selected.

When you select the Email button from within iPhoto, you can optionally select Titles and Comments to be added to the email message. At the same time, you can select the resolution of the images to be sent. We use 640 by 480 for the transfers, because that is easily displayed within a web page and is not high enough resolution to be concerned when someone copies the image from the site. The original titles are maintained to allow easy reference to the full-size photos for ordering.

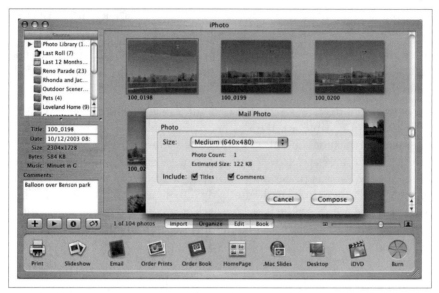

Figure 4-14. Email button selected in iPhoto

Mail

When iPhoto transfers the photos to Mail, it uses either the title for the subject with one image or something like *5 Great iPhotos* if you select five images. The subject is changed regardless and is used as a category name. So, if the photos are of some elk, the subject might be Animals. Likewise, a series of pictures of a sunrise might have a subject such as Scenery.

You can send as many photos as is practical at one time; just make sure they all belong to a single category/subject. The Comments can be changed within the email, though titles should be left unique as mentioned previously. When iPhoto transfers the information to the email, you'll see something like Figure 4-15. The subject needs to be changed to reflect its category.

You can edit the comments or insert them if they are not already provided. Once you've changed the subject and addressed the message, it's ready to send to the server.

sendmail

sendmail is the underlying program that processes email on MacOS X 10.2 (in 10.3, Postfix serves the same role). The server has a specific email account set aside to handle photos. By using the standard *.forward* file in that account's home directory, we can pass all incoming messages to a Perl program. That program processes the images, titles, and comments. There are several ways to prevent abuse on this account; the one I selected is to

Figure 4-15. The transferred image, followed by the title and comments

limit the email accounts from which it will process messages, from within the Perl code. In other words, it tosses any messages that don't come from my wife's account or a small list of other accounts.

The *.forward* file simply contains the following line:

```
"|/usr/adm/sm.bin/mailPhotoProcess.pl"
```

Be sure to include the quotes around the command and the pipe before the command name.

ImageMagick

ImageMagick (*http://www.imagemagick.org*) is a robust collection of tools and libraries offered under a usage license to read, write, and manipulate images in many image formats. The Perl program that processes the messages on the server sends the image portions of the messages to ImageMagick for some simple size reductions to build a thumbnail. ImageMagick provides a variety of other tasks, such as framing, watermarking, and so on. Since we keep the photos at a relatively small 640 by 480, there's no need for watermarking. However, if you want to add borders, drop shadows, or make any of a myriad of other changes to an image, ImageMagick is an excellent choice.

As part of the message processing, the Perl program also keeps track of the image type (e.g., JPEG, GIF, etc.). The image type is stored in the database and used when we display the image on the web page.

MySQL

The MySQL (*http://www.mysql.com*) database server is the world's most popular open source database, with more than five million active installations. Both the thumbnail and the original photo are stored in a MySQL database. The other fields that are added to the database table are a unique ID (generated by MySQL), image type (detected during the MIME parsing of the image), image title (extracted from the message body during MIME parsing), image comments (extracted from the message body during MIME parsing), and category (extracted from the message header during MIME parsing).

Here is the MySQL code to set up the database table:

```
CREATE DATABASE IF NOT EXISTS domain;
USE domain;

DROP TABLE IF EXISTS Gallery;

CREATE TABLE Gallery (
    ID        INT UNSIGNED AUTO_INCREMENT NOT NULL,
    Date      DATE NOT NULL,
    Image     LONGBLOB NOT NULL,
    Thumb     MEDIUMBLOB NOT NULL,
    Type      VARCHAR(20) NOT NULL,
    Title     VARCHAR(80) NOT NULL,
    Comments  TEXT,
    Category  VARCHAR(40) NOT NULL,
    PRIMARY KEY (ID),
    INDEX (Category)
);
```

The Code

Perl is often called "the duct tape of the Internet," and this application certainly fits that description. Now is the time to open an editor and create some Perl code. This code needs to go in a particular location, to allow the server to process it correctly. My iMac server is currently running Mac OS X

10.2.8, which uses sendmail. Accordingly, the Perl program needs to be located in the */usr/adm/sm.bin* directory. You'll need to create any directories along the way, such as *adm* and *sm.bin*.

> For more Perl shenanigans under Mac OS X, take a gander at "Mac::Glue Your Perl" **[Hack #19]**, "Update iChat Status with Mac::Glue" **[Hack #20]**, and "Hack Your Address Book with Perl" **[Hack #21]**.

The gist of the program is that we are going to receive an email message, which will have MIME attachments. Those attachments need to be extracted from the message, processed, and stored in a database. Once we're done processing the email, we'll send back a message indicating how many images were processed and the URLs to those images:

```perl
#!/usr/bin/perl -w
# load in the modules
use MIME::Parser;
use MIME::Entity;
use DBI;
use Image::Magick;
use Mail::Mailer;
use strict;

# get DBI vars and related info
my %dbHash = (
  "dbType"  => 'mysql',
  "dbName"  => 'domain',
  "dbHost"  => 'localhost',
  "dbUser"  => 'myUser',
  "dbPass"  => 'myPass'
);

DBI handles
my ($sth, $sql, $rv, $dbh, $dbData);

# set up DB connection
DBConnect(%dbHash)
  or DBError("Died in Connect");

# MIME parsing vars
my ($i, $parser, $entity, $head, $preamble,
  $epilogue, $num_parts, $part, $content_type,
  $body, $tmp);

# extract the pieces out of the email message
$parser   = MIME::Parser->new();
$parser->output_dir("data");
$entity   = $parser->parse(\*STDIN);
$head     = $entity->head;
```

```perl
$preamble = $entity->preamble;
$epilogue = $entity->epilogue;

# get the subject and use it as
# the category for all the photos
my $category = $head->get('Subject');
my $mailTo   = $head->get('To');
my $mailFrom = $head->get('From');
chomp($category);
chomp($mailTo);
chomp($mailFrom);
# get the domain name from the To mailing address
my $domain = (split('@', $mailTo))[1];

MIME vars
my ($bh, $filename, %file, @data, $title,
  $comments, @url, $id);
Image::Magick vars
my ($img, $imageData, $thumbData, $err);

# loop through the file attachments
$num_parts = $entity->parts;
for ($i = 1; $i &lt; $num_parts; $i++) {
  $part         = $entity-&gt;parts($i);
  $content_type = $part-&gt;mime_type unless
    ($part-&gt;mime_type =~ 'text');
  $body         = $part-&gt;as_string;
  $bh           = $part-&gt;bodyhandle;
  $filename     = $bh-&gt;path;

  if (($i % 2) == 1) {
    # handle the image file
    $file{'image'} = $filename;
  }
  else {
    # handle the data file and populate
    # the database
    $file{'data'} = $filename;

    # init the data array
    @data = ();

    # open the data file and load into
    # data array
    open(\*FILE, "&lt; $file{'data'}")
      or die "Error opening $file{'data'}: $!";
    while (&lt;FILE&gt;) {
      chomp;
      # ignore empty lines
      push @data, $_ if length > 0;
    }
    close(FILE)
      or warn "Error closing $file{'data'}: $!";
```

```
    # extract title and comments from data array
    $title = $data[0];
    shift @data;
    $comments = '';
    $comments = join ' ', @data if @data;

    # convert image to thumbnail
    $img = new Image::Magick;
    $err = $img->Read($file{'image'});
    die "Can't read image file: $err\n" if $err;
    $imageData = $img->ImageToBlob();
    $err = $img->Scale(geometry=>"200x200");
    die "Can not scale image file: $err" if $err;
    $thumbData = $img->ImageToBlob();

    # build, prepare and execute SQL command
    $sql = "REPLACE INTO Gallery
      (Date, Image, Thumb, Type, Title,
      Comments, Category)
      VALUES (NOW(), ?, ?, ?, ?, ?, ?)";
    $sth = $dbh->prepare($sql)
      or DBError("Died in prepare");
    $sth->execute($imageData, $thumbData,
      $content_type, $title, $comments,
      $category)
      or DBError("Died in execute");

    # get the last inserted ID to build a URL
    $sql = "SELECT ID FROM Gallery
      WHERE ID=LAST_INSERT_ID()";
    $sth = $dbh->prepare($sql)
      or DBError("Died in prepare");
    $sth->execute()
      or DBError("Died in execute");
    $dbData = $sth->fetchrow_hashref();
    $sth->finish();
    $id = $dbData->{'ID'};

    push @url, "http://www.$domain/cgi-bin/" .
      "gallery.pl?id=$id";
  }
}

# disconnect from the database
DBDisconnect();

# remove files from data directory
$entity->purge;

# return an email message to the sender
my $mailer = Mail::Mailer->new("sendmail");
# get the number of images sent
my $count = @url;
```

```perl
# build the message body
my $text = "$count new image";
$text .= "s" if ($count > 1);
# build the header
$mailer->open(
  {
    Subject => "$text added to $domain gallery",
    From    => '&lt;no-reply@' . $domain . '&gt;',
    To      => $mailFrom
  }
);

# print the message body
$text = "The following new image";
if ($count > 1) {
  $text .= "s were";
}
else {
  $text .= " was";
}
print $mailer "$text added:\n\n";
print $mailer "$_\n" for (@url);
print $mailer "\n";

# close the message
$mailer->close();

# DB connection subroutine
sub DBConnect {
  # convert the list to a hash
  my %dbHash = @_;
  # data source name
  my $dsn = "DBI:$dbHash{'dbType'}:" .
    "$dbHash{'dbName'}:$dbHash{'dbHost'}";

  # attributes
  my %attr = (
    PrintError => 0,
    RaiseError => 1
  );
  # connection command
  $dbh = DBI->connect($dsn, $dbHash{'dbUser'}, " .
    $dbHash{'dbPass'}, \%attr) or
    DBError("Cannot connect to $dsn");
}

# DB disconnect subroutine
sub DBDisconnect {
  $dbh->disconnect()
    or DBError("Cannot disconnect from DB");
}

# DB error subroutine
```

```
sub DBError {
  my $message = shift;
  # display a message
  warn "$message\nError $DBI::err " .
    "($DBI::errstr)\n";
}
```

Now, we've accomplished getting the images into the database. That's all well and good, but the other half of the task is to display them on a web site. Thankfully, we just got through the longer part. There are several gallery applications available that work with databases of images. This section extracts three thumbnail images to be used each day on a rotating basis. Each thumbnail is linked to its full-size image, which is displayed in a new window when the thumbnail is selected. The HTML output is presented after the Perl code:

```
#!/usr/bin/perl -w
use CGI;
use DBI;
use HTML::Entities;
use strict;
$|++;

# local vars
my ($id, $comments, $file, $url);

# set file name
$file = '/Library/WebServer/WebSites/' .
  'www.domain.com/include/gallery.shtml';

# get a CGI object
my $q = new CGI;

# DBI handles
my ($sth, $sql, $rv, $dbh, $dbData);

# DB connection values
my %dbHash = (
  "dbType"  => 'mysql',
  "dbName"  => 'domain',
  "dbHost"  => 'localhost',
  "dbUser"  => 'myUser',
  "dbPass"  => 'myPass',
  "dbTable" => 'Gallery'
);

# connect to the database
DBConnect(%dbHash);

# build the sql command
$sql = "SELECT ID, Comments FROM
  $dbHash{'dbTable'} ORDER BY RAND()
```

```
  LIMIT 3";
# prepare and execute the statement
$sth = $dbh->prepare($sql)
  or DBError("Died in prepare");
$sth->execute()
  or DBError("Died in execute");

open(\*FILE, "> $file")
  or die "Unable to open $file: $!";

while ($dbData = $sth->fetchrow_hashref) {
  $id = $dbData->{'ID'};
  $comments = $dbData->{'Comments'};
  # set HTML nbsp if no comments
  $comments = ' ' unless
    (length($comments) > 0);
  $url = "/cgi-bin/gallery.pl?id=$id";
  # send the results to the output file
  print FILE
    $q->td(
      {
        -align=>'center'
      },
      $q->a(
        {
          -href=>$url,
          -target=>'gallery'
        },
        $q->img(
          {
            -src=>"/cgi-bin/gallery.pl?" .
              "id=$id;thumb=1",
            -border=>0,
            -alt=>$comments
          }
        )
      ),
      $q->br(),
      $comments
    ),
    "\n";
}
$sth->finish();

close(FILE)
  or warn "Unable to close $file: $!";

# DB connection subroutine
sub DBConnect {
  # convert the list to a hash
  my %dbHash = @_;
  # data source name
  my $dsn = "DBI:$dbHash{'dbType'}:" .
```

```
    "$dbHash{'dbName'}:$dbHash{'dbHost'}";

  # attributes
  my %attr = (
    PrintError => 0,
    RaiseError => 1
  );
  # connection command
  $dbh = DBI->connect($dsn, $dbHash{'dbUser'}, " .
    $dbHash{'dbPass'}, \%attr) or
    DBError("Cannot connect to $dsn");
}

# DB disconnect subroutine
sub DBDisconnect {
  $dbh->disconnect()
    or DBError("Cannot disconnect from DB");
}

# DB error subroutine
sub DBError {
  my $message = shift;
  # display a message
  warn "$message\nError $DBI::err " .
    "($DBI::errstr)\n";
}
```

Here is some sample output from the preceding code. The output has been
prettied up, but it renders the same in HTML:

```
<td align="center">
  <a target="gallery"
  href="/cgi-bin/gallery.pl?id=28">
    <img alt="Georgetown Railroad" border="0"
    src="/cgi-bin/gallery.pl?id=28;thumb=1" />
  </a>
  <br />
  Georgetown Railroad
</td>

<td align="center">
  <a target="gallery"
    href="/cgi-bin/gallery.pl?id=85">
    <img alt="Lakeside morning" border="0"
    src="/cgi-bin/gallery.pl?id=85;thumb=1" />
  </a>
  <br />
  Lakeside morning
</td>

<td align="center">
  <a target="gallery"
    href="/cgi-bin/gallery.pl?id=95">
```

```
    <img alt="Elk in stream" border="0"
    src="/cgi-bin/gallery.pl?id=95;thumb=1" />
</a>
<br />
Elk in stream
</td>
```

Figure 4-16 shows the actual output.

| Georgetown Railroad | Lakeside morning | Elk in stream |

Figure 4-16. Script output as it appears on the Web

Final Thoughts

While this application is still under development, the techniques are used to show a daily sample of pictures, eCards, and photos by category. A database editor application can be used to change images from one category to another, or to change comments for an image.

—*Mike Schienle*

Keep a Digital Diary

Diaries enable us to document the big and little moments in life. And your pocket digital camera might be the greatest journaling tool of all.

Life moves so quickly. Before we know it, an entire year has raced by. Sometimes, we have difficulty remembering what we had for dinner last night, let alone what we did last month.

Keeping a diary helps give life perspective. Not only can we look back upon it and appreciate the richness of our existence, but it can also help us remember the specific dates that events happened. Many people don't want to take the time to explain, in words, the big and little moments as they occur. That's understandable. But our pocket digicams and camera phones can help us document our lives, and computers make organizing those images easy.

I'm going to walk you through an easy and effective way to keep a photo diary. Once you get a feel for the workflow and the types of tools you need, you can create a system that works better for you. Here are the necessary components:

Digital camera

You can use a pocket digicam, camera phone, or both. The key to a photo diary is having a camera available when events happen. It's not going to work if your only camera is a bulky digital SLR. In this case, portability is more important than image quality. Not only does your camera record the images of your life, it also captures when they happened. Every picture you take is time-stamped. For this to work properly, be sure to set the correct date and time on your camera.

Digital shoebox

As you record the events of your life visually, you need to have a place to store the images. In this hack, I use Apple's iPhoto (*http://www.apple.com/ iphoto*), because it is my usual digital shoebox. I can upload my images, write comments about each one, and output the diary to paper, CD, or even a web site. Other great digital shoeboxes, such as Adobe Album (*http://www.adobe.com*) and iView Media Pro (*http://www.iview multimedia.com*), work just as well.

Taking a picture every day is a good habit to acquire. It doesn't have to be a masterpiece, just something to show what kind of day it was. If it's autumn, a simple picture of colorful leaves will do. Caption it, "The maple trees in the front yard are in full color today and look beautiful."

Seems kind of boring doesn't it? You'd be surprised that, over time, those images are anything but boring. Have you ever wondered, in hindsight, when the trees in the front yard turn colors? You'll know the exact date by referring to your digital diary.

Once a week or so, upload the pictures to your digital shoebox. All shoeboxes allow you to create custom albums, so you'll want to make one exclusively for your diary, as shown in Figure 4-17.

The date and time are embedded in the image file itself, so you don't have to worry about when something happened; the software displays that information for you. But you might want to add a few words about what was happening when you took the photo. Don't worry about writing an essay here; just use a few words to describe where you were and what you were doing, as shown in Figure 4-18. This whole process should take only a few minutes. The idea is to make this easy; otherwise, you won't do it.

Over time, your digital diary will grow and become quite interesting. Even after a couple months, you'll find that looking back is more fun than you would have imagined when you started the project. But there's more.

Figure 4-17. A photo diary using iPhoto

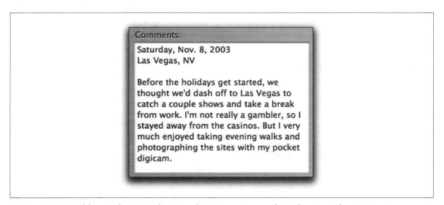

Figure 4-18. Adding a few words to each image to complete the record

A great benefit of the digital approach is its archiving ability. At the moment, optical discs, such as CDs and DVDs, are the best bet for preserving a diary. But what about software compatibility? I don't necessarily want to burn an iPhoto library onto a CD, because my nephew, who works on a PC, won't be able to read it.

To archive your diary, I recommend you export it as a web catalog that can be viewed on any computer with a simple web browser. Any good digital shoebox allows you to do this. In iPhoto, make sure that the album is selected and choose File → Export. You have some basic options to choose from, as shown in Figure 4-19. Most important is the "Show comment" box, which ensures that the text you've included with each photo is transferred to the web catalog.

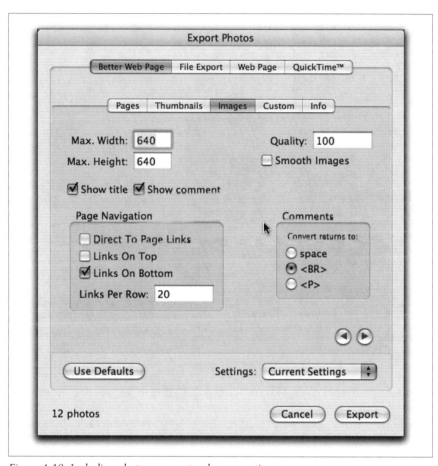

Figure 4-19. Including photo comments when exporting

After you click the Export button, the digital shoebox assembles your web pages and places them in the folder you designated. To check your work, simply open that folder and double-click on the *index.html* file.

Your web browser will open and you'll see a page of thumbnails with the date beneath each, as shown in Figure 4-20. The highlights and mundane events of your life are there before your eyes.

If you click on any image on the thumbnail page, the full version opens with the comment text below it, as shown in Figure 4-21. This is nothing like the

Figure 4-20. Your diary, transformed into a web page

diaries from the days of old. You have full-color images that capture the moments of your life with the precise dates and comments about what happened. Your diaries can be viewed on any computer by anyone you want to share them with.

At this point, I recommend you burn the web version of your diary to at least two CDs or DVDs: one to keep on hand at home and another to store offsite, such as at your office or safe-deposit box. This will ensure that your memories will be safe for years to come.

One last thought about sharing your memories: you might want to post your diary on your personal web site or even make a hardbound photo book. This is the great advantage of digital storage: once you have the information neatly tucked away in your computer, there are countless way to share it with others.

—*Derrick Story*

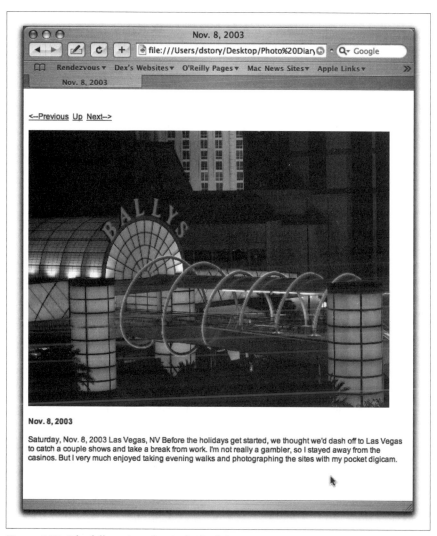

Figure 4-21. The full version of an individual day

HACK
#47

Rendezvous Picture Transfer

Everybody is using their Mac for storing and sorting photographs. But what if
the device you want to get a picture from is connected to a different Mac?
Rendezvous to the rescue!

There are many clever features in Mac OS X 10.3 that don't appear on the
cover of Apple's Panther page. One of my favorites is the new Image Capture application that enables you to network images directly from your
digital camera to others who can view them with a Rendezvous-enabled

browser. At first, this might seem more like a cool hack than anything truly useful. But depending on the features of your camera, this hidden Panther gem could bring new enthusiasm to your digital photography.

Our old friend, Image Capture (*http://www.apple.com/macosx/features/ imagecapture*), is at the core of this digital wonderment. While iPhoto gets all the headlines, Image Capture continues to work under the radar and improve with each version of the operating system. Panther includes Version 2.1.0, and I think you'll be impressed by some of its new goodies.

I first saw a discussion about some of these features on the O'Reilly Mac Editors list that I follow. Then, I heard that David Pogue was playing with remote capture, and he included a demo in his keynote at the Mac OS X Conference (*http://www.macdevcenter.com/mac/osx2003/*), while I configured the remote camera. Later that day, he did the same demo on Tech TV. David focused on the "*babysittercam*" aspect, and he documented his findings in this follow-up article for his Tech TV appearance (*http://www.techtv.com/ screensavers/howto/story/0,24330,3559134,00.html*). By the way, his demo was a big hit at the conference.

But now I'm going to broaden the conversation considerably and show you how to combine Image Capture and Rendezvous to add new flexibility for making your pictures available to others, as well as taking snapshots remotely. As a bonus, I'll show you how Mass Storage Device digital cameras can be used to easily broadcast any picture from your Mac over a Rendezvous network.

Setting Up Your Computer

Rendezvous should automatically be enabled on your Panther computer. You can check it by launching iChat and making sure you're logged in. Then, go to other computers on your network and open Safari. Add the Rendezvous button (shown in Figure 4-22) to the Bookmarks Bar (Preferences → Bookmarks → Include Rendezvous). This will come in handy once you start to actually broadcast images.

Now, launch Image Capture on your Mac. It's right there in your Applications folder. Open Preferences and click on the Camera tab at the top. Set the drop-down menu option to "When the camera is connected, open: Image Capture." This will prevent you from having to deal with iPhoto launching every time you plug in your camera. (This can be an irritating nuisance when you don't want to use iPhoto.) You can, of course, still use iPhoto by launching it manually when you do need it.

Connect your digital camera, put it in Playback mode, and turn it on. Go back to Preferences and now click on the Sharing tab (Figure 4-23). Check

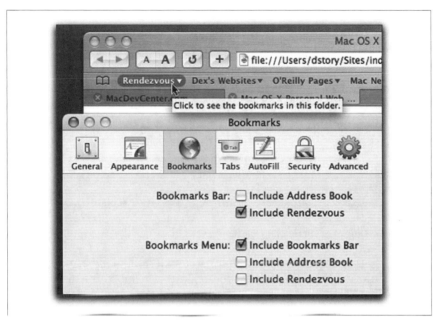

Figure 4-22. The Rendezvous button on Safari's Bookmark Bar

all of the boxes, and you should see your camera appear under "Share my devices." Click the OK button to close the Preferences dialog box.

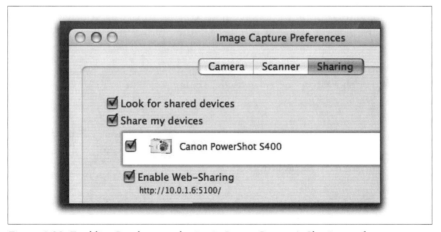

Figure 4-23. Enabling Rendezvous sharing in Image Capture's Sharing preferences

Now, go to another Rendezvous-enabled Mac on your network—it doesn't have to be running Panther; it could be running Jaguar—and open Safari. Click on the Rendezvous drop-down menu in the Bookmark Bar that you previously installed, and look for your shared device. You should see a Rendezvous-shared "page," as shown in Figure 4-24, just like that of any other computer in the vicinity.

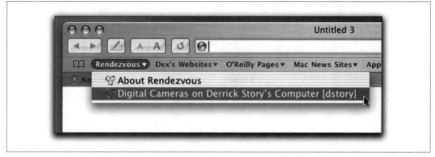

Figure 4-24. A digital camera found via Rendezvous.

Choose the page, and before you know it, you'll be looking at the pictures directly from the memory card on the remote camera! You can browse in thumbnail view, or, if you want to see a little metadata too, switch to list view for cool information such as file size, date captured, dimensions, bit depth, DPI, exposure, f-stop, flash setting, and color space. If you double-click any of the thumbnails, you can look at an enlarged view that will be constrained by the dimensions of your browser window.

But wait; there's more. You can actually download the image to the Rendezvous-connected computer and save it to your hard drive. And if you don't like the picture, you can delete it from the camera directly from the browser.

 If it's not your camera you're browsing, you might want to show some restraint with this feature.

If you connect a second camera to the Mac, Rendezvous will broadcast it too, and users can toggle between both cameras (as shown in Figure 4-25) and view the images on each of them.

Taking Pictures Remotely

Viewing pictures directly from the memory card of a remote camera is certainly useful and interesting. But with certain current models of digicams, you can also use Rendezvous-enabled Image Capture to actually fire the camera from any computer on the network. Once the camera records the image, it is then added to your browser window alongside the other images on the memory card.

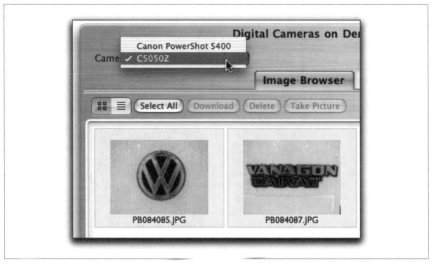

Figure 4-25. Toggling between multiple cameras in Rendezvous

Here are some of cameras that have this capability (thanks to David Pogue for this list):

- Canon A60, A70, S400, S50, and G5
- HP C618 and 912
- Kodak DC280, DC4800, and DC5000
- Nikon D1, D1X, and D1H

I tested this functionality with a Canon S400 Digital Elph, and the results were compelling, as shown in Figure 4-26. Image Capture instructed the camera to set the zoom to 7.4mm (the wide-angle setting), turn on the flash, and set the shutter speed to 1/60 of a second and the aperture to f-2.8. The camera used the assist light to focus before firing off the exposure. It also used the image resolution that I had previously set. The remotely fired images looked great. Very impressive.

 If you want the pictures to render faster on the screen, you can lower the resolution to 640×480. But don't do this if you plan on using these images later for prints; you won't have enough pixels for a decent enlargement.

You'll notice that next to the Image Browser tab there's another one called Remote Monitor. If you click on it, you go to a new window and the camera starts firing shots once a minute and displaying them on the screen. It doesn't save them to the memory card; rather, they are displayed only on the computer screen until they're replaced by the next shot.

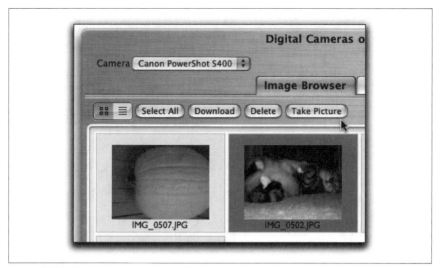

Figure 4-26. Firing the camera from the remote computer over Rendezvous

There is a Preferences switch on the left side of the window. In theory, it allows you to change the frequency of the camera firing, but it didn't work for me. Once I clicked the Preferences switch, my Mac asked me for a Shared Name and Password. I provided the correct information, but it was repeatedly rejected. So, the moral of the story, at least with a Canon S400, is to be happy with once-a-minute automatic firing, or use the control button in the Image Browser view to shoot pictures manually.

More Flexibility with Mass Storage Devices

So far, Rendezvous image sharing has been limited to pictures stored on the memory card or displayed from the camera right after exposure via remote firing. But what if someone you're chatting with in iChat wants to see a collection of pictures that you have saved on your hard drive?

You could send the images one by one (or in a compressed archive) via iChat and let the person open them on her computer. But it's a lot more fun (and easier) for your audience to view them in a browser window as thumbnails and enlarge or download only the images that interest them.

I connected an Olympus C-5050Z, which has USB Mass Storage capability, and tried adding pictures from my iPhoto album to the camera, then sharing them over Rendezvous. (Olympus calls this capability *auto connect*.) As shown in Figure 4-27, it worked!

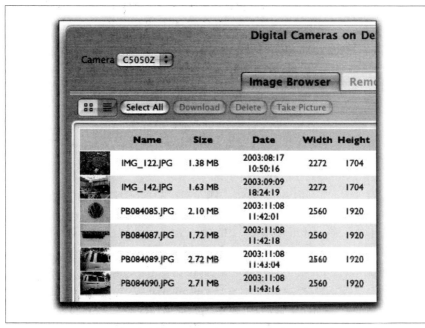

Figure 4-27. Pictures uploaded from iPhoto to a camera, then shared via Rendezvous

The first two pictures were taken with a different camera, the Canon S400, and copied from iPhoto to the Olympus C-5050Z. The Olympus displayed the S400 images right alongside the ones taken with the C-5050Z. Cool!

Here's the procedure for sharing images from your hard drive with a USB Mass Storage camera:

1. Connect the camera and turn it on.
2. When the device icon appears on your Desktop, open it and navigate to a folder that contains pictures.
3. Drag pictures from your hard drive into the folder. They will be copied to the camera's memory card.
4. Turn off the camera, and then turn it on again.
5. Open Preferences in Image Capture, and share the device.
6. View the complete image catalog from a Rendezvous-enabled browser.

Make sure you've already downloaded the native pictures that are already located on your memory card. There's a chance that, after you disconnect the camera, you'll get a memory-card error message and have to reformat the card. This happened to me only once during many tests, but beware and be prepared.

Real-World Use

For me, these new capabilities are going to be a handy way to distribute pictures to others directly from my camera. For example, I'm often asked to snap shots at work, which I don't mind. But I do hate uploading the images to my Mac, sorting through them, and sending the images that I think the requester might want via email.

Now, all I have to do is connect my camera and turn on Rendezvous sharing. Everyone can view the catalog in their browsers, grab the shots that they want, and I don't have to do a thing. Later, I can upload the pictures to my computer, if I want, at my convenience.

You'll need Panther on the computer that you use to serve the pictures. But any Rendezvous-enabled browser on the local network can view and download them. I successfully tested this functionality with an Olympus C-5050Z, Canon S400, Canon G2, and EOS 10D.

One thing to keep in mind is that your camera remains *powered up* while it's serving pictures across the network. If you have an AC adapter, this would be a perfect use for it. I don't have one, so I keep an extra battery on hand. I didn't run out of juice on any of the cameras while testing these procedures, so the *drain rate* must not be too bad. But, as with everything else in digital photography, be prepared; otherwise, you will certainly run out of power at the worst possible moment.

As for firing the camera remotely with this set up, well, it's fun, but since I don't have as much control over the camera's settings as I'd like, I don't see it as useful as the image-sharing functionality. But it makes for a great demo, and you might want to keep it in mind as an impressive Panther trick to show off Apple technology.

You can also use Image Capture to control scanners and share the images over a network. But that's another hack altogether.

—*Derrick Story*

Rotate Your Movie from Horizontal to Vertical

HACK
#48

Who says you have to shoot all your movies horizontally? Just as with stills, sometimes it's fun to turn the camera on its side. But when you upload your movies to your computer, they're turned the wrong way! Here's how to fix that.

When making movies with your digicam, you don't want your compositions limited any more than you do when shooting stills. Imagine if someone told you that you could shoot only horizontal pictures for the rest of your life. You'd tell them where to go stick their memory card.

The problem with movie making is that you might shoot your video with a vertical orientation, but when you upload the snippets to your computer, everything is horizontal. And 9 out of 10 chiropractors will tell you not to crane your neck sideways to watch these movies.

Fortunately, for the health of your entire viewing audience, there is a simple fix.

After you upload the video to your computer, open a snippet in QuickTime Player (you'll need a QuickTime Pro license for this), the versatile movie-viewing/editing application.

> If you've not yet upgraded to a QuickTime Pro license (*http://www.apple.com/quicktime/buy*; $29.99), I can't recommend the move more highly.

From the Movie drop-down menu, choose Get Movie Properties. You've just tapped into one of the most powerful areas of QuickTime Pro. There are two drop-down menus at the top of this dialog box. From the left one, choose Video Track, and from the right one, select Size, as shown in Figure 4-28.

Figure 4-28. Making selections in the QuickTime Movie Properties dialog box

You'll see that the dialog box changes content and options as you choose different items from the drop-down menus. In this case, two of the goodies you can access are found in those rotation arrows in the lower-right corner. Click on the one that rotates your movie in the desired direction, as shown in Figure 4-29. Like magic, your movie and its controls are now oriented the way you originally intended.

Figure 4-29. Rotating a movie in the QuickTime Movie Properties dialog box

Either way you do it, you can now edit, trim, and stitch together movie clips to your heart's content. Of course, all of your movies have to be oriented the same way; otherwise, you'll get some strange-looking results.

There's something inherently interesting about a vertically framed movie. And it's an option I encourage you to try as appropriate subjects present themselves.

See Also

- Simple Rotate (*http://www.imovieplugins.com/plugs/simplerot.html*) is an $1.50 shareware iMovie special effects plug-in.

—Derrick Story

HACK

#49   Store Pictures and Movies in Your iPod

Yes, iPods make terrific digital music players. They're also not so bad for storing movies and pictures from your digicam.

When I hit the pavement for street shooting or the trail for an afternoon hike, I usually have my digital camera and iPod tucked away in my backpack. I bring the camera for obvious reasons, but recently, the iPod has become just as important.

Yes, a little music is sometimes the perfect antidote to the relentless din of street noise, not to mention the fact that when I have my ear buds in place, fewer oddballs bother me. The iPod also stores all of my calendar information, in case I run into a friend who wants to schedule a lunch. It also holds handy reference notes, such as important restaurant locations and other vital statistics. Just about anything I can read on my computer can be transferred to my iPod. In fact, I recently read an article that reported that the dailies for the *Lord of the Rings* trilogy were whisked around the globe on an iPod.

The 40GB hard drive in my iPod is as big as the drive in my laptop. I have quite a bit of music, but that's not why I bought an iPod with such a big drive. The real reason is that I can upload movies and photos from my camera's memory card directly to the iPod. That means, as long as I have batteries to power my camera and two memory cards with me, I can shoot until my shutter finger cramps up in lactic-acid misery.

This scenario became particularly appealing when I got hooked on shooting movies with a Contax SL 300R T* pocket digicam (*http://www. kyoceraimaging.com*), shown in Figure 4-30. Even though it weighs just a tad more than four ounces and fits in the palm of my hand, it can record full-frame (640×480) movies at up to 30 frames per second (fps); that's the same frame rate as a dedicated digital camcorder. If you're interested in this amazing functionality but want to save a few bucks, check out the Kyocera FineCam SL300R, which uses the same technology but costs less than the Contax.

This bit of movie magic is enabled by RTUNE™ technology that allows the camera to write directly to a high-speed Secure Digital (SD) memory card until the card is full.

> The Contax also shoots still images at three frames per second until the memory card fills up.

Needless to say, at 30 fps, or even 15 fps, it doesn't take long to fill an SD card. So, I either had to invest a small fortune in memory cards or find another solution if I wanted to continue my obsession with digicam movies.

The other solution turned out to be the Belkin iPod Memory Reader (*http:// www.belkin.com*), shown in Figure 4-31. This device plugs into the iPod's Dock Connector (but not the iPod mini) and can accommodate five different

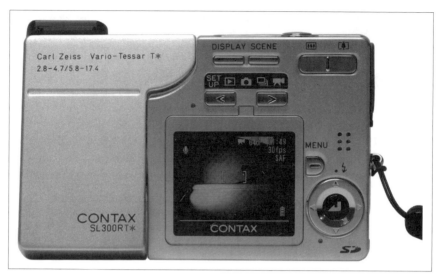

Figure 4-30. The Contax SL300R T*

types of media: CompactFlash (types 1 and 2), SmartMedia, Secure Digital, Memory Stick, and MultiMediaCard. You take the media out of the camera and upload its contents to the iPod while you insert your second memory card into the digicam and keep shooting. When the day is done, plug the iPod into your computer and upload all those photos and movies via the fast FireWire connection.

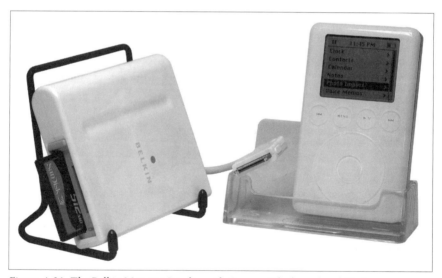

Figure 4-31. The Belkin Memory Reader with CompactFlash card and iPod

At time of this writing, 256 MB high-speed SD cards cost about $90. The Belkin reader runs $100. So, for about the price of one memory card, I can add gigabytes of storage to my digital camera.

You might be wondering why I carry two memory cards instead of just one. Unless you want to hang out and have a cup of coffee during the upload process, you'll need that second card to keep shooting. The Belkin might be convenient, but it isn't fast. I tested its speed by shooting a full-frame video at 30 fps with the Contax using a SanDisk Ultra II 256 MB SD card. I kept shooting until I got the "memory card is full" message, then inserted the card into the Belkin and initiated the upload. I timed the process with a stopwatch, and it took a whopping 10 minutes to complete the transfer.

I don't want to wait that long before I start shooting again, so I suggest you carry one, maybe two extra memory cards with you so that one can be uploading while you're shooting with the others. The good news is that you can put the iPod and media reader in your backpack during the transfer process and keep moving.

In case you're curious, it took only 16 seconds to upload that same 256MB of video from the iPod to the computer via the FireWire connection. Don't you just love bandwidth?

It's true; you'd go crazy trying to shoot a full-length feature movie with this rig. But the Belkin iPod Memory Reader does provide you with a reliable backup solution while you're on the go. And, thanks to the ample hard-disk space in the iPod, you can shoot many memory cards worth of video and pictures before having to retreat to your computer.

—*Derrick Story*

Gadgets and Hardware
Hacks 50–60

Living up to its position as the *digital hub*, the modern Mac is reaching out well beyond the bounds of Apple hardware—something all but unheard of in its early days. Through WiFi and Bluetooth wireless networking, FireWire and USB drives, dongles, and other assorted devices, it is drawing in and exchanging content and input with other Macs, Windows and Unix machines on the network, the PDA in your pocket, and even the cellphone in your hand.

For the most part, Mac OS X does a remarkable job of making all of these devices play nicely together without much in the way of configuration or fuss. But technology moves fast, many of the technologies that the newest devices use are cutting edge, and not everything is a seamless experience. There is still some room for improvement—and more than enough opportunity to hack.

HACK #50 Expand Your Screen Real Estate

Don't let a simple matter of screen real estate get in your mouse's way when you have a second display at hand.

Everyone can use a skosh more room on their Desktops. You can add the feel of more room with virtual desktop software [Hack #5], but that's perhaps akin to painting one of your walls a different color to "widen" the room. Short of laying out a goodly amount of cash on the luxurious 23" Apple Cinema HD Display or the more affordable 20" Apple Cinema Display or 17" Apple Studio Display (*http://www.apple.com/displays/*), you're pretty well stuck with the screen you have.

A rampantly unnoticed (or summarily ignored) feature of the Macintosh is a powerful little something called *screen spanning*. If you have a PowerBook or Power Mac of recent vintage, you can simply plug in an external (or second

external) monitor and turn on screen spanning to instantly tack on extra
screen estate. iBook, iMac, and eMac owners have unfortunately been shut
out of this screen spanning business—without a little hacking, that is. This
hack introduces you to the wonders of screen spanning and, if necessary,
fiddles with your Mac's Open Firmware to open up wider visual vistas to
some of those unsupported machines.

> I felt obligated to include some pun involving Alan Screenspan
> but just couldn't figure a way to work it in. —Rael

Span

Screen spanning stretches your Desktop across two monitors, such that your
mouse disappears off the side of one and appears on the other. You can use
each screen equally or relegate one to the task of holding your iChat chats,
collection of Photoshop palettes, or Microsoft Word toolbars.

Dust off that old 15" or 17" CRT (you know you have one lying about
somewhere) and plug it into your Mac. Depending on your Mac model, you
may need some sort of dongle in between; you'll most likely find it still
plastic-wrapped in your Mac's box and stowed away somewhere. That second monitor should spring to life, flicker for a moment or so, then display a
blank desktop sporting the same background image as your main screen.

If for some reason you don't see anything on the second monitor, try kick-
starting it by selecting Detect Displays from the Displays icon in the menu
bar (see Figure 5-1) or System Preferences pane (System Preferences → Displays). If you just see a mirror image (not literally so; nothing's reversed) of
your main screen on the second monitor, select Turn Off Mirroring from the
Displays icon in the menu bar (as shown in Figure 5-1) or uncheck the Mirror Displays checkbox in the Displays System Preferences pane (shown later
in Figure 5-2). The screen should flicker again and come up in spanned
mode.

If you're missing the Turn Off Mirroring option, you're most likely running
an unsupported Mac. Skip ahead to the "Enable Spanning in Open Firmware" section.

> I highly recommend you enable the Displays icon in the
> menu bar if you're going to be spanning and unspanning, or
> otherwise switching your display settings on a regular basis.
> Check the "Show displays in menu bar" checkbox on the
> Display tab in System Preferences → Display.

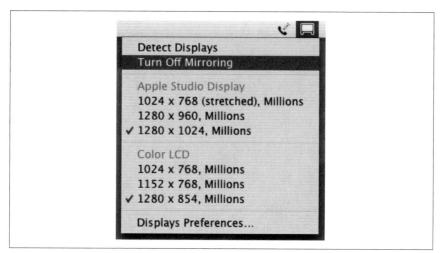

Figure 5-1. Detecting displays and turning off mirroring from the Displays icon in the menu bar

Arrange

Arrange your displays physically in any way that feels most comfortable to you: side-by-side, diagonally offset, one above the other, or anything in between. Try each for an hour or so, giving you time to get used to it before moving on to a different composition. Think of it as an art project—a tableau spanning the physical and virtual worlds, if you will—and have fun. Each time you shuffle your monitors in the physical world, let your Mac know where things stand by dragging the display representations on the Arrangement tab of the Displays Preferences pane, as shown in Figure 5-2.

You can further twiddle your settings for each individual display; each has its own Preferences pane, as shown in Figure 5-3, wherein you can set resolution and color. There's no rule that says the displays must have matching resolutions. In fact, one of your monitors might be more limited than the other; while your PowerBook's LCD goes only to 1024×768, your 17" CRT might go to 1280×1024. While this can be a bit nauseating, it does buy you even more room without costing you a penny more.

> You will notice that having one display of greater resolution than the other means you'll be bumping into the corners of the larger display with your mouse as you try to get to the smaller screen—like trying to get a futon through a narrow hallway. To ameliorate some of this odd effect, be sure the virtual arrangement in the Arrangement tab of the Displays Preferences pane matches your physical layout as closely as possible.

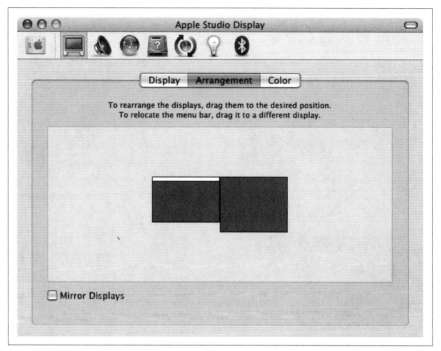

Figure 5-2. Arranging the displays in the Displays Preferences pane to reflect your physical layout

iCurve

There are various accessories available to raise your iBook or PowerBook from the Desktop to leave breathing and cooling room. While these can position your laptop a little better with respect to your second monitor, that's not their purpose and it shows; instead of a steep diagonal, you now have a shallower one.

Griffin Technology's iCurve (*http://www.griffintechnology.com/products/ icurve*; $39.99) is about the coolest piece of plastic you'll ever chance to meet. It raises and grades your laptop to bring it to proper eye level (no more staring down at your laid-back PowerBook screen) and at the same time makes room for a keyboard, mouse, book, or any other Desktop clutter you're prone to accumulating.

The best part, though, is that the iCurve is designed with spanning in mind—in particular, spanning between a PowerBook and the 17" Apple Studio Display, as shown in Figure 5-4. The top edge of the PowerBook sits perfectly aligned with the top edge of the display and almost so with the larger 23" Cinema Display.

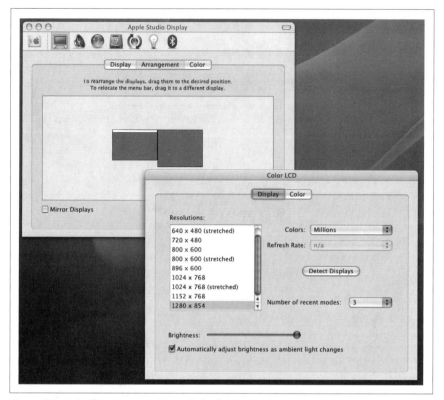

Figure 5-3. A Preferences pane for each display

Enable Spanning in Open Firmware

For those unfortunate souls who are without the ability to span (if Apple doesn't support spanning on your particular machine), there's a hack at the end of the tunnel. By poking about inside your Open Firmware, you might just be able to hack in support for screen spanning.

> Open Firmware is a small program built into your Mac. Its job is to check all your computer's hardware at startup and then find and boot an operating system from the hard drive.

The alteration affects your computer where hardware meets software, so this hack will enable extended Desktops in both OS 9 and OS X.

Figure 5-4. A 15" PowerBook G4 and 17" Apple Cinema Display, meeting eye to eye with a little help from iCurve

This hack involves making adjustments to the very undercarriage of your system. A mistake can prevent your machine from booting properly. Make sure you consult the chart of systems for which this hack works at *http://www.rutemoeller.com/ mp/ibook/supportlist_e.html*. This is particularly of note in the case of ATI Rage–based iBooks; from all reports at the time of this writing, the patch renders such machines dead as a proverbial doornail.

If your machine is not listed as supported, assume the hack will cause your computer harm and don't even think of trying it. Doing so could very well turn your Mac into a rather expensive paperweight.

There are extensive instructions (and oodles of warnings like the previous one) for laying hands on your Open Firmware and doing this hack manually at *http://macparts.de/ibook* (not to mention an entire set of forums devoted to the topic at *http://rutemoeller.com/mp/ibook/forum*). If all this sounds too risky for you, a handy Screen Spanning Doctor (*http://www.rutemoeller.com/ mp/ibook/ScreenSpanningDoctor.sit*; donateware) AppleScript does it all for you. Run it by double-clicking its icon; a simple AppleScript dialog box appears, as shown in Figure 5-5.

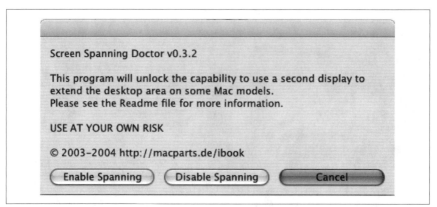

Screen Spanning Doctor v0.3.2

This program will unlock the capability to use a second display to
extend the desktop area on some Mac models.
Please see the Readme file for more information.

USE AT YOUR OWN RISK

© 2003–2004 http://macparts.de/ibook

Enable Spanning   Disable Spanning   Cancel

Figure 5-5. Using Screen Spanning Doctor to enable spanning on an otherwise span-free Mac

To turn on spanning, click the Enable Spanning button; conversely, turn off spanning again (there's really no reason to, though, since your Mac knows what to do when you unplug the second monitor) by clicking the Disable Spanning button. If you haven't yet checked the compatibility chart, heed the "USE AT YOUR OWN RISK" warning, click the Cancel button, and come back when and if you're ready.

Unhacking the Hack

If you simply overlooked or just ignored the earlier warnings about unsupported systems and tried the patch on your ATI Rage–based iBook, you are most likely wondering right about now how to resurrect your computer from its hack-induced coma.

Here's one solution that's been reported to work:

1. Take out your battery, leaving the AC adapter plugged in.
2. Restart your Mac and hold down the ⌘, Option, O, and F keys through the startup chime until you see the Open Firmware command line.
3. Type `reset-nvram` and press Return. Then, type `reset-all` and press Return again.
4. Cross your fingers, pray, or just think happy thoughts.

If all goes as hoped, your iBook should boot normally. Whatever you do, don't try that again in a hurry.

—C. K. Sample III and Rael Dornfest

iPod Tips and Tricks

There's nothing worse than when your trusty iPod starts acting up. It's like an angel falling from grace. Here's what to do when you need to take action and restore your iPod to its lofty place.

It never fails to amaze me that a device as small as the iPod can pack so much functionality. Every time I get close to taking it for granted, the thought of packing upward of 10 days worth of music into my pocket just amazes me all over again. And with only five buttons and a scroll wheel, it remains the most user-friendly MP3 player in the market. Imitated, but never duplicated, the iPod is truly the gold standard.

Despite all the kudos, though, the iPod isn't perfect. There are times when action is required. This hack shows you some ways to dig into your iPod.

Resetting an iPod

There are times when your iPod simply freezes and refuses to work. Sometimes, there's no explanation—unless you count the possibility of stray gamma radiation interfering with the iPod's electronics. In such an incident, you need to perform a reset on your iPod. To reset the iPod, press and hold the Menu and Play buttons at the same time for about 10 seconds. Let go of the buttons when you see the Apple logo again.

Restoring an iPod

If things really go wrong—for example, you erased your iPod using Disk Utility—or if you want to reset an iPod to its original, factory-fresh state before giving it to a friend, you can restore it using the iPod Updater. Here's how to do it.

You will not be able to retrieve the songs you have erased. The following steps will only help you to get your iPod to play music again.

Connect your iPod to your computer. Look in your */Applications/Utilities* folder for an iPod Software Updater application, which you'll have if you've been accepting all of your system updates. You can also download the iPod Software Updater at Apple's web site (*http://www.apple.com/ipod/download/*). When you run iPod Software Updater, you'll see the interface shown in Figure 5-6.

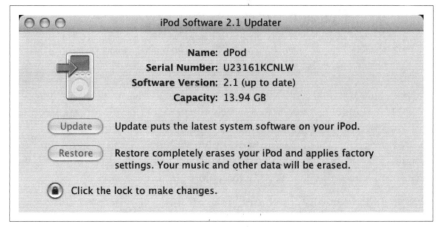

Figure 5-6. Restoring an iPod using the iPod Software Updater

Click Restore (you might need to click the padlock and key in an adminis-trator's username and password first). The iPod Software Updater applica-tion checks whether your iPod has the latest software. If your iPod is up-to-date, the Update button will be grayed out. An alert box appears to confirm you want to restore your iPod.

Click Restore. A progress bar appears. Depending on the model of iPod you have, you might need to unplug the iPod from your Mac and then recon-nect it. You'll be prompted if you need to do so.

In the iTunes Setup Assistant window, type a name for your iPod in the space provided. Then, wait until iTunes says the update is complete. Quit iTunes and disconnect the iPod. After a while, the Language display appears on the iPod screen. Select a language. Quit the iPod Software Updater application.

Your iPod now contains the music in your iTunes music library and playlists.

Performing Diagnostics on Your iPod

Your iPod contains built-in diagnostic routines to help troubleshoot your iPod when things go wrong. While the diagnostic tool can seem cryptic to end users, it is useful to technical support people when you send in your iPod for repair.

If you want to take a peek, here is how you can activate the diagnostic rou-tines on your iPod. First, reset your iPod (see the previous section on how to do this). Press and hold the REW, FFW and Select buttons. After a while, you will hear an audible chirp sound and a reverse image of the Apple logo will appear.

The test menu will then appear, as shown in Figure 5-7.

Figure 5-7. The iPod in diagnostic mode

You can use the REW and FFW buttons to navigate through the following test items:

```
A. 5 IN 1
B. RESET
C. KEY
D. AUDIO
E. REMOTE
F. FIREWARE
G. SLEEP
H. A 2 D
I. OTPO CNT
J. LCM
K. RTC
L. SDRAM
M. FLASH
N. OTPO
O. HDD SCAN
P. RUN IN
```

Use the Select button to select the test item you want to run. Be aware that using the hard drive scan test can take quite a bit of time—hours on the newer high-capacity iPods.

—*Wei Meng Lee*

HACK #52 Build an Emergency iPod Boot Volume

An emergency iPod boot volume can be just the thing when your drive goes south.

You're working on an important project and suddenly, poof!, out of nowhere your machine just up and dies. It plumb refuses to start back up again. Your deadline is looming, and at this point you don't much care about your computer; all you want is a few more minutes with that *Omnigraffle* file.

Assuming the file is still in existence and that your drive is accessible, even though not bootable, you reach for your trusty iPod, plug in, and calmly reboot.

Sure, you should have been backing up all along if the project was that important. But a backup won't get you far if you're the only person in the office with a Mac and you're using a Mac app without a Windows counterpart.

You see, sometimes, such a crash is caused by a hard-drive mechanical failure, but often enough, it's the system software that is corrupted. Your data is still safe, despite being locked up inside an otherwise nonbooting machine.

Using a Rev 1, 2, or 3 iPod (not the iPod mini, I'm afraid), you can create an emergency boot volume to keep on hand for just such emergencies. I use the word *emergency* because Apple does not recommend you use the iPod as a permanent boot volume. Doing so wears out your iPod's tiny hard drive quickly, because the iPod's hard drive is designed to be used in short spurts, not for the long haul. When you listen to music, the iPod's hard drive spins only to fill up the iPod's built-in RAM cache. It then quickly spins down and parks the hard drive's heads until they're needed again.

When used continuously, heat can build up inside the iPod case and literally fuse the hard drive platters together.

You can install any version of the Apple operating system on your iPod, as long as your particular machine can boot it. So, if you have a G5, don't bother installing OS 9 on your iPod (unless you want to access Classic within Panther). And if you have a beige G3, Panther will be useless to you. Instead, you'll need a previous version of Mac OS X.

With that decided, it's time to install OS X.

Plug in your iPod. Make sure you have enough room available for the OS; Panther needs approximately 2 GB (assuming you don't install the Developer Tools). Installing Panther or OS 9 on your iPod is just the same as for any other hard drive. This isn't true for Jaguar (OS X 10.2), though; to install Jaguar, you'll need to get a copy of Carbon Copy Cloner [Hack #85] and clone an already-installed version of Jaguar, then transfer it to the iPod.

You'll need to be able to access your iPod as a FireWire drive. If your iPod doesn't mount and show up on the Desktop, you haven't enabled FireWire disk usage for it. To do so, open iTunes, make sure you have the iPod selected, and click the iPod Preferences icon in the lower-right corner of the window (leftmost in Figure 5-8). In the iPod Preferences window, select "Enable disc use." Your iPod should now mount on your Desktop as expected.

Figure 5-8. Clicking the iPod button to reach the iPod Preferences pane

Before getting to the installation itself, make sure your iPod has at least 2 GB available (Control- or right-click your iPod on the Desktop and select Get Info). If it's too full, hop into iTunes and delete any songs on your iPod you've grown a little weary of.

You are now ready to install Panther. Insert Panther Install Disc 1. Once the CD mounts on your Desktop, open it and click the Install icon. The CD takes over, shutting down the computer, restarting it, and launching the Installer application. Follow the installation directions until you are asked to select a target drive on which to install OS X.

Because every little megabyte on your iPod is precious, let's do a Custom Install. Unless you are a polyglot, there shouldn't be any reason to have the 10+ languages that are included with Panther. You'll save a lot of disk space if you deselect all the language options you don't need; after all, this is an emergency boot volume, not a system that you'll be running for any other purpose. That done, you are ready to install. Do as your Mac tells you to until the installation is complete.

> You do not need to erase your iPod to install Panther. Indeed, you shouldn't! In fact, initializing your iPod through the installation process or through Apple's Disc Utility can cause problems.

If you want this boot partition to be a robust troubleshooting tool, you should consider installing Disk Warrior (*http://www.alsoft.com/DiskWarrior*), Norton Utilities (*http://www.symantec.com/nu/nu_mac*), and, for good measure, an antivirus tool such as Norton Antivirus (*http://www.symantec.com/ nav/nav_mac/index.html*) or Virex (bundled with every .Mac account and available from *http://www.networkassociates.com/us/products/mcafee/ antivirus/desktop/virex.htm*).

Now that you have Panther on your iPod, you can use it to boot up that ailing machine. Plug in your iPod and hold down the Option key while booting your Mac. After a few seconds, you'll see a list of all available startup volumes on your Mac and attached FireWire devices—most importantly, your iPod. For some reason, your iPod's name won't show up; look for a little FireWire icon instead. Select it, and you're good to go!

If your original machine's hard drive is usable but the system is corrupted, you can now either troubleshoot using your disk utilities or just grab or work with those vital project files you were after. Heck, you could do your presentation right from your iPod-powered Mac if necessary (assuming you have the right application available to you). Just remember not to spend any more time using the iPod as a boot volume than you absolutely need to.

The iPod makes for a terrific fallback in case anything goes wrong. And it plays music, to boot!

—Hadley Stern

HACK #53 Pair and iSync with Bluetooth Devices

You have a Bluetooth-enabled Mac and a Bluetooth-enabled cellphone, PDA, or other device, but how can you team them up to do something useful?

I recently spent some time with a friend of the family who surprised me by being rather technically adept—the family itself not being particularly so. She had noticed with glee that both her shiny new PowerBook and matching Palm Tungsten T3 had Bluetooth onboard and was wondering just what that meant in real terms. She understood this meant the two could communicate wirelessly and even keep each other in sync. But just how to set that up and what to expect from such a tie, she had no idea.

With Bluetooth finally hailed as a strong buy, it's surprising how little detailed information there is on what this so-called *cable-replacement technology* can do for you and just how to get it to go.

This hack steps you through the process of acquainting your Mac and Bluetooth device (a cellphone, in particular) and getting synchronization going between the two using iSync.

> If all you want to do is transfer files between two Bluetooth-enabled Macs or a Mac and a Bluetooth-enabled PDA or cellphone, pairing is unnecessary. If that's all you need, jump straight to [Hack #86].

Are You Bluetooth-Capable?

Many of you may well be lucky enough to already have Bluetooth built into your PowerBook or have optionally had it installed in your iBook, iMac, eMac, or G5 Desktop. A simple way to check is to launch System Preferences and see if you have a Bluetooth pane listed, as shown in Figure 5-9.

Figure 5-9. The Bluetooth pane listed in System Preferences

If not, you have the choice of either having Bluetooth installed internally (assuming your Mac is compatible with internal Bluetooth) or purchasing a USB Bluetooth dongle. Apple currently recommends the D-Link DBT-120 ($39.95 at *http://store.apple.com*), but you'll find quite a few available at your local computer store, Amazon.com, or eBay.

Pairing

The procedure for pairing your Mac with another Bluetooth-enabled device varies little, whether the other device is a PDA, cellphone, headset [Hack #57], mouse, or keyboard. About the only variance you'll encounter is in the amount of fiddling you'll need to do on the device side. With Bluetooth headsets, keyboards, and mice, just about everything is handled on the Mac side, with only the odd push of a button on the other.

For the purposes, then, of showing you about the most work you'll have to do to pair your Mac with another device, I've chosen a cellphone: the Nokia 6600. While the cellphone side of things will no doubt be different depending on which make and model you have, the steps should be easily extrapolated to fit your particular circumstances. When in doubt, you might consult the otherwise-ignored manual that came in the box with your cellphone; but don't expect much, because these things are notoriously badly written.

Since you're working with both your Mac and cellphone to get this all going, these instructions will interleave what you see and do on both ends.

On your Mac, visit the Bluetooth System Preferences pane (System Preferences → Bluetooth). Mine, shown in Figure 5-10, indicates that I already have a couple devices paired with my PowerBook: a Sony Ericsson P900 cellphone (aka *Raelity P900*) and Apple's wonderful Bluetooth keyboard (aka *rael's keyboard*).

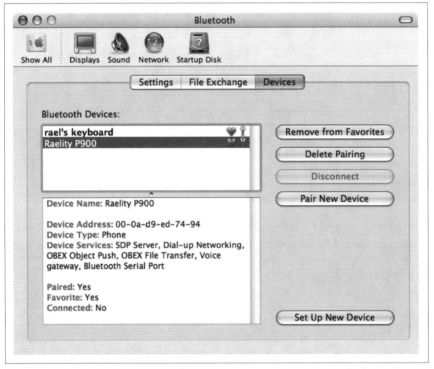

Figure 5-10. The Bluetooth System Preferences pane, showing two paired Bluetooth devices

Each device has its own friendly name so that you can tell them apart when a connection request comes in or when you're sending a picture or document to another device [Hack #86].

Click the Set Up New Device button to launch the Bluetooth Setup Assistant.

> You'd think you should click the Pair New Device button, wouldn't you? That would indeed do what you'd expect it to—pair your Mac with a new device—but it wouldn't then step you through preparing your device for iSync. It is better suited for simple Bluetooth devices such as keyboards, mice, and headsets.

From the greeting screen, click the Continue button. Select a Device Type—
in this case, a Mobile Phone, as shown in Figure 5-11.

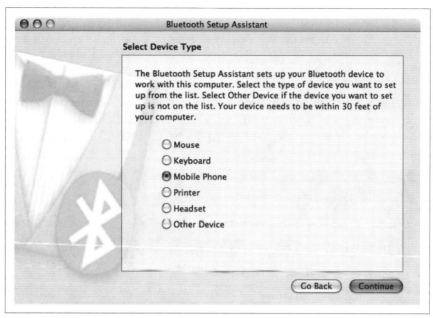

Figure 5-11. Selecting a device type with which to pair

Before clicking Continue, you should make sure your cellphone is *discoverable* (i.e., visible to devices around it). The specifics of just how to do this
vary from cellphone to cellphone, but the general idea is the same. Hunt
about in your cellphone's menu system for Bluetooth settings, turn on Bluetooth itself, and make it discoverable. On Nokia Series 60 devices (e.g.,
Nokia 3650, N-Gage, or 6600), you'll find what you're after under the main
menu → Connect folder → Bluetooth, as shown in Figure 5-12.

Figure 5-12. Turning on the cellphone's Bluetooth and making it discoverable

Notice my phone's name is set to *Raelity 6600*. By default it was something generic like *Nokia 6600*. While it's not necessary to do so, I changed it to something more personal—one part vanity, another part distinguishability amidst a crowd of Nokia 6600s. Whatever you name your cellphone, this is how it'll show up in the Bluetooth Setup Assistant when it's discovered.

Now, back in the Bluetooth Setup Assistant, click the Continue button and wait for your Mac to find your now-discoverable cellphone. Figure 5-13 shows that my Mac has stumbled across my Nokia 6600 (aka *Raelity 6600*).

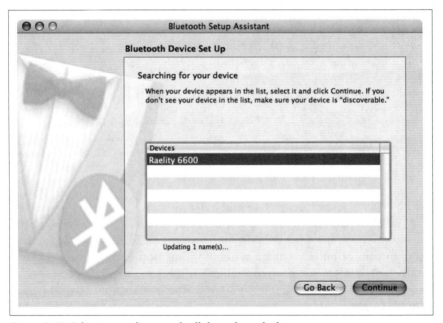

Figure 5-13. Selecting my discovered cellphone from the list

Select your cellphone from the list of discovered devices—usually a list of one—and click Continue.

The Bluetooth Setup Assistant generates a numerical passkey to use as an initial handshake between your Mac and cellphone, as shown in Figure 5-14. This provides a level of security so that both ends of the Bluetooth connection can trust that they (or at least you) know to whom they are speaking.

A second or two later, your cellphone should chirp and prompt you for this passkey, as shown in Figure 5-15. Tap it out on your keypad and click OK or its equivalent.

Figure 5-14. The Bluetooth Setup Assistant, generating a passkey

Figure 5-15. The cellphone, prompting for the shared passkey

You'll most likely not be able to see what you're typing (the password is hidden behind asterisks), which is a little silly given that it is more than visible in big black characters on your Mac's screen.

Your Mac now pairs with your cellphone and reconnects to assess its abilities. You'll probably be prompted to confirm that your Mac is allowed to connect to your cellphone; make sure it's your Mac that is knocking (check its name in the dialog box) and, if so, click the OK button or equivalent.

Depending on your cellphone's capabilities, the Bluetooth Setup Assistant will set it up to iSync with your Address Book and iCal, as well as make it available as a Bluetooth modem with which to access the Internet. As shown in Figure 5-16, my Nokia 6600 is capable of all these things.

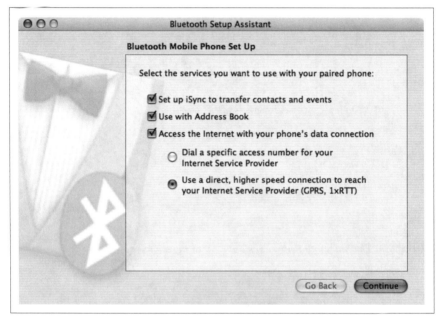

Figure 5-16. Selecting the services to use with the cellphone

You'll notice a couple choices for Internet access: dialup and GPRS/1xRTT. If you have a data plan with your cellphone provider, you'll want to leave the higher speed connection selected. Otherwise, to use your phone as a regular modem (of a sort) with your dialup account, select "Dial a specific access number...".

Click Continue. Assuming you left the "Access the Internet with your phone's data connection" box checked on the previous screen, you're prompted to provide some specifics, as shown in Figure 5-17. Leave this screen as is until you decide to use your cellphone as a Bluetooth modem [Hack #54].

Click Continue to come to the final screen, a polite confirmation that all has gone according to plan. Click Quit.

Back on the Bluetooth System Preferences pane, you'll notice your cellphone has been added to the list, marked both as a favorite (indicated by the heart icon) and paired (indicated by the lock) device, as shown in Figure 5-18.

Close System Preferences. You're paired!

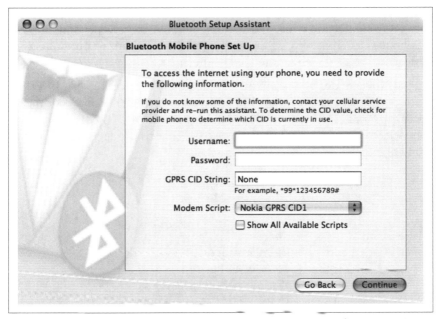

Figure 5-17. Setting up Internet connectivity using the cellphone as a Bluetooth modem

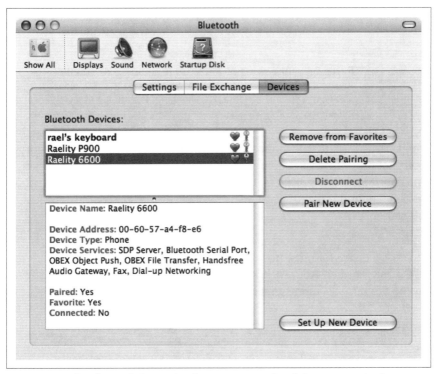

Figure 5-18. The Bluetooth System Preferences pane with cellphone now paired

Pairing might not be enough to stop your cellphone from prompting you with every connection your Mac attempts to make to it. Depending on your cellphone's paranoia level, you might need to authorize your Mac as a device to be trusted with unattended connections.

On the Nokia Series 60 (e.g., Nokia 3650, N-Gage, or 6600), visit the Bluetooth preferences again (Main Menu → Connect folder → Bluetooth) and select the Paired Devices tab. You should see your Mac listed; select it and then select Options → "Set as authorised" [*sic* (or not, depending on your brand of English ;-)], as shown in Figure 5-19.

Figure 5-19. Setting the Mac as authorized to connect unattended to your cellphone

> Rael's cellphone was sent direct from Europe and is configured for UK English. If you buy your 6600 in the United States, it will have the American spelling. Isn't living in a global society great? —Duncan

You'll be warned that "Connections will take place automatically without confirmation." Since this is precisely what you want it do, press the Yes button. Your Mac now appears as a trusted device, indicated by the lock icon in the right column in Figure 5-20.

iSync

The raison d'être for most people who pair their Bluetooth phone with their Mac is to sync their Address Book with their phone so that they never again have to tap out—let alone remember—a phone number.

> It's quite shocking how soon we forget all those phone numbers we were sure would never be shaken loose from memory; for the first time in my life, I don't actually know my parents' number. My phone and Mac do, and that's what counts, right?

Figure 5-20. The Mac, appearing as a trusted device

The pairing stage has already prepared your cellphone for use with iSync (that is, unless something untoward happened or you have a brand-spanking-new cellphone not yet supported by iSync). Now, you need to tell iSync all about it.

Launch iSync (*Applications/iSync*) and select Devices → Add Device (or ⌘-N). A list of devices that were recently paired but have not yet been enabled with iSync pops up; you should find your cellphone listed among them. iSync shows two such devices in my list: a Sony Ericsson P900 (aka *Raelity P900*) and Nokia 6600 (aka *Raelity 6600*), as shown in Figure 5-21.

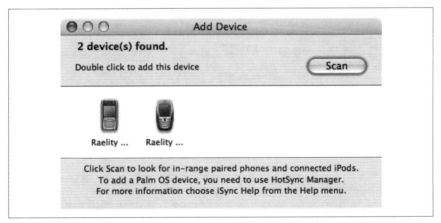

Figure 5-21. Two paired cellphones to add: Sony Ericsson P900 (left) and Nokia 6600 (right)

Double-click the device you'd like to enable with iSync and close the Add Device dialog. Your cellphone appears alongside .Mac, your iPod, and any other devices you already have set up to sync, and iSync opens a sheet for altering the sync settings for your newly added cellphone, as shown in Figure 5-22. I usually leave everything as it is by default, merging anything I already have on the phone with my Mac and syncing all my contacts and calendars from a week ago onward.

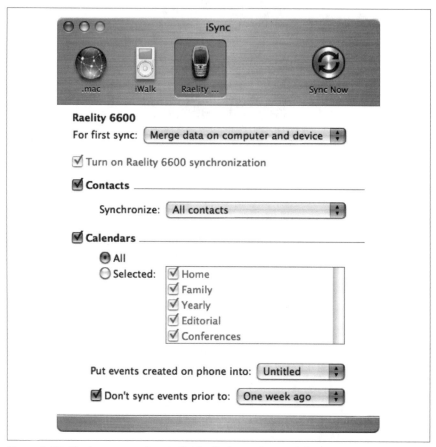

Figure 5-22. Honing sync settings individually for each paired device

 Your cellphone might not be able to accommodate all of the many contacts you have in your Address Book. My otherwise-wonderful Sony Ericsson Z600 and currently rather common T610/T616 have rather limited memory and so cut off after some number of contacts.

If this happens, you can create groups of contacts in Address Book and sync only those with your cellphone. Since Address Book entries can live in more than one group, perhaps even create a group called Must Haves and choose only that group in the iSync settings for your cellphone.

When you have the settings as you like them, click your cellphone's icon in iSync to wrap up the settings sheet.

Now sync iSync. This might take some time, because iSync isn't the fastest of beasts and Bluetooth isn't the fattest of wireless pipes. Don't wander off, though; depending on your iSync preferences (iSync → Preferences... or ⌘-,), you might be prompted to confirm changes to your contacts and appointments on your cellphone and Mac.

That's about all there is to it. iSync and a Bluetooth cellphone mean never having to say "I don't have her number with me."

HACK #54 Use Your Cellphone as a Bluetooth Modem

Avoid the WiFi HotSpot hop and take the Internet on the road with you wherever you might find yourself: on a bus, train, or walk in the woods.

With WiFi all the rage these days, you can about as easily hop onto the Internet at (or near) your local burger chain or coffee shop as at your office or home. But WiFi only solves the *last-yard problem*. You have to be within range of a HotSpot or otherwise open wireless network to get anywhere at all. If you find yourself with a few hours to spare on layover at a WiFi-disabled airport or on a train or bus with nothing but unwired, gorgeous scenery as far as the eye can see, you're relegated to reading a book or chatting with a fellow traveler or three. What's a wireless wonder to do without WiFi?

Choosing a Plan and Cellphone

Get yourself a data account from your cellular provider to bring you the Internet alongside your voice connectivity. At the time of this writing, all-you-can-eat data plans range from around $10 (T-Mobile is my current favorite) to $80 (AT&T) per month. If you don't anticipate using the Internet from your phone much, you might consider a pay-as-you-go plan, which will run you around 2 cents per KB on up to around $20 for 8MB (AT&T). U.S. providers are rolling out faster services—you may have heard of EDGE, for example—but currently, those are available only in limited locales and with limited choices of handset.

You'll also need a phone with the right capabilities for what you have in mind. Some lesser models provide only Wireless Access Protocol (WAP)—think HTML light—access to the Web, while others have a real web browser and email client onboard. Still others come with Bluetooth onboard, such that you can use your cellphone as a Bluetooth modem for connecting to the Internet when you're otherwise out of range of a wired or

WiFi connection. It's slow (around 19K per second) and more than a little flaky, but it's better than being relegated to a Net-free existence for a couple of hours, no?

For the purposes of this hack, I chose a Nokia Series 60 (the 6600, to be precise) and an all-you-can-eat data General Packet Radio Service (GPRS) plan from T-Mobile US.

 If you don't, for whatever reason, have a data plan with your cellphone provider yet have a Bluetooth-enabled phone that's capable of connecting to the Internet, you can still get online using analog dialup access. Read "Dialing Mobile," later in this hack.

Pairing with Your Cellphone

This hack assumes you've already paired your Mac and cellphone. If you've not already done so, read "Pair and iSync with Bluetooth Devices" [Hack #53] and come back when you're good and paired.

Goin' Mobile

Using knowledge gleaned from friends, bits and bobs from reliable sources, and grease from my well-worn elbows, here are some hopefully crystal-clear instructions on getting online using your Bluetooth-enabled Mac (built-in or Bluetooth dongle), Bluetooth-enabled cellphone, and a data plan from your cellphone provider.

Mac OS X relies upon modem scripts to know just how to talk to the particular modem at hand. While your Mac is already chock-full of scripts for all the popular modems, it most likely does not have those necessary for talking to your cellphone. Thankfully, Ross Barkman's mobile phone scripts (*http://www.taniwha.org.uk*: free/pintware) are the main missing link in this puzzle. Scroll down Ross's page to the Mobile Phone Scripts section and find the GPRS package for your cellphone make and model. For my Nokia 6600, I grabbed *http://www.taniwha.org.uk/files/NokiaGPRS2004-05.sit*.

Extract the *.sit* archive and drag the script or scripts (some packages have scripts for specific phones, while others have a more generic collection) to your *Macintosh HD/Library/Modem Scripts* folder (where *Macintosh HD* is the name of your Mac's hard drive as it appears on your Desktop). For my Nokia, I chose *Nokia GPRS CID1* (I use *Ericsson GPRS CID1* for my Sony Ericsson P900, Z600, or T610/T616).

Open Internet Connect (*Applications/Utilities/Internet Connect*) and select the Bluetooth tab, shown in Figure 5-23.

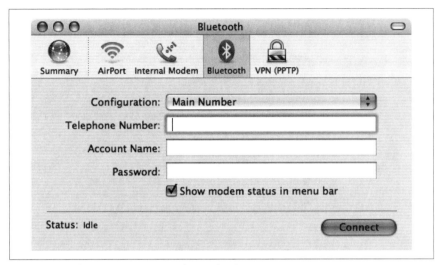

Figure 5-23. The Internet Connect Bluetooth tab

From the Configuration pull down menu, select Edit Configurations.... Hit the plus (+) button to create a new Bluetooth connection configuration and give it a name; I chose *Nokia 6600*.

Now, head over to Ross Barkman's GPRS Info Page (*http://www.taniwha. org.uk/gprs.html*). Here, the fabulous Ross provides a table of GPRS settings for providers around the world. Find your provider and account type (Figure 5-24 shows mine) and copy the settings into the Telephone Number, Account Name, and Password fields, as shown in Figure 5-25.

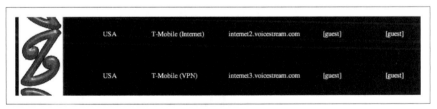

Figure 5-24. A snippet of Ross Barkman's GPRS Info Page

Click the OK button to return to the Bluetooth Internet Connect panel.

Now, you're ready to dial. Click the Connect button and cross your fingers. Internet Connect whirs to action, contacting your service provider, establishing a connection, authenticating, and, finally, showing that you're connected, as shown in Figure 5-26.

You should see some indication on your phone that it too is aware of what's going on. The Nokia Series 60's little G (for GPRS) blinks while connecting,

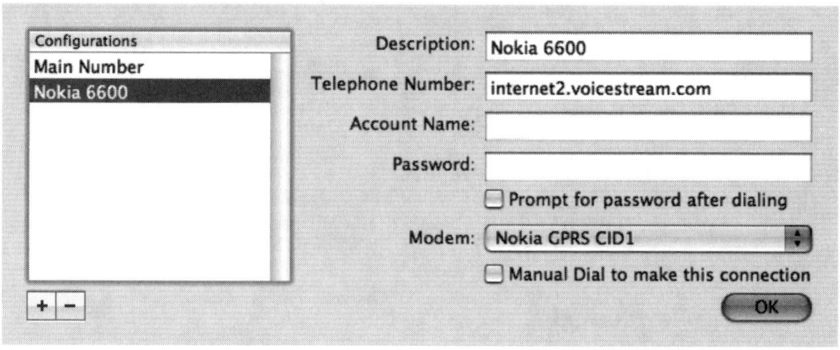

Figure 5-25. Filling in the Bluetooth Internet Connect configuration

Not-So-Clear Settings

Pay close attention to the fact that more than one set of settings might exist for your provider. In my case, I have a T-Mobile Internet rather than T-Mobile VPN account, so I use the first settings in Figure 5-24.

Also, be sure to pay attention to the Key to Table section at the bottom of Ross's page. Check any settings that appear in brackets against the key. For instance, though [guest] appears in both Username and Password fields for my provider, I should not type [guest] literally in those fields. Instead, according to the key, [guest] indicates that I should use the Guest option of Remote access or leave the field blank in Internet Connect. Inserting a space in the Password field stops Internet Connect from asking for a password every time I connect.

and turns to a solid [G] when you're online. The Sony Ericsson P800/P900 and Z600 display a little globe (as in World Wide Web) icon.

If all went to plan, you should be able to open your web browser and issue the international greeting (*http://www.google.com*) or visit anywhere else you wish. If packets flow (you should see them doing so in the Internet Connect panel) and your favorite site comes up in your browser, congratulations! You're on the Net using your Bluetooth phone as a wireless modem.

When you're done, click Disconnect to disconnect. Leaving your connection going can really rack up megabytes without your realizing it (downloading email in the background, for instance) if you're not careful.

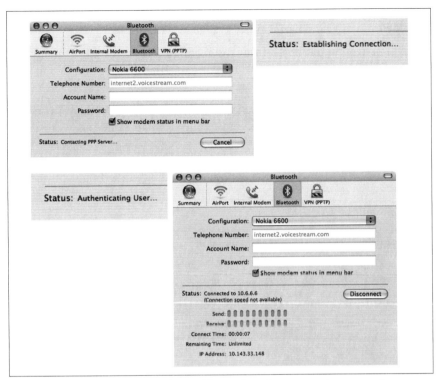

Figure 5-26. Internet Connect making a Bluetooth modem connection: contacting, establishing, authenticating, and connected

Dialing Mobile

If you don't have a cellular data plan (you might consider it unnecessary for your usage requirements or perhaps you are happy spending a few voice minutes on dialup), find yourself in an area with cellular but no GPRS data coverage, or just want to use up your monthly minute allotment rather than paying per megabyte on your pay-as-you-go data plan, you can still get online using your cellphone as an analog dialup modem.

It's slow as molasses (I got 9.6K at most) and a little fiddly, but it's a useful trick nevertheless.

Visit Ross Barkman's Mobile Phone Scripts page again and find the GSM scripts package for your cellphone make and model. (This is different than the GPRS package used earlier for turning your cellphone into a data device.) For my Nokia 6600, I grabbed *http://www.taniwha.org.uk/files/ NokiaGSMFeb2003.sit*.

Open Internet Connect (*Applications/Utilities/Internet Connect*) and select the Bluetooth tab shown previously in Figure 5-23.

Select Edit Configurations... from the Configuration pull-down menu and hit the plus (+) button. Give it a different name than your GPRS dialup configuration (if you have one); I chose *Nokia 6600 Dialup*.

In the Telephone Number field, enter a real phone number (that of your ISP or company's dialup access) and your dialup username and password in the Account Name and Password fields, respectively. Select a GSM script from the list, starting with the lowest speed and working your way up if all goes as expected. Figure 5-27 shows the configuration that worked right off the bat for me.

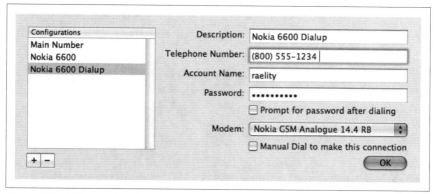

Figure 5-27. Filling in the Bluetooth Internet Connect configuration with ISP's dialup settings

Click the OK button to return to the Bluetooth Internet Connect panel and click Connect to give it a whirl. You should see about the same set of stages in the Internet Connect panel's Status display as when making a GPRS data connection. Your cellphone will probably show something altogether different. My Nokia 6600 looked like it was actually making a call, which, of course, it was. I knew this was different only because the little Bluetooth activity icon—it looks a little something like (0)—at the top-right was on, as shown in Figure 5-28.

Once you're up and running, surf, mail, and chat as usual.

> Realize that using your cellphone as a dialup modem does eat into both your cellphone plan's voice minutes and your ISP dialup minutes.

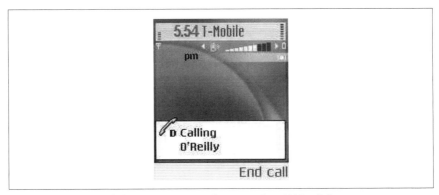

Figure 5-28. Analog dialup access, as seen from a Nokia 6600 cellphone

Final Thoughts

No more hotspot hopping for you—you're now your very own hotspot, sure to have onlookers agape as you surf the Net on your morning train commute.

That said, I should note that this isn't a one-size-fits-all hack. There are about as many tweaks and twiddles, depending on phone model and service provider, as there are hacks in this book (*GPRS Modem Hacks*, anyone?), but success is usually just a few minutes of fiddling or Googling away. If you're having trouble, you might browse or search my site, Mobile-Whack (*http://www.mobilewhack.com* or *http://www.mobilewhack.com/ ?find=os+x+gprs&plugin=find*), or spend a little time on HowardForums (*http://www.howardforums.com*), a massive database/forum of GPRS usefulness.

It's also worth noting that you can use an Infrared-equipped cellphone in much the same manner, just so long as your Mac has IR on board (the 12" PowerBook, for instance, doesn't). You'll need to keep your cellphone and Mac's IR ports nicely aligned with one another with little margin for error. Still, it works well enough to avoid talking to your fellow train travelers.

HACK #55 Share Your Mac's Net Connection with a Bluetooth Phone

Instead of wasting time and kilobytes on GPRS, use the Bluetooth functionality of your mobile phone to access your Mac's Internet connection.

Soon after going Bluetooth with my Nokia 3650 in the summer of 2003, I discovered that one of my favorite programs from my Palm OS days, Avantgo, would not sync between the 3650 and the Mac. Rather, Avantgo is designed to sync via the phone's GPRS connection. I ran the sync once over that connection and quickly blew through the 1MB per month of connectivity that my cellular account provided me. According to the logs, 3.46MB of data had been downloaded to my phone. Because of that one sync, my bill that month was three times what it was supposed to be. I needed to find a better and less expensive way to get the information I wanted on my phone.

At the time, I knew it was possible to set up the 3650 as a wireless modem for my Mac and had even tested that connection. I thought that if an Internet connection works in this direction, it should also be possible to reverse it. I started poring over pages and pages of Google searches, Mac OS X Hints (*http://www.macosxhints.com*), and every discussion forum I could find to discover a way to do this.

Early in this process, I discovered TechnoHappyMeal's Bluetooth Internet Sharing AppleScripts (*http://www.technohappymeal.com/archives/ 000070.html*), but I quickly found that they did not work for my phone. Upon discovering this, I tried three or four more times, howling curses into the night and flinging my 3650 (gently) across the sofa into the pillows. After calming down a bit, I opened up the TechnoHappyMeal scripts in Apple's Script Editor to take a look at the code:

```
do shell script "sudo /usr/sbin/pppd /dev/tty.Bluetooth-PDA-Sync 115200 \
   noauth local passive proxyarp asyncmap 0 silent persist :10.0.1.201 &" \
   with administrator privileges
do shell script "sudo /usr/sbin/sysctl -w net.inet.ip.forwarding=1"
do shell script "sudo /usr/sbin/natd -same_ports -use_sockets -log \
   -deny_incoming -interface en1"
do shell script "sudo /sbin/ipfw add divert natd ip from any to any via en1"
```

I then read Peter's TechnoHappyMeal article on how to set up this connection (*http://www.technohappymeal.com/archives/000069.html*). I tried all the steps in the article without the scripts. Twice. Then I tried the scripts again. Nothing worked.

But according to the comments at TechnoHappyMeal, it was working for some people, so I knew it was possible. So I kept looking. I found two useful things. I first discovered a Mac OS X Hint for sharing a Bluetooth connection out to a Palm (*http://www.macosxhints.com/article. php?story=20021103062212288&query=bluetooth*). I posted about all this on my site, and Terry Chay emailed me to point me to another bit buried in the comments of another post at Mac OS X Hints (*http://www. macosxhints.com/article.php?story=20030616191119129*) about creating a consistent Bluetooth link between a phone and an Address Book. Jim Wright commented that he was able to ping between his phone and his Mac, but he couldn't get the DNS to resolve.

When I emailed Jim about this, he said that it had since started working for him, albeit sporadically, but for some reason Avantgo syncing continued to fail. Jim pointed me to an Apple Discussion thread (which has since disappeared) and a post by a JRLove, whom I have never managed to contact. On the Apple Discussion thread, JRLove posted a group of commands to run from the Terminal, and he later posted these commands on the original Mac OS X Hint where Jim had posted.

I entered these commands in order, substituting my phone's MAC address in the first command line and removing -p800, which was necessary only for P800/P900 users. It connected. The Mac and the 3650 both indicated a connection, just like when I ran iSync. I followed instructions on the Apple Discussion thread to fool my 3650 into thinking that the paired connection between the 3650 and my PowerBook was a GPRS access point. Avantgo still wouldn't work. Browsing worked if I typed in the IP address of the site I wanted, but, as Jim had experienced, the DNS was not resolving.

Terry, Jim, and I emailed back and forth for about a week about this issue. Ultimately, Terry noted that sudo named was the command that starts running the DNS on the Mac and he had discovered two ways of forcing it to work: by reloading a web page with a reference to a static IP or by running sudo named again to start up another nameserver daemon.

Remembering the TechnoHappyMeal scripts, I added another line of sudo named to the code and slapped it into some AppleScripts between do shell script and with administrator privileges. I came up with a basic and stupid name that I thought would never conflict with any existing products with actual lawyers behind them, posted the scripts to my web site, and the first raw and rather unpredictable version of Share2Blue2th was born.

When I wrote these scripts, I did not fully understand what all of the command-line code did. I just wanted my Mac and my phone to do something that I knew was possible, and I dug around on the Internet until I found the *how-to* of it all. Once I found that and got it working, I decided I wanted to automate it, so I packaged the command-line code in an AppleScript wrapper.

In these early phases, because of my ignorance about all the command-line code, I was superstitious about the scripts. Jim discovered that adding pauses between the commands ensured that everything ran properly. I put the additional code in the scripts, and they suddenly started to run much more consistently.

Continued communication with Jim Wright and Terry Chay, help from the readers of my web site, and conversations with people like Jon in the

MacScripter BBS AppleScript Forum (*http://bbs.applescript.net/viewtopic. php?p=26388*) have enabled me to refine the scripts over time and have helped me come to understand what is going on with most of the code. The Share2Blue2th scripts are less my own accomplishment than they are a testament to the collaborative power of the Internet and the Mac community.

The Code

First, let's look at the commands as you can type them manually into the Terminal application. All these commands must be run as an administrator, thus the sudo before each command. This is necessary because the commands use bits and pieces of your system that iSync has access to, but which you normally (and rightfully) don't have permission to use. You will be prompted for your administrator password after entering the first command.

Here are the commands in order, with my commentary:

```
sudo sh -c \"cd ~; nohup \
  /System/Library/SyncServices/SymbianConduit.bundle/Contents/Resources/¬
mRouter \
  -a 00:00:00:00:00 -t 180 -btt 180 -p -v >~/mrouter.log 2>&1 &\"
```

This is one long string, used to invoke mRouter. As you can see, mRouter is part of the *SymbianConduit.bundle* within *System/Library/SyncServices*. iSync uses this little program to establish connections with Symbian-based devices. If you type the complete path to mRouter in the Terminal, you will receive a list of valid options.

The first option is -a *addr*, which specifies the 48-bit device address of the target. For our purposes, this is the MAC address for the paired device with which you want to share your computer's Internet connection. I've substituted 00:00:00:00:00 for the MAC address; you'll need to replace this with your device's MAC address (which is listed as the Device Address of your paired device in System Preferences → Bluetooth → Devices).

Next, the -t *time* option specifies the timeout, in seconds, for the mRouter connection, and -btt *time* specifies the Bluetooth timeout. I have set both of them to 180 to give everything plenty of room. The -p switch tells mRouter not to use a pipe and is necessary if you run mRouter as standalone code. Next, for compatibility if you are using a P800 or P900 phone, you will need to add the -p800 switch. Finally, -v specifies the verbose switch. Running this command from the command line establishes a Bluetooth connection between your device and your Mac.

These variables are specific to the version of mRouter bundled in Mac OS X 10.3.2 and later running iSync 1.4. The code is slightly different if you are running an earlier version of iSync. Try the following command instead:

```
sudo sh -c \"cd ~; nohup \
  /System/Library/SyncServices/SymbianConduit.bundle/Contents/Resources/¬
mRouter \
  -p -a 00:00:00:00:00 -vv -t 180 >~/mrouter.log 2>&1 &\"
```

Now we can do something with this connection:

```
sudo /usr/sbin/sysctl -w net.inet.ip.forwarding=1
```

Unlike mRouter, sysctl actually has a manpage, so launch the Terminal and type man sysctl if you want to find out all about it. Basically, we are invoking sysctl to change the kernel's default IP forwarding to 1 (which, in the world of ones and zeros that the kernel speaks, translates into "turn on Internet Sharing, please"), effectively making your Mac a gateway.

Next, we need to start the NAT daemon:

```
sudo /usr/sbin/natd -interface en0 -use_sockets -same_ports -dynamic ¬
-clamp_mss
```

This command invokes natd, the Network Address Translation daemon (type man natd to read its manpage). Basically, natd does what its name implies: it translates the network address. What does that mean? Well, the command tells natd to use the Ethernet connection (-interface en0) to share over Bluetooth. If you want to share your AirPort connection instead, substitute en1 for en0. If you are connected via a USB modem that uses a PPP connection, you have to use the -nat switch to ppp(8), rather than -interface en0 (I've never tested this, so let me know if it works!). The -dynamic command ensures that if your Mac's IP address changes, that change will be translated for the shared connection as well.

Now that the NAT daemon is running, we must divert traffic to it:

```
sudo /sbin/ipfw add divert natd ip from any to any via en0
```

ipfw is the IP firewall and traffic shaper control program (type man ipfw in the Terminal to read up on it). This command adds a rule to ipfw, diverting all packets that pass through natd from any IP number to any IP number via the defined interface port (en1 for AirPort and en0 for Ethernet).

The following command runs named, which is a Domain Name System (DNS) server (type man named in the Terminal for more information):

```
sudo named
```

Run this command twice to force DNS resolution over the connection. If, after running named twice, you are still unable to connect to a web site without typing in the IP address for the site, wait a few seconds and run named again. In the early, superstitious days of using these commands, I used to run sudo named four or five times in a row just to be sure I would connect, but that was overkill.

Running these commands, substituting your MAC address for *00:00:00:00:00* and using the interface appropriate for your purposes, should share your Mac's Internet connection to your Bluetooth paired device. In order for your device to realize that this connection is available for Internet, you will need to trick it into accessing the Bluetooth paired connection with your Mac as an Internet access point. You can do this by setting up an Internet access point with the same name as your Mac's shared Bluetooth name normally appears on your device's pairing. The configuration will differ depending upon your device.

On the Nokia 3650, navigate to Connections → Bluetooth, turn on Bluetooth, and make sure your phone and your Mac are paired, if you haven't already done so.

Next, navigate to Tools → Settings and choose the Connection settings tab. When you click on Access Points, a screen should display your available access points. Select Options: New Access Point and Use Default settings. Change the connection name to the name of your computer as it appears in the paired device list on your phone. Change the Access Point name to the same name. Leave everything else set to the defaults.

Navigate back to the Connection settings and select GPRS. Make sure "GPRS connection" is set to "When available," and make sure that the access point you just created is selected under Access Point.

After successfully establishing this Internet sharing, you need to know how to kill this connection. Again, from the Terminal, type the following command to kill the DNS routing over the shared connection:

```
sudo killall named
```

Next, use this command to clear the natd firewall settings that you defined through ipfw when you established the connection:

```
sudo /sbin/ipfw -f flush
```

This command kills the Network Address Translation over the shared connection:

```
sudo killall natd
```

This command switches IP forwarding back to 0, tuning it off:

```
sudo /usr/sbin/sysctl -w net.inet.ip.forwarding=0
```

This command ends the mRouter connection between your device and your computer:

```
sudo killall mRouter
```

Finally, this optional command removes the mRouter log from your home folder:

```
sudo rm -f ~/mrouter*
```

If you are curious, or if you are troubleshooting the connection, you might want to delay erasing this file. Navigate to your *Home* folder and double-click *mrouter.log* to read a log of all that has happened during your connection.

As you can see, this is a lot of information to type into the Terminal each time you want to share your Internet to your Bluetooth-enabled device. The next step to making this a real hack is to automate the process, and the easiest way to do this is via AppleScript. Here is the final code for the script:

```
--Open this script in a new Script Editor window.
property your_phones_MAC : missing value
property userchoice : "Ethernet"

--set the MAC address once:
if your_phones_MAC = missing value then
    set your_phones_MAC to text returned of \
    (display dialog "Enter your phone's MAC address:" & return \
    & "(This can be found under System Preferences-->Bluetooth-->Devices \
    under your phone's paired name. Make sure you use colons!)" & return \
    & return \
    & "e.g., 00:00:00:00:00:00" default answer "" buttons {"Cancel", "OK"} \
    default button 2 with icon 1)
end if

--remember the last port chosen and default to that button:
set userchoice to button returned of (display dialog "Select port to share:" \
buttons {"Cancel", "AirPort", "Ethernet"} default button userchoice with \
icon 1)
if userchoice = "AirPort" then
    set thePort to "en1"
else
    set thePort to "en0"
end if

do shell script "sh -c \"cd ~; nohup \
  /System/Library/SyncServices/SymbianConduit.bundle/Contents/\
Resources/mRouter \
  -a " & your_phones_MAC & " -t 180 -btt 180 -p -v ¬
>~/mrouter.log 2>&1 &\""
with administrator privileges
do shell script "sleep 10"
do shell script "sudo /usr/sbin/sysctl -w net.inet.ip.forwarding=1"
do shell script "sleep 2"
do shell script "sudo /usr/sbin/natd -interface " & thePort & \
" -use_sockets -same_ports -dynamic -clamp_mss"
do shell script "sleep 2"
do shell script "sudo /sbin/ipfw add divert natd ip from any to any via " \
& thePort
do shell script "sleep 2"
do shell script "sudo named"
do shell script "sudo named"
```

The first section of this script checks to see if your device's MAC address has previously been defined. If it is missing, the script displays the dialog box shown in Figure 5-29, prompting you to enter your phone's MAC address and telling you where you can find this information.

Figure 5-29. Prompting for a MAC address

After this value is defined, it is saved as the variable your_phones_MAC, which is substituted in the first bit of command-line code regarding mRouter. As a result, this variable is saved in the script, so this dialog box will not pop up on subsequent launches of the script.

Before I added this portion to most recent release of the scripts, users had to open the scripts in Script Editor (found in */Applications/AppleScript/*) and manually edit the first bit of command-line code with the correct MAC address. I tried various methods of grabbing the MAC address from the system, but this always broke mRouter, because the system displays the MAC address with dashes rather than with colons and mRouter thought each dash was followed by a command that it did not understand.

The next section of the script uses the display dialog function to launch a dialog box (see Figure 5-30) that asks you to choose the port you want to share over Bluetooth: Airport or Ethernet.

Figure 5-30. Prompting for a port

The dialog defaults to the port that was selected the last time the script ran. If you choose AirPort, the thePort variable is set to en1; if you choose Ethernet, the thePort variable is set to en0. Selecting Cancel ends the script.

The remainder of the script runs the previously discussed command-line commands by wrapping them in quotation marks following do shell script. As you can see, the first command lacks sudo but is followed by with administrator privileges, which amounts to the same thing.

Since you are running these commands through an AppleScript, rather than directly from the command line, a third and final dialog box will launch, prompting you for your administrator password. The values you input in the previous dialog boxes are substituted for the variables thePort and your_phones_MAC within the commands. Notice that sleep commands have been added between the different commands. This ensures that each command has time to execute before the script kicks out the next command.

In the Share2Blue2th package, all the scripts are included both as standalone script applications and as regular scripts that can be placed in the Scripts folder (~/Library/Scripts/) and launched via the Script Menu (/Applications/ Apple Script/Install Script Menu). The package consists of four scripts: Share Internet Over Bluetooth, Share Ethernet Over Bluetooth, Share AirPort Over Bluetooth, and Kill Net Over Bluetooth. The only difference between the Share Internet Over Bluetooth and the Ethernet and AirPort scripts is that the latter two simply default to their specific ports, without launching the port dialog that prompts the user's input. Here's the code for the Kill Net Over Bluetooth script:

```
do shell script "killall named" with administrator privileges
do shell script "sudo /sbin/ipfw -f flush"
do shell script "sudo killall natd"
do shell script "sudo /usr/sbin/sysctl -w net.inet.ip.forwarding=0"
do shell script "sudo killall mRouter"
do shell script "sleep 15"
do shell script "sudo rm -f ~/mrouter*"
```

As you can see, the Kill Net Over Bluetooth script is simply the command code to kill the connection, wrapped in quotation marks following do shell script. Again, the first command lacks sudo but is followed by with administrator privileges. Since you are running these commands through an AppleScript, a dialog box will prompt you for your administrator password.

Running the Code

Before running the scripts, make sure that iSync isn't currently running, because attempting to run mRouter while a sync is in progress will guarantee failure. If the scripts fail the first time you run them, run the kill script and run them again. For some reason, this seems to happen the first few times you try the scripts, but after you get it running it works like clockwork from then on.

You can run the code directly from the Script Editor by clicking Run. To always have the scripts a click away, move the script folder to the */Library/ Scripts/* folder to make it available via the Script Menu. Run the scripts at any time by selecting Script Menu → Share2Blue2th. Sometimes, the scripts make your phone's connection run much faster than a regular GPRS connection; other times, they seem to run at just about the same speed.

Hacking the Hack

These scripts share your Mac's Internet connection over Bluetooth with any paired Bluetooth device. The only problematic part of the equation is getting your device to see this connection as a viable source for Internet access.

I wrote these scripts specifically for use with a Nokia 3650, but numerous readers of my site have reported being able to use them with the Nokia 7650, 3660, 3620, and N-Gage, Sony Ericsson P800 and P900, and the Palm Tungsten T3. A Salling Clicker v.2.1 (*http://homepage.mac.com/jonassalling/ Shareware/Clicker/*) plug-in version of the scripts is also available from my site (*http://3650anda12inch.blogspot.com*).

One person reported using the scripts to share an Internet connection between two Macs, and another between a Mac and a PC. I've not tried any of these combinations myself and have no idea how they managed it, but give it a shot. Play around with the code and contact me about anything you discover. I'll mention it on my site. Happy hacking!

—*C. K. Sample III*

HACK #56   Control Your Mac with a PDA

With your Palm as remote control and your Mac a few feet away, you have a powerful presentation tool at hand.

You've bought your first Mac with Bluetooth, and now you're wondering what it's good for. Or, you've had a Bluetooth Mac, and now you have a Bluetooth PDA, but you figure there must be something cool the two can do together, especially given all the Bluetooth hype you've heard. The answer is Salling Software's Clicker, a cool application that allows your Bluetooth devices (phones and PDAs) to act as a remote control for your Mac.

The first version of Clicker won two Apple Design Awards at WWDC 2003: Best Mac OS X Product (Best of Show) and Most Innovative Mac OS X

Product. That version—covered in the O'Reilly Network article, "Using Your Bluetooth Phone as a Remote Control" (*http://www.macdevcenter.com/ pub/a/mac/2003/08/22/bluetooth_remote.html*)—was great, but Version 2.0 (*http://homepage.mac.com/jonassalling/Shareware/Clicker/*) added entirely new functionality, allowing you to control your Mac with your PDA. In this hack, we'll walk through how to install and use Clicker, and then we'll look at some examples of Clicker in action, using PowerPoint and iPhoto.

Installing and Using Clicker

For Sony Ericsson Bluetooth-enabled phones, Clicker Version 2.0 still works much like the way Version 1 did (as described in the "Using Your Bluetooth Phone as a Remote Control" article mentioned in the previous section), with the addition of some cool new stuff, and it still costs $9.95. Clicker for Bluetooth-enabled Palm OS devices costs $14.95, but it does everything the phone version does and more. Together, both will set you back $24.90 (there's no bundle discount), which isn't much, once you consider what Clicker can do.

After you've downloaded Clicker, you simply install it as you would any other application for your Palm. Launching Clicker on your PDA results in a screen similar to the one in Figure 5-31.

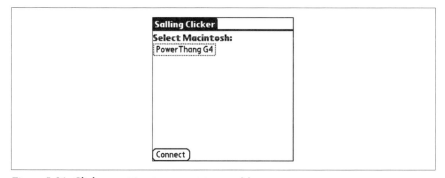

Figure 5-31. Clicker, waiting to connect to your Mac

 If you've never paired your PDA to your Mac, check out "Bluetooth on Mac OS X" (*http://www.oreillynet.com/pub/a/ wireless/2002/08/13/bluetooth_osx.html*) for information on pairing, or Chapter 6, "Bluetooth," of *Mac OS X Unwired* by Tom Negrino and myself (O'Reilly).

Tapping on the name of your Mac brings up a dialog like the one in Figure 5-32; if all works well, the connection will succeed and you'll then get the Salling Clicker menu shown in Figure 5-33. At this point, Clicker can control any of the applications shown: DVD Player, iPhoto, iTunes, Keynote, PowerPoint, and the Finder itself.

Figure 5-32. Clicker, trying to connect to your Mac

Figure 5-33. Clicker, connected and ready to serve

Clicker in Action: PowerPoint

When I was speaking at the recent O'Reilly Mac OS X Conference, I used Clicker on my PDA to control my PowerPoint presentation. Choosing PowerPoint from the list in Figure 5-33 displayed the menu shown in Figure 5-34. The most useful of the items shown is the one with the least descriptive name: Control.

Selecting Control told my PDA to do several things simultaneously:

- Act as a remote control that allows me to move forward (and backward) through my presentation by using the navigator buttons.

- Act as a timer, showing how long I've been speaking (and therefore, how much time I have left).

- Act as a note displayer, showing the notes that I've entered in PowerPoint for my own reference.

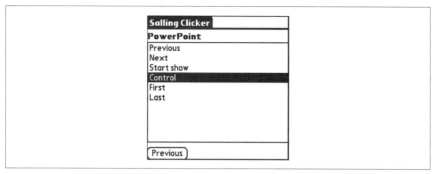

Figure 5-34. Controlling PowerPoint with my PDA

So, while the slide shown in Figure 5-35 was displayed on the screen for the audience, my PDA showed me Figure 5-36. Unlike sessions in which I've used a mouse to control my slides, I wasn't tied to sitting at my seat. Also, unlike sessions in which I've used an IR remote, I didn't have to have a direct line of sight with my Mac.

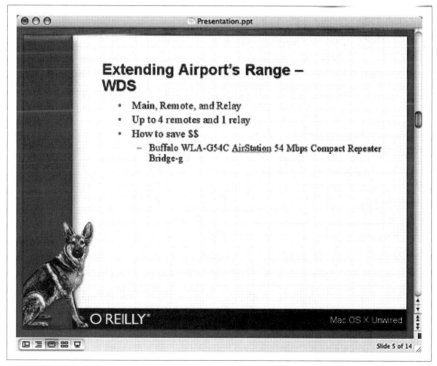

Figure 5-35. A typical PowerPoint slide

Here's a hot presentation tip: when using Clicker to control your presentations (via either phone or PDA), turn on Presentation Mode (either from the

Figure 5-36. Session timer and speaker notes for the PowerPoint slide in Figure 5-35

menu bar or from Clicker's Preferences pane), as shown in Figure 5-37. This tells your Mac and paired device to do a number of useful things: do not invoke phone events, aggressively try to reconnect if the connection is lost, and keep your Mac from sleeping/dimming (even when you aren't actively using Clicker). It won't turn off your phone, though, so be sure to turn yours off when you're presenting; this is just as true for speakers as it is for conference-goers!

Clicker in Action: iPhoto

Let's say I'm speaking at a conference, and the subject of my cat (*http:// www.pixel.mu*) arises (you might be surprised by how frequently this actually happens).

I would, of course, then want to show the attendees exactly why he's worth their attention, and that involves showing one of his many pictures in my iPhoto library. But I don't want to show all of them to the attendees (that could take longer than the session itself), so I have to choose just the right image to present. Clicker allows me to go through the images on my Mac's hard drive, look at them on my Palm, and choose which one to display on my Mac.

To do this, I choose iPhoto from the list of applications in Figure 5-33, which then causes the list of commands to appear, as shown in Figure 5-38.

Choosing iPhoto Slideshow displays a list of photo albums. I can pick the one I want and get a list of image names. Selecting an image makes it appear on my PDA, as shown in Figure 5-39.

I can then do any of the following:

- Click down on the navigator to advance to the next picture.
- Click middle or right on the navigator to display the current image on the screen.

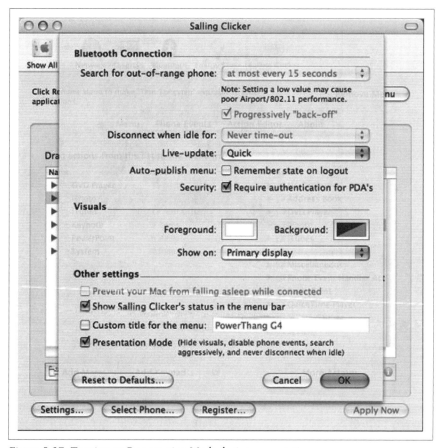

Figure 5-37. Turning on Presentation Mode during presentations

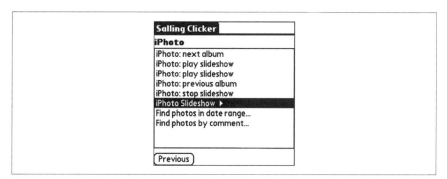

Figure 5-38. iPhoto's list of commands

- Click up on the navigator to view the previous photo.
- Click left on the navigator to go back to the list of images.

Figure 5-39. Not my cat's best angle, so I won't choose this one

 There are, of course, many other useful things you can do with Clicker and iPhoto. For instance, you can run an iPhoto slideshow in a way similar to the PowerPoint slideshow covered earlier.

Here's a hot iPhoto tip: you can reduce the level of JPEG compression (and thereby improve the quality, although transfer times will increase) of images shown on your Palm by changing a hidden setting. Quit Clicker, open Terminal, and type:

```
defaults write com.salling.SallingClickerHelper JPEGCompressionFactor 0.7
```

See Also

This hack covers only a small amount of the functionality that Clicker ships with. Given that, under the hood, Clicker's commands are simply AppleScript, the only limits are your imagination and your scripting skills. If you want to know more, check out:

- The article "Using Your Bluetooth Phone as a Remote Control," mentioned previously, briefly covers scripting Clicker Version 1.
- Chapter 6 of *Mac OS X Unwired* covers Bluetooth on Macs.
- Salling Software has a page on developer resources (*http://homepage. mac.com/jonassalling/Shareware/Clicker/developer/*).

- *AppleScript: The Definitive Guide* (O'Reilly) doesn't cover scripting Clicker, but it's a good start if you decide you want to learn more about the AppleScript language itself.
- Clicker has an active support forum (*http://groups.yahoo.com/group/ericssonclient/*) at Yahoo! Groups.

—Dori Smith

Listen to Bluetooth

Using iChat AV with a Bluetooth-enabled headset has great potential and some immediate benefits. We wrestled with the configuration and show you what works, what almost works, and what to look out for.

I once read a review of a *bug zapper*: a product that killed flying insects. The reviewer concluded that once you took into account the product's pros and cons, your best value for the dollar was to buy one and then give it to your next-door neighbor. You ended up with most of the pros and none of the cons. Using iChat AV with a Bluetooth-enabled headset has a lot in common with that product, including the way that both of them leave you complaining about bugs.

Here's the hardware you'll need for this hack:

- A Mac running OS X 10.3.2 or later
- A Bluetooth module, either internal (all supported) or external (only some supported)
- A Bluetooth-enabled headset, such as the Jabra BT200

And here's the software you'll need:

- Bluetooth Firmware Updater 1.0.2 or later
- Bluetooth Software 1.5 or later
- iChat AV 2.1

I've been pairing the Jabra BT200 headset with my Sony Ericsson phone for months now and have found it to be very handy. Wearing it at last October's O'Reilly OS X Conference, the most common question I was asked was "Does that work with a Mac?" I was sorry to disappoint people and tell them no, and I was happy to hear that with the recent release of Bluetooth 1.5 that answer had changed.

 The second most common question I heard was whether the headset made me look more like a Bajoran or a Borg, but that's another story altogether.

What You'd Expect

You're a Mac user, so you expect that you can plug things in (or in this case, pair things), and they'll just work. So, you'd expect that a Bluetooth headset pairing would allow you to use your Mac and your headset to do things like voice recognition, listen to iTunes, and, in general, use the audio input and output features of the headset to replace the audio input and output of the Mac. Unfortunately, it's not quite that simple.

The Installation Process

There are three separate downloads, all of which are required: the Bluetooth firmware updater, the Bluetooth software, and iChat AV 2.1. The firmware updater has the most ominous warning message I've ever seen in an Apple product, with five separate warnings, as shown in Figure 5-40.

Figure 5-40. Apple's Bluetooth Firmware Updater warning messages

Even with this many warning messages, things can still go wrong. If you were an early adopter and bought the original Bluetooth adapter sold by Apple (the D-Link DWB-120M), you'll get an error message that says your adapter isn't suitable and its firmware isn't updateable. The Belkin F8T003 isn't updateable either, but the current adapter Apple sells (the D-Link DBT-120) works fine.

But if you do have a compatible adapter, even with all those warning messages, Apple missed one: don't try to run the firmware updater with Bluetooth turned off. The updater won't ever find your Bluetooth device, and it won't stop trying. This leaves you with only one option, which is specifically warned against: canceling the update. Thankfully, no harm appeared to be done to my test machine, and the updater ran just fine after Bluetooth was turned on.

If you've gone to Apple's Bluetooth page (*http://www.apple.com/bluetooth*) to download both the Bluetooth software and the firmware updater, you might then think that you have everything that's necessary. After all, the page says "You can also use a Bluetooth headset to talk to your friends and colleagues during an iChat AV session." But the page forgets to mention that you need to have the latest version of iChat AV (Version 2.1 as this book goes to press; download from *http://www.apple.com/ichat*). While the only feature Apple documents adding in 2.1 was the ability to video-conference with AOL 5.5/Windows users, installing 2.1 fixed a number of hairy Bluetooth chat bugs on my test system, including application freezes and an inability to turn off Bluetooth devices.

Getting Started

As mentioned previously, even though you've installed three different downloads, it's still not quite plug-and-play. Your iChat preferences (Figure 5-41) and Sound System Preferences (Figure 5-42) each have separate settings for sound input and output.

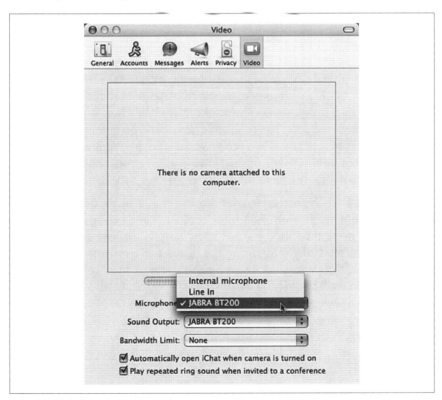

Figure 5-41. iChat AV Video Preferences pane

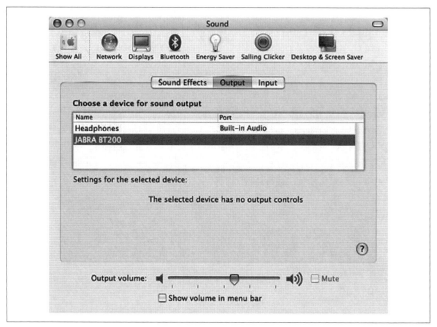

Figure 5-42. Sound System Preferences pane

While this seems counterintuitive at first (two separate inputs and two separate outputs?), it starts to make sense shortly after you've tried using the headset for all system sounds. For instance, if your Mac hasn't made any sounds in a while, it drops the connection to your headset. If an application then beeps, the connection has to resume before the beep can be sent, causing a delay that makes you wonder just which recent action went with that beep. And listening to iTunes through the headset is near painful; listeners compared it unfavorably to AM radio through a cheap speaker.

As for setting your System Preferences to use the headset for sound input, there's not really much point, as Apple documents fairly clearly that "Speech recognition is not a supported feature." And despite the Speech System Preferences pane successfully recognizing the headset as a microphone and then displaying that it's hearing sounds, you can't use it to enter speakable items. The days when we'll be able to talk to our Macs wirelessly is coming, but it's not here yet. Between the issues with system sounds, iTunes quality, and lack of speech recognition, there's no point in setting your Sound preferences (either input or output) to use your Bluetooth headset.

Setting Things Up

After all that negativity, I'm happy to say that setting up a Bluetooth head-set was fairly straightforward, although somewhat more than plug-and-play:

1. Launch the Bluetooth Setup Assistant.

2. Choose the new-to-Bluetooth 1.5 Headset radio button.

3. Set your headset to be discoverable, and wait for your Mac to find it.

4. At the prompt, enter the passkey associated with the headset; if you have the Jabra BT200, it's 0000.

5. Launch iChat AV.

6. Visit iChat → Preferences → Video (because you'd expect to find the audio settings under the video preferences, right?).

7. Set the Microphone and Sound Output pop-up menus to your headset, as shown previously in Figure 5-41.

8. Start talking to your buddies.

Thankfully, all those steps have to be done only the first time; after that, when necessary, you'll simply be prompted to pair the device again, as shown in Figure 5-43.

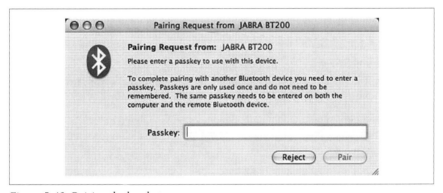

Figure 5-43. Pairing the headset

Don't believe that line about "Passkeys are only used once and do not need to be remembered"; you'll need to repeat this step every time you turn off the headset (which includes recharging it) or go out of Bluetooth range and come back again. And even though your Mac knows that it's a headset and that you can't enter a passkey on a headset, it'll tell you that "[t]he same passkey needs to be entered on both the computer and the remote Blue-tooth device," so be sure to remember your passkey!

iChatting with Bluetooth

Finally, you've got everything set up, just the way you want it, and you'll find that it works well, although not perfectly. If you've used iChat before, you'll find that the greatest new feature is being able to pace while chatting—no more having to talk directly into your iSight or PowerBook's microphone. And the combination of iChat, an iSight, and your Bluetooth headset is the virtual equivalent of VOIP calling.

I got mixed reports from the people I chatted with about the relative audio quality. While they all agreed that the headset was considerably better than my 15" PowerBook's built-in microphone, they split just about evenly on whether the headset was better or worse than the iSight's mic. The most common evaluation was that the two were fairly even in quality but their tone was different, and different people preferred one over the other (sometimes strongly).

I was hoping that the headset would clear up what I consider to be iChat AV's greatest failing: the echo effect. It's distracting to hear everything I say repeated on the other end. The good news is that the headset does kill off the echo. The bad news is that it kills it off for the person you're chatting with, not you. So, you'll still hear an echo, but the person on the other end won't. Consequently, I found that I got the greatest enjoyment from the headset when I gave it to someone else to use while I was chatting with them.

You'll also want to be careful how you seat the headset in and around your ear; while it's supposed to fit everyone, nothing that's one-size-fits-all ever quite does. Proper positioning of both the earbud and the mic improves the quality of both the sound input and output.

Final Thoughts

If it's important to you (as it is to me) to pace while you talk, you owe it to yourself to get a Bluetooth headset to use with iChat AV. If you don't currently have any audio input to your Mac and you already have Bluetooth, this is a simple way to be able to start audio chatting.

But beyond that, this technology is still not quite there yet. The big benefits, I found, were those available when I gave the headset to others to use instead of me: primarily, the end of the echo issue (on my end). I also had access to other sound input (internal PowerBook mic, iSight) and the recipient (with a tower) didn't, allowing us to audio chat for the first time.

Eventually, Apple will support features such as speakable items and voice recognition. In the long run, we'll get functionality that will let your Mac/cellphone/headset interoperate, such that you can be listening to quality music on your headset until a phone call comes in. At that point, iTunes will pause, caller ID will show up on your Mac to say who's calling, and you'll be able to take that call via the headset. While we're close, we're not quite there yet.

(Thanks to Tom, Matt, Al, Chug, Steven, Eric, Lynn, Chuck, and Dan for help with the audio tests.)

—*Dori Smith*

HACK #58 Print Without Wires

WiFi Internet and long battery life have freed us from the wires that bind us while we work on our laptops—except, that is, when we want to print. Here's how to cut the printing umbilical cord and generate documents with wireless freedom.

Panther is WiFi savvy and Bluetooth adept. Generally, we think of these protocols for file transfer and Internet connection. But doesn't it seem silly to browse the Web from any chair in your home, touch base with friends via iChat, send pictures from your camera phone to your laptop—all wirelessly—then have to go plug in to print this stuff?

You don't have to. Both Rendezvous and Bluetooth enable wireless printing. At the moment, one works better than the other, but I'll show you both and let you choose.

Rendezvous Printing

If you're using an AirPort Base Station for your wireless network, you can connect an inkjet printer to the Base Station and enable network connectivity. All AirPort Extreme Base Stations have the magical USB port in the back. Via this port, you can plug in your printer and enjoy wireless freedom.

The printer is accessible not only to you, but also to anyone you allow on your AirPort network. This is far and away the easiest way to share one printer among many. Here's how to set it up:

1. Connect your inkjet printer to the USB port on the back of your AirPort Extreme Base Station and turn it on.

2. Load the printer drivers on every Mac that will be accessing this printer on the network. If the drivers aren't loaded, folks will be able to see the printer on the network, but they won't be able to use it.

3. Log into the AirPort network and make sure Rendezvous is active. The easiest way to check this is to launch iChat and enable Rendezvous mode (iChat → Log into Rendezvous).

4. Open the Printer Setup Utility in your Utilities folder. Click the Add Printer icon and select Rendezvous from the drop-down menu, as shown in Figure 5-44. After a few seconds of searching, your printer should now appear in the list under Name.

5. Click on the printer name to highlight it, and then select the appropriate driver from the Printer Model drop-down list. Then, click the Add button.

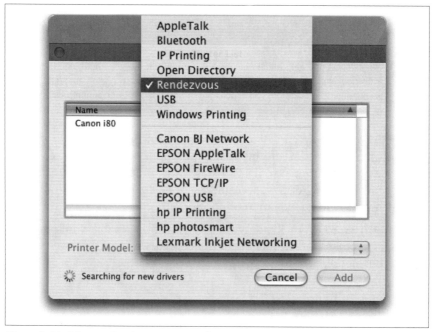

Figure 5-44. Selecting Rendezvous to reveal a printer on the network

Your little ole inkjet printer is fully networked and ready to use. Open an application, make sure the Rendezvous printer is selected in the Page Setup and Print dialog boxes, and send a test page. Within seconds, your printer will start churning away, obeying your command.

The beauty of this configuration is that Rendezvous is simply serving as an alternative to your USB cable. Your Mac is using the printer-specified drivers that you loaded and only the connection has changed.

Unfortunately, Bluetooth printing isn't quite as refined yet, as you'll see now.

Bluetooth Printing

Bluetooth-enabled printers are easier to find these days, especially among the smaller inkjet varieties for mobile computing. I've been working with the

Canon i80 mobile printer (*http://www.usa.canon.com*) that offers an accessory Bluetooth module (BU-10). The i80 is Panther-compatible, and its drivers offer Mac users plenty of functionally, including borderless printing of photographs.

Also included in the software bundle is the i80 Setup Utility. Make sure you have this loaded on your Mac, because you can use it to change your passkey when you set up pairing between the printer and Bluetooth devices, including your mobile phone, PDA, and Mac.

Speaking of your Mac, Bluetooth printing wasn't enabled with the original shipment of Panther. Be sure you've updated your Bluetooth software to Version 1.5 or later. If you haven't done so already, you can download the update from Apple's web site (*http://www.apple.com/bluetooth*). Of course, your Mac needs Bluetooth connectivity in the first place. If you don't have a built-in module, you can purchase the D-Link Bluetooth USB adapter from the Apple Store.

Before you get too excited about Bluetooth printing, however, I should tell you that it works much better with my mobile devices than with the Mac. I've successfully printed text and images from a Sony Ericsson Z600 mobile phone and Palm Tungsten T2 PDA; both are Bluetooth-enabled. I have also printed from the Mac, but I haven't been able to control the formatting as well as I would like.

The challenge with Bluetooth printing on the Mac, unlike with Rendezvous, is that many printer manufacturers don't have their own Bluetooth drivers for Mac OS X yet and depend instead on Common Unix Printing System (CUPS) and Gimp-Print drivers. Over time, I'm sure manufacturers such as Canon will offer their own Mac Bluetooth drivers, but if your printer doesn't have one available, you need to use CUPS and Gimp-Print. You can download the latest version from the SourceForge web site (*http://gimp-print.sourceforge.net/MacOSX.php3*). Currently the drivers work for Epson, Canon, Lexmark, and HP printers.

As of this writing, the most stable version of Gimp-Print is 4.2.6. It does enable communication with Canon's i80, but formatting is not "what you see on the screen is what you get on the paper." Over time, I think these issues will be resolved. So, in that optimistic spirit, I'll walk you through the setup procedure:

1. Make sure Bluetooth is enabled on your Mac (System Preferences → Bluetooth → Turn Bluetooth On; the button should show as Turn Bluetooth Off if Bluetooth is already on) and the printer is turned on.

2. Open the Printer Setup Utility (Utilities → Printer Setup Utility) and click the Add printer icon (the one with a printer and + sign).

3. Select Bluetooth from the drop-down menu. Your Mac searches for Bluetooth-enabled printers within range and list them. When it finds your printer, it asks your for the passkey so that the two devices can trust and pair with one another, as shown in Figure 5-45.

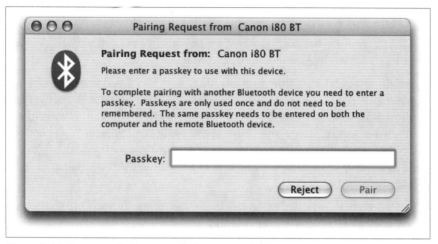

Figure 5-45. Pairing with the printer before it's available

4. Enter your printer's passkey. If you don't know what it is, try the default (0000); that works more often than not. If it doesn't work, launch the Canon's i80 Setup Utility to establish your passkey with the printer. Once you've paired with the printer, it appears in the list of available printers.

5. Click on the name of the printer to highlight it, and then choose a driver from the Printer Model drop-down list. Chances are, you won't have a specific driver for your computer as you did with Rendezvous printing. Select any of the versions of the CUPS+Gimp-Print drivers available, as shown in Figure 5-46.

6. Click the Add button. Your printer should now be available for Bluetooth printing.

You might want to distinguish the name of this setup with others, just so you know which is the regular USB connection and which are the connections for Rendezvous and Bluetooth. You can do this by clicking the printer name again in the Print Setup Utility and clicking the Show Info button. The Printer Name field is editable, enabling you to give it a descriptive label.

Since we're early in the Bluetooth printing game, your results will vary from printer to printer. The good news is that the drivers will come and soon Bluetooth printing with a Mac will be as reliable as the Rendezvous and USB connections.

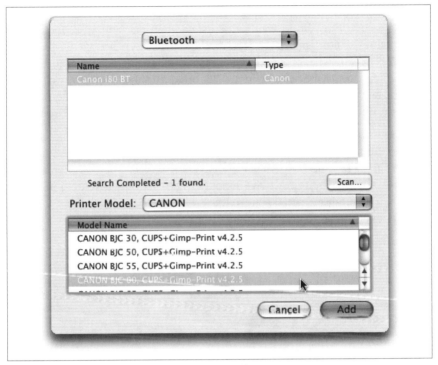

Figure 5-46. Choosing a driver to enable Bluetooth printing

In the meantime, mobile phones and PDAs seem to work quite well with these printers, and you have lots to keep you busy while you wait for refinement of the Mac drivers.

—Derrick Story

Zip, Zap, and Sync Your Gizmos

Charge and sync your gizmos without toting that weighty and ungainly tangle of chargers, cradles, and cables. Behold the magic—and power—of USB.

Just as Bluetooth [Hacks #86 and #58] is finally coming into its own as dongle replacement (USB replacement in particular), I've been coming to see USB as Bluetooth with power, suffering only from a mild but tolerable bit of tethering.

> I should give fair warning that this hack will be chock-full of D and Z words like *dongle*, *doodad*, *gizmo*, and *whizbang*. I assure you, this is the unavoidable side effect of the subject at hand and does not reflect what you should expect to find in any of the other hacks or O'Reilly books in general.

Zip, Zap, and Sync Your Gizmos

I'm a gadgeteer, pockets bulging and pack consistently laden with cell-phones, PDAs, FireWire drives, cameras, camcorders, and USB doodads of many shapes, colors, and purposes. And as if these gizmos weren't enough to tote around, each comes with its own set of chargers, cradles, and bales of sync cables—some, like the Palm cradle, bulkier than the gizmo itself. With both the additional dimensions and heft to consider, these really do count in large amounts—not to mention that they alarm airport security personnel.

For a few months now, though, I've been carrying a lighter load. Rather than lug all those heavy charging bricks, cradles, and cables, I have a fistful of whizbang Zip-Linq (*http://www.ziplinq.com*) cables. These miniature marvels stretch out to an impressive 30 inches or so, yet only take up 4 inches or so in their natural, retracted state (Figure 5-47), which makes them fit easily in the pockets of cargo pants or laptop bags.

Figure 5-47. A typical Zip-Linq cable—in this case, a 6-to-6 pin FireWire

Zip-Linqs come in an assortment of types and subtypes. There are USB (*http://www.ziplinq.com/retractable-cable-usb.html*) A-to-Bs for printers, A-to-Mini USB 4s and 5s for digital cameras and MP3 players, and A-to-As for extending your reach even further. FireWire Zip-Linqs (*http://www.ziplinq.com/retractable-cable-firewire.html*) connect DV camcorders to multimedia PCs and connect drives to laptops and to each other. The RJ-12, RJ-45, and RJ-45 (*http://www.ziplinq.com/retractable-cable-modular.html*) crossovers mean never having to say you can't reach the phone or data jack. Leave that USB cradle behind and sync your PDA (*http://www.ziplinq.com/retractable-cable-pda.html*)—iPAQ, Palm, or Blackberry, to name but a few—through your laptop's USB port. And that's just for openers.

While I'm always in a personal area network of Bluetooth, WiFi, IR, and GPRS, I'm now a rather comical sketch of tethered power, a Zip-Linq or three draped over a laptop, hanging out of a bag, or thrown over a shoulder.

"So," I hear you saying, "I get that they're handy, but why's this guy getting so worked up over something as trivial as cables?"

Well, there's power in these little beauties—quite literally.

The Power in PowerBook

In various meetings, gatherings, and social visits, I keep finding folks con-fused by the concept, delighted by the prospect, or just not knowing that there's more in a USB cable than data. There's also a trickle of power (around 5V DC), enough to charge your cellphone, PDA, or other gadget you might not have thought of charging the USB way.

Think of your laptop as an occasionally AC-connected battery for your mobile devices.

 You'll want to be sure, whenever possible, to plug in your laptop; otherwise, you'll find out rather quickly that even a trickle of charge shared here or there can drain even the har-diest of laptop batteries in no time flat.

Settling in for the night at a strange hotel in an even stranger city? Plug your laptop into the power outlet and share the restorative power with your PDA and cellphone, one per USB port, and iPod off a FireWire port; Figure 5-48 shows my Sony Ericsson P900 with the Zip-Linq cellphone charger cable and various handset-specific connectoids. There's no need to comb the room for spare power outlets. In the morning, all will be charged (don't for-get to sync that PDA while you're at it) and ready for another day, another city. And you won't have to waste precious time or precoffee thought searching every nook and cranny of your room for strays before checking out.

You'll need a Charge-N-Sync (*http://www.ziplinq.com/retractable-cable-pda.html*) cable for each PDA, a cellphone charger (get a full set at *http://www.ziplinq.com/retractable-cable-cell.html* or see *http://www.keyspan.com/cables/homepage.Cell.spml* for handset-specific kits) per phone, and a FireWire 6-6 (*http://www.ziplinq.com/retractable-cable-firewire.html*) for the iPod.

 Be sure to choose the right cellphone package for your handset. While each comes with interchangeable heads to fit a number of popular brands, Kit 1 supports Ericsson, Motorola, Nokia, and Siemens (see the compatibility chart at *http://www.ziplinq.com/m01-compatibility.html*), while Kit 2 supports Samsung, Kyocera, LG Mobile, Sanyo, and Motorola (compatibility chart at *http://www.ziplinq.com/m02-compatibility.html*). Also, Kit 1 includes a 6V booster for some phone models, while some Nokia models need a 9V boost, available separately.

Figure 5-48. My various cellphones siphon power nightly from my PowerBook thanks to the Zip-Linq cellphone charger kit

Managed to convince your significant other to put up with your Palm Tungsten T3 and Nokia phone on your holidays, but your power brick (iBook, that is) is a no-no? Don't bother digging about in your discarded dongle drawer for that disused cradle and one anonymous adapter among several. Pick up the handy-dandy Zip-Linq AC Wall Adapter and/or 12V DC (*http:// www.ziplinq.com/retractable-cable-pwr.html*), shown in Figure 5-49, for regular outlet or auto/boat/RV cigarette lighter, respectively.

Figure 5-49. Simulating 5V of USB power with a wall or auto adapter

Your phone's running low on juice while you await that all-important call at your local coffee shop; what's a gadget geek to do? Look around for someone with a laptop—even a Windows laptop will do, if you can stand being seen within 30 feet of one—and make a new friend while grabbing a quick trickle of charge.

 Just be sure to disconnect and wander off when you answer that call; otherwise, you're liable to be considered both a power leech and just plain annoying.

This also works if you've visiting any friend with a free USB port on her laptop or Desktop. All you need on you is the cellphone charger (*http:// www.ziplinq.com/retractable-cable-cell.html*) and appropriate snap-on attachment for your phone.

Set up a one-wire network [Mac OS X Hacks, Hack #69], Mac-to-Mac over RJ-45 FireWire (6-6 pin, *http://www.ziplinq.com/retractable-cable-firewire.html*) or RJ-45 Ethernet, Mac-to-PC over Ethernet, or PC-to-PC over crossover RJ-45 (*http://www.ziplinq.com/retractable-cable-modular.html*).

Or, just limit the tangled web your Mac and assorted devices weave on your Desktop, replacing those super-long and unnecessarily thick cables with the thin, just-the-right-length goodness of Zip-Linq.

They range in price from around $10 for a USB cable to $20 for a cellphone kit. Pick them up piecemeal at your local computer superstore. They're unevenly distributed at best; I've never found the full set at a single store. Or go whole hog at your favorite e-tailer; Zip-Linq themselves and the always Mac-friendly Keyspan (*http://www.keyspan.com/products/homepage-Cables.spml*) provide links to the usual (Zones, CDW, etc.) and not so usual suspects.

I really can't say enough about these little wonders. And now that I have put it all down in writing, everyone will be glad to know I'll be saying less about them in person. ;-)

Hacking the Hack

PowerBook 12" users, don't forget to grab one of the A-to-A extenders (*http:// www.ziplinq.com/retractable-cable-usb.html*), because some cellphones (the Nokia 3650, for example) require the 6V booster, which gets in the way of the second USB port. You can make it work with a wiggle and a shove, but it's a tight squeeze and might put undue stress on your USB ports.

Add more zing to your zip when you're away from an outlet by plugging your laptop into an external battery pack. A friend of mine is rather happy with his Electrovaya Powerpad 160 (*http://www.electrovaya.com*), to name just one possibility. It delivers 19V, 160 Watt hours, powering his Power-Book for 12 to 15 hours. Plug it into your laptop's power jack—it pretends to be a DC Apple power supply—and soak up and share the power with your Zip-Linq'd devices.

And for when you run out of USB ports—you know you will, when you start charging your friends' cellphones and their friends' PDAs—pack one of those mini USB hubs and do a little daisy chaining. My favorite (and not because it glows blue, but that's a plus) is the harmonica-like Macally 4 Port MiniHub (*http://www.macally.com/spec/usb/connecting_device/hubmini.html*).

HACK #60   iOscillate

Get in enough face time with your fans by means of an iSight, an oscillating fan, a little ingenuity, and a well-developed sense of play.

If you've ever actually tried to do any video-conferencing using iChat and an iSight (or equivalent camera [Hack #34]), you've no doubt found that it works surprisingly well. Sure, there are sound hiccups and video burps, but most of these can be ameliorated. Add a tad more bandwidth (e.g., DSL instead of 56K modem dialup). Don't download large MP3 files during the call. Shutting off email stems the tide of those large attachments washing in from the office. Or simply use an actual telephone (gasp!) for audio.

But try it with a roomful of people spread unevenly around a conference table and you're sure to find yourself staring at a stray notepad, box of tissues, hopelessly out-of-date organizational chart, or the one person in the room not saying a thing or moving a muscle. Now, you'd think some kind-hearted soul would move the camera every so often, pointing it at least at another unmoving, unblinking participant or different notepad; they probably won't. You'd hope someone would be nominated to or just take charge of pointing the camera at whoever is speaking; it doesn't usually happen. Even when talking directly to the poor schlub on the far end of the call, people will actually stare at the side of the camera, as if doing so somehow provided more presence.

So, what's a telecommuter with poor iSight to do? Why, oscillate, of course.

An iSight mounted to the top of debladed oscillating fan, as shown in Figure 5-50, sweeps out up to a 180-degree field of view. While this doesn't mean you're necessarily going to be looking at the person speaking for more than a split second or so, it does provide more of a sense of actually being there—albeit in an admittedly nauseating fashion.

Intrigued? I was too when the idea first struck, so I set about building one.

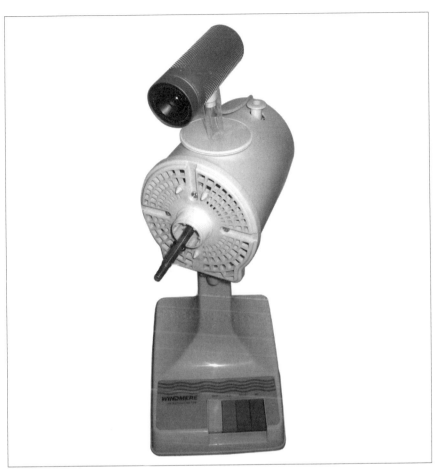

Figure 5-50. iSight + oscillating fan = iOscillate

Building an iOscillate

Throwing together an iOscillate of your very own is trivial, eating up a scant 15 minutes or so. It requires little in the way of parts, and no tools are necessary.

Prepare the fan. Appropriate a disused or otherwise available oscillating fan—probably not best done on the hottest day of the summer.

Strip it of its blade and metal or plastic cage. Your average Walmart unit ships with these parts preremoved for your convenience. If it's already assembled, disassembly usually entails only two or three steps and requires no tools. Unclip the cage edges to separate the front portion. Unscrew the nose (usually clockwise in the U.S.) that holds the blade in place and remove the blade. Unscrew the washer that holds the back portion of the cage in place and remove it. If possible, replace the nose so that the spinning metal shaft doesn't hurt anyone.

Mount the camera. Attach one of the various plastic connectoids that came with your iSight or other webcam to the top of the fan. I found that the flat, sticky-based iMac mount worked nicely with my iSight.

You can even just use Scotch or duct tape if all else fails. This, however, does mean that it'll be difficult to impossible to point the camera up or down as needed to catch the faces rather than ties or toupees of the participants.

Try to keep the camera itself away from the fan, to avoid vibration and cut down on the noise of the motor (if your webcam has a built-in microphone).

Do make sure that the camera is upright. And whatever you do, don't even think of strapping it to the soon-to-be-spinning metal shaft.

Run the USB or FireWire cable. Drape or stick down the webcam's USB or FireWire cable in such a way that it has more than enough play yet is well clear of the metal shaft that is used to turn the blade, the mechanics involved in oscillation of the fan head, and anything else electro-mechanical on the fan.

That's all there is to building this wondrous Rube Goldberg device (*http://www.rube-goldberg.com*). Let's give it a whirl, shall we?

Oscillating

Place this contraption on a conference table, such that it is most likely to provide a sweeping view of all participants—not to mention the occasional glimpse of that gorgeous oak tree outside the window. This generally works best with all participants arranged in an arc slightly shorter than 180 degrees, close enough together so that the camera doesn't try to focus on the wall behind when there's a wide enough gap between two people.

Hook the iOscillate up to a Mac (or PC if compatible), orienting the screen so that most of the participants can see the person on the other end of the line.

Start your engines!—or sufficiently quiet, steady, and well-geared motor. While the speed setting you choose should have no bearing on oscillation, I did find that my fan's High setting made for a smoother ride.

Fire up iChat or the equivalent and ring your remote peer.

You might suggest he pop some Dramamine or wear those oddly effective seasickness wristbands. These things do whiz along at quite a clip and the camera can sometimes get confused while trying to maintain focus.

Hacking the Hack

Picking your oscillating fan is key. While any old fan will do, if you're going to go out and buy one—really you shouldn't, not unless you're hot, that is—you might see if you can find one with an adjustable oscillation speed. Also, pay attention to the vibration-to-dollar ratio of some of the cheapest models.

A friend suggested actually leaving the fan blade and cage assembly intact, so as to actually cool the participants and make for a nice, wind-blown supermodel effect. If you mount the webcam behind the cage, know that the blades will confuse the iSight's autofocus to no end. If you mount it to the top, you'll find it vibrates considerably and there's a risk of catching some part of the USB or FireWire cable in the blade.

For a decidedly manual version of this hack, try placing your webcam on a lazy Susan: that revolving tray one finds in the center of large round dining tables. You'll still have to remember to aim the camera at whoever is talking, but it then becomes a group endeavor (and makes for a smoother ride than the usual jiggly reorientation). Place the laptop that's hosting the session next to the camera so that participants can see to whom they are speaking. Put the speakerphone on the tray too for greater sound quality on the listener's end. Or, if it's a lunch meeting, use it as intended: to pass the Kung Pao and rice.

Networking and Network Apps
Hacks 61–67

The ubiquity of networking—both locally and worldwide—has made it the killer application for the computer. In fact, there's something quite lonely about using a computer that isn't networked. The only time it is remotely palatable is when you are stuck on an airplane. (And soon you may even be able to get easy WiFi access at 30,000 feet.) Mac OS X has opened its doors to an ever-widening collection of protocols while stitching them all together in as seamless a way as possible. Rendezvous makes local networking that much easier by removing any need for configuration whatsoever. Mac provides a home on the Net for backing up and syncing, not to mention housing your home page and allowing you to share files without needing a server of your own. Add third-party applications for collaboration to the mix and you all but erase the already fine distinction between your Desktop and those of others.

HACK #61 Share Your Address Book and iCal

Use iSync's machine-to-machine synchronization to share your Address Book and iCal calendars with your boss, assistant, spouse, or housemates (if you're just that close).

iCal's publish-and-subscribe feature is all well and good if only one person "owns" a particular calendar and everyone else is accorded read-only access. This doesn't work particularly well, though, when you have two people who both need to actively maintain the same calendar—boss and assistant, for instance. While each can "own" their own and subscribe to the other's, this doesn't allow for the boss to reschedule, cancel, or otherwise alter appointments set by her assistant (a good thing, perhaps) and vice versa. And there's currently no way to share an Address Book by publish-and-subscribe, Rendezvous (as with iTunes), or otherwise.

One workaround is for this group of two or more persons (beyond two, though, things get a little out of hand) to "co-own" the same set of iCal calendars, To Do Lists, and Address Books. With a little clever tweaking, you can keep the assistant's and his boss's computer in perfect sync, propagating changes between iCal and Address Book on each machine every hour.

iSync

iSync isn't just for syncing between your laptop and PDA or Bluetooth-enabled cellphone. Its core use is to sync iCal, Address Book, and Safari bookmarks with .Mac, Apple's online service for Mac folk. .Mac also acts as a middleman for one's contacts, calendars, to-do lists, and bookmarks in sync between two or more computers (e.g., between a G5 at work, eMac at home, and iBook on the road), but it lends itself rather well to the boss/assistant situation at hand. But who says all these computers—and the .Mac account itself—have to be owned by just one person?

Aye, there's the hack.

Buy one .Mac account. For illustrative purposes, let's pretend you choose *the_boss*. Set up the boss's and assistant's machines to use the same .Mac account. Visit the .Mac tab of the .Mac System Preferences pane. Fill in the .Mac account name and password, as shown in Figure 6-1.

Figure 6-1. Setting both machines to use the same .Mac account

As an added bonus, you can share an iDisk between you, automatically synchronizing important documents, driving directions, and anything else on the iDisk between the two machines and .Mac. To do so, click the iDisk tab, check "Create a local copy of your iDisk," and choose automatic or manual syncing (the former means you'll never have to remember to sync), as shown in Figure 6-2. Close System Preferences when you're finished.

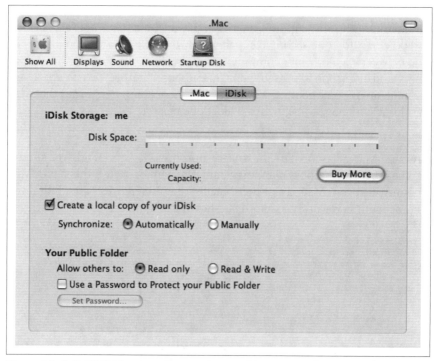

Figure 6-2. Split 50 MB between the two of you and keep in sync by sharing an iDisk

Open iSync (*Applications/iSync*) and click the .Mac icon to open the iSync .Mac configuration drawer. Before you can sync, you'll have to register each of the computers with the shared .Mac account. Give each a memorable name—something obvious, like *Assistant* for the assistant's (as shown in Figure 6-3) and *Boss* for the boss's. Click the Continue button and wait a moment or two while the computer introduces itself to .Mac.

When you're done, you'll be dropped into the iSync .Mac configuration drawer proper, as shown in Figure 6-4. For the first sync, you'll most likely want to merge what you have on your computer with what's already on . Mac, if anything. Check the "Automatically synchronize every hour" checkbox so that you don't have to synchronize manually (and avoid the

Figure 6-3. Registering the assistant's account

risk of forgetting to do so). Make sure the "Address Book Contacts" and "iCal Calendars and To Do items" checkboxes are checked. (You'll probably want to uncheck Safari Bookmarks so that each of you can maintain your own list of favorite sites.)

Click the .Mac icon in iSync again to close the configuration drawer. Click the Sync Now button and wait until the sync finishes.

Then, do the same thing on the other system. From here on out, any change made to an iCal Calendar entry, To Do item, or Address Book Contact will automatically flow through .Mac to the other computer—and vice versa.

 Bear in mind that syncing happens only once an hour, which means there might be a period of an hour or so when the boss doesn't know her assistant's moved an appointment or the assistant doesn't know his boss has gone ahead and cancelled it. Don't assume short-notice changes get through in time; pick up the phone and confirm.

Address Book Proviso

The Address Book has the concept of designating the entry (known as a *card*) that contains the contact information for the owner of the Mac as *My*

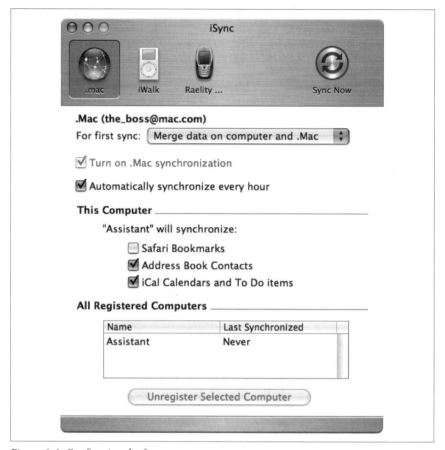

Figure 6-4. Configuring the first sync

Card. To claim one of the Address Book entries as your card, first you'll
have to find it among the other cards. Either scroll through the list or press
⌘-F, and then enter your name in the Find box to search for it. Select your
card in the middle pane and choose Make This My Card from Address
Book's Card menu, as shown in Figure 6-5.

> *Only one of you should do this*—most likely, the boss. Other-
> wise, with each subsequent .Mac sync, you'll fight a battle
> over whose Address Book card takes precedence; in each
> case, the most recently selected one wins. You'll both be
> either the boss or the assistant, depending on who chose last.

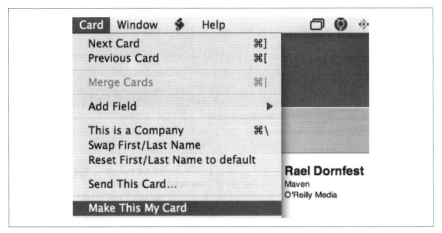

Figure 6-5. Identifying an entry as My Card in Address Book

This is the one big proviso, so if there's anything in this process you should be sure to remember, it's this.

iChat Proviso

Now, this little proviso affects you only if you both use iChat or AIM. Your .Mac account comes with one iChat/AIM login—in this example, *the_boss@mac.com*. You can't both use that one login, especially not at the same time. For one, you'll confuse the heck out of any of your buddies. You'll also end up sharing the same buddy list—again, not a good thing. And finally, while iChat/AIM does allow you to be logged in from more than one location (read: machine) simultaneously, you'll both see every incoming message without being able to talk to one another; this is enough to drive anyone mad.

The solution is for only one of you (in this case, the boss) to use the .Mac AIM/iChat login. The other person (the assistant) should sign up for a free AIM account; point your browser at *http://my.screenname.aol.com/*, click the Get a Screen Name link, fill out the form shown in Figure 6-6, and register for one.

iChat's tendency is to want to use the AIM name associated with your Address Book card as its login name. This is just fine for the one account (the boss's), but it won't work for the other person (the assistant). The latter needs to visit iChat → Preferences... → Accounts and enter his newly registered AIM name and password as the account to use for iChat. Each time he logs into iChat thereafter, he'll be correctly identified by his AIM name and have a Buddy List of his very own.

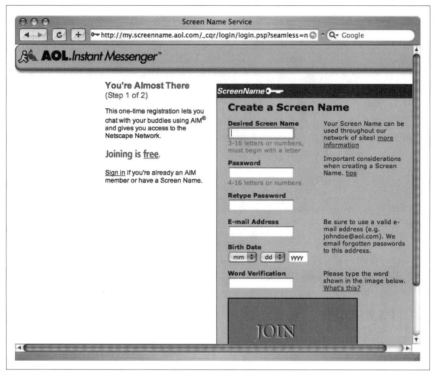

Figure 6-6. Signing up the second person for an AIM account

Hacking the Hack

iSync isn't just for syncing machines and .Mac accounts; the boss's and assistant's shared Address Book and iCal spaces can be extended out to any cellphones, PDAs, or even iPods they own.

HACK #62 Collaborative Editing with Rendezvous

Using Rendezvous-based collaborative editing tools, you can share the job of taking notes at a meeting with a peer or build an augmented transcript of a conference session with those around you.

Rendezvous is an intriguing technology that simplifies certain networking tasks in Mac OS X. It allows you to connect to the network and use services offered by other devices on the network, all without any of the usual messy configurations (see the sidebar, "How Rendezvous Works," for an explanation of how Rendezvous works).

One of the innovative uses of Rendezvous is collaborative editing, which allows multiple users to edit a document simultaneously through the

How Rendezvous Works

The first step toward understanding how Rendezvous works is to realize that every device, including your Mac or a printer, that participates in a wired or wireless network must have an IP address. This IP address can be allocated from a DHCP server or it can be self-assigned. When a device participates in a network without having an IP address (due to the absence of DHCP or an explicit self-assignment), Rendezvous automatically assigns an IP address by using local-link addressing. Basically, Rendezvous randomly assigns an IP address from a predetermined range of addresses—set aside for local-link addressing by the Internet Assigned Numbers Authority (IANA)—and assigns it to the device. The IP address range used by Rendezvous is 169.254/16.

The device then broadcasts a message to all other devices on the network to see if its IP address has already been used by another device. If it has already been used, Rendezvous assigns another IP address and the procedure repeats. If it has not already been used, the IP address is assigned and the device is ready to communicate with other devices on the network.

network. In this hack, I introduce two collaborative-editing tools, SubEthaEdit and iStorm, and talk about their various features.

Collaborative Editing with SubEthaEdit

One of the challenges of working in a group is maintaining version control on the documents that are created. SubEthaEdit from The Coding Monkeys (formed by a group of three computer-science students) redefines the meaning of collaborative work. Using SubEthaEdit, multiple users can edit a single document at the same time. SubEthaEdit uses Rendezvous to discover other users who need to edit the same document.

You can download SubEthaEdit from *http://www.codingmonkeys.de*. Once you have successfully installed SubEthaEdit, an icon will appear on your Desktop.

You can start editing your document at the text-editing area. To share this document with someone using Rendezvous, click on the Share button (see Figure 6-7).

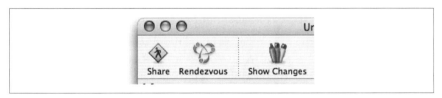

Figure 6-7. Sharing a document

SubEthaEdit reveals the access control list that shows the people who are currently editing this document, as shown in Figure 6-8.

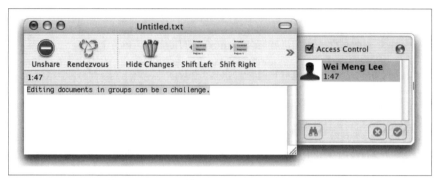

Figure 6-8. Viewing the access control list

Other users who want to share the task of editing the document also need to run SubEthaEdit. To see which document is being shared, click on the Rendezvous button. Figure 6-9 shows that Wei Meng Lee is editing a document called *Untitled.txt*.

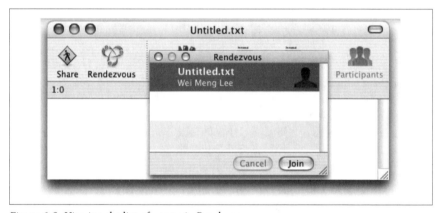

Figure 6-9. Viewing the list of users via Rendezvous

Double-click on the document you want to edit, and your name appears in the access control list of the document master, as shown in Figure 6-10. The document master simply selects the username and clicks on the check (to allow access) or cross (to deny access) buttons.

By default, text that any user types is highlighted with a pink background. To differentiate your text, go to SubEthaEdit → Preferences and set your own color. You can now use the different background colors to differentiate who typed what, as shown in Figure 6-11.

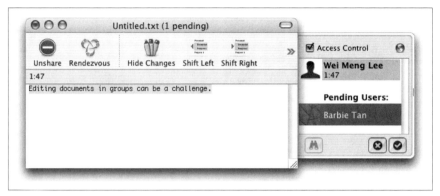

Figure 6-10. Granting (or denying) permissions to a user

Figure 6-11. Multiple users editing a document

Multiple people can now edit the same document simultaneously.

> SubEthaEdit, formerly known as Hydra, was a first-place win-
> ner in the second Mac OS X Innovators Contest. You can
> learn more about the application and its creators by reading an
> interview with one of the Coding Monkeys, Martin Pittenauer
> (*http://www.macdevcenter.com/pub/a/mac/developer/2003/08/
> 20/innovators.html*).

Brainstorming with iStorm

iStorm is a collaborative-editing tool from Math Game House Software. It is
similar to SubEthaEdit and is available for download at *http://www.
mathgamehouse.com/istorm/*. The trial version allows users to collaborate for
20 minutes; pricing starts at $10 per user for the unlimited version.

Once iStorm is downloaded and installed, you should see a familiar editing window with a few buttons at the top. Figure 6-12 highlights the significant buttons.

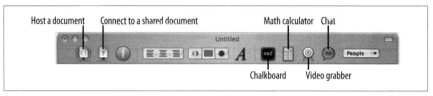

Figure 6-12. The various buttons in the iStorm window

To share the document with other users, simply click the "Host a document" button (the one of the far left in Figure 6-13).

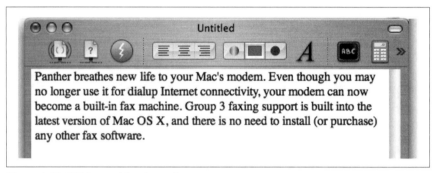

Figure 6-13. Editing and hosting a document

iStorm then asks you for some information, such as the document name and your name, as well as your server information (you can just accept the defaults). To share the document, click Serve (see Figure 6-14). Your Mac is now be the hosting computer for this document.

At the bottom of the screen, you should see a green button (see Figure 6-15 and just trust me that it's green ;-). The green button signifies that the document is available for editing. Since, at the moment, you are the only one editing the document, you have full control over the document.

Let's assume that another user is using iStorm on another Mac. To edit the shared document, the user just needs to click on the "Connect to a shared document" button (the second button from the left in Figure 6-15). The user will be shown which documents are available for editing, as shown in Figure 6-16. Select the document you want to use and click Connect.

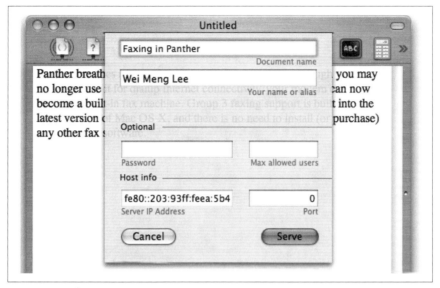

Figure 6-14. Sharing the document

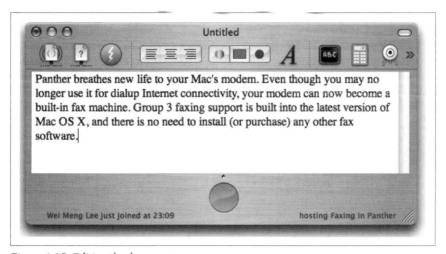

Figure 6-15. Editing the document

By default, iStorm uses Rendezvous to locate other users on the local network. You can disable Rendezvous and manually enter the IP address and port number of the hosting computer.

Figure 6-16. Connecting to a shared document

Notice that, once you start editing your document, the button turns blue (see Figure 6-17), signaling that you have gained control of the editing rights of the document. In the meantime, other users will see a red button, which means the document is currently being modified by someone (see Figure 6-18). To release the editing right of the document so that others can edit it, click on the blue button; it will change to green (see Figure 6-19), which means the document is free to be edited by others.

> Thankfully, iStorm supplements its color-coordination with labels ("your name," "being modified by…," and "up for Grabs"), both for color-blind persons and the purposes of making sense of it all in a two-color book such as this one.

One cool feature of iStorm is the *shared chalkboard*. To activate the shared chalkboard, click the Chalkboard button (see Figure 6-20). (I noticed that this window has some problems with the layout of the various controls, so you might need to make some adjustments before you can see the screenshot shown in the figure).

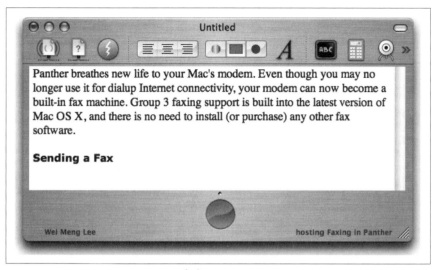

Figure 6-17. Blue—document currently being edited by yourself

Figure 6-18. Red—document being edited by someone else

Figure 6-19. Green—document available for edits

Another cool feature is Video Grabber, which allows you to use a video camera [Hack #34] to take snapshots of yourself. To take a snapshot of yourself, just drag and drop the Grab Video window (its content) onto your shared document. You can even use the snapshot as the background of your chalkboard, as shown in Figure 6-21.

Finally, you can also do the usual chatting stuff on iStorm (see Figure 6-22).

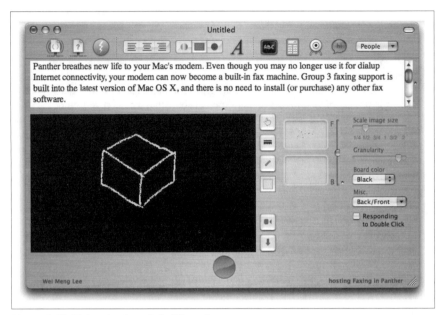

Figure 6-20. Using the shared chalkboard

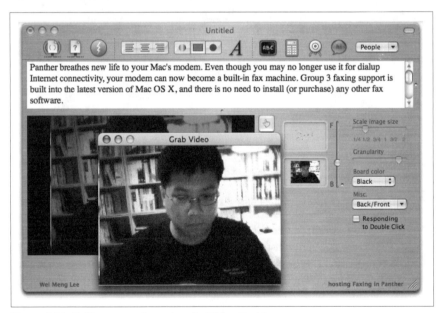

Figure 6-21. Taking a snapshot using the Video Grabber

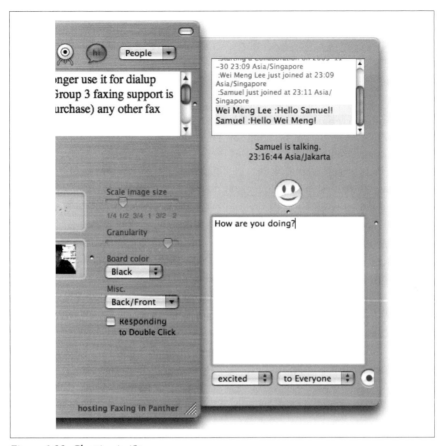

Figure 6-22. Chatting in iStorm

Final Thoughts

The nice thing about using a Mac is that you always have an abundance of innovative software to make your life easier and more pleasant. SubEthaEdit and iStorm are two applications I am going to use to collaborate with coworkers. Give them a try and let me know what you think.

—Wei Meng Lee

HACK #63 See Spike Share His Clipboard

Share text snippets, images, documents, and files of any type with Spike, a peer-to-peer networked clipboard.

The lion's share of talk around sharing (of the online sort) revolves around files—from Word documents to questionably legal MP3s and movies—of usually considerable content and often of large size. But it's the sharing of microcontent that I find most interesting. I'm talking about those bits and bobs of text, snippets of code, URLs, snail-mail addresses, and so forth that we think nothing of copying and pasting yet can't readily share with someone across the room or across the world.

Sure, you can just instant-message them over, but only if they're small enough and of limited formatting. That nicely formatted chunk of text from Microsoft Word will most likely choke iChat and simply not go due to size restrictions, or it will make it across yet appear to its receiver as plain text at best. You can email it, but that's a bit of work. There's all that saving, attaching, and addressing to do first—let alone creating a special temporary version of your document if you want to send only a piece of the whole. And it gets exponentially worse if you're doing more than the simplest collaboration.

Spike (*http://www.porchdogsoft.com/products/spike*) is a peer-to-peer networked clipboard that makes whatever you cut or copy available to those with whom you choose to share, whether across the room or across the seas. It runs on both Mac and Windows, over networks far and near, the latter thanks to the wonders of zero-configuration (aka Zeroconf or Rendezvous) networking.

The interface, shown in Figure 6-23, resembles an Open... dialog, with local and remote clipboards on the left and their contents on the right. Your History clipboard holds everything you've recently copied or cut, with older items falling off as newer ones are added (this history is configurable).

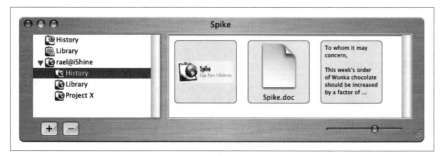

Figure 6-23. Sharing local and remote clipboards with Spike

The Library is a default permanent clipboard, where anything you copy to it is kept until explicitly deleted (using right- or Control-click → Delete). In Figure 6-23, notice my shared History, Library, and a Project X folder being shared from my shiny PowerBook.

Spike was written thoughtfully enough to allow for multiple instances running on the same machine. You'll see them show up as *username@machine* (e.g., *rael@emac* or *asha@emac*). Thus, Spike is just perfect for passing files and clippings between users of the same machine with ease.

Building on the clipboard metaphor, there's no need to explicitly drag things into the shared space to make them available; just Edit → Copy (⌘-C) or Edit → Cut (⌘-X) and they're shared, as if by magic. To borrow from a friend's shared clipboard, click it in Spike and Edit → Paste (⌘-V) or drag and drop it where you want it, as shown in Figure 6-24. Only when you paste or drag and drop is the content actually pulled from the shared space over the network, so as not to waste bandwidth for something you have available to you but might never end up using.

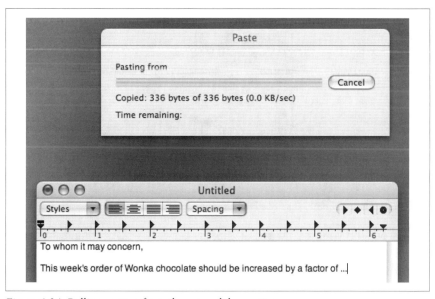

Figure 6-24. Pulling content from the network by pasting

In addition the default History and Library, you can create any number of your own shared clipboard spaces by clicking the + button. To add something to a particular clipboard, simply drag it there, as shown in Figure 6-25.

All of this is also rather configurable, from the size of the History and user-defined hotkey to what you're sharing. The Preferences pane is rather self-explanatory. You can choose to limit who has access to your clippings by assigning a global password to your Spike shares (Preferences → Network).

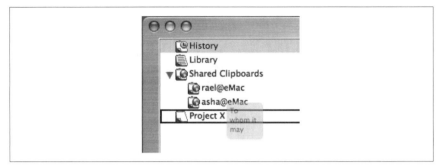

Figure 6-25. Dragging clippings to any user-defined clipboard

At the time of this writing, you cannot assign different passwords to different clipboards. You can, however, decide which clipboards to share and which to keep close to the vest. Right- or Control-click a local clipboard and check or uncheck Share (Figure 6-26) to share or not share it.

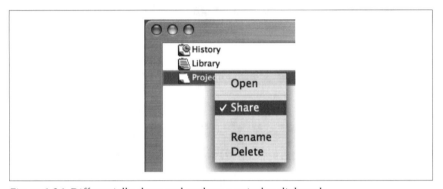

Figure 6-26. Differentially share and unshare particular clipboards

Spike works on your local wired or wireless network with absolutely no setup, thanks to Rendezvous. To get to a remote clipboard somewhere else in the world, you'll need to know its IP address and the port (think CB radio channel) on which it is running; ask the person running Spike at the other end for this information. That in hand, click the + button and select New Remote Clipboard... (or press ⌘-Shift-N), enter the IP address and port, and click Connect, as shown in Figure 6-27. If all goes to plan, you should see a new share (labeled with the IP address at which it lives) show up in Spike's left pane.

Before you can share your clipboard in kind with anyone on the Internet, you'll need to specify a port (Spike → Preferences... → Network → Specify port number) and make sure that port is open on your firewall and traffic is flowing to the appropriate Desktop or laptop computer on your local network. For that, I leave you in the hands of your local system administrator, Internet service provider, or firewall's manual.

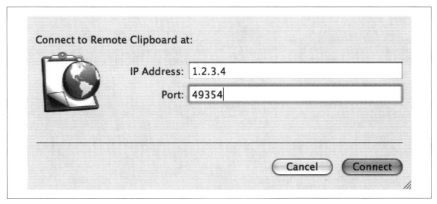

Figure 6-27. Connecting to a clipboard clear on the other side of the Net

Whether you're collaborating on a Keynote presentation with someone a continent away, leaving a phone number to be picked up later by someone on the same machine, or passing a note to yourself on the computer down in the basement, Spike scores a touchdown.

HACK #64 Detect Wireless Networks

Learn all about the networks available in your area.

If you are simply looking for an available wireless network to hop onto, you can usually get by with the built-in AirPort client. It does a decent job of telling you the public networks that you can connect to. But if you are trying to find out more than the ESSIDs of the networks in range, you need a more powerful tool. This hack presents three useful survey tools for OS X.

MacStumbler

Sharing nothing but a name with the popular NetStumbler (*http://www.stumbler.net*), MacStumbler (*http://www.macstumbler.com*) is probably the most popular network scanner for OS X. It is easy to use and provides the details that you are probably most interested in: available networks, the channels they use, and their received signal strength. It also displays received noise, whether WEP is enabled, and a bunch of other useful details, as shown in Figure 6-28.

Like many other OS X apps, MacStumbler is capable of text-to-speech, so it can even speak the ESSIDs of networks that it finds as they appear. Although it is still in beta, I have found MacStumbler to be a reliable tool. It currently supports network scanning with the built-in AirPort card only.

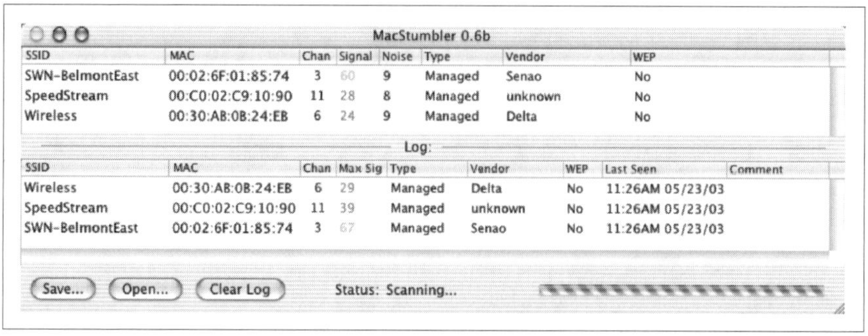

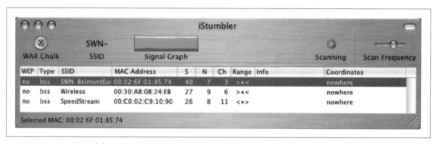

Figure 6-28. MacStumbler's main screen

iStumbler

iStumbler (*http://homepage.mac.com/alfwatt/istumbler*) is another popular network discovery tool. This tool is even simpler than MacStumbler, because there is really nothing to configure. Just fire it up and it finds all available networks for you, complete with a real-time signal and noise meter.

As shown in Figure 6-29, iStumbler has eventual plans for GPS support, but as of v0.6b, the Coordinates field is meaningless. GPS support is planned for the next release, which might be out by the time this book goes to press.

Figure 6-29. iStumbler's simple, brushed-metal interface

Like MacStumbler, iStumbler supports scanning with a built-in AirPort card only.

KisMAC

KisMAC (*http://www.binaervarianz.de/projekte/programmieren/kismac/*) is another OS X tool that shares a name with another popular monitoring tool—namely, Kismet *http://www.kismetwireless.net*). This is a much more advanced network-discovery and monitoring tool than either of the previous two tools.

MacStumbler and iStumbler work by sending out probe requests to all available access points. The access points respond to the probes (as they would for any legitimate wireless client), and this information is then collected, sorted, and displayed by the scanners. Since these scanners rely on responses to active probing, it is possible for network administrators to detect the presence of tools such as MacStumbler and iStumbler—or any other tool that makes use of active network probes.

KisMAC is a *passive* network scanner: rather than send out active probe requests, it instructs the wireless card to tune to a channel, listen for a short time, then tune to the next channel, listen for a while, and so on. In this way, not only is it possible to detect networks without announcing your presence, but it also makes it possible to find networks that don't respond to probe requests: namely, *closed* networks (APs that have beaconing disabled). But that's not all. Passive monitors have access to every frame that the radio can hear while tuned to a particular channel. This means that you can detect not only access points, but also the wireless clients of those APs.

The standard AirPort driver doesn't allow passive monitoring, so KisMAC uses the open source Viha AirPort driver (*http://www.dopesquad.net/security/*). It swaps the Viha driver for your existing AirPort driver when the program starts and automatically reinstalls the standard driver when it exits. To accomplish this driver switcheroo, you have to provide your administrative password when you start KisMAC. Note that while KisMAC is running, your regular wireless connection will be unavailable. KisMAC also supplies drivers for Orinoco/Avaya/Proxim cards, as well as Prism II–based wireless cards.

KisMAC's main screen provides much of the same information as the first two scanners we looked at. But double-clicking any available network shows a wealth of new information, as shown in Figure 6-30.

One interesting side effect of passive scanning is that channel detection isn't 100% reliable. Since 802.11b channels overlap, it is sometimes difficult for a passive scanner to know for certain which channel an access point is tuned to and can be one off from time to time. The AP in Figure 6-30 is actually set to channel 3, although it is reported as channel 2.

KisMAC allows you to specify which channels you would like to scan on, as shown in Figure 6-31. This can help if you are trying to find access points that use the same channel as your own.

KisMAC has a slew of nifty features, including GPS support, raw frame injection (for Prism II and Orinoco cards), and even a real-time relative traffic graph (see Figure 6-32). Yes, it can even read discovered ESSIDs aloud.

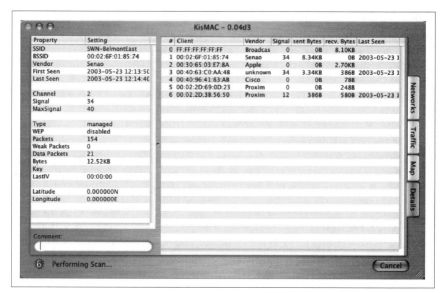

Figure 6-30. Wireless network details in KisMAC

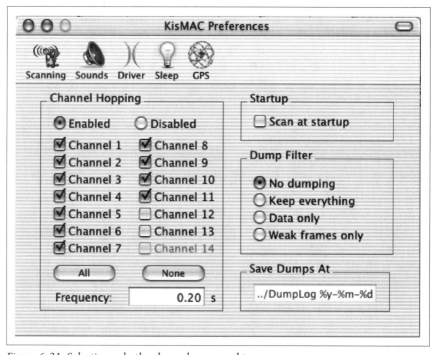

Figure 6-31. Selecting only the channels you need to scan

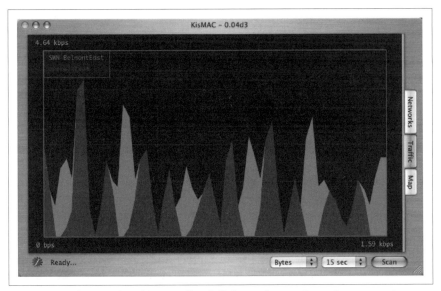

Figure 6 32. Showing the relative traffic of all detected networks, without transmitting a single bit

Perhaps the most powerful feature of all is KisMAC's ability to log raw 802.11 frames to a standard pcap dump. Check the Keep Everything or the Data Only option in preferences to save a dump file that can be read by tools such as Ethereal (*http://www.ethereal.com*).

KisMAC is probably the most advanced wireless network tool available for OS X, although it is still quite beta. I still keep MacStumbler and iStumbler handy, because they both are slightly more stable and can operate without removing the AirPort driver. By making use of these three free tools, you can find exactly how 802.11b is being used in your area.

—Rob Flickenger

HACK #65 Secure Your AirPort Network with WPA

Move over WEP; now there's something far more secure. Wireless Protected Access on your AirPort extreme base station will keep those snoops next door from watching while you browse, email, and chat.

With the release of Mac OS X 10.3 Panther, Apple provided a firmware upgrade for the AirPort Extreme Base Station and AirPort Extreme clients, which support the Wireless Protected Access (WPA) security standard for securing your wireless network. WPA is far more secure than Wireless Equivalent Privacy (WEP).

However, before you rejoice in this news, make sure you meet the following requirements:

- You must be running Mac OS X v10.3 or later. If you still have not upgraded, well, it's time to do so.
- You must be using an AirPort Extreme wireless network. That means your base station and your AirPort card must both be compatible with AirPort Extreme. If you are using the 802.11b AirPort network, you have to stick to WEP.

Upgrading Your AirPort Extreme Base Station

Download the firmware upgrade for your AirPort Extreme base station from Apple's web site (*http://docs.info.apple.com/article.html?artnum=120268*).

Launch the AirPort Admin Utility (*/Applications/Utilities/AirPort Admin Utility*). Select your base station from the list and click the Configure button. You might be prompted to enter the password for your base station. Click the Upload icon in the toolbar or select Upload from the Base Station menu. Choose the Airport Extreme firmware file you downloaded and click OK to begin uploading it to your base station.

When all is done, your base station will restart.

What Is WPA?

WPA is an enhanced security standard developed by the WiFi Alliance and IEEE to increase the security of wireless networks. As you probably know, WEP is inherently insecure, which means that any person intent on eavesdropping on your network communication can do so with the appropriate tools. To address this concern, WPA was designed as an interim solution (the longer-term solution lies in the 802.11i workgroup) to protect the privacy of wireless networks.

WPA contains the following components:

- Temporal Key Integrity Protocol (TKIP) for encrypting wireless packets
- 802.1X and Extensible Authentication Protocol (EAP) for user authentication
- Message Integrity Check (MIC) for checking the integrity of the packets sent over the air

To log into a WPA-protected network, you first need to supply a network password. TKIP then uses this password to mathematically generate an initial encryption key. All packets sent over the air will then use this encryption key. To prevent this key from being discovered (by someone who collects and analyzes many packets), TKIP routinely changes and rotates this key so that it is never used twice.

In AirPort Extreme, WPA supports two modes:

Enterprise mode
> This mode uses a Remote Authentication Dial-In User Service (RADIUS) for user authentication.

Personal mode
> This mode uses a network password for user authentication.

802.1X

The 802.1X specification is a port-based network-access control mechanism: when a client is authenticated, the port is granted access; if the client is not authenticated, access to the port is denied. Although 802.1X was originally designed for Ethernet networks, it can be applied to wireless networks as well.

Configuring for WPA Access

Now, let's configure our AirPort Extreme base station to enable WPA. As usual, configure your base station by using the AirPort Admin Utility.

Click the Name and Password button on the left. In the right pane, click the Change Wireless Security... button to change the security standard that is used to secure your AirPort Extreme network (see Figure 6-33).

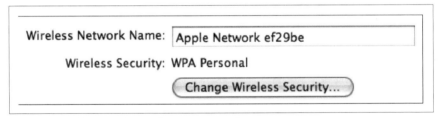

Figure 6-33. Changing the wireless security mode

In the Wireless Security drop-down listbox, select WPA Personal if you do not have a RADIUS server in your network (Figure 6-34). This option is useful for home or small-business networks. Select the Password option and key in the password twice. This password will be used to authenticate you on the network when you log into the network for the first time. When you enter a password in the configuration dialog, an industry-standard hashing algorithm is applied to generate the full 64-byte preshared key.

Figure 6-34. Using WPA Personal with a password

You can also select the Pre-Shared Key option to enter a key manually, as shown in Figure 6-35. This option is provided as an additional option only, just in case you are using non-Apple client software that does not do the proper hashing. The Pre-Shared Key is 64 hexadecimal (0-9, A-F) digits.

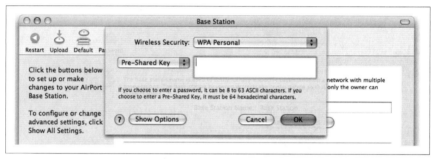

Figure 6-35. Configuring a preshared key manually

You can also click on the Show Options button to review more information about the encryption information. You can change the Group Key Timeout text box to change the frequency of key rotation, as shown in Figure 6-36.

Users with a RADIUS server for authentication should select the WPA Enterprise option, as shown in Figure 6-37. Using a RADIUS server, your AirPort Extreme network will use 802.1X authentication to authenticate your wireless users. Your RADIUS server will contain user login credentials.

Once the AirPort Extreme base station is configured and updated, you should now be able to see the network on your Mac, as shown in Figure 6-38.

Select the Apple Extreme wireless network and you will be prompted to enter the password to log into the network, as shown in Figure 6-39.

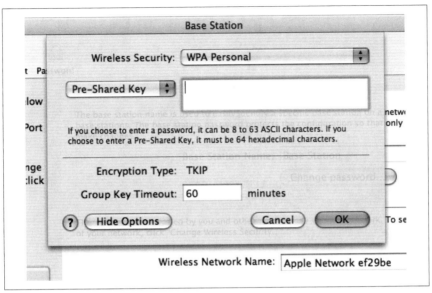

Figure 6-36. Viewing options for changing Group Key Timeout

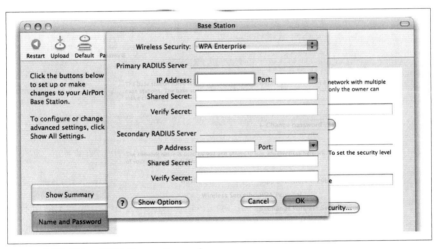

Figure 6-37. Using WPA Enterprise mode

 If you use the WPA Enterprise mode, you will no longer be able to configure your AirPort Extreme base station to use MAC address filtering using a RADIUS server.

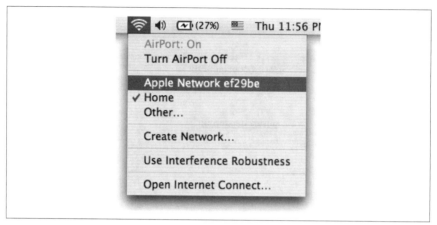

Figure 6-38. Connecting to an AirPort Extreme network

Figure 6-39. Entering the password to connect to an AirPort Extreme network

Final Thoughts

One thing to note about the use of WPA is that it greatly reduces the ability of people to eavesdrop on your wireless conversations. In security terms, it means the integrity of your wireless packets is protected. It does not, however, provide a strong authentication mechanism, because all users have to use a common network password, as shown in our example using WPA Personal. To ensure that only authorized users are connected to the wireless network, you need to use 802.1X authentication together with a RADIUS server.

—Wei Meng Lee

Manage Multiple AirPort Base Stations

#66

Managing one AirPort Base Station is easy enough, but managing multiple stations can be an exercise in repetition. But it doesn't have to be.

Managing an AirPort Base Station is easy enough using the AirPort Admin Utility (*/Applications/Utilities*). In fact, one of the strong selling points of the AirPort Base Station over other wireless access points is the ease of use of the configuration tools compared to the web configuration interfaces found on the others. But there is a feature of the AirPort Admin Utility that you might not be aware of: the ability to save and load configurations.

At first glance, the ability to save and reload an AirPort Base Station's configuration might seem superfluous. After all, once the base station is configured, what's the point? Well, there's at least three that we can think of:

- Having a backup of your configuration is never a bad idea. If you have a simple configuration using just DHCP and no access control, losing your configuration is not a big loss. But if you've spent quite a bit of time adding lots of AirPort IDs (née *MAC addresses*) into the access control settings, you'll want to preserve that work somewhere.

- It allows you to have multiple configurations, which is handy for when you travel with your base station. For example, you could save your home configuration before you leave, then tweak the base station to work with whatever hotel or conference-room networks you encounter, and then reload your home configuration when you return.

- If you have multiple base stations, having one configuration that you can upload to all of them, making small tweaks as necessary, can be a godsend compared to manually making sure that all of their settings are correct.

To save your configuration, open your base station in AirPort Admin Utility and go to File → Save a Copy As. This saves your file with the extension *.baseconfig*. Once you have a configuration file, you can open it with AirPort Admin Utility, modify it, and then save it again.

To upload a configuration to a base station, completely replacing its current configuration, go to the File → Import and select the *.baseconfig* file to use.

A Power Tool for Configuration Management

As nice as it is to be able to store and modify *.baseconfig* files for individual base stations, it's not the greatest solution for network administrators who need to take care of multiple base stations, especially when they need to update a particular setting across all of their base stations at once. In April 2004, Apple released a new tool, the AirPort Management Utility, to help manage networks with a number of base stations. You can download this tool as part of the AirPort Management Tools download located at *http://www.apple.com/support/airport/*.

AirPort Management Utility trades the hand-holding interface of AirPort Admin Utility for a power user's interface that gives you direct access to all of the tweakable properties of each base station, as shown in Figure 6-40.

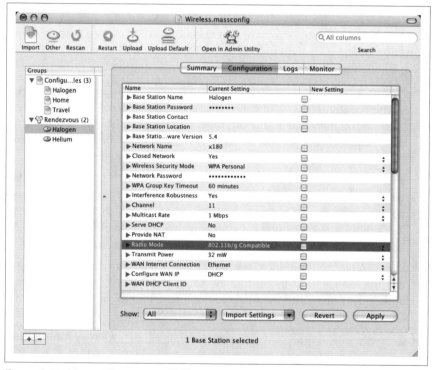

Figure 6-40. Airport Management Utility in action

Where AirPort Management Utility really shines is in its ability to edit the same property on more than one base station at once. For example, if you want to change the network name for multiple base stations on the local network, you can select the base stations and make a change to a single line, as shown in Figure 6-41.

AirPort Management Utility will take care of updating the value on all of the base stations simultaneously.

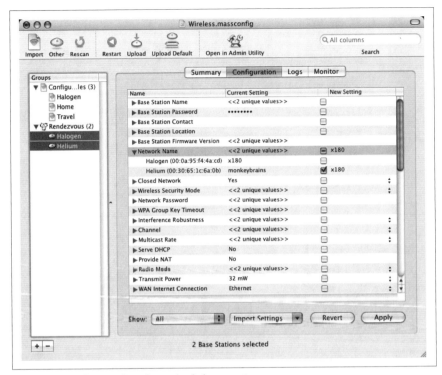

Figure 6-41. Editing values for multiple base stations

Tweaking Placement of Base Stations

Another task that falls to administrators of wireless networks is the placement of base stations to best serve the machines for the network. Quite frankly, the signal strength meter on the menu bar leaves quite a bit to be desired as a tool to help get the best signal possible. Luckily, we now have the AirPort Client Monitor, another tool that comes as part of the AirPort Management Tools package. This tool not only reports signal strength much more accurately than the menu bar meter, but it also reports the noise on the connection, as well as the bandwidth available, as shown in Figure 6-42.

By using the AirPort Client Monitor, you can gather information about any computer and position it for best network performance. This tool fails, however, when you need to balance the position of a base station against multiple machines. Sure, you could run back and forth between Macs and see their signal strengths one at a time as you make adjustments. But that would be the proverbial pain in the rear, not to mention a major threat to the soles of your shoes.

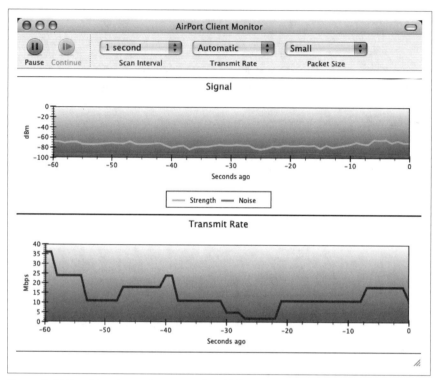

Figure 6-42. Tracking the performance of an AirPort connection

Never fear; your soles are safe. Simply fire up AirPort Management Utility, select a base station, and click on the Monitor tab. This produces a chart of the signal strengths of all of the computers that are using that base station, as shown in Figure 6-43.

The only thing needed from you is a translation of the AirPort IDs reported to the actual machines, but once you know which AirPort ID belongs to which machine, you'll be able to tweak the position of the computers and the base station to get the best signal possible to all machines.

HACK #67   Access Remote Desktops

Whether you need to administer multiple computers in the workplace or classroom, or connect to that Unix fileserver or Windows print server downstairs, remote desktop software will make your life easier.

You *can* go home again—that is, if your home is running remote desktop software. Using the likes of Virtual Network Computer (VNC) and Apple Remote Desktop (ARD), you can control, administer, and make general use

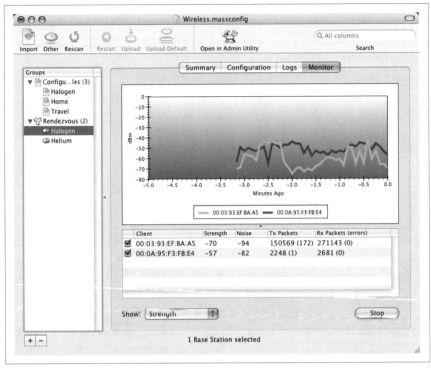

Figure 6-43. Tracking signal strength for clients of a base station

of Macs, Windows PCs, and Unix boxes, whether they're across the world or downstairs in the basement.

Each of the two options discussed here offers its own feature set and cost/benefit ratio. VNC starts at $0 and involves some rather geeky setup, which some of you might rather pass. ARD is all GUI all the time, but it will set you back a few hundred bucks. VNC allows connections from Windows to Mac, Mac to Unix, Unix to Windows, and everything in between. ARD connects Mac to Mac only. VNC requires a little knowledge on the part of the end user, while ARD is a Mac-simple Apple product.

In the end, you'll get to remote-control that desktop. Just what's involved and how much you're prepared to pay is up to you.

Virtual Network Computer (VNC)

One of the attractive features of Mac OS X is the ease with which you can integrate a Mac OS X system into an environment that consists of multiple Unix workstations that typically rely on X11 for their GUI. The reverse process is also possible. You can log into a remote Mac OS X machine from another computer, launch an application on the remote Mac OS X machine, and display the application on your local machine. The local machine, meanwhile, can be running the X Window System, Microsoft Windows, Mac OS X (of course), or any another platform supported by VNC.

VNC consists of two components:

VNC server
    Must be installed on the remote machine

VNC viewer
    Used on the local machine to view and control applications running on the remote machine

The VNC connection is made through a TCP/IP connection.

Not only can the VNC server and viewer be on different machines, they can also be installed on different operating systems. This allows you to, for example, connect from Solaris to Mac OS X. Using VNC, you can launch and run both X11 and Aqua applications on Mac OS X but view and control them from your Solaris box.

VNC can be installed on Mac OS X with the Fink package manager (look for the *vnc* package), but that version (the standard Unix version of the VNC server) supports X11 programs only, not Aqua applications. This standard Unix version of VNC translates X11 calls into the VNC protocol. All you need on the client machine is a VNC viewer. An attractive Mac-friendly alternative to the strictly X11-based VNC server is OSXvnc (*http://www.redstonesoftware.com/vnc.html*).

The standard Unix version of the VNC server is quite robust. Rather than interact with your display, it intercepts and translates the X11 network protocol. (In fact, the Unix version of the server is based on the XFree86 source code.) Applications that run under the Unix server are not displayed on the server's screen (unless you set the DISPLAY environment variable to :0.0, in which case it is displayed only on the remote server, not on your VNC client). Instead, they are displayed on an invisible X server that relays its virtual display to the VNC viewer on the client machine.

OSXvnc works in a similar manner, except it supports the Mac OS X Aqua Desktop instead of X11. With the OSXvnc server running on your Mac OS X system, you can use a VNC client on another system (for example, a Unix system) to display and control your Mac OS X Aqua Desktop. You can even tunnel these VNC connections (both X11 and Aqua) through SSH.

Launching VNC. If you installed VNC on your Mac OS X system via Fink (or on any Unix system, for that matter), you can start the VNC server by issuing the following command:

```
% vncserver
```

If you don't have physical access to the system on which you want to run the VNC server, you can log into it remotely and enter the command before logging out:

```
% nohup vncserver
```

This command starts the VNC server, and nohup makes sure it continues to run after you log out. In either case, the first time you start vncserver, you need to supply a password, which you need to supply anyway when connecting from a remote machine. (This password can be changed using the command vncpasswd.)

You can run several servers; each server is identified by its hostname with : *number* appended. For example, suppose you start the VNC server twice on a machine named abbott; the first server will be identified as abbott:1 and the second will be identified as abbott:2. You need to supply this identifier when you connect from a client machine.

By default, the VNC server runs twm, the Tab Window Manager for X11. So, when you connect, you will see an X11 desktop instead of the Mac OS X Desktop. You can specify a different window manager in *~/.vnc/xstartup*. To terminate the VNC server, use the following command syntax:

```
% vncserver -kill :display
```

For example, to terminate abbott:1, you must issue the following command while logged into abbott as the user who started the VNC server:

```
% vncserver -kill :1
```

VNC and SSH. VNC passwords and network traffic are sent over the wire as plain text. However, you can use SSH with VNC to encrypt this traffic.

A derivative of VNC called TightVNC is optimized for bandwidth conservations. (If you are using Fink, you can install it with the command fink install tightvnc). TightVNC also offers automatic SSH tunneling on Unix and backward compatibility with the standard VNC.

If you want to tunnel your VNC connection through SSH, you can do so even without TightVNC. To illustrate this process, let's consider an example using a Sun workstation named *mrchops* running Solaris and a Power-Book G4 named *tichops* running Panther. In the following example, the

VNC server is running on the Solaris machine and a VNC client is running on the Mac OS X machine.

To display and control the remote Solaris GNOME desktop on your local Mac OS X system, log into the Solaris machine, *mrchops* (log in via SSH if you must log in remotely). On *mrchops*, enter the following command to start the VNC server on display :1:

```
% nohup vncserver :1
```

In your ~/.vnc directory, edit the *xstartup* file so that GNOME will start when you connect to the VNC server with a VNC client. In particular, your *xstartup* file should look like this:

```
#!/bin/sh
xrdb $HOME/.Xresources
xterm -geometry 80x24+10+10 -ls -title "$VNCDESKTOP Desktop" &

exec /usr/bin/gnome-session &
```

Log out of the Solaris box, *mrchops.*

From a Terminal window (or *xterm*) on your Mac OS X machine, log into *mrchops* via ssh:

```
% ssh -L 5902:localhost:5901 mrchops
```

Any references to display :2 on your Mac will connect to the Solaris machine's display :1 through an SSH tunnel (display :1 uses port 5901; display :2 uses 5902). You might need to add the -l option to this command if your username on the Solaris machine is different than the one you're using on your Mac OS X machine. For example, if your username on *mrchops* is *brian,* but on *tichops* your username is *ernie,* you need to issue the following command instead of the previous one:

```
% ssh -L 5902:localhost:5901 mrchops -l brian
```

Additionally, you might need to open ports through any firewalls you have running. Open ports 5900 to 5902 for VNC, and open port 22 for ssh.

On your Mac, you can either start X11 or run vncviewer from the command line:

```
% vncviewer localhost:2
```

You can also run an Aqua VNC client such as VNCDimension (*http://www.mdimension.com*) or Chicken of the VNC (*http://sourceforge.net/projects/cotvnc*). Figure 6-44 shows a VNCDimension connection to a Solaris GNOME desktop.

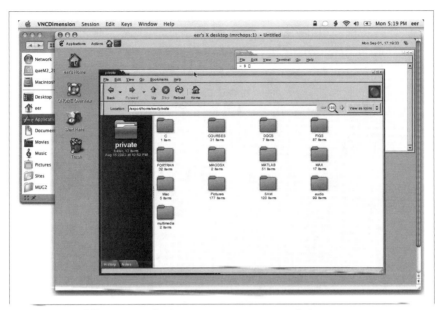

Figure 6-44. VNCDimension displaying a remote GNOME desktop

Connecting to the Mac OS X VNC server. To connect to a Mac OS X machine that is running a VNC server, you need a VNC viewer. We mentioned two Mac OS X viewers (VNCDimension and Chicken of the VNC) in the previous section, and additional Mac OS X viewers can be found at Version-Tracker (*http://www.versiontracker.com/macosx*) or MacUpdate (*http://www.macupdate.com*) by searching for VNC. VNC or TightVNC provide viewers for Unix systems. These viewers can be used to display and control the Mac OS X Aqua Desktop.

To connect, start your viewer and specify the hostname and display number, such as chops:1 or chops:2. If all goes well, you'll be asked for your password and then be connected to the remote Mac OS X Desktop. VNC connections to Mac OS X Aqua Desktops can be established through SSH tunnels.

To illustrate this process, let's do the reverse of our last example—that is, make an SSH-secured connection from a Solaris machine to the Mac OS X machine that's running the VNC server. Again, let's assume that the name of the Solaris machine is *mrchops* and the Mac OS X machine has a hostname of *tichops*.

On *tichops* double-click the OSXvnc application. Select a display number (we've selected 1 in this example). The port number will be filled in automatically once you've selected the display number. Next, enter a password that will be used to connect to the VNC server and click the Start Server button, as shown in Figure 6-45.

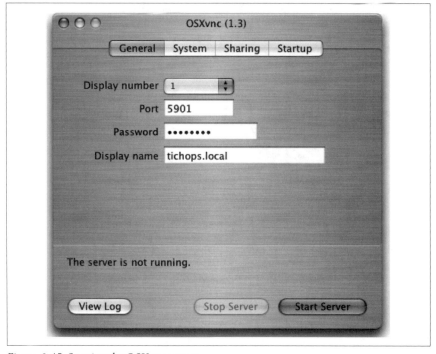

Figure 6-45. Starting the OSXvnc server

You can also ssh to *tichops* and start OSXvnc from the command line. For a list of command-line options, enter:

```
/Applications/OSXvnc.app/OSXvnc-server -help
```

On the Solaris machine, *mrchops*, enter:

```
ssh -L 5902:localhost:5901 tichops
```

In another *xterm* window on *mrchops*, enter:

```
vncviewer localhost:2
```

Figure 6-46 shows the resulting VNC connection.

> Although we were able to control the Mac OS X Desktop from the Sun Solaris machine, the image quality of the Mac OS X Desktop shown in Figure 6-46 is rather poor on the systems that we used (Sun Ultra 10-440 running Solaris 8 and a PowerBook G4 running Mac OS X Panther).

Figure 6-46. Mac OS X Desktop, displayed and controlled on a Solaris GNOME Desktop

A wrapper application for OSXvnc, Share My Desktop (SMD), is available from Bombich Software (*http://www.bombich.com/software/smd.html*) and is licensed under the GNU General Public License. This handy little application reduces launching the OSXvnc server to a one-click operation. To start the VNC server, just launch the SMD application and click the Start Sharing button—it'll change to a Stop sharing button, as shown in Figure 6-47.

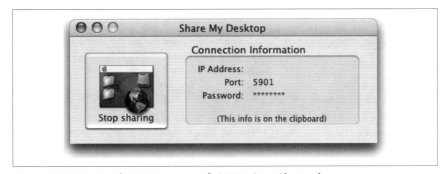

Figure 6-47. Starting the VNC server with SMD's Start Sharing button

A random password and port for the VNC server is automatically chosen. You can modify the default setting in SMD's Preferences pane. In particular, you can keep the password private (it is displayed as asterisks in the SMD main window) and either generate a random password (the default) or specify your own password. Additionally, you can select two energy saving settings: allow the screen to dim and allow the computer to sleep.

If you want the VNC server to run whenever the Mac OS X system is running, SMD provides a way to install and configure a systemwide VNC server that will, optionally, start when you boot up your Mac OS X system. To take advantage of this feature, you need to be logged in as an administrative user. Open the SMD application and select File → Manage System VNC Server to open the dialog window shown in Figure 6-48.

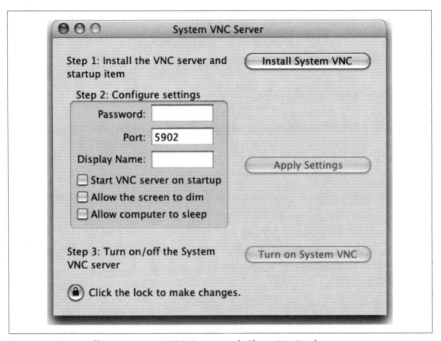

Figure 6-48. Installing a System VNC Server with Share My Desktop

Click the lock to make changes and supply your administrative password (you must be an administrative user to do this). This pop-up window allows you to install the VNC server and startup item, configure settings (password, port, display name, start VNC server on startup, allow the screen to dim, and allow the computer to sleep), and to turn on/off the system VNC server. If you click the Install System VNC button, the *OSXvnc-server* and *storepasswd* binaries is installed in */usr/local/bin* and a startup item is installed in *Library/StartupItems/*. A backup of the *etc/hostconfig* file is also made, in case you later want to uninstall the systemwide VNC server and return to the settings you had prior to the installation of the system VNC.

The settings for the systemwide VNC server are stored in *etc/vnc_settings*, and the password is stored in *etc/vnc_pass*. Changing the "Start VNC server on startup" option resets the value of VNCSERVER in the *etc/hostconfig* file. If you've installed the systemwide VNC server using this procedure, you can uninstall it (along with its configuration files) by clicking the Uninstall System VNC button in the same Manage System VNC Server pop-up window. This uninstall procedure also restores the *etc/hostconfig*, which was backed up when you installed VNC server. Since this can overwrite system configuration changes you've made since installing VNC, we suggest you instead edit the VNCSERVER line so that it is set to -NO- instead of -YES- and restart (see Chapter 2 for more information on the *hostconfig* file).

> VNC clients and servers are available for Windows machines, so Windows clients can connect to Mac OS X and other Unix VNC servers. Mac OS X clients can also connect to and control Windows VNC servers. (See *http://www.realvnc.com* for more information about VNC servers.) As an alternative to VNC, you can use Microsoft's free Remote Desktop Client (RDC), available at *http://www.microsoft.com/mac/otherproducts/otherproducts.aspx?pid=remotedesktopclient*, to control a Windows desktop from a Mac OS X machine.

Apple Remote Desktop (ARD)

If you work in an environment where you need to manage a large number of Macs (such as in a classroom) and need to set up something a little simpler and slightly less geeky than VNC, you might want to take a look at Apple Remote Desktop (*http://www.apple.com/remotedesktop*: $299 for 10-Client Edition, $499 for Unlimited Client Edition). It's pricey (but you expected that; otherwise, you'd have used VNC) but effective software; you can easily control and manage all the Macs on the network. Windows users probably take this functionality for granted, because that platform includes Remote Desktop Connection.

So, what do you get for that hefty ding in your budget? Let's take a closer look.

Client installation. Installing Remote Desktop is straightforward. You have two packages: one for the administrator and one for the client. You put the *administrator* package on your machine, and everyone else gets the *client* software. Once everything is installed on the client side, you'll see the

Remote Desktop icon in the System Preferences window, as shown in Figure 6-49.

Figure 6-49. Locating the Remote Desktop icon in the System Preferences window

Click on Remote Desktop, and then click on the Sharing... button to config-ure the software, as shown in Figure 6-50.

Figure 6-50. Configuring Remote Desktop on the client machine

In the Sharing window, click on the Services tab and check the Apple Remote Desktop checkbox. This starts the Apple Remote Desktop service so that the administrator (which is most likely you) can remotely manage this Mac using the IP address shown at the bottom of the screen (see Figure 6-51). Click Access Privileges to determine the account that the administrator will use. Check the "Show status in menu bar" checkbox to display the status of Apple Remote Desktop on the menu bar.

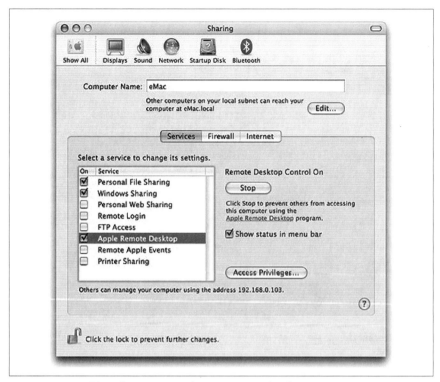

Figure 6-51. Enabling the Remote Desktop service on the client

You can then select the user account to allow for monitoring. You can also refine the permissions for each user, such as the ability to let the administrator delete items, send text messages, and so on, as shown in Figure 6-52. Click OK to continue.

That's it! The client setup is complete. One last thing to note is that the client can send a message to the administrator when that machine is being monitored, as shown in Figure 6-53.

Administrator installation. Once the administrator package is installed, you can find the Remote Desktop icon in the Applications folder, as shown in Figure 6-54.

Double-click on the Remote Desktop icon to launch Apple Remote Desktop. If you're using the application for the first time, you'll see the prompt shown in Figure 6-55. Click the Add Computers Now button to search for all of the Macs you want to administer remotely.

You can click on the Search button to find Macs to administer (see Figure 6-56). You can search all computers on the local network or search

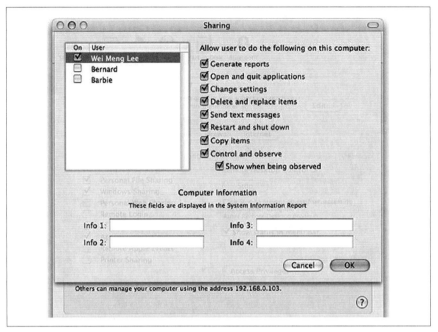

Figure 6-52. Providing access privileges to certain user accounts

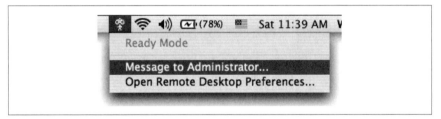

Figure 6-53. Sending a message to the administrator

Figure 6-54. Locating the Remote Desktop administrator application in the Applications folder

using a range of IP addresses. To add a Mac, click the Add >> button. You will be prompted for a username and password. This username is what you configured earlier on the client to allow for administration.

Once the computers are added, you should see the Computer Status window shown in Figure 6-57.

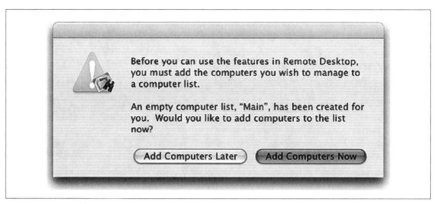

Figure 6-55. Adding computers to administer

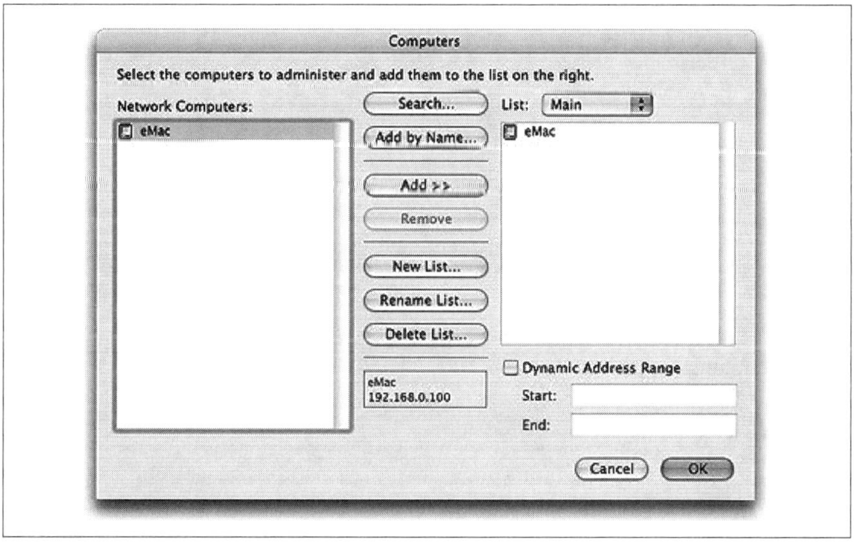

Figure 6-56. Searching for computers to administer

You can observe what the remote computer is doing by clicking on the Observe button. In my case, the screen of the remote computer is displayed in a window (currently surfing web sites using Safari), as shown in Figure 6-58. This feature is useful if you want to monitor the kind of activity taking place on the user's computer, such as in a classroom environment.

If you want to control the Mac remotely, you should click on the Control button. Once you do that, you can use your mouse to control the Mac. This feature is useful when you need to administer multiple Macs remotely, such as when installing new applications or updates.

Figure 6-57. The Computer Status window

Figure 6-58. Observing a remote computer

In some cases, you might want to show the remote user how to perform a certain action. To do so, you might broadcast your own screen to the remote user. In this case, click the Share Screen button to show the remote user your own screen.

You can also lock the screen of the remote computer by clicking the Lock Screen button, as shown in Figure 6-59. The remote Mac's screen will then display the locked screen message.

Figure 6-59. Locking a remote screen

To chat with the remote user, as shown in Figure 6-60, click the Text Chat button.

Figure 6-60. Chatting with a remote user

The Sleep and Wake Up buttons force the remote computer to sleep and wake up, respectively. You can also copy files between the client and the remote computer by using the Copy Items button.

Under the Report item in the main menu, you can perform a software search on the remote computer by using the Software Search... menu item, as shown in Figure 6-61.

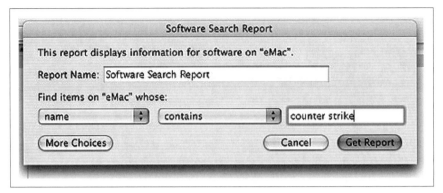

Figure 6-61. Searching for software on a remote computer

You can also gather detailed information about the remote computer using the System Information... menu item, as shown in Figure 6-62.

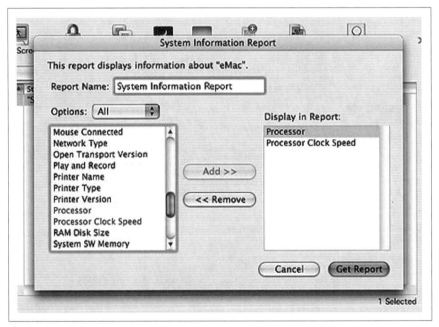

Figure 6-62. Selecting options to report

The information gathered will then be displayed in the System Information Report window, as shown in Figure 6-63.

Apple Remote Desktop is a really cool addition to your administrator's tool-box if you need to maintain a large number of Macs. However, my own gripe is that it is not included in Panther itself; instead, you need to pay

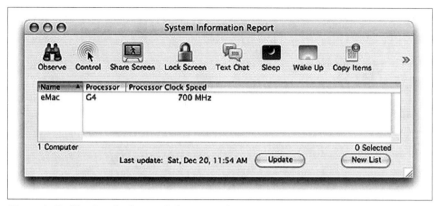

Figure 6-63. Viewing the System Information Report

quite a tidy sum ($499) for an unlimited license. But budget concerns aside, I am definitely impressed with how well it works!

—*Brian Jepson, Ernie Rothman, and Wei Meng Lee*

Servers

Hacks 68–76

Mac OS X is not just a personal desktop machine. Beneath its candy-coated shell beats the heart of a full-blown Unix system, along with the software that Unix systems are famous for: servers. Apple reserves some of the fancy server software for Mac OS X Server (a great solution for corporate users), but there's quite a number of server software packages built into every Mac OS X system. And since the system is Unix, it's easy to add your own servers for any need.

This chapter flips all the right switches to turn up the built-in Apache web server and steps you through installing, configuring, and bringing up your own Mac mail server.

HACK #68 Apache Behind the Scenes

To go beyond the basics of using the world-class web server built into Mac OS X, you'll have to learn a bit about its configuration files.

Mac OS X comes with one of the most popular and widely used web servers on the planet as part of its standard equipment list. Panther ships with Version 1.3.29 of Apache; to turn it on, just click a single button in your System Preferences application, as shown in Figure 7-1.

Once you've enabled Apache, you can point your web browser at your machine's IP address, hostname, or *http://localhost* and see the default Apache home page—yes, the one with the big "Seeing this instead of the Web site you expected?" caption. This rather bland default home page is located in */Library/WebServer/Documents*, the home of your web site on this machine. Easy, huh? To create your own web site, just add your files to this folder. But this folder isn't the only place you can build a web site.

If you've ever had a web site hosted at an Internet Service Provider (ISP), you're probably used to having a URL that looks a little something like this: *http://www.myisp.com/~me*, where *me* is your login name. In addition to the

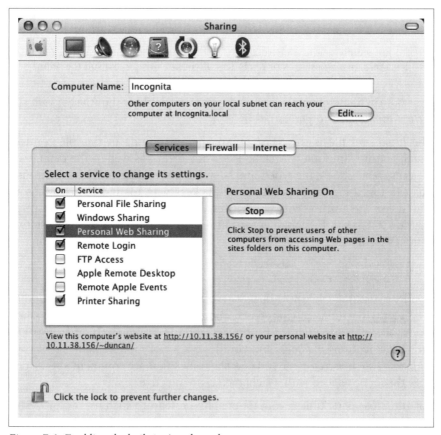

Figure 7-1. Enabling the built-in Apache web server

main web site you now have running on your Macintosh, each user (remember, whether you're the only user or not, OS X is a multiuser system) also has his very own site.

The files for your user site live in the Sites folder in your home directory. Point your web browser at *http://localhost/~me*, where *me* is the short name associated with your user account. You'll be greeted with a friendly "Your website here" message, along with further instructions on building your own web site. That page is actually a file called *index.html*, which sits in your Sites folder; edit it by using your favorite text or HTML editor and reload the page in your browser to see the results.

The Main Configuration File

If you want to do more than serve files with the built-in server, you'll probably find yourself needing to get down and dirty with Apache's configuration files. The standard Apache configuration file, located at */etc/httpd/httpd.conf*, is as large as it is well documented. Take its introductory warning to heart:

> Do not simply read the instructions...without understanding what they do. They're here only as hints or reminders. If you are unsure, consult the online docs. You have been warned.

For your own reference, the online docs are available at the Apache web site (*http://httpd.apache.org/docs/*).

The *httpd.conf* file is the heart of Apache; everything in this file controls which features (modules) Apache loads at startup, as well as the default set of access restrictions, file types, and so much more. When searching through this file for something specific, the quickest way to find and learn is to search for the feature you want to enable. For example, if you want to enable CGI, start by looking for CGI in the file. Here are the first two matches we find:

```
LoadModule cgi_module libexec/httpd/mod_cgi.so
AddModule mod_cgi.c
```

You'll see a number of these lines within the Apache *httpd.conf* file. If you've ever worked with a plug-in–based program, you'll easily recognize their intent; these lines load different features into the Apache web server. Apache calls these features *modules*, and you'll see a lot of module names that start with mod_, such as mod_perl and mod_php. Lines that are commented out (i.e., lines that are prefaced with a # character) are inactive.

For the most part, unless you are enabling a feature such as PHP [Hack #70], you shouldn't mess around too much with the main configuration file. Not only is it long and complicated, but the system updates that Apple provides might also one day blotto your configuration. Luckily, the *httpd.conf* file is already configured with the following line:

```
Include /private/etc/httpd/users/*.conf
```

This instructs Apache to pick up additional configuration information from the files in the */etc/httpd/users* directory that have a *.conf* extension.

Editing User Configuration Files

Not only does Apple configure *httpd.conf* to use configuration files in the */etc/httpd/users* directory, but it also automatically creates one for each user on the system. For example, the following is a listing of my */etc/httpd/users* directory:

```
$ ls /etc/httpd/users
duncan.conf rael.conf
johnjacobjingleheimerschmidt.conf
```

Inside each of these files, a configuration block controls the settings for a user's site, as shown here:

```
<Directory "/Users/duncan/Sites/">
 Options Indexes MultiViews
 AllowOverride None
 Order allow,deny
 Allow from all
</Directory>
```

These are pretty common default settings for directories under Apache; you'll see similar entries in the main configuration file for Apache's default document root (for OS X, that's /Library/WebServer/Documents). Editing either the user configuration file or httpd.conf involves authenticating as an administrative user and then making your changes. For example, the following change blocks outside access from other computers:

```
<Directory "/Users/morbus/Sites/">
 Options Indexes MultiViews
 AllowOverride None
 Order deny,allow
 Deny from all
 Allow from 127.0.0.1
</Directory>
```

Even though these files are called *user configuration files* and are named after the various users on a system, there's no reason to limit their use to just tweaking settings on an individual user's site. After all, these files are included in the main configuration of Apache by the Include directive in httpd.conf. Therefore, we recommend that any time you want to add configuration directives, you should do so in one of the user configuration files. Just be sure to not place the directives inside a <Directory> block unless you want your settings to be restricted to that directory.

Restarting Apache

Each time you make alterations to any of Apache's configuration files and save your changes, you'll need to restart Apache by issuing the following command:

```
% sudo apachectl restart
httpd restarted
```

apachectl is a simple interface for controlling (e.g., starting, stopping, and restarting) Apache. Type man apachectl for more information on the various command-line switches. Once Apache has restarted, your configuration changes will be active.

—*Kevin Hemenway and James Duncan Davidson*

Turn on WebDAV

Share a space on your web server for remote file sharing and collaboration.

WebDAV (Web-based Distributed Authoring and Versioning, also called *DAV*) is a set of extensions to HTTP/1.1 (Hypertext Transfer Protocol, the protocol spoken by web browsers and servers) that allows you to edit documents on a remote web server. DAV provides support for:

Editing
>   Creating, updating, deleting

Properties
>   Title, author, publication date, and so on

Collections
>   Analogous to a filesystem's directory or Desktop folder

Locking
>   Prevents the confusion and data corruption caused by two or more people editing the same content at the same time

WebDAV is platform-independent, in terms of both client and server. This means that Macintosh, Unix, and Windows users can collaborate on web content without all the usual conversion problems. Furthermore, it doesn't matter whether your documents are hosted on an Apache or Microsoft IIS server.

WebDAV is software agnostic. As long as your web-authoring tools are DAV-compliant, the particular product you're using makes little difference. It is (at least should be) seamless. Because DAV is simply a set of extensions to HTTP, it's easy for companies to build support into any product that already understands the Web. And, since DAV rides on top of HTTP, firewalls tend not to get in the way of accessing your web content remotely.

WebDAV makes use of the standard authorization and authentication methods built right into every web server. In the same manner as one restricts access to a portion (a file, folder, or entire site) of one's web site to a particular set of users or machines, so too can one finely tune WebDAV access to resources.

Best of all, WebDAV is built into the Apache web server that is part of Mac OS X.

Configuring WebDAV in Apache

Open the Apache server's main configuration file, */etc/httpd/httpd.conf*, for editing [Hack #78]. You'll need to authenticate yourself as an administrator by using sudo [Hack #88]:

```
$ sudo pico /etc/httpd/httpd.conf
```

You'll need to hunt down two lines in your Apache configuration and uncomment them. These are the two lines to look for in */etc/httpd/httpd.conf*:

```
# LoadModule dav_module libexec/httpd/libdav.so
...
# AddModule mod_dav.c
```

Since these lines are commented out by default, we'll have to uncomment them in order to make WebDAV functional. Do so, and the lines should now look like this:

```
LoadModule dav_module libexec/httpd/libdav.so
...
AddModule mod_dav.c
```

Once the WebDAV module is activated, you'll need to add a configuration directive to enable a DAV share. Zoom down to the end of the file and add the following lines:

```
DAVLockDB /etc/httpd/dav/DAVLock
DAVMinTimeout 600
<Location /dav/>
 DAV On
 AuthType Basic
 AuthName "WebDAV Restricted"
 AuthUserFile /etc/httpd/dav/.passwd
 <LimitExcept GET HEAD OPTIONS>
 Require valid-user
 </LimitExcept>
</Location>
```

The first line sets up a database file that WebDAV uses to track who's editing which file. It locks a file to prevent something dangerous from happening, such as two people trying to update it at once. The second line tells the web server not to wait forever if the remote computer loses the connection with it. The <Location> tags set the context of the WebDAV settings to the */dav* directory, which we will set up under the document root.

We're using AuthTypeBasic security, which requires a username and password to make modifications. We'll store the password in a file called */Library/WebServer/.passwd*, and the required username is *webdav*.

There is a risk to using basic authentication. The username and password are weakly encoded, so it is possible that someone could listen to your network and steal the password. A few years ago, a new authentication scheme called *digest authentication* was developed for Apache. This scheme uses strong encryption to protect the password.

Unfortunately, the digest-authentication module that ships with Apache Version 1.3 (the one that comes with Mac OS X) is old and not compatible with most browsers and client software. My attempts to use it with iCal failed. There is a more recent version of the module, but it requires Apache Version 2.0, which is not trivial to set up and is therefore beyond the scope of this hack. Hopefully, Apple will upgrade Apache to a more modern version, but in the meantime, keep an eye out for an Apache v2 package that will compile on Darwin (perhaps from the Fink project).

The `<LimitExcept>` directive gives us some protection from malicious intent. First, it locks down all the actions that can be performed on WebDAV files, except those actions that are read-only. Second, it limits the write privileges to one user, named *webdav*. The only ability this user has on the system is to write files in this directory.

Setting Up Directories

First, you need to set up the realm of WebDAV documents. Based on what we put in the configuration file, this will be in a subdirectory of the document root called */dav* (that's */Library/WebServer/Documents/dav*). You'll need to create that directory yourself and change the permissions and ownership so that the web server can write to it:

```
$ sudo mkdir /Library/WebServer/Documents/dav
$ sudo chgrp www /Library/WebServer/Documents/dav
$ sudo chmod 775 /Library/WebServer/Documents/dav
```

Next, you need to find a place for the WebDAV lock database file. For lack of a better place, I created a directory alongside the *httpd.conf* configuration file, */etc/httpd/dav*. Again, set the permissions so that the server can write files here:

```
$ sudo mkdir /etc/httpd/dav
$ sudo chgrp www /etc/httpd/dav
$ sudo chmod 775 /etc/httpd/dav
```

Creating Users

While our configuration specifies that only valid users are allowed to alter the contents of the */dav* directory via WebDAV, we haven't yet created said users. We'll do so now.

Don't use an existing username and password. A malicious hacker sniffing your communications can grab that username and use it to sneak inside your system. The username we will create will be limited to WebDAV files only, which will be useless to a would-be intruder.

First, create a password file by using the htpasswd utility. (Again, to keep everything related to DAV together, I used */etc/httpd/dav/*.) You'll simultaneously create a user account and password for *webdav*. You'll be prompted for a password. Invent something secure and save it someplace safe. Make the password unique (don't use one that you use elsewhere), because of the basic authentication risk I mentioned earlier:

```
$ sudo htpasswd -c /etc/httpd/dav/.passwd webdav
New password:
Re-type new password:
Adding password for user webdav
```

Restarting the Server

An Apache control script, apachectl, does away with the need to kill and restart the Apache server by hand. Simply issue a start, stop, or restart, and apachectl will comply. In this case, you want to restart the server, so type:

```
$ sudo apachectl restart
/usr/sbin/apachectl restart: httpd restarted
```

If Apache isn't already running, apachectl is smart enough to go ahead and start it up for you:

```
$ sudo apachectl restart
/usr/sbin/apachectl restart: httpd not running, trying to start
Processing config directory: /private/etc/httpd/users
Processing config file: /private/etc/httpd/users/rael.conf
/usr/sbin/apachectl restart: httpd started
```

Your WebDAV server is now ready for use by anyone (with the proper authentication, that is) who can reach your web server. Mac OS X has built-in support for mounting WebDAV shares [Mac OS X Hacks, Hack #74] and treating them like just about any other hard drive.

Did you know that iDisk is WebDAV-based?

See Also

- WebDAV Resources (*http://www.webdav.org*)

—Erik T. Ray and Rael Dornfest

Turn on PHP

HACK
#70

PHP is a fabulous scripting language for beginners to try their hands at serving up dynamic web content.

Have you ever wanted to add a guest book to your web site? Or show a web counter? Well, PHP is just the ticket to get started. PHP (short for *PHP: Hypertext Processor*, yet another geeky recursive name) is a widely used scripting language that is designed from the ground up to be used in web pages. When you include PHP code in a page, it is interpreted by the web server when the page is requested. The code itself doesn't make it to the user, but the result of it does. This allows you to put all sorts of dynamic content on your web site.

There are lots of online guides and books out there to teach you how to use PHP, but to get started, you must have PHP. Most guides start out by telling you to download and compile the PHP distribution. Well, there's no need for that, because it's already built into Mac OS X. All you need to do is hunt down two lines in your Apache configuration and uncomment them. These are the two lines to look for in */etc/httpd/httpd.conf*:

```
# LoadModule php4_module libexec/httpd/libphp4.so
...
# AddModule mod_php4.c
```

Since these lines are commented out by default, we'll have to uncomment them in order to make PHP functional. Do so, and the lines should now look like this:

```
LoadModule php4_module libexec/httpd/libphp4.so
...
AddModule mod_php4.c
```

Once you make this change, the following configuration block in your *httpd.conf* file takes care of the rest of the necessary configuration, including setting the *php* file type handler and adding *index.php* to the list of index pages used:

```
<IfModule mod_php4.c>
# If php is turned on, we repsect .php and .phps files.
AddType application/x-httpd-php .php
AddType application/x-httpd-php-source .phps

# Since most users will want index.php to work we
# also automatically enable index.php
<IfModule mod_dir.c>
DirectoryIndex index.html index.php
</IfModule>
</IfModule>
```

Save the Apache configuration file, and restart the web server:

```
$ sudo apachectl restart
httpd restarted
```

Let's take a look at our Apache error log for a second to illustrate a simple yet helpful bit of information. Each time you start Apache, it spits out a single line that tells you everything started successfully. With a plain-vanilla Apache server, the line usually looks something like this:

```
[Wed Apr 14 23:53:56 2004] [notice] Apache/1.3.29 (Darwin) configured --
resuming normal operations
```

When you add a third-party module or feature (such as PHP, mod_perl, mod_ssl, etc.), Apache graciously makes mention of it in this startup line. If you just restarted the Apache web server now, take a look at the error log by typing the following command:

```
$ tail /var/log/httpd/error_log
```

You should see Apache wax poetic with this line:

```
[Sat Apr 17 00:50:20 2004] [notice] Apache/1.3.29 (Darwin) PHP/4.3.2
configured -- resuming normal operations
```

Apache tells us that PHP is enabled, but how do we really know for sure? Rather easily, actually. Create a file named *index.php* in your Sites directory, using the following as its contents:

```
<? phpinfo( )?>
```

When you load *index.php* in your browser (*http://127.0.0.1/~morbus/index. php*, for example, replacing *morbus* with your short username), you should see a long page full of PHP diagnostic information. PHP has been successfully configured for use.

Now that you have enabled PHP, you're ready to dive in and start playing. The PHP web site (*http://www.php.net*) is a great place to start.

— *Kevin Hemenway and James Duncan Davidson*

Advertise Web Sites with Rendezvous

#71 Announce your web site to all the other Macs on your local network.

Rendezvous (also known as *Zeroconf Networking*) has brought us a wealth of benefits. We can chat with people [Hack #33], trade files, and even edit documents collaboratively [Hack #62] on the local network with ease and without having to perform any tedious configuration of the network settings on our machines. Even the Safari and Camino web browsers have gotten in on the action and can display the available web sites on machines that happen to be on the local network. This can be great fun at conferences where you have hundreds of Macs and can scope out what other people are serving from their machines.

What isn't so clear is how Apache, the web server built into Mac OS X, advertises web sites to the network. Well, it's controlled by the configuration directive for the mod_rendezvous_apple module that is included with Apache on Mac OS X. This module is configured with the following block, which is located toward the end of the /etc/httpd.conf file:

```
<IfModule mod_rendezvous_apple.c>
# Only the pages of users who have edited their
# default home pages will be advertised on Rendezvous.
RegisterUserSite customized-users
#RegisterUserSite all-users

# Rendezvous advertising for the primary site is off by default.
#RegisterDefaultSite
</IfModule>
```

As configured, Apache advertises any user's site on your system that has had its default home page edited. This means that once you edit the ~/Sites/index.html file, it will show up in the Rendezvous section of Safari, as shown in Figure 7-2.

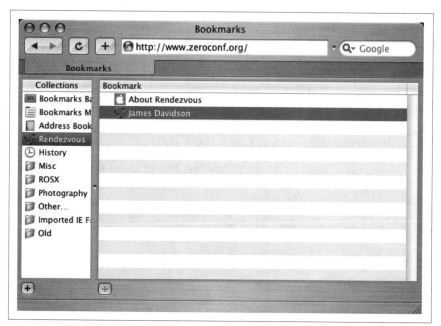

Figure 7-2. Rendezvous advertised sites in Safari

If you want to advertise sites other than the one in the user home directories on your machine, you can edit this block. Here's a list of the directives you can use:

RegisterUserSite

> This directive can be followed by either customized-users or all-users. Using customized-users (the default) advertises sites of only those users who have edited their ~/Sites/index.html file. When followed with all-users, every user's site on the system will be advertised, even if they haven't edited their ~/Sites/index.html file.

RegisterDefaultSite

> This directive creates an advertisement for the server using your Mac's name. When enabled, users on the network can find the web content located in the /Library/WebServer/Documents folder. This directive is disabled by default.

RegisterResource

> This directive, which doesn't appear in the default httpd.conf configuration file, lets you advertise a particular section of your site and must appear with the following syntax:
>
> ```
> RegisterResource name path
> ```
> For example, to advertise the Apache user manual located on your system, you could add the following directive to your Apache configuration:
>
> ```
> RegisterResource "Apache Manual" /manual
> ```

The mod_rendezvous_apple module was designed to advertise sites on your local machine. But what if you want to provide pointers to web sites on another machine, perhaps a remote machine across the Internet? It's actually easy to do; after all, this is the über-configurable Apache. Here's the configuration directives you need to use to create an advertisement to a remote web site:

```
RegisterResource "O'Reilly Conference Website" /conflink
Redirect /conflink http://conferences.oreilly.com/
```

The first line advertises a location of /conflink on your local machine that will show up as "O'Reilly Conference Website" in the browser. The next line sets up a redirect so that when a request comes into your machine for /conflink, the request will be redirected to the O'Reilly web site. Figure 7-3 shows this advertisement in the browser.

Now you can advertise any web site anywhere.

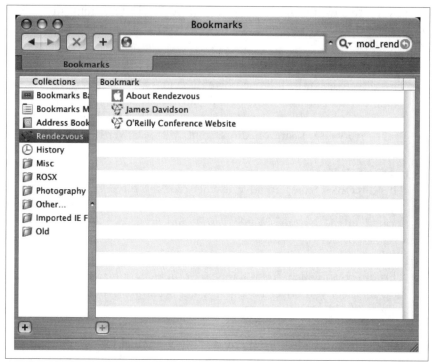

Figure 7-3. Advertising other web sites via Rendezvous in Safari

HACK #72 Set Up a Postfix Mail Server

Previous versions of Mac OS X shipped with the powerful, but complicated, sendmail. Now, Mac OS X comes with Postfix to handle your SMTP needs.

You might not know it, but there is a fully functional mail server built into Mac OS X Panther: the Postfix mail server. Postfix is a new addition to Mac OS X as of Panther and replaces sendmail, the legendary, hard-to-configure mail server that shipped with Mac OS X 10.0 through 10.2.

If you have Mac OS X Server (well worth the money for business use), enabling and using Postfix is as easy as turning on the Mail Service in the Server Admin application, as shown in Figure 7-4. Once enabled, Mac OS X Server will accept mail for users of the system.

The client version of Mac OS X Panther ships with the same basic underlying Postfix system as Mac OS X Server, but it doesn't come with the nice configuration tools. This means that setting up the Postfix is a do-it-yourself proposition.

There are two levels at which Postfix can handle mail duties:

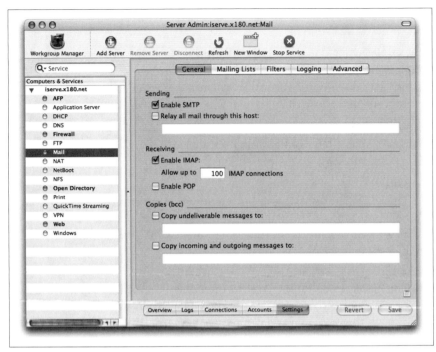

Figure 7-4. Enabling mail with Mac OS X Server

- As a local mailer that lets you send mail from your machine (including from the command line) but doesn't listen for SMTP connections from other machines
- As a first-class SMTP server that can accept mail from the world at large and let you send messages

Enabling Local Mail

You system is already configured, as best it can be, by Apple to let you send mail from the command line. By default, the */etc/hostconfig* file contains the following line:

```
MAILSERVER=-AUTOMATIC-
```

This line causes the Postfix installation on your Mac to run a program called *postfix-watch*. This program watches the local mail queue. When a message is added to the queue—for example, by using the mail command—it causes the rest of the Postfix system to launch and attempt to deliver the mail in the queue. At this point, the success of that attempt is dependent on the IP address of your machine's primary network interface. If your Mac's primary interface has an IP address that's resolvable to a DNS name, even one as

baroque as *dsl093-174-038.pdx1.dsl.speakeasy.net*, then Postfix has everything it needs deliver mail.

If, however, your Mac is using an IP address that does not resolve to a legal
hostname in the DNS system—a frequent occurrence in these days of NAT-
enabled gateway routers—Postfix will not report itself correctly to other
mail servers on the Internet and mail will not be delivered.

If your Mac falls into this situation of not having an IP with a DNS name,
you can change a few configuration settings in the */etc/postfix/main.cf* file to
allow Postfix to send mail successfully:

myhostname

> This parameter sets to the hostname you want Postfix to claim mail is
> being sent from. This name should be, but does not need to be, resolv-
> able to an IP address. All that is required is that the domain part of the
> hostname is valid.

mydomain

> This parameter should be set to the domain name that Postfix will use.
> This domain name must exist in the DNS system and should be set to a
> domain that you own and can receive mail from.

For example, to set up Postfix to report itself correctly using a domain
named *foo.com*, make the following settings in */etc/postfix/main.cf*:

```
myhostname = powerbook.foo.com
mydomain = foo.com
```

You can edit these properties by hand in the *main.cf* file, but a nifty little
tool called postconf allows you to modify Postfix configuration settings
without finding the right properties in the file. To make the same edits
shown in the previous example, use the following commands:

```
$ sudo postconf -e ' myhostname = powerbook.foo.com '
$ sudo postconf -e ' mydomain = foo.com '
```

Once you've made these changes, you'll be able to send email (and so will cron
and other Unix tools!) from the command line by using the mail command. It
won't matter whether the IP address your machine is using can be resolved to a
valid DNS hostname or not. The mail command is easy to use, as shown here:

```
$ mail youremail@domain.com
Subject: this is a test

This is only a test, if this were an actual message... wait, it is.
.
EOT
```

Be sure to end your message with a single period (.) on a line by itself. This
tells mail that you are done with the message and that it should send it.

If you've tried to send mail before making changes to */etc/postfix/main.cf*, the mail system will be active and take a minute or so to see that you've changed its configuration. To force Postfix to reload its configuration, use the following command:

```
$ sudo postfix reload
```

If you need to troubleshoot Postfix, you'll find the log at */var/log/mail.log*. You can view this file easily by using Console (*/Applications/Utilities/Console*), as shown in Figure 7-5.

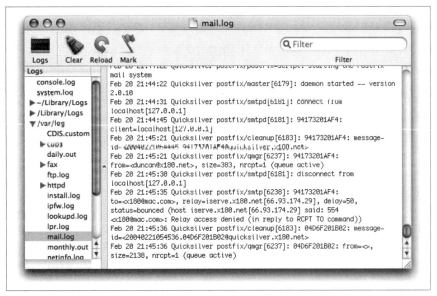

Figure 7-5. Using Console to view the Postfix log file

Where Postfix Delivers Mail

When Postfix is given a message, it faithfully delivers it according to the following rules:

- If the message is addressed to a user on the local machine in the form of *user@localhost* or *user@myhostname*, Postfix sees if there is a user on the local system with the given username and, if so, appends the message to the a file named after the user in the */var/mail/* directory. For example, Postfix delivers mail for a user named *alan* to */var/mail/alan*.

- If the message is addressed in the form of *user@somedomain.com*, Postfix attempts to contact the SMTP server that handles mail for the domain and sends the message.

- If the message is addressed in the form of *user*, Postfix appends the hostname set by the `mydomain` parameter in */etc/postfix/main.cf* and attempts delivery of the message.

If, for some reason, Postfix can't deliver a message, it bounces it back to the sender. In the case of mail sent from the command line, it bounces the mail back to an address determined as *user@mydomain*.

Once mail has been delivered to a local user in the */var/mail* directory, you need either a POP or an IMAP server to access that mail with Mail; or, you need to use the `mail` command-line utility.

Forwarding Mail

If you don't want to install a POP or IMAP server or don't want to use the `mail` utility to check your mail, you can define an address to forward mail to in a *.forward* file in your home directory. The format of the file can be quite simple and can contain an email address. For example, if a user named *mary* wants to have mail forwarded to *mary.jane@mac.com*, she can put the following line in *~mary/.forward*:

```
mary.jane@mac.com
```

When mail arrives at the server addressed to *mary*, Postfix sees the *.forward* file and then sends the message along to *mary.jane@mac.com*.

Turning on the SMTP Server

Once you've made the configuration changes to send mail from your machine, it's a short hop to set it up to be a first-class Simple Mail Transport Protocol (SMTP) mail server on the Internet.

Edit the */etc/hostconfig* file and change the `MAILSERVER` line to read `MAILSERVER=-YES-`.

Edit the */etc/postfix/master.cf* file and uncomment the line that begins with `#smtp`, as shown here:

```
# =========================================================================
# service type private unpriv chroot wakeup maxproc command + args
# (yes) (yes) (yes) (never) (100)
# =========================================================================
smtp inet n - n - - smtpd
```

After making these edits, restart the Postfix system with the following commands:

```
$ sudo postfix stop
$ sudo postfix start
```

After most configuration changes, you can use postfix reload. But when dealing with SMTP server settings, we've found it to be a bit more reliable if you use the stop and start commands.

After executing this command, Postfix will listen on port 25 on the *localhost* interface to accept incoming email via the SMTP protocol. If you want to check whether the SMTP server is indeed running, you can telnet to port 25 (the SMTP port) on your machine:

```
$ telnet 127.0.0.1 25
Trying 127.0.0.1...
Connected to localhost.
Escape character is '^]'.
220 incognita.x180.net ESMTP Postfix
QUIT
221 Bye
```

You can now have applications on your system, such as Mail, use your Postfix installation as an SMTP server.

By default, when you turn on the SMTP server, it accepts mail only on connections that originate from your machine (i.e., *localhost*). In order to allow other hosts on the network to access the SMTP server, you need to tweak an additional setting.

Before you configure Postfix to accept SMTP connections from other machines, you should consider whether you want the responsibility of operating a mail server on your private network or even on the public Internet.

To allow your SMTP server to be accessed via any network interface, and thereby via any host on a network your computer is connected to, set the inet_interfaces configuration setting as follows, and then restart Postfix:

```
inet_interfaces = all
```

Remember, you can use the postconf command:

```
$ sudo postconf -e ' inet_interfaces = all '
```

After making these edits, restart the Postfix system with the stop and start commands:

```
$ sudo postfix stop
$ sudo postfix start
```

After you restart Postfix, any machine that can connect to yours can send you email. At this point, Postfix is restrictive about the mail it accepts for delivery. It will accept only mail addressed to a user on the local machine. Postfix rejects any mail addressed to a user that doesn't exist or which is destined for some other system. These settings prevent your machine from being used as an *open-relay*: a mail server that can be used by anyone and has become a rampant way for spammers to distribute unwanted email.

Handling Mail for Entire Domains

If you have configured the DNS records for a domain to send mail to your server and you want to loosen Postfix's rules a little bit to accept mail for an entire domain, you can use the mydestination parameter in */etc/postfix/main.cf*. For example, to handle mail for the domain set in the mydomain parameter, add the following line:

```
mydestination = $myhostname,localhost.$mydomain,$mydomain
```

This line is a little more involved than you might expect. This is because, by default, Postfix handles mail to $myhostname and localhost.$mydomain automatically. Therefore, when you want to add additional destinations to this list, you have to call out those two settings specifically. If you don't, Postfix might get itself into a jam.

If you want to handle mail for more domains, simply add them to the end of the list, like so:

```
mydestination = $myhostname,localhost.$mydomain,$mydomain,bar.com, foo.com
```

You can add as many domains to this list as you want to accept mail for. You should keep in mind, however, that because Postfix maps the user part of an email address to a user on the system, mail to *alan@bar.com* and *alan@foo.com* will both be delivered to */var/mail/alan*.

HACK   Relay Mail with Postfix
#73   Once you have configured Postfix to send and receive mail, the next step is to let it relay mail for you when you are using a different machine.

Postfix doesn't like *relaying email* (i.e., accepting email that is then forwarded on for final delivery on another server) from sources that aren't trusted in one way or another. A long time ago, when the Internet was young and everyone trusted everyone else, SMTP servers accepted and relayed any message for delivery anywhere. But then people started taking advantage of the openness of the system to send spam and other unwanted email. System administrators started cracking down. Now, running an open relay is considered very bad mojo.

As configured by Apple, Postfix relays only mail that originates on the local machine. If you are running a mail server for anything more than just forwarding messages from various cron jobs, you'll probably want to expand the number of machines that can relay mail through your server. There are two ways to do this:

- Tell Postfix which network addresses it is okay to accept mail from.
- Authenticate an SMTP session so that anybody who has an account on the system can send mail through the server from anywhere.

Setting Trusted Hosts

There are two ways to tell Postfix which network addresses it should relay messages from. The first is to use the mynetworks_style parameter in the */etc/postfix/main.cf* file. This parameter can specify one of the following settings:

host

> This setting means that only the local machine should be trusted. This is the setting that a freshly installed Mac OS X system uses.

subnet

> This setting tells Postfix to trust machines that are on the networks to which the server is connected.

class

> This setting tells Postfix to trust connections from any machine in the A/B/C class network of which the server is a part. Normally, this setting should not be used.

By default, the */etc/postfix/main.cf* file contains the most restrictive parameter:

```
mynetworks_style = host
```

If you want to trust any machine on the same network subnet to which your server is connected—that is, any machine that shares a router with yours— use the following parameter:

```
mynetworks_style = subnet
```

To gain more control over which network addresses Postfix trusts, you can use the mynetworks parameter. This parameter takes a list of network blocks in CIDR (network/mask) notation. For example, to trust all connections coming from the 192.168.1 network, as well as any connections from the 17.254 network, specify the following parameter in */etc/postfix/main.cf*:

```
mynetworks = 192.168.1/24, 17.254/16
```

If all this talk of CIDR notation sounds like Greek to you but you want to specify a single host to trust, you can do so by listing the host's IP address followed by /32. For example, to trust connections from 10.0.1.34, specify the following parameter:

```
mynetworks = 10.0.1.34/32
```

Enabling SMTP Authentication

In addition to checking the IP address from which a message is sent, Postfix can allow mail clients to authenticate themselves with a username and password. If the user exists on the system and the password is correct, Postfix allows relaying of the sent mail. This is known as *SMTP authentication* (or *SMTP AUTH* in geek circles). To enable this in Postfix, add the following configuration settings to */etc/postfix/main.cf*:

```
$ sudo postconf -e 'smtpd_sasl_auth_enable = yes'
$ sudo postconf -e 'smtpd_use_pw_server=yes'
$ sudo postconf -e 'smtpd_pw_server_security_options=plain,login'
$ sudo postconf -e 'smtpd_recipient_restrictions = ¬
permit_sasl_authenticated,permit_mynetworks,¬
reject_unauth_destination,permit'
```

Now that the configuration is done, you'll need to tell Postfix to reload its settings:

```
$ sudo postfix reload
```

To make sure that the settings took effect, you can telnet to port 25 on your server and look at the output of the EHLO SMTP command. Here's an example session:

```
$ telnet 127.0.0.1 25
Trying 127.0.0.1...
Connected to localhost.
Escape character is '^]'.
220 quicksilver.x180.net ESMTP Postfix
EHLO localhost
250-quicksilver.x180.net
250-PIPELINING
250-SIZE 10240000
250-VRFY
250-ETRN
250-AUTH LOGIN PLAIN
250-XVERP
250 8BITMIME
QUIT
221 Bye
Connection closed by foreign host.
```

We find the magic bits we are looking for in the line that contains AUTH LOGIN PLAIN. This advertises to mail clients, such as Mail, that the server supports authentication.

To configure Mail to work with SMTP AUTH on your mail server, you'll need to tweak the server settings for your outgoing mail server. Access the dialog box shown in Figure 7-6 by going to Preferences → Accounts → Account Information → Server Settings.

```
                    SMTP Server Options

    Outgoing Mail Server:  my.server.net


    Check with your system administrator before changing any of
    the advanced options below:

             Server port:     25
                          ☐ Use Secure Sockets Layer (SSL)
          Authentication:  Password                    ▲▼
              User Name:  duncan
               Password:  ••••••••••••

       ⊘                        Cancel       OK
```

Figure 7-6. Configuring SMTP Authentication in Mail

This works great, except for the fact that a major security issue exists with this setup: your username and password travel over the network unencrypted. This means that anyone who has the ability to snoop on your network communications can get your password and use it to log into your server. If you are using a couple desktop machines on a home network, you are probably fine. But if you access your email server from the local coffee shop or at a conference, your username and password are visible to anyone with the right tools, which is not a good thing. But there is something that can be done about it.

Protecting Your Sessions with TLS (SSL)

Postfix is compiled to allow you to encrypt your mail sessions using Transport Layer Security (TLS), formally known as Secure Sockets Layer (SSL). This encryption protects the communications between a TLS/SSL-enabled mail client (such as Mail or Entourage) and the server and encrypts your username and password when you use SMTP authentication.

> Using TLS protects your email from prying eyes only on the way to the server. After that, a message is visible on the way to its final destination. However, the point is to protect that all-important password of yours.

To use TLS, you need to make an X509 certificate. For most private purposes, a self-signed certificate is all you need. To make one, use the following commands. You will be asked a few questions as part of the process of making this certificate.

```
$ sudo mkdir -p /etc/sslcerts
$ sudo openssl req -new -x509 -nodes -out /etc/sslcerts/smtpd.pem -keyout /
etc/sslcerts/smtpd.pem -days 3650
Generating a 1024 bit RSA private key
........++++++
....................++++++
writing new private key to '/etc/sslcerts/smtpd.pem'
-----
You are about to be asked to enter information that will be incorporated
into your certificate request.
What you are about to enter is what is called a Distinguished Name or a DN.
There are quite a few fields but you can leave some blank
For some fields there will be a default value,
If you enter '.', the field will be left blank.
-----
Country Name (2 letter code) [AU]:US
State or Province Name (full name) [Some-State]:Oregon
Locality Name (eg, city) []:Portland
Organization Name (eg, company) [Internet Widgits Pty Ltd]:Mac OS X Hacks
Organizational Unit Name (eg, section) []:World Headquarters
Common Name (eg, YOUR name) []:Mary Jane
Email Address []:mary@somewhere.com
```

Now, we need to add the appropriate configuration properties to /etc/postfix/main.cf:

```
$ postconf -e 'smtpd_use_tls = yes'
$ postconf -e 'smtpd_tls_keyfile = /etc/sslcerts/smtpd.pem'
$ postconf -e 'smtpd_tls_cert_file = /etc/sslcerts/smtpd.pem'
$ postconf -e 'smtpd_tls_auth_only = yes'
```

The first line tells Postfix that it can use TLS. The second and third lines indicate where the TLS certificate is stored. And the last line indicates that Postfix should allow SMTP Authentication to occur only in the scope of a TLS session. Reload Postfix:

```
$ sudo postfix reload
```

To make sure the settings took effect, you can telnet to port 25 on your server and look at the output of the EHLO SMTP command. Here's an example session:

```
$ telnet 127.0.0.1 25
Trying 127.0.0.1...
Connected to localhost.
Escape character is '^]'.
220 quicksilver.x180.net ESMTP Postfix
```

```
EHLO localhost
250-quicksilver.x180.net
250-PIPELINING
250-SIZE 10240000
250-VRFY
250-ETRN
250-STARTTLS
250-XVERP
250 8BITMIME
QUIT
221 Bye
Connection closed by foreign host.
```

Notice the line containing STARTTLS. This advertises to mail clients, such as
Mail, that the server supports encryption. Also note that the line containing
AUTH LOGIN PLAIN is gone. This is a result of setting the smtpd_tls_auth_only
property.

To enable your Mail client to send mail to your server, you'll once again
need to tweak the server settings for your outgoing mail server. Access the
dialog box in Mail (shown in Figure 7-7) by going to Preferences → Accounts
→ Account Information → Server Settings.

Figure 7-7. Configuring SMTP Authentication with TLS

Now, when you send mail, your username and password will be protected
by the best encryption available. There's only one catch. Because we used a
self-signed certificate, your Mail client will complain that it can't verify the
certificate in use, as shown in Figure 7-8. Though this error is distracting at

first, it's harmless enough. After all, you created the certificate, so there's no problem with using it. Don't worry, this message won't pop up *every* time you send a message. In Mail, it pops up only the first time you use the SMTP server after you launch the application.

Figure 7-8. Mail, letting you know a self-signed cert is being used

If you would rather not see this message, you'll need to venture into the world of certificate authorities and shell out some money. If you are setting up a mail server for a company, you should do this, but if you are just setting up a mail server for yourself, there's really no need.

Bypassing Captive Routers

One problem you might notice while using hotel and café wireless connections is that outbound mail can't be delivered when you are using SMTP Authentication. This is because these network providers are capturing port 25 at the router and feeding it to their own SMTP server. The theory behind this is that computer users aren't savvy enough to deal with a multitude of different mail configurations, so the network providers are trying to make it easy. Unfortunately, this breaks SMTP Authentication badly, because their server can't authenticate you and your mail client is set up to use authentication.

The solution is to set up an alternate port on your SMTP server so that you can bypass the captivity and send mail directly to your server. For example, to configure Postfix to listen to port 2525 as well as 25, add the following line to */etc/postfix/master.cf*:

```
# ============================================================================
# service type  private unpriv  chroot  wakeup  maxproc command + args
#               (yes)   (yes)   (yes)   (never) (100)
```

```
# ==========================================================================
smtp      inet  n      -     n     -     -     smtpd
2525      inet  n      -     n     -     -     smtpd
```

Reload Postfix with the following command:

$ **sudo postfix reload**

Now, configure your Mail client to use port 2525, as shown in Figure 7-9.

Figure 7-9. Configuring to send mail to port 2525

Set Up Secondary Mail Servers

HACK #74

The problem with running your own mail server is that sometimes the connection to it goes down. When this happens, mail bounces—not a good thing. To prevent this, you'll need to set up a secondary mail server.

If you are running a mail server for a domain, you need to prepare for the inevitable drops in network connectivity to your server. No matter how good your connection is to the Internet, at some point, your ISP will perform some maintenance or a construction worker will dig up the fiber line though which your packets travel and your server will be disconnected from the Net. When this happens, mail addressed to your domain can't be delivered.

The way the mail system works, as long as your server comes back on within a couple days or so, mail usually gets through. But the people who sent you the mail get an email from the server that states in large letters, "The message you sent could not be delivered." Further down in the message, there is a note that the server will attempt redelivery for a while. It seems, however, that most people never see that and instead freak out, call your cellphone, and wonder what on earth happened.

The solution is to set up a backup mail server (a *backup MX* in DNS jargon), which requires two steps. First, you need to find a backup server to handle mail for when your server isn't available. Second, you need to place a backup MX record into the DNS record for your domain.

> So how do you place a backup MX record into your DNS settings? That depends on who runs your DNS services for you. If you are using the DNS servers provided by your domain name registrar, there should be a way to add an MX record in the domain administration screens.

So, how do you find a backup server? You really have two choices. The first is to find a friend who is also running a server and ask her to configure her server to accept mail for your domain and then forward it to your machine when it becomes available again. And, of course, in exchange you'll do the same for her, right?

Setting up Postfix to serve as a backup mail server involves two configuration properties in */etc/postfix/main.cf*. The first, smtpd_recipient_restrictions, should contain the key reject_unauth_destination. If you followed the instructions on relaying mail [Hack #73], this key is already set up:

```
smtpd_recipient_restrictions = permit_sasl_authenticated, permit_
mynetworks,reject_unauth_destination,permit
```

Next, the domain names you want your server to relay mail for should appear in the relay_domains list. By default, this list contains only $mydestination. To add relay mail for the *foo.com* domain, use the following command:

```
$ sudo postconf -e 'relay_domains = $mydestination foo.com'
```

Then, reload Postfix's settings:

```
$ sudo postfix reload
```

Your server is now configured to be a backup mail server for your pal's domain.

If you can't find anybody to trade backup mail server duties with, you should take a look at using DynDNS.org's MailHop Backup MX services (*http://www.mailhop.com*). For a little cash, you can get a good backup mail infrastructure.

Create Mail Aliases

HACK #75

Email aliases direct mail sent to webmaster@, me@, and so forth to the right email address.

A fancy bit of email functionality in common use, especially among those with their own domain, is to create *aliases* to forward mail sent to a variety of so-called *vanity* email addresses to a single email address. Perhaps you'd like *webmaster@* on your web site so that you can have your email application filter requests to another folder. *me@* is a popular one, though I can't quite fathom why. Others popular aliases include *info@*, *support@*, *sales@*, and *godlike@*—okay, so that last one's not all that common.

Prior to Panther, Mac OS X used sendmail as its Mail Transfer Agent (MTA). The included version of sendmail was configured to look to NetInfo for alias information, which required diving into NetInfo to create aliases or making sure that sendmail was configured to look at the */etc/aliases* file. In Panther, sendmail has been replaced with Postfix, which is configured to use a database based on the */etc/alises* file by default.

> This hack assumes Postfix is properly configured [Hack #72]. You may need to do nothing, or you might have a little work to do.

Alias File Format

The format of the */etc/aliases* file is simple. Each line of the alias file consists of the name to alias followed by one or more target addresses to deliver mail addressed to the alias. Lines that begin with a # are treated as comments. By default, the first few lines of the */etc/aliases* file look like this:

```
#
# Sample aliases file. Install in the location as specified by the
# output from the command "postconf alias_maps". Typical path names
# are /etc/aliases or /etc/mail/aliases.
#
# >>>>>>>>>> The program "newaliases" must be run after
# >> NOTE >> this file is updated for any changes to
# >>>>>>>>>> show through to Postfix.
#

# Person who should get root's mail. Don't receive mail as root!
# root: you

# Basic system aliases -- these MUST be present
MAILER-DAEMON: postmaster
postmaster: root
```

To deliver to your user any mail addressed to *root*, you just need to edit this file as an administrator. Simply uncomment the *root* alias and edit it to something like this:

```
root:         duncan
```

You aren't limited to defining aliases to local users. You can also have aliases send mail to other users on other machines. For example, if you want to redirect mail to an external address, you can define the following alias:

```
john:         johnjacobjingleheimer@mac.com
```

When you make a change to the */etc/aliases* file, you need to run the `newaliases` command:

```
$ sudo newaliases
```

This rebuilds the database derived from the */etc/aliases* file into a format that Postfix can quickly use.

Homegrown Mailing Lists with Aliases

Aliases are useful for more than just redirecting email for a single user. They are also handy for building up small mailing lists. For example, I maintain a small mailing list for my family. There are only 10 people on the list, so there's no need for a full-fledged mailing list manager such as Mailman (*http://www.list.org*). Instead, I just define an alias that looks like this:

```
family:       duncan, mom@somewhere.com, dad@elsewhere.com, sis@school
```

Then, I quickly reload the aliases database:

```
$ sudo newaliases
```

I now have a fully functional mailing list for my family to use.

HACK
#76   Set Up IMAP and POP Mail Servers

There's tremendous value in having all your email with you at all times. Unfortunately, this usually means being tied to a particular mail client. IMAP allows you to have this particular cake and eat it too. This hack focuses on IMAP but installs POP along the way, since it's just so simple to do.

Switching email clients can mean a pile of work and a plethora of less-than-great import/export/conversion functions and scripts. Wouldn't it be great to switch seamlessly between Entourage's gorgeous GUI, Mail's simplicity, Eudora's feature set, and the powerful, text-based Pine Unix mail app?

Internet Message Access Protocol (IMAP) is usually considered a Post Office Protocol (POP) mail replacement. POP accumulates all your incoming mail on your service provider's or enterprise's mail server, to be downloaded on a regular basis to your desktop or laptop and from then on saved and manipulated (filed in folders and such) locally. IMAP stores and manipulates all your mail on the server; your mail client is fed the headers (To, From, Subject, etc.) and retrieves each message from the server on demand. Since everything's done on the server, you can switch mail applications on a whim, according to the functionality you need or just when the mood strikes.

But what if you're offline? Aye, there's the rub. Most mail applications can be set to keep a cache of messages locally for offline use, syncing with the server on occasion. This is hardly an efficient way to do things; messages get duplicated and require ongoing synchronization between server and Desktop—not to mention the fact that you don't have offline access to messages that just don't happen to be cached locally on your Desktop.

What if you moved the IMAP server to your desktop or laptop? You'd have all your mail right where you need it, but you wouldn't suffer the tax of being tied to a particular mail application.

Unfortunately, IMAP software doesn't ship by default on Mac OS X. Fortunately, it's easy to get, compile, and set up. We're going to use the University of Washington's IMAP server, but we'll need the Mac OS X Developer Tools installed before proceeding.

Downloading and Building the IMAP Server

Downloading and building the IMAP server is a relatively straightforward process when you know exactly what to type. Of course, the trick is to know exactly what to type, which is sometimes no easy thing. When Apple upgraded Mac OS X to Panther, the way the system performed authentication changed and broke the instructions that worked in Jaguar. After quite a bit of sleuthing, inspired by many of the comments at the Hacks web site (*http://hacks.oreilly.com*), we're happy to bring you a recipe that works.

First, you need to download the latest IMAP distribution from the University of Washington FTP server (*ftp://ftp.cac.washington.edu/imap*). The instructions in this hack are based on the latest distribution at the time of this writing: *imap-2004.RC*. You'll want to check the FTP server, however, and make sure to grab the latest available version.

That said, here's an easy script to download the distribution:

```
$ curl ftp://ftp.cac.washington.edu/imap/imap-2004.RC.tar.Z > imap.tar.Z
$ uncompress imap.tar.Z
$ tar xf imap.tar
$ cd imap-2004.RC8
```

Next, we need to compile the code. If you've built the UW IMAP server before, you might notice that the target has changed from osx to oxp:

```
$ make oxp SSLTYPE=nopwd SSLDIR=/usr SSLCERTS=/etc/sslcerts
$ sudo mkdir -p /usr/local/bin
$ sudo cp imapd/imapd /usr/local/bin/imapd
$ sudo cp ipopd/ipop3d /usr/local/bin/ipop3d
```

There. That wasn't so bad, was it? You now have fully functional IMAP and POP servers compiled and installed. Now, you just need to configure them.

Configuring the Servers

We need to do two things to configure the servers. First, we need to set up SSL certificates for each server to use. Second, we need to enable the servers to handle requests.

To install a self-signed certificate (perfectly adequate for our needs), use the following commands. You will be asked a few questions as part of the process. The answers I used are highlighted in bold; yours will be different.

```
$ sudo mkdir -p /etc/sslcerts
$ sudo openssl req -new -x509 -nodes -out /etc/sslcerts/imapd.pem -keyout /
etc/sslcerts/imapd.pem -days 3650
Using configuration from /System/Library/OpenSSL/openssl.cnf
Generating a 1024 bit RSA private key
...................................................++++++
..........................++++++
writing new private key to '/etc/sslcerts/imapd.pem'
-----
You are about to be asked to enter information that will be incorporated
into your certificate request.
What you are about to enter is what is called a Distinguished Name or a DN.
There are quite a few fields but you can leave some blank
For some fields there will be a default value,
If you enter '.', the field will be left blank.
-----
Country Name (2 letter code) [AU]: US
State or Province Name (full name) [Some-State]: California
Locality Name (eg, city) []: San Francisco
Organization Name (eg, company) [Internet Widgits Pty Ltd]: x180
Organizational Unit Name (eg, section) []: Home Mail
Common Name (eg, YOUR name) []: James Duncan Davidson
Email Address []: duncan@x180.net
```

Now, do the same for the POP server using the same values for the fields; only the command-line invocation changes:

```
$ sudo openssl req -new -x509 -nodes -out /etc/sslcerts/ipop3d.pem -keyout /
etc/sslcerts/ipop3d.pem -days 3650
...
```

Next, we need to configure Mac OS X to start up the IMAP server when it sees requests to the IMAP over SSL (port 993) and the POP server for POP SSL requests (port 995). In Jaguar and previous versions of Mac OS X, this duty was handled by inetd. In Panther, it is handed by xinetd, which patiently listens for requests for particular services and farms them out to the appropriate applications to handle. Tell xinetd about the new IMAP server by adding a file to the */etc/xinetd.d* directory:

```
$ sudo pico /etc/inetd.conf/imaps
```

This file needs to contain the following lines:

```
service imaps
{
 disable = no
 socket_type = stream
 wait = no
 user = root
 groups = yes
 flags = NOLIBWRAP
 server = /usr/local/bin/imapd
}
```

We need do the same thing for the POP server:

```
$ sudo pico /etc/inetd.conf/pops
```

This file needs to contain the following lines:

```
service pops
{
 disable = no
 socket_type = stream
 wait = no
 user = root
 groups = yes
 flags = NOLIBWRAP
 server = /usr/local/bin/ipop3d
}
```

The next step is to set up Mac OS X's authentication system so that it can perform the proper authentication for the servers:

```
$ sudo cp /etc/pam.d/ftpd /etc/pam.d/imap
$ sudo cp /etc/pam.d/ftpd /etc/pam.d/pop3
```

To activate the IMAP and POP servers, we need to tell xinetd to start them up:

```
$ sudo /sbin/service imaps start
$ sudo /sbin/service pops start
```

Congratulations! You're done. Now, you just need to set up your mail client to use SSL, using its configuration settings.

## CHAPTER EIGHT

Files and Backup
Hacks 77–87

Files and folders lie at the heart of everyone's digital life. While using a file-system has become all but second nature to us over the past few decades of GUI computing, we still find ourselves struggling with the chore of storing, organizing, maintaining, and backing up our personal filestore.

You'll find a lot in this chapter on backup: the final frontier in personal data. We're often shocked to find how people who are so reliant upon what lives on their drives spend so little time making sure it doesn't all disappear with a resounding "poof!" if (read: when) something goes wrong. Trust us; there's never a good time to lose a hard drive. Everyone needs to have a backup plan.

While backup is about as personal as the files you store, there's sure to be something here that fits your particular needs—in combination and with some minor adjustment.

HACK #77 Synchronize Your Files

If you own multiple Macs, keeping all of your work everywhere can be challenging. But a couple of tools can help you work seamlessly between PowerBook and PowerMac.

I usually use a couple of computers to do my daily work. I use my Power-Book to write my articles when I am on the road or when I am in the office. When I come back home I usually use my PowerMac G4, because I prefer a bigger keyboard than the one on the PowerBook. And I often need to synchronize the stuff I have on my PowerBook with my PowerMac. Confusion sometimes arises when I have a hard time figuring out which is the latest version of the work I have worked on.

.Mac

One of the simplest ways to work with your files on multiple Macs is to use .Mac's iDisk (*http://www.mac.com/1/iTour/tour_idisk.html*; .Mac is $99 per year, 60 day free trial available). If you have a .Mac account, the iDisk icon is always there in your Finder. Just click on it to connect to your iDisk folder automatically. Since it is a shared filesystem on the network, every Mac you set up with your .Mac account will be able to see files on your iDisk.

This works great if your Mac is always connected to the network, but what about when you are using your laptop on an airplane or somewhere else without a nice, fast Internet connection? The answer is simple. You can create a local cached copy of your iDisk by going into the .Mac System Preference panel and setting iDisk to create a local copy of your iDisk. This copies the contents of your iDisk to your machine and keeps them in sync with the network copy of the files. When you change a file on your local machine, it gets copied to the iDisk automatically. If you aren't connected when you modify a file, iDisk updates the next time you have a network connection.

This solution works well, as long as you don't have a lot of data. But if you have more data that you need to keep on multiple Macs than you have pocketbook for .Mac storage space, read on.

You Synchronize

To solve this synchronization problem, I use You Synchronize (*http://www.yousoftware.com/products/synchronize.php*; $49.95, trial available) from You software. You Synchronize is an application that performs file synchronization between two folders, whether they're on the same server or distributed over the network. It can also detect when files have been modified in both folders and let you choose which modified file you want to keep.

One of the significant features of You Synchronize is that it supports four different methods of synchronizing files:

- Checksum
- File signature
- Checksum and modification date
- Modification date

The checksum method offers the most robust synchronization method. Conventional synchronization software is error-prone, because it relies on modification dates to decide on the synchronization process. This can be risky, because the modification dates for the two files might not be accurately set.

The checksum method uses CRC32-bit checksums to determine if a file, not the modification date, has changed. However, the checksum is resource intensive, so You Synchronize provides the other three methods for synchronization, depending on your usage.

Once you launch You Synchronize, you should see the window shown in Figure 8-1.

Figure 8-1. Setting the options in the Settings tab

The most important tab is the Settings tab, where you configure the local and remote folders to synchronize. So, the content of the local and remote folders will have identical contents after synchronization.

You can choose the type of synchronization: Two Way Synchronization, Local Replace Remote, or Remote Replaces Local. You can also choose the comparison method: Checksum, File Signature, Checksum & Modification Date, or Modification Date.

Once you have configured the options, click Sync to synchronize the two folders.

To set up multiple sets of folders to synchronize, click Projects. A drawer window appears, as shown in Figure 8-2. You can add, rename, delete, or duplicate projects. Each project synchronizes two folders.

Figure 8-2. Adding new projects via the Projects drawer

In addition to manually clicking the Sync button to perform synchronization, you can also automate the synchronizations process by clicking on the Schedules button, as shown in Figure 8-3.

Chronosync

Chronosync (*http://www.econtechnologies.com/site/Pages/ChronoSync/chrono_ overview.html*; $30, trial available) from Econ Technologies is another good piece of synchronization software you can use for your Mac. Chronosync is an easy-to-use data-management tool that allows you to efficiently synchronize files and folders from one disk location to another.

To synchronize two folders, you need to specify the two folders involved in the synchronization process. Then, you can click Save to save this information as a synchronization set. Each synchronization set specifies a pair of folders to synchronize, as shown in Figure 8-4.

You can also specify some simple rules to customize the synchronization, as shown in Figure 8-5.

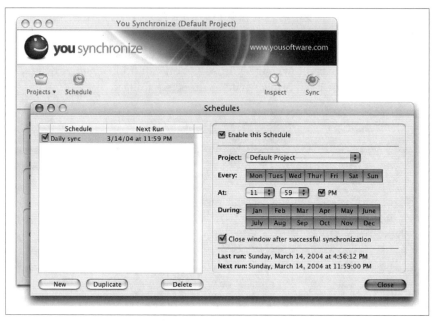

Figure 8-3. Scheduling a synchronization process

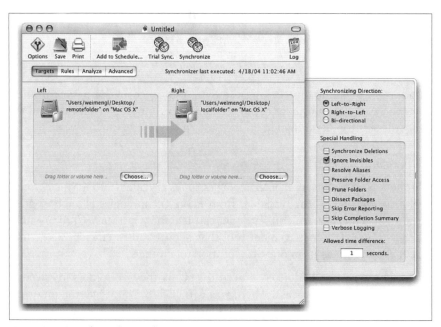

Figure 8-4. Specifying the synchronization set

To schedule a synchronization automatically, click Add to Schedule and specify the schedule, as shown in Figure 8-6.

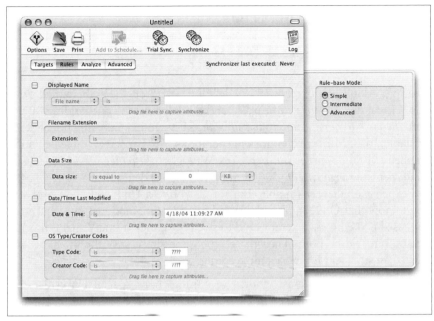

Figure 8-5. Specifying rules

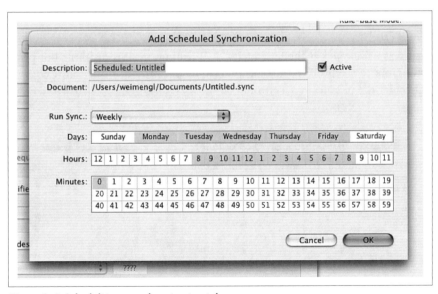

Figure 8-6. Scheduling a synchronization job

Now that you have configured synchronization, be sure to perform it regularly to keep all your files in sync and to avoid conflicts.

—*Wei Meng Lee*

Edit Special Unix Files
#78

*Special Unix files need special handling. You can't simply edit them in Word
and expect things to work. Here's a crash course in editing using the pico
command-line editor and TextEdit GUI editor.*

You've no doubt discovered OS X's default text editor, the aptly named Text-
Edit. Hopefully, you've also heard of and downloaded the outstanding BBEdit
(*http://www.barebones.com/products/bbedit*; $179, 30-day fully functional demo
available), the favorite text editor of generations of Mac users. Or maybe you've
grabbed BBEdit's little brother, TextWrangler (*http://www.barebones.com/
products/textwrangler*; $49, 30-day fully functional demo available), which is
less expensive but very capable. But unless you're a Unix jock, you probably
don't know that OS X ships with several other feature- and history-rich Terminal-based text editors. Veterans tend to swear by either vi (the Visual Editor) or
Emacs, but seldom both. Then there's pico, the simplest of the three, yet still
more than sufficient for most simple editing work.

This hack provides a crash course in editing those special Unix files discussed in this book: *httpd.conf*, */etc/inetd.conf*, *plist* files, and the like. We'll
skip the two with the steepest learning curve (vi and Emacs) and stick with
pico and TextEdit.

Using Pico

Pico was developed at the University of Washington. It is a simple but powerful Unix text editor. To fire up pico, type `pico` (by itself or followed by a
particular file to edit) in a Terminal window (see Figure 8-7).

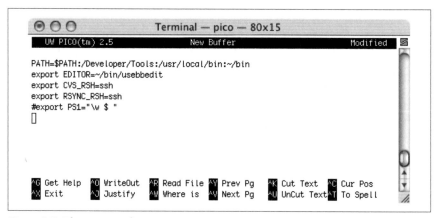

Figure 8-7. The pico interface

Pico's interface, while perhaps a little Unixy for the uninitiated, is pretty
straightforward. Rather than click buttons in menu bars, you issue commands

by typing Control-character shortcuts; the bottom two rows of pico's interface provide a list of commonly used shortcuts. That ^ character prefixing all the shortcuts stands for the Control key on your keyboard; thus, ^G signifies that for more comprehensive help (see Figure 8-8), you should press Control-G.

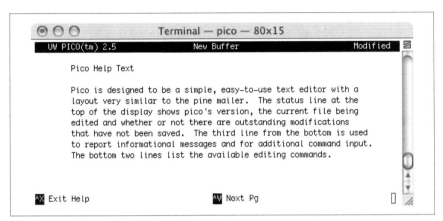

Figure 8-8. Getting help in pico

Press Control-X to leave Pico Help.

Now that you have pico warmed up, let's take it for a spin with some common operations.

Moving about. You can move about within the text file you're editing, as you might expect, by using the arrow keys. Beyond basic character-by-character movement, however, your old habits will fail you. None of the ⌘- sequences work here. To scroll through long text, you cannot use the Page Up and Page Down keys on your keyboard; you must use Control-Y to page up and Control-V to page down. To jump to the beginning of a line, press Control-A. To jump to the end, type Control-E.

To search within the current file for a snippet of text, press Control-W, enter the text to find at the Search: prompt, and press Return. To search for the same text again, press Control-W, followed by Return. To change your mind and cancel a search, press Control-C.

Saving. To save a file (see Figure 8-9), press Control-O (write out—go figure!).

Figure 8-9. Saving a file in pico

Type a filename or fully qualified path (e.g., /tmp/test.txt) to which to save, and press Return.

You can also use the built-in file and directory browser (press Control-T) to locate a particular directory in which to save your file (see Figure 8-10). Use the arrow keys to move about, Return to move into a directory, .. to move up a directory, and E to select a directory and return to the File Name to write: prompt. You can also select a filename; whatever you save over-writes the contents of a preexisting file with that name.

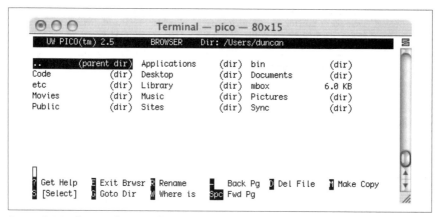

Figure 8-10. The pico directory browser

Opening. Oddly enough, pico doesn't have an Open File command. Instead, you insert the contents of a file into the editor. Press Control-R, and every-thing's pretty much the same as it was with saving, directory browser and all. The only difference is that you press Return rather then E to make your final selection. The selected file's contents appear in the editor, appended to anything you've already been editing.

Selecting text. Selecting a block of text in pico is not as straightforward as using your mouse. In fact, the mouse is utterly useless in pico and just about every other command-line application.

To select a block of text, use the arrow keys to position your cursor at the start of the text you want to select and press Control-Shift-6. Pico responds with [Mark Set]. Move about until you've selected all the text you wish; selected text is called out in inverse colors.

To unselect the text, simply press Control-Shift-6 again.

To cut the selected block, press Control-K. To paste it somewhere, move the cursor to the right place and press Control-U. Note that there's no copy function in pico. To copy, just cut and paste (Control-K, Control-U) in place and then paste again with Control-U anywhere and as many times as you wish.

> You can always use Terminal's cut and paste features (⌘-X, ⌘-C, and ⌘-V). Just keep in mind that these are being accessed from the Terminal and not from pico.

Deleting. Use your Delete key as usual to delete the character before your cursor. To delete the character after the cursor, press Control-D. Delete an entire line with Control-K.

Leaving. To get out of pico at any time, press Control-X. If you haven't saved what you're currently editing, pico offers you one last chance to Save modified buffer.

Setting Your Default Command-Line Editor

The default command-line editor is vi—not a great choice for beginners. Commands such as crontab -e use the default as their editor of choice, rather than allow you to use the pico editor you now know and love.

To set your command-line editor of choice to pico, create a file called *.tcshrc* in your home directory to contain the following single line:

```
setenv EDITOR /usr/bin/pico
```

The next time you invoke a Terminal command that requires a default editor (and respects the EDITOR environment variable), pico will be used instead of vi.

Using TextEdit

TextEdit (Applications → TextEdit) is the default GUI text editor. More like any other application you've used than pico, TextEdit is also much more novice-friendly.

As in most Mac applications, you can drag and drop selections made with your mouse. Saving, opening, cutting, copying, and pasting work as expected. Moving about with the arrow keys and modified arrow keys (i.e., using Shift-arrow) also holds no surprises. Page Up and Page Down shift up and down a page, respectively.

The big issue when working with TextEdit is that it doesn't deal well with editing Unix files—especially those files that you don't have permission to edit without becoming an administrative user.

The Best of Both Worlds

If you are going to be doing a lot of text editing and want seamless integration between the command line and a GUI-based editor, you should take a look at either BBEdit or its little brother, TextWrangler. Both of these tools can open files owned by the administrator and require an administrator password when you save them, as shown in Figure 8-11.

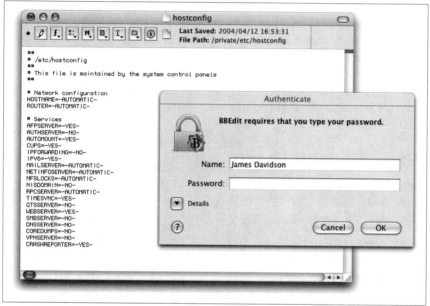

Figure 8-11. The /etc/hostconfig file loaded in BBEdit

When you run BBEdit for the first time, it prompts you to install its command-line tool, bbedit (TextWrangler also prompts you to install its tool, edit). After you do so, you'll be able to open files with the following command:

```
$ bbedit /etc/hostconfig
```

Unlike the command-line editors that allow you to specify a file that doesn't already exist, you have to tell bbedit to explicitly create a new file when needed. To do so, use the -c argument:

```
$ bbedit -c newfile.txt
```

Use BBEdit as your EDITOR. BBEdit can even serve as your command-line editor, replacing pico, vi, or Emacs. Simply save the following script as *~/bin/usebbedit*:

```
#!/bin/sh
/usr/bin/bbedit --wait --resume "$@"
```

This script launches BBEdit in such a way that it keeps the process that requested the editor waiting until you close the window for the file. After the file is closed, the Terminal window from which the editor was called pops back into the foreground.

After you save the script, make it executable:

```
$ chmod +x ~/bin/usebbedit
```

Now, set your EDITOR environment variable (in your *.bash_profile* if you want to make it permanent) to the following:

```
export EDITOR=~/bin/usebbedit
```

Writing and executing shell scripts. BBEdit also allows you to write and execute shell scripts without ever going to the command line. Simply write your script in a BBEdit window and then use the Run → Run menu. BBEdit runs the script and then puts its output into a new window as shown in Figure 8-12.

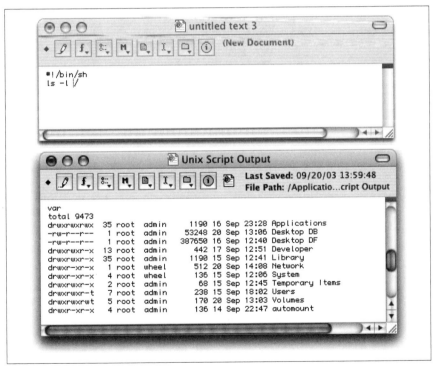

Figure 8-12. Running a script in BBEdit

—*Wei Meng Lee*

HACK #79 Find and Unerase Misplaced and Deleted Files

Several options are available for recovering data that has been taken down by a crashing app, mistakenly erased, or simply misplaced somewhere on one of your many memory cards, USB jump drives, and external drives.

You, your software, a crashed hard drive, or a piece of removable media has just mistakenly made inconveniently unavailable (read: deleted) a vital presentation or favorite digital photograph.

First things first: take a deep breath and don't panic.

Fortunately, a variety of tools are available for Mac OS X to help you recover your lost information. They cost a bit of cash, but they all run less than pay-as-you-go, service-based software such as VirtualLab™ Data Recovery Software for Macintosh (*http://www.binarybiz.com/vlab/mac.php*) or the thousands of dollars charged by data-recovery specialists such as DriveSavers (*http://www.drivesavers.com*). These services can be of great help in the case of a catastrophic drive crash or dropped laptop, but for individual files that have been mislaid or trashed by accident, they're probably overkill.

Recovering Word Files

As hard as it is to believe, Microsoft Word is not entirely bug free and is even known to crash from time to time. When this happens, Word usually realizes that something has gone awry and, upon relaunching, attempts to recover whatever you were just working on. You'll notice your nearly departed document (in some form) pop right up, its name suffixed with the word *recovered* in parentheses.

If the recovered file doesn't immediately appear upon restarting Word after a crash, don't despair. Word (and some other programs) usually saves temporary files to an invisible folder on your computer. Close Word, launch the Terminal [Hack #91], and type the following on the command line:

```
$ open /tmp/501/TemporaryItems
```

If you aren't the only user on your Mac, you need to substitute your numeric user ID for 501 in the path. To find your numeric user ID, execute the id command in Terminal.

In the Finder window that jumps to the fore, look around for *Word Work Files*. Drag these to the Desktop and try to open them one after the other. Chances are, at least part of your lost document is somewhere in the text of these files.

If you don't like mucking about in the Terminal, get yourself a copy of Presto-Chango (*http://www.applelinks.net/lubod/*), a set of scripts that automates this process.

Recovering Digital Media

SubRosaSoft (*http://www.subrosasoft.com*: $24.95 per individual application, $49.90 for the whole bundle) offers a trio of specialized apps for recovering missing information and accidentally deleted files.

If you have badly scratched or damaged CDs, CDRestore scans the damaged disk, copies it temporarily to your hard drive, and immediately burns a full replacement copy—all with a single mouse click.

FlashRestore is compatible with most Memory Sticks, SmartMedia, CompactFlash I & II, and SD/XD Cards. Select a mounted piece of removable media and set FlashRestore on it, scanning for deleted files and copying anything recoverable to a folder on your hard drive.

Some cameras securely erase their files (i.e., erase the files and then immediately write over the area from which they were erased). In this case, FlashRestore will not be able to recover your files, so make sure you give the demo a try with some of your media before paying the full purchase price. If the FlashRestore demo doesn't work with your media, you might try DataRescue's PhotoRescue (*http://www.datarescue.com/photorescue*: $29; demo available), which provides advanced picture recovery from SmartMedia, Memory Stick, and Compact Flash.

MP3Restore is nearly identical in form and function to FlashRestore, but instead of recovering image files from removable media, MP3Restore scans your hard drive, iPod or other MP3 player, and removable media for deleted MP3s. It copies any files it finds to a folder of your choice. As with FlashRestore, a fully functional demo is available to test against your MP3 player and other media.

If you work with more varied types of audio and video files and are looking for something a little more robust for media recovery, you should give MediaRECOVER Image Recovery Software for Mac OS X (*http://www.mediarecover.com/image_recovery_mac.html*: $29.95; limited demo available) a whirl. It recovers deleted or lost pictures, audio, *and* video from a wide array of media, including SmartMedia, CompactFlash, Memory Stick, MicroDrive, xD Picture Card Flash Card, PC Card, Multimedia Card, Secure Digital Card, Zip Disks, floppy disks, and others. According to the MediaRECOVER web site, the program recognizes and recovers any of the following file types: JPEG, EXIF, TIFF, PNG, GIF, BMP, Canon CRW, Nikon NEF, Kodak DCR, AVI, MOV, and MPG/MPEG.

ProSoft's Data Rescue X

If you've got a really messed up hard drive or some piece of removal media that contains vital files of types different than those discussed in the previous sections, you're going to want to invest in a program such as ProSoft's Data Rescue (*http://www.prosoftengineering.com/products/data_rescue_info.php*: $89). Data Rescue has been around since the pre–OS X days (ProSoft still offers an OS 8.1–compatible version of its software) and was recently bought by ProSoft. I have come to love and rely upon Data Rescue over the years.

It's a little pricey, but if you have a seriously problematic hard drive that won't even mount but that contains data you *need* to access, Data Rescue is that rare, powerful program that could quite possibly save the day. It won't repair your drive, but it will diligently scan it and find every recoverable file that you have erased. (Once again, with anything you've securely erased, all bets are off.)

You can run Data Rescue from its bootable installation disk or mounted disk image. You will need a separate hard drive for Data Rescue to use while scanning the source drive for files; it will save anything it finds to that second drive.

You have the option to perform a Quick Scan or a Thorough Scan, both of which scan your entire drive for all recoverable files, or a Content Scan, which focuses the scan for particular file types. As with the previously discussed programs, Data Rescue can also be used to recover MP3s from a dead iPod or images from your digital camera. Data Rescue can take a long time to work, depending on the drive's size and amount of data corruption. When it finishes running, it displays a list of results from which you can choose the files you want to salvage.

Hacking the Hack

This hack discusses various ways to fix a problem. If you want to avoid this problem altogether, the easiest way is to practice safe backup. In that vein, you'll find oodles of backup hacks in this chapter; one or more are likely to apply to your particular circumstances.

—C. K. Sample III

Store and Search Your Records as PDF

Replace paper with PDF and keep your files with you without the weight of the filing cabinets.

For decades now, we've been hearing about the paperless office. Computers were supposed to save us from drowning in seas of letter-sized paper and eliminate filing cabinets everywhere. Alas, that hasn't happened. Instead, we're making more paper than ever before, because it's so darn easy to print nice-looking documents. And there probably will always be the coworker who insists on printing out his email to read instead of dealing with it onscreen.

To be fair, there has been a strong argument for paper printouts. Paper is a format that can be kept for a long time and still be read, unlike that electronic document you created 10 years ago using whatever word-processing software you had. But with the advent of PDF as a standard portable format that can be read on many operating systems and by many programs, we can be sure that any document stored as a PDF will be readable for decades to come.

But even though PDF has been around for a while, only the advent of Mac OS X has made it drop-dead easy for anybody to create PDF files. All you have to do is print from any application and hit the Save as PDF button, as shown in Figure 8-13. This makes it easy to store a PDF copy of whatever you want for permanent retrieval.

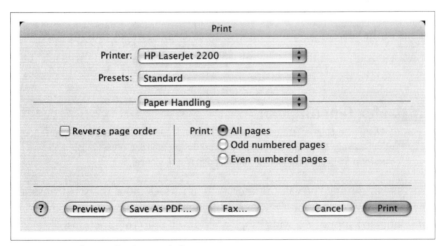

Figure 8-13. The standard Print dialog

What kinds of documents should you keep this way? Well, it depends on your needs, but I store the following kinds of files as PDF documents on my computer:

- Bank statements, downloaded from my bank or printed out with Safari
- Important emails, including those that contain information important to my job
- Copies of legal documents, such as contracts
- Receipts from online purchases, such as from Amazon.com or the Apple Store
- Scanned receipts
- Tax forms, printed from TurboTax

Not only does having all of this information in PDF form save me from filing a bunch of paper, it also means I can keep a copy of my important records on a spare hard drive in a safe-deposit box and another copy on my laptop. That way, I have all my data, regardless of where in the world I might be.

Searching Through Documents

The advantages of the PDF format don't stop with portability and the ability to archive documents; PDFs also lend themselves to easy searching from the Finder. For example, if you want to see all the documents that contain the phrase "Whole Foods," you can use the File → Find menu in Finder and then search by content, as shown in Figure 8-14. Figure 8-15 shows the results of the search.

Now that you have all your documents with you, don't forget to back them up!

HACK #81 Flex OmniOutliner

When is an outliner not just an outliner? When it can as easily export to your iPod as your calendar, lay the groundwork for an amazing presentation, and perform feats of calculation usually found in a spreadsheet.

When is an outliner not an outliner? When it does more than just outlines. The latest version of OmniOutliner (*http://www.omnigroup.com/applications/omnioutliner/*) supports a wide range of additional useful functions.

OmniOutOfTime

Let's start with something easy, like the ability to export your outlined data into iCal or even into your iPod. Many people think of an outline as a kind

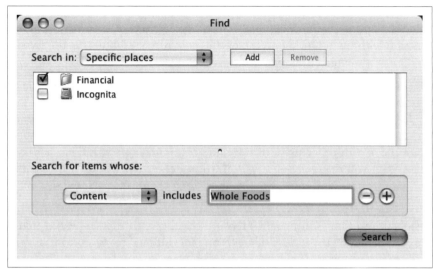

Figure 8-14. Finding by content in the Finder

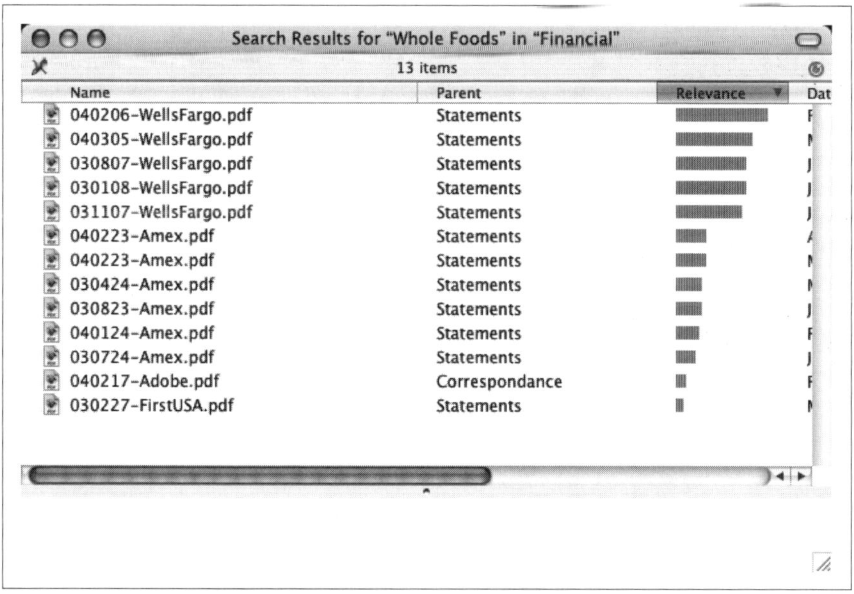

Figure 8-15. Results of a content search

of supercharged to-do list, but there are other practical applications for an outliner. Ever considered maintaining web pages, writing a book, or even backing up your brain (*http://www.macdevcenter.com/pub/a/mac/2003/08/05/outboard_brains.html*) with an outliner?

The nice folks at the Omni Group maintain a list of useful scripts (*http://www.omnigroup.com/applications/omnioutliner/extras/*) you can use in conjunction with OmniOutliner. One of the most recent additions is the *Export To iCal* script, which is easy to use.

All you need to do is grab the *.dmg* file, unpack it, and drag the script file to your */Library/Application Support/OmniOutliner/Scripts* folder. Yes, this could mean any of several different folders on your computer, but it depends on whether you intend to use the scripts only under your user account, share them with other users of the same computer, or share them across a network. If you're unsure of how you will use the scripts, stick with the first option for now and put the file in */Users/<Your User Name>/Library/Application Support/OmniOutliner/Scripts*.

Then, fire up OmniOutliner, and you'll see the script has appeared under the Scripts menu. To successfully export your outlined to-do list to iCal, you first need to set up your outline in a certain way. To get dated to-do items to appear as iCal to-dos, you need to list them in a column with the word Due in the title and set the Column Type as Date in OmniOutliner's Info inspector, as shown in Figure 8-16.

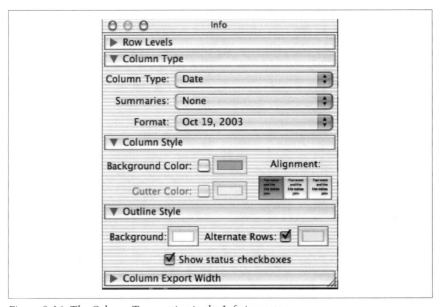

Figure 8-16. The Column Type setting in the Info inspector

Similarly, to get priority settings to show up nicely in iCal, you need a column titled Priority, with a Column Type of Number. Priorities need to entered as integers from 0 to 3, with 0 being lowest priority.

Once your columns are arranged and your data is entered, you're ready to export your outline to iCal (see Figure 8-17).

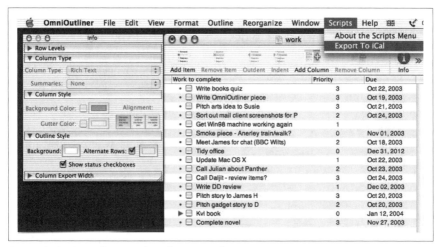

Figure 8-17. An outline, ready to be exported

Once the export is done, iCal starts automatically (if it was already running, the script can quit the program and relaunch it for you). You'll find all your outliner items listed in your To Do Items pane, with the appropriate priorities and due dates visible (see Figure 8-18). The Info pane shows even more detail.

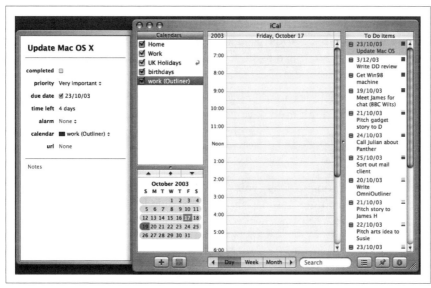

Figure 8-18. iCal, showing exported data from OmniOutliner

You might be asking the obvious question: why not just create the to-dos in iCal in the first place? Or, if OmniOutliner is your preferred tool, why not just keep them there? Well, if you use OmniOutliner for special lists (not necessarily to-do lists), you might find it useful to be able to see those lists alongside all your other usual to-dos. Alternatively, if you like having to-dos and calendar events in one place but don't like iCal's system for adding new events (I'll fess up: I don't get along with iCal at all), this is one possible way of getting around that problem.

As a final extra nugget of goodness, OmniOutliner allows you to put scripts on the toolbar, alongside all of the other controls. Just use the Customize Toolbar menu as usual, and drag your chosen script to where you want it. As long as you have installed the script in the correct folder (as described earlier in this hack), this will work. Figure 8-19 shows the Export To iCal script in the toolbar.

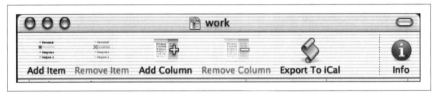

Figure 8-19. OmniOutliner's toolbar, customized with the Export To iCal script

OmniOutAndAbout

How about taking your OmniOutlines around with you in your pocket? You can do this too, if you have an iPod. There are two AppleScripts available from Omni Group's Extras page (*http://www.omnigroup.com/applications/ omnioutliner/extras/*), rolled together in a disk image with some helpful extra information.

The disk image includes another script you can run to open the right installation folder; you don't even have to go digging around in the Finder. Then, you copy over the script of your choice: Export as Contact for older iPods, or Export as Note for owners of newer machines (third generation) that support text notes.

There are limitations to what you can view comfortably on the small iPod screen, so multicolumn outlines should be avoided. Also, the status of individual items (checked or unchecked) won't show, nor will indentations that indicate child/parent relationships within the outline.

All of that said, moving outlines from your Mac to the iPod is just plain cool, and it might even be useful. Once you grab the script and the package opens, you get the screen shown in Figure 8-20.

Figure 8-20. Installation screen for the iPod export script

Follow the instructions on this screen, and soon you'll be exporting directly from OmniOutliner via the Scripts menu, as shown in Figure 8-21.

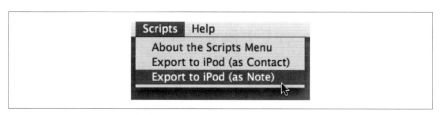

Figure 8-21. Export to iPod (for 3G models) added to the Scripts menu

For additional OmniOutliner-to-iPod export caveats, here are the notes directly from the *README* file:

- Though these scripts can be used with multicolumn outlines, doing so is of limited usefulness, because the iPod can't display this type of text well on its narrow screen.

- Extremely large OmniOutliner documents might cause AppleScript to fail with a Stack Overflow error.

- Exported outlines don't show their checked/unchecked status, indent level, or note text.

- To delete an outline from the iPod, open its Contacts folder in the Finder and delete the file whose name matches the name of the outline you want to delete.

- The "as Contact" script requires Mac OS X 10.2 with the optional BSD package installed in order to properly encode non-ASCII text. (It can still be run without the BSD package, but special characters and international text will appear as gibberish.)

OmniOutOfYourImagination

Some say that OmniOutliner could even be put to use as a tool for professional writers (a journalist and an author provide two of the three testimonials for the software at the top of its home page: *http://www.omnigroup.com/applications/omnioutliner/*), but using the program this way might require a certain adjustment of the writer's way of thinking.

Writers tend to work with text files in editors and word processors designed for the task. However they design their working routine, they will usually have a draft of their work saved as a text file, which they will use as the basis for future drafts. The text is treated as a single unit, to be sculpted into shape. That's how I tend to work, anyway.

Before writing this review, though, I tried starting a new work of text in OmniOutliner. It was an interesting new way of working. Each time you press the Return key in OmniOutliner, you create a new outline item. You have to press ⌘-Return to make a carriage return within the item itself. This lends itself to a means of writing that I, for one, have not tried before: paragraph-by-paragraph control.

I just write as I used to (OmniOutliner uses the built-in, systemwide spell checker), pressing Return as I normally would, and the program turns my ramblings into a outlined document. I can study my masterpiece in different views, collapsing chapters or subheadings that I don't want to see so that I can concentrate on the ones I do. This works surprisingly well, helping to chop the text up into meaningful chunks without getting in the way of reading it as a whole.

That said, OmniOutliner is no word processor. Sure, it can process words, but that's not really what it was designed for. It's better for processing *thoughts* and *ideas,* but you could argue that any work of text, be it a high-school essay or the next best seller, is comprised of a series of thoughts and ideas turned into a coherent whole. There's certainly the potential for a writer to use this program to achieve that, but it takes a bit of getting used to.

If you use Microsoft Word as your word processor, Omni-Outliner enables you to export your outlines as Word documents and preserve the outline styling. You'll need OmniOutliner 2.2 or later; download the *Export from OmniOutliner to Microsoft Word* script from the Extras page (*http://www.omnigroup.com/applications/omnioutliner/extras/*). See "OmniExportExpert," later in this hack, for more information on export options.

OmniSpreadsheet

Think of a Mac OS X–native spreadsheet application; you'll probably struggle to come up with anything other than Excel, or maybe AppleWorks—although, after doing a quick check, I did stumble across BC Spreadsheet (*http://homepage.mac.com/gotterdamn/*), which looks kind of interesting. OmniOutliner's next hidden treat is the ability to act as an effective cruncher of numbers, offering some nice spreadsheet-like functions.

Throw some numbers into an outline, use the Info panel to make sure those columns are of Number type, and then switch on the Calculated Summaries option.

Lo and behold, OmniOutliner totals up all the child items in a parent-item figure. It's an ideal way to keep track of expenses or the sales figures for a small business.

I've found some additional tips for OmniOutliner accounting over at Loud Thinking (*http://www.loudthinking.com/arc/000081.html*). You might want to take a look at them if you're contemplating ditching Excel for simple accounting. The *Sample Documents* download on the Extras page (*http://www.omnigroup.com/applications/omnioutliner/extras/*) includes a pretty good spreadsheet template.

OmniExportExpert

If there's one thing you can't accuse OmniOutliner's creators of, it's skimping on the export options. There are so many ways to get your information out of OmniOutliner that some people might find it hard to pick one.

Export options for HTML, XML (as in Keynote, too, as you'll see later in the hack), OPML, plain text, or RTF are built into the program. The Omni Group's Extras page also includes a script that will export an outline into Microsoft Word, another potentially useful feature for wordsmiths. You need to download and install Late Night Software's XSLT Tools 1.0 (*http://www.latenightsw.com/freeware/XSLTTools/index.html*) to make it work.

The exported file is HTML and, if you open it in Word under Outline mode, it retains all of its outline features. Figure 8-22 and Figure 8-23 show shots of an outline before and after being exported to Word.

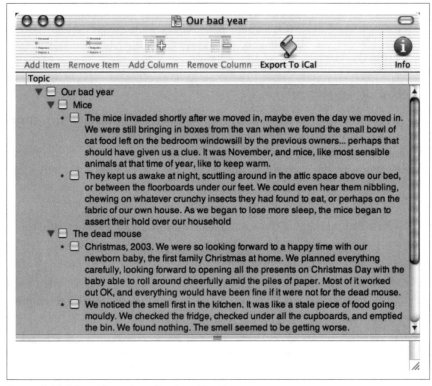

Figure 8-22. The outline viewed in OmniOutliner

OmniSteve

One of the best uses for OmniOutliner might be to use it as a brainstorming tool for your next Keynote presentation. You can take advantage of Omni-Outliner's simple tools to organize your thoughts and then export them to Keynote, where you can create and refine the design elements.

For many tech types, OmniOutliner is a more comfortable environment (i.e., a *text* environment) for working out ideas than Keynote's interface, which can distract you with the need to manage visual elements while you're still at the *thinking* stage. OmniOutliner added XML-export capability in Version 2.2 and specifically called out Apple's Keynote application in the preferences and export options.

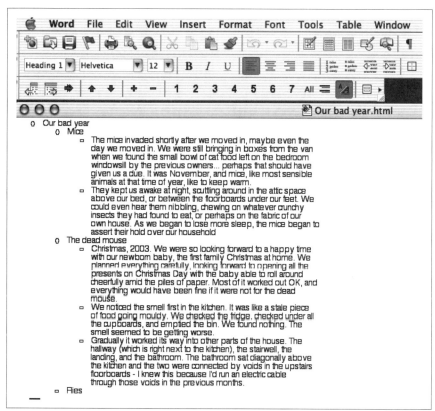

Figure 8-23. The outline after being exported to Microsoft Word

Not only can you export your outline to Keynote, but you can also specify the template and some basic styling in OmniOutliner's Preferences pane (see Figure 8-24), so much of the work is done before you ever open Apple's presentation application.

Then, when you are working in Keynote, you can open Outline view in the sidebar, and it should look just like what you created in OmniOutliner. Figure 8-25 shows the outline that I dashed off in OmniOutliner. I didn't have to spend any mental capital thinking about templates and other design elements. I merely focused on the ideas themselves.

Then, I opened the exported OmniOutliner file in Keynote and switched to the outline view in the sidebar, as shown in Figure 8-26. It looks just like my original outline, but now I have a big start on the design work.

I really like having a pure-text environment to use for brainstorming and organizing, before getting into the design phase of a presentation. Even if I

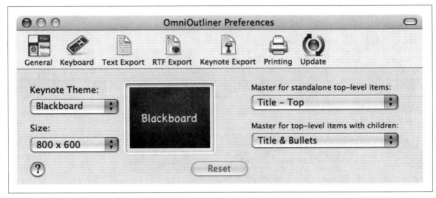

Figure 8-24. OmniOutliner Preferences

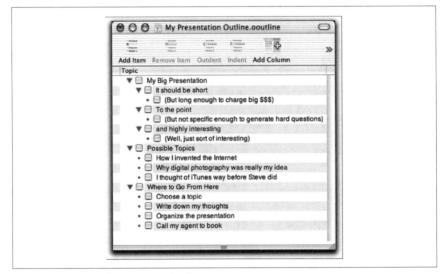

Figure 8-25. My outline in OmniOutliner

didn't use any of the other OmniOutliner goodies, I would consider keep-ing it in my Applications folder just for this use.

If you're interested in learning more about Keynote and XML, check out David Miller's Mac DevCenter article, "Key-note's XML Connections" (*http://www.macdevcenter.com/pub/a/mac/2003/11/18/keynote.html*).

OmniOmni

Still, we've only scratched the surface of OmniOutliner's hidden talents. Other delights on the Extras page include a widget to turn outlines into BrainForest

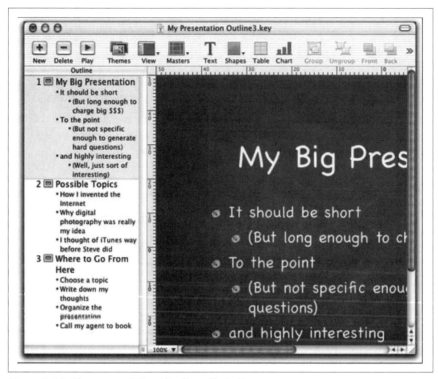

Figure 8-26. The exported OmniOutliner file in Keynote

Professional (*http://www.ultrasoft.com/BrainForest/overview.shtml*), documents for viewing your outlines on Palm OS, a tool that exports to LaTeX (*http://www.opendarwin.org/~landonf/software/Omni-LaTeX/*), and yet another tool that extends the built-in HTML export, giving you greater control over the look of the exported web page.

Further afield, Steve Ivy has created another HTML renderer for OmniOutliner (*http://www.redmonk.net/stories/omniOutlineRenderers*); the Studio Log (*http://www.blankreb.com/studioarticles.php?ID=10*) offers a fascinating look at using OmniOutliner as a script editor; and Mark Guzdial has been using OmniOutliner for initial outlining of articles before using homemade scripts (*http://coweb.cc.gatech.edu/guzdial/28*) to export to LaTeX via BBEdit and TeXShop. Nifty.

There's plenty to keep even the most devoted OmniAddict busy for weeks.

—Giles Turnbull

HACK #82   Decide What to Back Up

The toughest part of backing up is figuring out what needs to be saved and what can be safely lost.

If you've never done a backup before, figuring out what you should back up is the first hurdle you'll need to get over. There are two types of backups you can perform:

Complete backup
> You back up *everything* on your hard drive, including the system software.

Partial or incremental backup
> You back up only certain files.

For example, longtime Mac users know the importance of keeping a backup floppy of your Preferences folder (*/System Folder/Preferences*). With earlier versions of the Mac OS, the greatest source of startup problems had to do with extension errors, which often traced their way back to a corrupt preference file. If you had a recent copy of your preferences, you could simply pop in your backup floppy, drag the Preferences folder onto your System Folder, and restart. Sure, you'd lose any preferences that were set since the last backup was made, but at least you could get into your system. If you backed up your Preferences folder once a week, the risk of you being locked out of your system reduced greatly. In that case, the act of dragging the Preferences folder onto a floppy disk would be considered a *partial backup*.

What you back up depends greatly on how you use your system and how important you determine its data to be. For me, my Mac is my life. If my hard drive were to crash and burn, or if my house were broken into and my Mac were stolen, my only recourse for getting my information back would be to have a complete backup. But I also do partial backups.

Confused? Don't be. This is a fairly standard practice.

Backing up your entire system can be time-consuming, but it's worth it. I typically do a complete backup once a week on Sunday and partial backups nightly. The weekly backup saves everything on my hard drive to a set of CDs, while the nightlies save specific folders to an external FireWire drive connected to my PowerBook.* That way, if my system crashes midday on Wednesday, I can restore my system to the complete backup performed on the previous Sunday and then restore files from Monday's and Tuesday's nightly partial backup. Without the combination of complete and partial

---

* I also back up files to my iDisk daily, but the backup to my iDisk is limited to just a few things, mainly for redundancy.

backups, who knows how much work I would have lost, and trying to remember what I've edited or written in a week is impossible.

Backups—both complete and partial—are a way to protect yourself from partial or permanent loss of data. Take the time to consider what's important to you, and back it up accordingly.

At a minimum, here are some things you should consider backing up:

Email
> Depending on how much mail you receive in a day, you might need to back up your email on a weekly basis only. However, if you receive a lot of email and it's a critical part of your daily communications, you should consider backing it up every day. If you are using Mac OS X's Mail application, your mail is stored in ~/Library/Mail.

Preferences
> Old habits never die. Backing up your Preferences (~/Library/ Preferences) can save you a lot of time from having to reset your application and system preferences if something goes amiss.

Home directory
> Backing up your Home directory can simplify the task of selecting which files to back up. By selecting your Home directory to be backed up, you will catch everything in all of the directories you see in the Finder when you click on the Home icon. This includes the contents of the following folders:

> * Desktop (only the files on your Desktop, not the contents of any mounted drives)
> * Documents
> * Library
> * Movies
> * Music
> * Pictures
> * Public
> * Sites

Mind you, if you have a lot of files, a complete backup of your Home folder can take a long time, and you probably won't be able to back up everything to your iDisk. However, if your Mac is equipped with a Combo or SuperDrive, you will be able to back up to CD or DVD instead, or to a networked or external drive that's mounted on your system.

These are just a few ideas of things you should consider backing up. One thing you don't need to back up, at least according to Apple, is all of the information on your iDisk. Apple makes nightly backups of all .Mac members' iDisks.

—*Chuck Toporek*

Automate Backups with Existing Tools

#83   You don't have to buy fancy software to perform backups. There's a whole slew of tools already installed on your Mac.

The big difference between the world of Unix and that other place is that in the other place they have *applications* and we have *tools*. Applications require learning not just parameters and keystrokes, but a whole way of working. If the programmer who created the word processor thinks you should spell-check your documents before you save them, then check them you shall.

Tools, on the other hand, also require learning, but instead they ask, "What do you want to do?" The choice is yours. And with a good toolbox full of these, anything is possible.

To back up my iMac, I bought a small FireWire hard disk and used Carbon Copy Cloner to make my backups. Although this software is simple and effective, there were two flaws. First, the backups happened only when I remembered to initiate them, and second, I had only one backup, whenever I last made it. I wanted something that addressed these issues, so I sat down and listed my requirements:

- Automatic backup, preferably when I'm not using the Mac
- Several generations of backup available
- As cheap as possible

I took a look at some commercial software. In addition to the cost of the software itself, however, I would need to get a bigger drive and learn how to use the application. The application and I did not get along, it soon found itself on eBay, and I was back where I started, along with the investment of a 120 GB disk. It was time to dig into my existing toolbox and see what I could cook up.

Apple already provides a tool to make backups: Apple Software Restore (ASR), which allows one volume to be cloned onto another. In addition to this, we also have the multifunctional hdiutil, which can create, mount, and unmount disk images. With these and a handful of standard Unix tools, we are well on our way to a happy ending.

All we need to do is create a disk image of the required size on the external drive, mount it, clone the source drive into the image, and unmount it.

The Code

Let's write the code. First, we need to name a few things. SOURCE is the volume we are backing up—in this case, root. FILEDEST is the volume where the backup will be stored. All disk images require a VOLUMENAME; otherwise, they get called untitled, which is really not a lot of use to anyone, so we set it to backup_YYYY-MM-DD and use it as the basis of the IMAGENAME:

```
#!/bin/sh

#############################################
Set some variables
#############################################

### The name of the volume we wish to backup
SOURCE='/'

### The volume onto which we are putting the backup
FILEDEST='/Volumes/Overflow'

### Creating the backup disk image file and volume name
VOLUMENAME=backup_`date +%Y-%m-%d`
IMAGENAME=$FILEDEST/$VOLUMENAME.dmg

#############################################
#Create the image
#############################################

hdiutil create -srcfolder $SOURCE -fs HFS+ \
   -format UDRW -volname $VOLUMENAME $IMAGENAME
```

Scary, isn't it? hdiutil creates an image file called IMAGENAME on volume FILEDEST based on SOURCE. In this case, SOURCE is my root volume, but it could be a folder such as */Users/peterhickman* if I wanted to back up only my user files. It took only 15 lines, including comments. This is the power of hdiutil, and it can do a whole lot more.

By default, this script creates an uncompressed image, but by removing -format UDRW, the script creates a compressed image. Compressed sounds good, but a compressed image backup takes in excess of two hours, whereas an uncompressed image backup takes 69 minutes, based on backing up a 10 GB root volume on my Mac. Additionally, mounting the compressed image takes an age (minutes as opposed to seconds), which reduces the utility of a backup. If getting the data out of the backup is too much trouble, you will wonder why you went to all the trouble of creating one.

Making Things Even Easier

So, we have a tool that backs up a designated volume into an image file. To run it (which must be done as root), we have to enter sudo backupimage, and almost everything we wanted is ours.

Now, we want to automate it so that we no longer have to remember to do this chore and it can execute when we are tucked safely in bed. In the world of Unix, we have cron, which runs tasks for us at regular intervals. So, we need to set up a cron entry as root to run our script once a week (or the frequency you prefer):

```
[peterhickman]$ sudo crontab -e -u root
0 0 * * 0 /usr/local/bin/backupimage
```

Should things go wrong, cron mails you if it can, but if Postfix is not configured or running on your machine (by default, it does not run), look at */var/mail/root*, which tells you what the problem was.

So, there we have it. All we ever needed to do our backups, other than the external disk, was in our toolbox all the time. External hard disks are cheap, and there is no reason to buy additional software.

> If you need additional power tools to help you manage backups on the command line, check out rsyncbackup. It's a Perl script that helps automate various kinds of backups. You can find it at *http://erlang.no/rsyncbackup/*.

Other Issues

It's important to remember that your external hard disk, although large, is not infinite. Every now and then, check to make sure you're not going to run out of space. That too could be automated, but doing so would detract from the simplicity of our current solution—another problem for another day. Also, just because the script runs without error does not mean it has worked; open your backup image file and rummage around. Are the files there? Are they correct?

You can automate your chores, but you cannot automate your responsibility.

Final Thoughts

Thanks to solid built-in tools like these, Macs are putting the power back into the hands of users who like to fiddle under the hood. Almost everything we need is there. We just forget sometimes.

—*Peter Hickman*

Back Up Your Digital Music Collection

Hard drives don't last forever, so it's best to start thinking now about how you can safely back up your digital tunes.

So, you have your thousand-CD collection ripped to you computer, as well as the hundred or so songs you've purchased from the iTunes Music Store. Your CDs have now been given away or sold for a buck a piece (if you're lucky) to a second-hand music store. You're all digital, all the time—good for you!

Until that massive hard drive decides to bite the dust, that is. All that work converting your CDs and all those songs purchased are as good as gone. This hack helps you prepare for that all but inevitable day. Hard drives do crash, and when yours does, you want to be sure you have your music backed up somewhere safe.

The first decision you need to make is what media to use. Backing up to CDRs, DVDs, and a hard drive each have their advantages and disadvantages. Blank CDs are great because they are cheap (only a few cents a piece—if not free—if you bother to mail in that rebate); however, they hold only approximately 650 MB (100 or so songs). DVDs hold a lot more data (up to 4.5 GB, or around 450 songs, give or take a couple dozen) but are more expensive and burn at a much slower rate than CDs.

A typical CD burner can burn at 10–50×, whereas a DVD burner maxes out at 2×.

An external hard drive is super-fast but might be outgrown quickly unless you go all out and get a whopping great one, at which point it is much more costly. The best way to make your decision is to look at the size of your music collection you are backing up. Only have 20 GB on you computer? Then either blank CDs or DVDs are probably the way to go. If your collection is 100 GB or larger, you might consider purchasing an external FireWire (faster) or USB 2.0 (slower) hard drive. The time you save should more than make up for the cost of the hard drive over that of a pile of cheap CDs.

Regardless of which media you choose, you have to figure out a way to transfer all of your music. If you purchase a hard drive, this is just a matter of plugging it in and drag-and-dropping your music folder onto the new hard drive. Wait for the files to copy over, and you're done! You might want to consider keeping the hard drive at a location different than your computer (at work is good, since you can listen to your tunes there too), just in case physical damage happens to your computer (as a result of fire, flood, child pouring juice over computer, etc.).

If you choose to back up to CDs or DVDs, it helps to use some kind of backup software that automates some of the job for you. Yes, you can back up to CDs using iTunes, but the task is an arduous one at best. You have to create a playlist, drag the songs to that playlist, and then hit burn for each and every CD. But what if you want to back up a serious amount of music?

iPod

If you have one of the larger capacity iPods (the 40 GB model is nice), it's useful to remember that you already have a handy backup right there in your back pocket. Obviously, this works only for any music in your iTunes library that you actually have copied over to your iPod.

If you have the room, might I suggest you have iTunes automatically keep your iPod in sync with your entire library? You can always change your mind later. With your iPod connected to your Mac, click the iPod button (leftmost in Figure 8-27) in iTunes to bring up the iPod Preferences.

Figure 8-27. Clicking the iPod button to reach the iPod Preferences pane

Select the "Automatically update all songs and playlists" radio button and click OK, as shown in Figure 8-28. Both your Mac's hard drive and your iPod should growl for a bit as all the music not yet on your iPod is copied across. (This can take some time, depending on the size of your music library.)

If you're not blessed with a sufficiently large iPod, or if you are blessed with a sufficiently large music library, you might need to choose either to "Automatically update selected playlists only" or to "Manually manage songs and playlists" (both choices are located in the iPod Preferences pane).

Backup Applications

If you don't have an iPod but still have music to back up, there are a few backup solutions available to you. Good backup software does something called *disk spanning*. This means that if you have 10 GB of music to back up to a handful of CDs, the software automatically figures out how many CDs you need and prompts you to feed each in turn throughout the burning process.

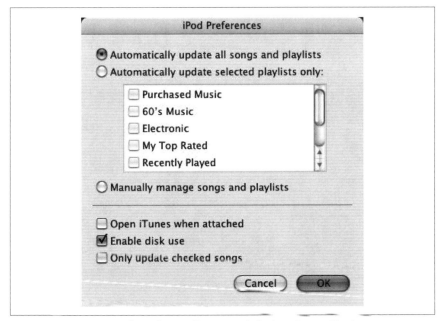

Figure 8-28. Automatically updating all songs and playlists for iPod backup

One such application is Apple's Backup (*http://www.apple.com/support/ downloads/backup.html*), included with .Mac membership or Dantz's Retrospect (*http://www.dantz.com*).

Apple's Backup, while downloadable even without a .Mac account, unfortunately doesn't allow you to back up to CD, DVD, or another drive without a .Mac account. If you have a .Mac account, though, it's a rather friendly app with some nice features. You'll find a tour of Backup (and the rest of .Mac) at *http://www.mac.com/1/iTour/tour_backup.html*.

For the non-.Mac folk out there, let's take a look at backing up with Dantz Retrospect. When you launch the app, the main window pops up, as shown in Figure 8-29. You have four main options: Backup, Restore, Duplicate, and Archive. To back up to a series of CDs or DVDs select Backup.

Here, you name your backup project and select a type. Since in this case we are doing a straightforward backup, click the Backup button. The Backup Set Creation dialog pops up, as shown in Figure 8-30. Choose to back up to a hard drive or CD/DVD. If you select CD/DVD, Retrospect figures out the number of CDs or DVDs you need, based on the amount of data (in this case, music) you have to back up.

Retrospect then prompts you to select a *source folder* (the folder from which it should copy files). By default, iTunes keeps its music in an *iTunes Music*

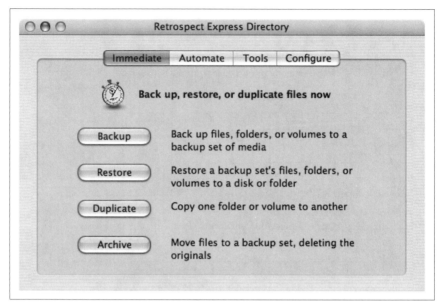

Figure 8-29. The main window in Retrospect

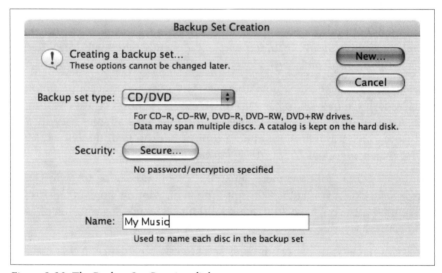

Figure 8-30. The Backup Set Creation dialog

folder within the *Music* folder in your home directory. Even though you are backing up to CDs or DVDs, Retrospect needs to create a document in which to keep data about your backup—not your backup itself. Hit Save to let it save this *backup set*.

Click the Start button to get things rolling. Retrospect prompts you to insert a disc, spends a few minutes burning and verifying the disc, and then ejects the disc and asks for another. Shampoo, rinse, and repeat until all your music is backed up.

While feeding Backup or Retrospect CD after CD or DVD after DVD (you should be cursed with so much music!) might seem rather tedious, at least the program takes care of all the rest for you.

Whether you use CDs, DVDs, or another hard drive, make sure you back up. Those iTunes music purchases will be worthless if anything should happen to your one and only copy.

—Hadley Stern

 ## Make a Carbon Copy
#85
Use Carbon Copy Cloner, Apple Software Restore, and Disk Utility to back up and (more importantly) restore your hard drive and important data.

Sure, you could drop a load of cash on a commercial backup solution for your Mac, but that's really not necessary. With a few powerful and versatile tools included in Panther and some third-party freebies, you have a nice option for making a restorable backup of your hard drive and all your important media, files, and information. This of course will take a lot of space, so you need either a second internal or external hard drive, a second Mac booted in target mode over FireWire, or an iPod.

 You can mount one Mac's hard drive onto another Mac over a FireWire cable (assuming both have FireWire, of course) quite easily. You simply tie them together with a FireWire cable and reboot the one you'll be using as a slave drive while holding down the T (for *target*) key. After just a few seconds, the Mac boots into what's known as *target mode*, the screen blinking a FireWire logo where usually there'd be the Mac OS X login screen. After a click, spin up, and whir, you'll see its drive show up right on your other Mac's Desktop.

I'll start with the easiest, then move on to the slightly more difficult options, saving the rather cool-if-you-can-summon-the-courage possibilities for the pop quiz at the end.

Carbon Copy Cloner

My absolute favorite utility for Mac OS X, and the choice of Apple Geniuses at your nearest Apple Store, is Mike Bombich's Carbon Copy Cloner (*http://www.bombich. com /software/ccc.html*; $5 donateware, free for educational use). The name pretty much tells you exactly what it does; it makes a carbon-copy clone of your hard drive.

If, on the other hand, you are a do-it-yourselfer and have no fear of the Terminal and esoteric Unix commands, you might prefer to put that $5 toward a double latté and use ditto, the command-line tool upon which Carbon Copy Cloner is based. Mike has a detailed walk-through of how to create a bootable backup of Mac OS X on the command line (*http://www.bombich.com/mactips/image.html*). This nets you the same results, though not nearly as easily, nor in anything even approaching the same amount of time.

After downloading Carbon Copy Cloner (CCC) and copying it to your Applications folder, go ahead and launch it. Figure 8-31 shows its main interface.

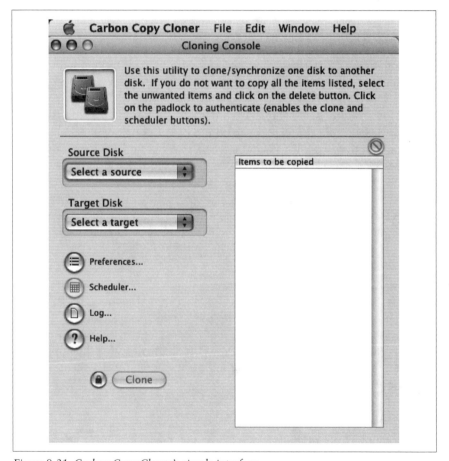

Figure 8-31. Carbon Copy Cloner's simple interface

For Source Disk, select the drive you want to clone. The "Items to be copied" field should be populated with all the files and directories, visible and invisible, found in your Source Disk's root directory. If there are portions of the drive you don't want to clone, highlight them and click the red delete button at the top of the column to remove them from the list.

If you want a true carbon copy of your source drive, you'll want to leave the list as it is. Selectively choosing files to be backed up, however, can be useful. For instance, if you want to back up only users' home directories, remove everything but Users from the list.

From the Target Disk pull-down menu, select the drive to which you'd like to save the cloned data.

To set preferences in Carbon Copy Cloner, click the Preferences... button to bring up CCC's Preferences pane, as shown in Figure 8-32.

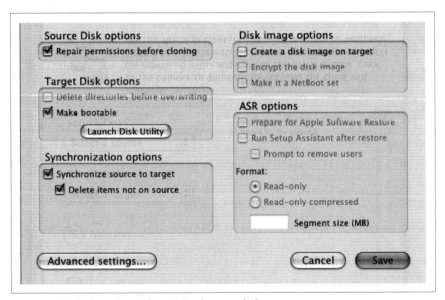

Figure 8-32. Carbon Copy Cloner's Preferences dialog

Here is where you can fiddle with all the details for your cloning. Most of the settings are rather self-explanatory:

- You can (and should) choose to repair permissions on the source drive.
- Make the target disk bootable and overwrite any existing files currently on the disk.
- You can synchronize the source with the target for faster backups. Check Delete Items Not on Source, unless you want to make an aggregate backup of your drive over a period of time with old deleted files alongside new ones.

- Rather than use the entire drive as a backup, you can choose to create a disk image on the target and even encrypt it for extra security.

- You can also make the image read-only or read-only compressed, which takes up less space but makes for a much slower restore.

- The option to make a NetBoot restore is useful if you run a small network of computers that you will be imaging over a network connection.

- "Run Setup Assistant after restore" and "Prompt to remove users" are specialty settings for those running a computer lab or otherwise involved with deploying multiple systems. Perhaps you're selling your machine and want to strip it down to give its new owner that fresh-from-the-store feeling.

I have a little 20 GB portable FireWire drive I've had for several years and which is perfect for backing up my 12" PowerBook. Once a week, I grab that drive, plug it in to my PowerBook's FireWire port, select my source drive, select PortaHD (the little drive's name) as the destination drive, and check "Repair permissions before cloning," "Make bootable," "Synchronize source to target," and "Delete items not on source."

The first time I ran a backup with these settings, it took about an hour and a half on my 867 MHz PowerBook with approximately 15 GB of data on the hard drive. The good news is that after doing this once, checking "Synchronize source to target" cut the backup time in half, unless there'd been a good deal of housecleaning or new installations between backups.

Click the Save button to save your preference changes.

Back in CCC's main interface (Figure 8-31), click the little lock next to the Clone button, provide your administrator password, and click Clone to begin the cloning process.

You *could* continue working (albeit slowly) on your computer while CCC runs, but I don't recommend it. Things will slow to a crawl during the backup and any files you are currently working on will have to be added to the queue as if new. Although I have never had a problem with a backup, this is just the sort of thing that could introduce cloning problems. Instead, push yourself away from the computer, wait a minute or so for your eyes to readjust to real life, and go spend some quality time with loved ones, mow the lawn, or read a book.

It is a good idea to always keep the "Repair permissions before cloning" box checked. Although doing so slows down the entire backup process, it is an important safety precaution. Uncheck this box only if you have just finished repairing permissions with some other utility, such as Disk Utility or Cocktail (*http://www.macosxcocktail.com*).

If you can get into the habit of running a CCC backup before any major software installations or other system changes, you can easily roll your system back to the prefiddle version you created by booting from the cloned drive and running CCC in reverse: point Source Disk to the backup drive and the Target Disk to your main drive. Make sure the "Delete items not on source" preference is checked, to ensure that everything is recreated as it was originally before the update.

This setup works well for me, because my PowerBook is always either in use or in its bag and the only way it is ever getting backed up is if I consciously remember to do so. You, however, might have an always-on iMac, G4, or G5 that you would rather have do all this busywork for you while you're not around. To do so, you can make use of CCC's handy scheduler. Set up a default drive or partition on your machine that is always available for backups. Launch CCC and set everything as you'd like—as if you were about to create a backup right this moment. Between entering your administrator password and pushing the Clone button, click the Scheduler button. Up pops the Scheduler window, as shown in Figure 8-33.

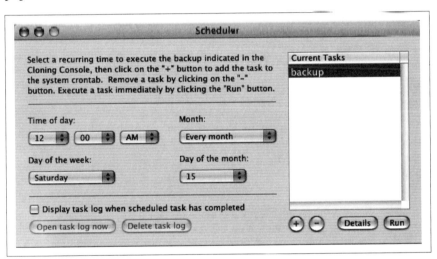

Figure 8-33. Carbon Copy Cloner's Scheduler interface

In the Scheduler interface, you can schedule CCC to run the backup as it is currently configured on a recurring basis by using your system's internal scheduler (aka crontab, for those of you in the know). In Figure 8-33, I've set CCC to run my standard clone operation at 12:00 a.m., every Saturday *and* on every 15th day of every month. After setting the schedule, click the plus (+) button under the Current Tasks column and provide a name for this cloning task (I used the rather original *backup*). To remove an existing task from the schedule, simply highlight its name in the list and click the minus (–) button.

> When you set up a schedule in CCC, it creates a custom shell script, scheduling it to run straight from the shell without launching CCC. If you're curious (or if you're a programmer looking to hack the script), you can open your crontab file, find the CCC-generated script, open it in your favorite text editor, and poke and prod away. If you just want a quick peek at the script, just highlight the task's name in the Scheduler window and click the Details button.

In addition to making one-to-one clones, CCC also offers various other options. Check the "Create a disk image on target box" in the Preferences window to clone to an image file and (optionally) check "Encrypt disk image" to secure your cloned image with a password. If you've been looking for an excuse to buy a 40 GB iPod, consider that it is a convenient place to store such an encrypted disk image; rather than cart around a bag of drives (and get concerned looks from airport security personnel), take your music and backups with you on the road in one convenient and rather pretty package. This type of backup will not be bootable, unless you check the Prepare for Apple Software Restore option. With this option enabled, you can use the image to fully restore your hard drive by using Apple Software Restore from the command line (we'll get to this in a moment) or from within Disk Utility.

For advanced users who are working with a large number of machines or in a computer lab, there is an option to make your image a NetBoot set and another option (found in Preferences... → Advanced settings...) to tag preflight and postflight scripts to run before and after your restore.

> Any of the disk-cloning options discussed in this hack can help you partition an existing hard drive into two smaller partitions with ease. Simply clone your drive to another drive temporarily, and then boot from the new drive. Launch Disk Utility (Applications → Utilities → Disk Utility) and select the original drive. Click the partition tab, and create as many partitions as you like; just make sure you leave enough room for your original drive on one of the new partitions. Click the Partition button and wait for Disk Utility to erase (and I do mean *erase*) and repartition the drive. Then, clone your new drive back onto one of the new partitions, select that drive as the startup disk in the Startup Disk System Preferences pane, and reboot the machine.

Apple Software Restore

Apple Software Restore (ASR), part of Disk Utility (Applications → Utilities → Disk Utility) is a powerful tool for copying disk images to volumes and cloning drives; and it's included right in the OS X box. ASR is basically a scripted graphical frontend to the command-line asr tool, designed to restore your computer's original contents (including the Mac OS 9 system software, factory settings, and applications that came with your computer) without reinstalling OS X itself.

> You can either run Software Restore with the disks that came with your system to do a full reinstall and reset your Mac to factory settings, or you can choose the Restore in Place option to install your original system software, factory settings, and applications that came with your computer, leaving everything else on your disk untouched. You should know that this might cause some of your preferences to be lost.

To utilize the full power of Apple Software Restore, you have to run it from the command line (or use Disk Utility to access its features, as described later in this hack). Open a Terminal window and type man asr to pull up the man (as in *manual*) pages for the version of Apple Software Restore included in Panther. ASR works like the ditto backup utility (upon which CCC is based); however, unlike ditto, which copies directories, asr is concerned solely with cloning and copying disk images to volumes.

Before you clone a drive with asr, you should reformat the target drive and repair permissions. This isn't entirely necessary, but it is a good step to take for the sake of cleanliness. On the command line, type:

```
sudo asr -source <sourcevolume> -target <targetvolume> -erase
```

Replace *<sourcevolume>* with the path to the source drive and replace *<targetvolume>* with the path to the target drive. You need to use sudo to become an administrative user for a moment, because asr needs to be run as the *root user*. You will be prompted for your administrator password.

The -erase command erases the data on the target drive, ensures that any *blessed* (read: special) folders on the source will also be blessed on the target, and retains all permissions between the two drives. If you use this command, you will be asked if you are sure you want to erase the target drive before continuing. To disable this warning, add -nocheck to what you type on the command line, but be sure you really want to erase everything before doing so.

> A *blessed* folder in OS X (and OS 9) is one that the computer trusts as being a worthy candidate from which to boot. Without being blessed, your Mac won't trust a System Folder simply copied over and will refuse to boot from it. If you're curious, type `man bless` on the command line for more information.

Here's how the beginning of such a session usually goes. In this case, I am copying my root hard drive to a FireWire drive named File Cabinet.

```
$ sudo asr -source / -target /Volumes/File\ Cabinet
Password:
 Validating target...done
 Validating source...done
     Validating sizes...done
 Restoring...
 Copying "/" (/dev/disk0s9) to "/Volumes/File Cabinet" (/dev/disk2s3)...
```

As you can see, I left off the -erase flag, because there is additional data on the drive that I do not want to erase. After cloning a drive in this manner (without erasing), you still need to bless that drive to make it bootable. Notice that asr validates the target, source, and sizes before running. ASR will not run if your target drive is not as large as your source drive, even though you might have less data on the source drive than on the target drive. This is one of the main reasons that I generally use CCC or ditto (rather than asr) for cloning my drives.

I do, however, use asr to restore compressed images I've created either in CCC or Disk Utility to a target volume. To do so, type the following on the command line:

```
sudo asr -source <compressedimage> -target <targetvolume> -erase
```

Replace <compressedimage> with the path to the source image and replace <targetvolume> with the path to the target disk that you want to replace. If the image you want to restore was not originally prepared to be used with asr via CCC or Disk Utility, running the following command prepares the image for you:

```
sudo asr –imagescan <compressedimage>
```

You can create disk images of parts of your data by using Disk Utility or even CCC and then use asr to copy this information to the root directory of your existing installation by simply leaving off the -erase tag. Or if, like me, you prefer a simpler solution than going to the Terminal, you can access all of Apple Software Restore's features through Panther's Disk Utility.

Disk Utility

My second favorite backup utility, after CCC, is Panther's Disk Utility. It is probably one of the most versatile, powerful, and underappreciated programs. Most of you are probably already familiar with it as a means of formatting and partitioning drives or repairing permissions on your computer. I use this application to make backups of all the software I purchase and basically every piece of removable media that goes into my computer. I also use it to make encrypted backups of my important files and folders.

Launch Disk Utility (Applications → Utilities → Disk Utility, or directly from Panther Installation Disk 1 if you are unfortunate enough to have a fragged installation disk). Select Images → New; you'll be given the choice between a Blank Image..., Image from Folder..., or Image from (Select a Device)..., as shown in Figure 8-34.

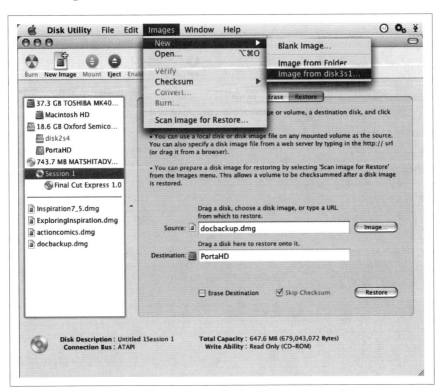

Figure 8-34. Disk Utility, with the Restore tab selected and Images → New menu displayed

Notice three devices at the top of the left column in Figure 8-34, each with its partition(s) listed immediately beneath: Macintosh HD, Final Cut

Express Installation Disk, and my FireWire hard drive, PortaHD. If I choose one of the devices in the column and select Image from (Select a Device)..., the name of the device will replace (Select a Device). I can then create a disk image from this device—read/write, read-only, or compressed and either encrypted or unencrypted.

If I want to make a backup of my Final Cut Express installation disk, for instance, I select the session name on that drive under the device, navigate to Image from disk2s1..., and choose a name and location to which to save the disk image. Since this is a CD image, I have the additional option to create a CD/DVD Master, which can be used as the master image for burning multiple copies of the disk. This is what I generally do when backing up software I've bought, keeping a copy of the master image with others like it on a hard drive or DVD and burning a copy from within Disk Utility whenever my current copy gets too scratched up for general usage. This is also how I made the first two disk images that show up in the second part of the column in Figure 8-34.

This method can also be used to back up commercial DVDs, but unfortunately, because most commercial DVDs weigh in at over 4.7 GB (the default size for DVD-R media), you won't be able to burn the image to a new DVD to replace a scratched one.

As you can see, I also have a *docbackup.dmg* image, which is an encrypted and compressed copy of my Documents folder that I made by selecting Image → New → Image from Folder and navigating to my Documents folder, choosing a name and location to which to save the image, and compressing and encrypting it.

> If you choose to encrypt an image, you will be prompted for a password with which to gain access to it later. Whatever you do, don't forget that password; without it, your image is inaccessible and therefore utterly useless.

Notice in Figure 8-34 that I've selected the Restore tab. Using the Restore function in Disk Utility basically calls on the power of Apple Software Restore. If you have previously created a bootable backup disk image of your hard drive using CCC or Apple Software Restore, you can boot from your original Panther Install Disk 1, launch Disk Utility (under the Installer menu), drag the backed-up image into the source field and the drive you want to replace into the destination field, and check the "Erase destination" box to write the image over the destination drive.

You can also clone disks on the fly by using this method. Boot from the Panther Install Disk 1, launch Disk Utility, select your source and destination drives from the column on the left, and choose "Erase destination."

> You can also select a disk image on a remote server as the source image to restore locally. To do so, either type the *http://* URL of the remote image as the source or drag a hyperlink to Disk Utility's source field from your browser.

Notice also that I have my *docbackup.dmg* file in the source field and my PortaHD in the destination field (Figure 8-34). I haven't checked "Erase destination," so the contents of the *docbackup.dmg* will simply be copied onto the root directory of PortaHD. For this reason, when choosing to make an image from a folder, it's a good idea to put that folder inside another folder from which you make the image, to prevent your files from being spread all over your drive when you run a restore. Alternately, you can simply double-click the image file, enter the password, and have it mount in the Finder, from which you can drag its contents to whatever location you desire.

Hacking the Hack

Sure, you could script several different scheduled backups, one for every night of the week, that make a separate encrypted bootable image on some enormous drive, but that's for rank amateurs. The industrious among you could use these tools to create a bootable CD or DVD with the necessary troubleshooting files to help fix your ailing Mac whenever something goes wrong.

A Cocoa application from CharlesSoft (*http://www.charlessoft.com*) called BootCD automates the task of making a bootable CD and can been made to produce a bootable DVD with the proper tweaking. Unfortunately, the current version doesn't run on Panther, so you have to find a friend who is still running Jaguar to get it going.

Even without this utility, if you have a SuperDrive, you could theoretically create a custom blank disk image in Disk Utility that weighs in at under 4.7 GB. Make it read/write and mount it, and then carefully pick and choose the necessary files to copy to it using Carbon Copy Cloner (you need to save this disk image on a separate drive/partition from your boot partition for this to work, because CCC won't allow you to write to a file located on the source drive).

> I've used Carbon Copy Cloner to clone files to a mounted image before, but never on this scale. If this doesn't work for you, you could alternately try to script asr to do all of this via the command line.

Make sure to include Disk Utility and any other troubleshooting tools you might want in your list. Once you have completed the image, eject the mounted image to save it to disk. Launch Disk Utility, select the image you have just created, and burn a copy. If the burning completes successfully, restart your computer with the new DVD in the drive, hold down the C key to boot from CD/DVD, and cross your fingers.

—C. K. Sample III

HACK #86 Bluetooth File Exchange and Browsing

Rendezvous and wireless networks have made it easier than ever to swap files. But if your Mac is Bluetooth-enabled, there's an easier way, if all you want to do is quickly swap a file.

A common sight in the hallways at conferences and in meeting rooms everywhere is that of two Mac users setting up a temporary network connection to trade a few files. Of course, it's easy enough to set up a one-wire network [Mac OS X Hacks, Hack #69] with a direct Ethernet connection between two laptops or even set up an ad hoc wireless network. But if you are using a newer PowerBook with built-in Bluetooth, or if you have a Bluetooth USB dongle, it's even easier and faster just to transfer over Bluetooth.

Basic File Swapping

To transfer a file via Bluetooth, launch the Bluetooth File Exchange application located in the */Applications/Utilities* folder. You'll see a file browser, as shown in Figure 8-35.

Once you've selected a file to send, click the Send button. A list of devices is displayed, as shown in Figure 8-36. This list shows the devices that are available to send files to. If, for some reason, you don't see the name of the computer or device you want to send the file to, click the Search button. Once you've found your target, click on its name and then hit the Send button.

Once you send a file to a computer or other device, the user on the other side sees a dialog that asks whether to accept it. Once accepted, the transfer proceeds.

You can configure your Mac to automatically receive items sent by Bluetooth without any need for authorization. This is useful in the home environment, where ease of use outweighs the security concerns. To receive items with authorization, go to System Preferences and select Bluetooth. In the File Exchange tab, change the "When receiving items" selection to "Accept files without warning."

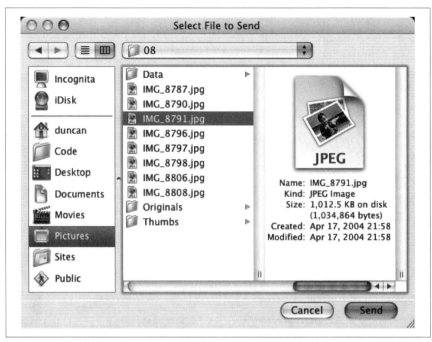

Figure 8-35. Sending a file via Bluetooth File Exchange

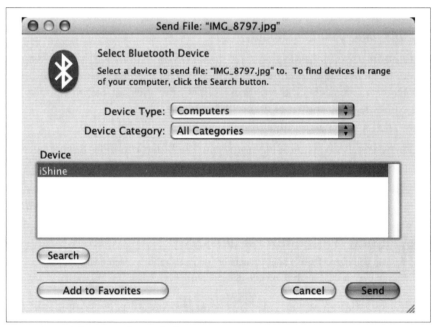

Figure 8-36. Selecting a Bluetooth device

Sending Files from the Finder

You can also send files via Bluetooth via the Services menu [Hack #8] in the Finder. Simply select a file in the Finder, and then select Finder → Services → Send File to Bluetooth Device (⌘-Shift-B), as shown in Figure 8-37.

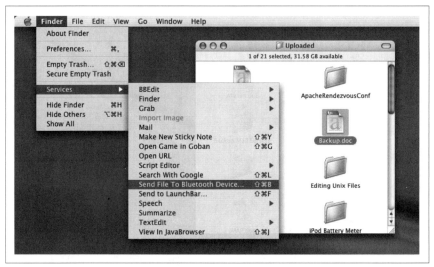

Figure 8-37. Sending a file via the Services menu

File Browsing Using Bluetooth

In addition to sending files to other devices, you can also allow other computers to browse your computer. Launch System Preferences → Bluetooth → File Exchange and check the option "Allow other devices to browse files on this computer," as shown in Figure 8-38. Make sure to select an appropriate folder to share. We recommend sharing your ~/*Public* folder.

To browse a Mac using Bluetooth, launch Bluetooth File Exchange and select File → Browse Device. Once you select a device to browse, you can then see the target device's folder, as shown in Figure 8-39.

—*Wei Meng Lee and James Duncan Davidson*

Secure File Sharing with SSH

HACK
#87

Do you distrust AFP's built-in security? Good. Use SSH to secure your shares or even access them safely over the Internet.

Apple's file-sharing services use a venerable protocol called AppleTalk Filing Protocol (AFP) that dates back at least to Mac OS System 7. It is handy

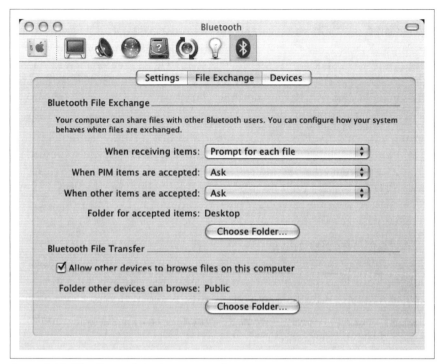

Figure 8-38. The Bluetooth Preferences panel

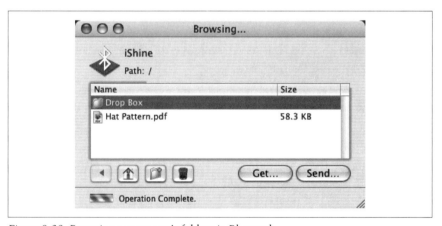

Figure 8-39. Browsing a computer's folder via Bluetooth

for sharing files between Macs or even to Linux and BSD boxes using
netatalk (*http://netatalk.sourceforge.net/*).

While shares on your network are protected by a password, some servers
and clients might use that password in the clear. The protocol itself uses no

encryption, so the contents of files transferred over AFP are exposed to local packet sniffers. While you have the option to use AFP over SSH (when using an Apple Xserve), the client silently falls back to standard AFP if an SSH connection is unsuccessful (*http://www.securityfocus.com/archive/1/355548/ 2004-02-25/2004-03-02/0*). This is a Very Bad Thing, because you could unknowingly end up passing sensitive data over the network, even if you picked the "safe" options.

Fortunately, since AFP uses TCP as its transport, it's easy to tunnel it over your own SSH connection. Doing this not only protects your connection, but it also prevents the possibility that the client will fall back to an insecure protocol. AFP servers typically run on TCP port 548. To establish a secure connection to your file server, simply run a command like this from a Terminal window:

```
ssh fileserver -L5548:localhost:548 -N
```

This establishes an SSH connection to your AFP fileserver and forwards all traffic to your local port 5548 to the AFP server's port 548. Of course, you need an account on the file server in order to establish an SSH connection.

Now, on your Mac client, press ⌘-K in the Finder to make a new AFP connection, and type this address:

```
afp://localhost:5548
```

Presto! You are automagically connected to the AFP server, only now all of your passwords and file data are protected by SSH's strong encryption and authentication mechanisms. Note that this means you can easily and securely connect to your AFP server even over untrusted networks, such as wireless hotspots and the Internet.

When you are finished using the share, simply eject it to disconnect and then press Control-C in the Terminal window to kill the SSH session.

If you decide to run AFP on a file server connected to the Internet, don't forget to firewall off port 548 coming in on any network interface. This protects your server from potential security issues in the AFP protocol and doesn't affect users connecting over SSH (because they connect over the loopback (127.0.0.1) interface, not a real network interface.)

—*Rob Flickenger*

System Administration
Hacks 88–100

We'd be flat-out lying if we said it didn't take a little system administration every now and again to keep your Mac running smoothly and reliably. We're looking forward to the day when we don't have to, but for now there are tasks to run, bits of cruft to clean up, and—rare but true—pieces of the system you just have to reinstall when something goes wrong. While Mac OS X does its best to keep a handle on all that happens behind the scenes, it's not 100% foolproof and needs a helping hand every so often.

HACK #88 Become an Administrator for a Moment

Your Mac does its best to protect you from yourself and your family by requiring authentication, both in the GUI and on the command line, when you're about to do something potentially problematic.

OS X, being a multiuser Unix system at its heart, tries to prevent you (or your family) from doing anything that might adversely affect your Mac. It does so by denying access to particular files that keep your system running and disallowing actions that it considers potentially harmful. Every now and again, however, you need to install a piece of software or touch a vital Unix configuration file to get something done. Before it lets you do so, OS X requires that you authenticate yourself as an administrative user, known in Unix parlance as *root*.

Desktop Root

While most applications can be installed simply by dragging them into the Applications folder, some require a little more tomfoolery. Application and package installers often need to create folders, drop files into place, and adjust configuration settings in restricted parts of the operating system.

At these times, you're either not allowed to continue if you're not listed as an administrative user of the system (take a look at the System Preferences →

Users pane) or prompted for your password if you are. Figure 9-1 shows a typical Authenticate dialog.

Figure 9-1. The Authenticate dialog

You'll notice that there is a Details arrow button in the window. Clicking this will let you see exactly which application is requesting the use of the password.

After you type in your password, the Installer continues. In effect, you've become an administrator with full power over your system, if only for a moment. You've then granted the Installer similar power to do what it needs to do.

 Whenever you authenticate yourself to an application, realize that it's going to fiddle with your system and make sure you have some idea what it's trying to do. Read the notices displayed by installers carefully.

You'll also encounter times when you need to authenticate yourself to make a configuration change in System Preferences or the like. If you're unable to change some settings that seem as if they should be editable, look around the window for a little lock icon. If it's locked (see Figure 9-2), you might need to unlock it (click on the lock icon) and authenticate yourself.

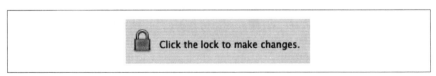

Figure 9-2. Locked settings

If you feel the need to lock the settings again when you're done, click the lock again.

Command-Line Root

On the command line, there is no fancy dialog for authenticating you as the root user. The sudo utility (the name is a shortened form of *substitute-user do*) allows you to gain temporary root privileges on a per-command basis. To use sudo, simply preface the command you want to run as root with sudo and a space; sudo prompts you for your (not root's) password. If you have administrator privileges, entering your password runs the sudoed command as if the root user were doing it.

 Use sudo with care. You can easily make mistakes with sudo that could require a complete reinstallation of the OS to get going again. If that thought makes you queasy, you're better off avoiding it.

Typical sudo use looks like this:

```
$ sudo apachectl restart
```

Here are a few notes about sudo:

- The first time you run sudo, you'll see another reminder to use sudo with care.
- You need to enter your password only when you haven't already used sudo within the last five minutes.
- It's not necessary to activate the root account or do anything else special to start using sudo.

If you need to execute several commands as root in a row and don't want to type sudo continually, you can get a shell as the root user by using the following command:

```
$ sudo -s
Password: *****
#
```

The prompt changes to # to indicate that every command typed will run as the root user.

 Even though it takes more work, you can and should avoid opening root shells by using the sudo command. By making the extra effort, you are less likely to make a horrific mistake and hose your system.

If you want to run a particular shell as root, say tcsh, you can also use the following command:

```
$ sudo tcsh
```

Enabling the Root Account

Some people really want to be able to log into their system as root. For some reason, having administrative privileges and the ability to execute any command by using sudo isn't enough. If you are one of these people, you can enable the root user so that you can log into either the GUI or the command line and have unfettered and unmonitored access to your system. We don't recommend you do this, but if you insist, here's how:

1. Launch NetInfo Manager (*/Applications/Utilities*).
2. Authenticate yourself by using the Security → Authenticate menu.
3. Enable the root user by using the Security → Enable Root menu.
4. Give the root user a password that is as secure as you would give any administrator of the system.

If you follow this procedure, you will have a fully functional root user.

Logging in as Root

Log in as root just as you would log in as any other user. The only difference is that root won't appear in the list of users and their associated cute icons. Click Other, enter root as the Name, and enter the password you assigned to the root account as Password.

—*Chris Stone and Rael Dornfest*

HACK #89   Understand Your User Account

Before Mac OS X was released, there wasn't really a concept of a user or account in the Macintosh environment. This hack introduces you to what it means to have an account and what this business of a Home directory is all about.

When Mac OS X first appeared, a lot of old-school Mac users were aghast at the concept of user accounts, especially when they were the only ones using their computer. "Why go through all the hassle when I'm the only one who uses my computer?" they asked. The complaints only intensified as users were asked to enter an administrator password for access to certain files, sometimes even denied access to settings and files on their very own computers—the gall of it!

The reasoning is twofold: to protect you from yourself and to support Mac OS X's multiuser environment.

The concept of protecting you from yourself might at first blush appear intrusive, but we've all had an instance in which we've deleted an innocent file from our OS 9 System Folder, only to discover our idiocy when our system didn't reboot, our printer didn't print, or our modem didn't sizzle. In this regard, OS X has your back; crucial files necessary for everyday operation are protected from overzealous removal.

The multiuser environment of OS X is based on technology that's been around for a while in the Unix world: a system of checks and balances that stop your kid sister from gleefully deleting that Photoshop file you've been working on all weekend. Whether you're the only user isn't a concern; protection from the inside (e.g., yourself or your kid sister) and protection from the outside (e.g., malicious crackers, viruses, and Trojans) becomes paramount.

While a determined user can delete any file on his OS X machine with enough effort (the easiest way being to boot into OS 9), Apple has wisely made it difficult to do so through Mac OS X.

What's in a Name?

When creating an account (System Preferences → Accounts → New User)— either the initial account upon installing Mac OS X, or an additional account—you're prompted for both your Name (e.g., John Jacob Jingleheimer Schmidt) and something called a Short Name, as shown in Figure 9-3.

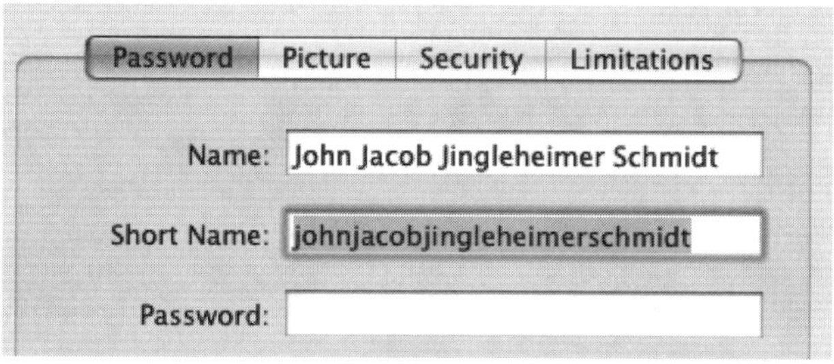

Figure 9-3. Selecting a Name and Short Name

Your Short Name is your actual username, or *login name*, the name by which your computer knows you. It is usually three to eight characters long, composed of letters or numbers. While OS X attempts to choose a Short Name for you based upon what you entered as your Name, it doesn't do a particularly good job if your name isn't as simple as Sam Smith. And, trust me, you don't want to spend your days being known by your computer as johnjacobjingleheimerschmidt. Choose something short and quick to type, like john, johnj, or schmidt. Here's why....

Your Home Directory

Your home directory, shown in Figure 9-4, is where you'll be keeping all your stuff. In it you'll find special directories for your documents, pictures, movies, and settings (that's what the Library is). Of course, you're not forced to organize your stuff this way, but it is a good convention. Feel free to settle in, create new folders, and shuffle things about. It's generally a good idea not to throw out the special folders, because the operating system and its applications often make use of them and expect them to be there. In particular, don't touch your Library folder; it's the home of your preferences, settings, and other pieces used by particular applications.

Figure 9-4. Finder view of a typical home directory

If you chose john as your Short Name, your home directory is Macintosh HD → Users → john. By creating a central place for all your important data, OS X ensures easy backup or deployment on other machines. Instead of having to single out your favorite control panels or extensions from OS 9, you can simply back up your home directory. When you're ready to restore, simply copy it over to the same location, and your environment (iTunes music library, Desktop pictures, added software tweaks, etc.) takes effect the next time you log in.

From the command line's point of view, your home directory (again, assuming your Short Name is john) is */Users/john*. You'll sometimes see it referred to on the command line as ~; that's a shortcut that saves you from having to type your full login name when you refer to your home directory. So, *~/Documents* actually refers to */Users/john/Documents* (Macintosh HD → Users → john → Documents in the Finder).

Who's the Boss?

As the primary user of your computer (or at least as the user you created when you installed the system), you're automatically afforded administrative privileges, which means you can install just about any software, modify settings that affect how OS X functions, and create and delete other accounts. Needless to say, if you don't want your kid sister messing up your computer, you shouldn't make her an administrative user. Give administrative access only to those people (read: accounts) that truly need it.

Deleting an Account

Deleting an account under Mac OS X is easy using the Accounts System Preferences pane (System Preferences → Accounts → Delete User). This removes the account and disables the associated home directory.

Deleted accounts, however, are gone but not completely forgotten. If you take a moment to actually read the confirmation dialog shown in Figure 9-5, you learn that the contents of the now-deleted account's home directory are archived as a disk image in Macintosh HD → Users → Deleted Users.

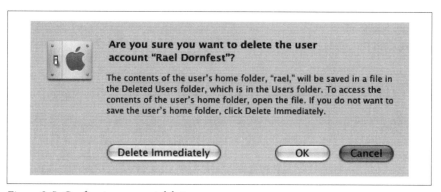

Figure 9-5. Confirming account deletion

When and if you're ready to delete the contents of an archived home directory permanently, simply drag its disk image to the Trash.

Rename a User Account

While OS X makes it easy to create new accounts, alter their capabilities, or change and delete their passwords, it's less than helpful when it comes to renaming an account (i.e., changing its Short Name).

There's no quick and easy way to change the username of an account, but it's not impossible. For example, to fix our johnjacobjingleheimerschmidt user [Hack #89], renaming the account (aka Short Name) to john requires us to do the following:

1. Change the Short Name in NetInfo, the part of the system that manages user account information.

2. Rename the user's home directory.

Changing Information in NetInfo

To modify user information, we're going to use the NetInfo Manager utility, found in the */Applications/Utilities* folder. After you've launched the NetInfo Manager, you'll see an interface with two parts. The top part of the interface is a browser that allows you to navigate through the tree hierarchy of the NetInfo database. The leftmost column of the browser displays a forward slash (/), which is the root of the NetInfo tree. The column to the right is the set of top-level directories (not to be confused with filesystem directories!) that are in the database. We're interested in the *users* directory, as shown in Figure 9-6.

When you select johnjacobjingleheimerschmidt in the *users* directory, the various information keys associated with the account show up in the bottom part of the interface. To change the username, you need to change the values of the following keys from johnjacobjingleheimerschmidt to john:

- name
- _writers_passwd
- _writers_hint
- _writers_picture
- _writers_tim_password
- _writers_realname

To change each key, click the value in the right side and replace johnjacobjingleheimerschmidt with john, as shown in Figure 9-7.

Last, you'll need to change the home key from /Users/johnjacobjingleheimerschmidt to /Users/john. Once you've done this, save your changes using the File → Save Changes menu (or ⌘-S). You'll

Figure 9-6. NetInfo Manager

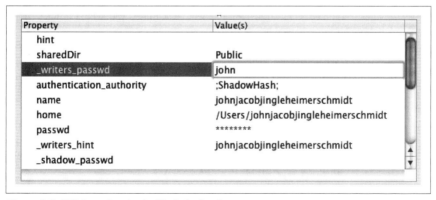

Figure 9-7. Editing a key in the NetInfo database

notice that the username in the browser changes to john, as shown in Figure 9-8.

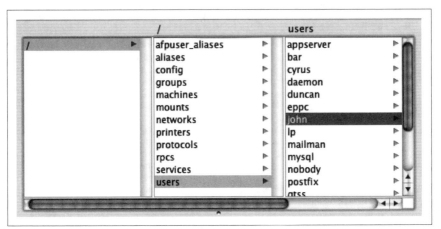

Figure 9-8. The new username john in NetInfo

Renaming the User's Home Directory

Now that we have changed the user information in NetInfo, we need to change the user's home directory name. To do this, launch the Terminal (*/Applications/Utilities*) and use the following command:

```
$ sudo mv /Users/johnjacobjingleheimerschmidt /Users/john
Password: ******
```

This changes the name of John's home directory to match what we put into NetInfo. Give the account a try by logging in and fiddling about.

Use the Terminal   HACK #91

Much of a Mac user's life is spent using the GUI. But under the Technicolor surface lies the command-line environment, which gives you access to the nuts and bolts of the system.

There's no way we can give you an exhaustive tour of the Terminal. Complete books could be—and have been—written about using the various Unix shells available to you. But we'll get you started with this brief tour.

Launching the Terminal

If you've never gone looking for the Terminal before, you probably don't know where to look for it. Maybe it's one of those things that for some people is best left out of sight, out of mind. However, the fact that you are reading this book shows that you aren't one of those kinds of people. You'll find the Terminal hiding in the */Applications/Utilities* folder, as shown in Figure 9-9.

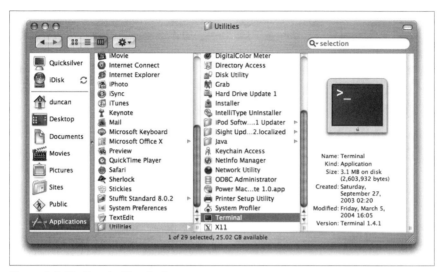

Figure 9-9. Finding the Terminal

Double-click the Terminal folder to create a fresh Terminal window in which to work, as shown in Figure 9-10. When you launch the Terminal, it tells you the last time you logged in and welcomes you to Darwin, the core of Mac OS X.

Figure 9-10. A fresh Terminal window

After the "Welcome to Darwin!" greeting, you'll see a prompt. If you are using a fresh installation of Panther and haven't yet modified the Terminal, you'll see a dollar sign ($), the prompt for the *bash* shell. If you've updated your system from Jaguar or a previous version of OS X, you'll see a percent sign (%), the prompt for the *tcsh* shell.

Need another Terminal window? Simply click File → New
Shell or ⌘-N to open a new window.

All that `Quicksilver:~ duncan$` jazz is known as the *prompt* and provides
some useful information about your current working environment. The bit
before the : is your computer's name (set in the System Preferences → Sharing pane). After the : is your current path, your whereabouts on your hard
drive. In this case, I'm in my home directory, referred to colloquially as ~
(that's a tilde, found on the top left of your keyboard); were I in the Applications folder, my location would read as `:/Applications`. The bit just before
the $ is your username—duncan, in this case.

You'll issue all your commands at the prompt; the cursor (that big block)
keeps track of your typing in much the same way the I-beam does in your
text editor.

Using the Shell

In a nutshell, the *shell* is a mediator between you and the internals of the
Unix system. Its job is to interpret the commands that you type and invoke
the various programs on your system to satisfy those instructions. The *bash*
and *tcsh* shells differ in how they let you interact with the system and have
been the subject of many fierce debates in the community of über-geeks
(second only to *emacs* versus *vi* discussions), but for the most part, they
work the same. If you've never used the shell, you'll do just fine sticking
with the now default *bash* shell.

Now, let's take a look at some basic commands to get you started with using
the shell.

Current working directory. Let's make sure we know where we are, shall we?
Type `pwd` (short for *print working directory*):

```
Quicksilver:~ duncan$ pwd
/Users/duncan
```

Unless you've gone anywhere since opening your Terminal window, you
should be in your home directory: */Users/<login>*, where *<login>* is your
Short Name **[Hack #89]** on the system. Again, this is the same as the ~ shortcut.
That's all well and good, but where exactly is */Users/duncan* with respect to
the folders in the more familiar Finder? It's the same location as your home
folder in the Finder.

While in the Finder we have *folders*, in the Terminal we call them *directories*. Subdirectories are delimited by a forward slash (/) character. Switchers,

note that Windows uses a backslash (\) to delimit subdirectories—for example, c:\mydocu~1. Remember to use / on the Mac command line.

> Backslash, under Unix, has magical properties of its own. It's used to escape or call out special characters such as spaces, question marks, or the like. You'll use it most often on the command line to deal with filenames that contain spaces, letting Unix know that you're still talking about the same file and haven't moved on to another. Notice the semantic difference between a single file, this\ is\ one\ file, versus a string of files, file1 file2 file3.

Listing files and folders. Now that you know your whereabouts, let's take a gander at the content of the current directory. The ls (list) command displays the content of a particular directory:

```
Quicksilver:~ duncan$ ls
Applications Documents Music Sites
Code Library Pictures
Desktop Movies Public
```

In this example, the ls command displays the content of the current directory. You can also ask ls to list the contents of a specific directory and display the result in a particular format by passing it command-line options and a directory name.

In the Terminal, commands are in the format command -options parameter. Options are prefixed by a hyphen (-); when you use are more than option, they're pushed together.

As shown in the following example, ls -al Documents asks ls to list all (-a) the files in the home directory, using a longer (-l) listing format:

```
Quicksilver:~ duncan$ ls -al
total 112
drwxr-xr-x 31 duncan duncan 1054 14 Apr 18:06 .
drwxrwxr-t 7 root admin 238 14 Apr 16:54 ..
-rw-r--r-- 1 duncan duncan 3 18 Mar 02:22 .CFUserTextEncoding
-rw-r--r-- 1 duncan duncan 12292 14 Apr 16:54 .DS_Store
drwxr-xr-x 3 duncan duncan 102 19 Mar 14:07 .MacOSX
drwx------ 103 duncan duncan 3502 14 Apr 16:25 .Trash
-rw------- 1 duncan duncan 6109 14 Apr 18:00 .bash_history
-rw-r--r-- 1 duncan duncan 138 14 Apr 18:00 .bash_profile
-rw-r--r-- 1 duncan duncan 137 23 Mar 17:26 .bash_profile~
drwxr-xr-x 3 duncan duncan 102 23 Mar 17:25 .emacs.d
drwxr-xr-x 3 duncan duncan 102 21 Mar 03:01 .java
-rw-r--r-- 1 duncan duncan 25 4 Apr 14:26 .lpoptions
drwx------ 4 duncan duncan 136 31 Mar 15:30 .ssh
drwxr-xr-x 40 duncan duncan 1360 12 Apr 16:58 Applications
drwxr-xr-x 6 duncan duncan 204 12 Apr 17:03 Code
```

```
drwx------ 30 duncan duncan 1020 14 Apr 16:54 Desktop
drwx------ 24 duncan duncan 816 12 Apr 18:02 Documents
drwx------ 35 duncan duncan 1190 14 Apr 18:05 Library
drwx------ 15 duncan duncan 510 21 Mar 03:39 Movies
drwx------ 5 duncan duncan 170 29 Mar 21:38 Music
drwx------ 5 duncan duncan 170 4 Apr 13:29 Pictures
drwxr-xr-x 4 duncan duncan 136 18 Mar 02:22 Public
drwxr-xr-x 8 duncan duncan 272 31 Mar 17:09 Sites
```

By default, ls does not display any files that begin with a dot (.). To display them, use the -a option. The two files listed with names . and .. are special files known as the *current* and *parent* directory, respectively.

Occasionally, you might have a long file listing, with output flowing off the top of the screen. To page through the output one screenful at a time, send—known as *piping* because of its use of the pipe (|) character—the output to the more command:

```
$ ls -al | more
```

Clearing the screen. After trying out these commands, your screen will no doubt be full of files and directories. To clear the screen, type clear or press Control-L.

Changing directories. To move about, issue a cd (change directory) command, specifying a directory as the parameter. This is akin to opening a folder in the Finder. For example, let's meander over to the Public directory:

```
Quicksilver:~ duncan$ cd Public
Quicksilver:~/Public duncan$
```

Notice how the current directory (the bit after the : in your prompt) changes to ~/Public. This is a constant reminder of where you are at any moment in time; there's no need to keep typing pwd to find out. Remember that the ~ refers to your home directory; so, in this case, I'm actually in */Users/duncan/Public*.

There are two ways to specify a particular directory. The first is to use the *absolute* or *full* path (e.g., cd /Users/duncan/Public). The second way, which is much shorter when you're moving down the path relative to your current location, is to use the *relative* path (e.g., cd Public). Assuming you're in your home directory, these examples are equivalent.

Let's now turn our attention to the contents of the Public folder:

```
Quicksilver:~/Public duncan$ ls
Drop Box
```

Inside of Public, there is one subdirectory, Drop Box, and no files. Change to the Drop Box directory by typing cd Drop\ Box. You can also use tab completion to save yourself a little typing; simply type cd D and press the Tab key.

Bingo! The directory name is automatically completed for you. This works on both files and folders, relative and absolute paths. If there's another file or folder with the same initial letter, type the second letter and press Tab, and so on, typing as much of the name necessary to distinguish it from others.

Moving on up. To move up one step in the directory hierarchy, use .. to refer to the special parent directory:

```
Quicksilver:~/Public/Drop Box duncan$ cd ..
Quicksilver:~/Public duncan$
```

Move up multiple levels by combining .. and /, like so:

```
Quicksilver:~/Public duncan$ pwd
/Users/duncan/Public
Quicksilver:~/Public duncan$ cd ../..
Quicksilver:/Users duncan$ pwd
/Users
```

 The command cd ., in effect, does nothing, because it simply changes the current directory to, well, the current directory. But . will come in handy in a moment when we start copying files.

To go to the top of the directory (known as the *root* directory), use / all by itself:

```
Quicksilver:/Users duncan$ cd /
Quicksilver:/ duncan$
```

To return to your home directory, simply use the cd command with no parameters, the equivalent of cd ~ and cd /Users/*login* (where *login* is your Short Name):

```
Quicksilver:/ duncan$ cd
Quicksilver:~ duncan$
```

Creating directories. To create a new directory, use the mkdir (make directory) command, followed by the directory name, which can be either a relative or an absolute path. Note that if your new directory name contains spaces, you need to escape them or enclose the entire directory name in double quotes (""). Otherwise, mkdir will think you mean to create multiple directories, as shown in the following failed attempt to create a new folder called *Temp Folder*:

```
$ mkdir Temp Folder
$ ls -l
total 0
drwxr-xr-x 2 weimengl staff 68 Dec 11 08:50 Folder
drwxr-xr-x 2 weimengl staff 68 Dec 11 08:50 Temp
```

Either of the following two versions work as expected:

```
$ mkdir Temp\ Folder
$ mkdir "Temp Folder"
```

Removing directories. To remove a directory, use rmdir (remove directory), the polar opposite of mkdir. The space issue applies as expected; either of the following will do:

```
$ rmdir Temp\ Folder
$ rmdir "Temp Folder"
```

Copying files. To copy a file, use the cp (copy) command, followed by the file to copy and its intended destination. Use either a relative or absolute path for each. For example, let's copy the file *index.html* from the Sites directory to Documents:

```
Quicksilver:~ duncan$ cp Sites/index.html Documents
Quicksilver:~ duncan$ cd Documents
Quicksilver:~/Documents duncan$ ls
index.html
```

To copy a file to the current directory, use the special . filename, like so:

```
Quicksilver:~/Documents duncan$ cp Sites/index.html .
```

Deleting files. To delete a file, use the rm (remove) command. The following example deletes that *index.html* we just copied to Documents:

```
Quicksilver:~/Documents duncan$ rm index.html
```

Moving files. To move a file from one directory to another, use the mv (move) command, followed by the space-separated name and destination path. The following example moves the file *index.html* from the Sites directory to Documents:

```
Quicksilver:~ duncan$ mv Sites/index.html Documents
Quicksilver:~ duncan$ cd Sites/
Quicksilver:~/Sites duncan$ ls
images
Quicksilver:~/Sites duncan$ cd ../Documents
Quicksilver:~/Documents duncan$ ls
index.html
```

The mv command is also used for renaming files. The following example renames the file from *index.html* to *index.txt*:

```
Quicksilver:~/Documents duncan$ mv index.html index.txt
Quicksilver:~/Documents duncan$ ls
index.txt
```

Let's put everything back, shall we? Type mv index.txt ~/
Sites/index.html to return everything to as it was when we
started this ride.

Viewing the content of a text file. At times, you might want to take a quick
peek at the contents of a text file. To do so, use cat (concatenate), specifying the file or files to display, like so:

```
$ cat ~/.lpoptions
Default _192_168_254_149
```

Copy and paste, drag and drop. The standard editing suite (select all, copy,
and paste) works as expected in the Terminal, whether invoked with ⌘-A,
⌘-C, and ⌘-V or pulled down from the Edit menu.

A nice bit of interaction between command line and GUI is the ability to
drag a file, directory, or bookmark from anywhere you are in the Finder
right onto the command line. Want to edit a file in a Terminal-based editor
[Hack #78] without navigating the directory hierarchy to get to it? Type pico (or
the appropriate command for your editor of choice), followed by a space,
and drag the file right into the Terminal window. It's a shortcut that comes
in handy more often than you'd think.

Consulting the Manpages

There is only so much that can be covered in this quick tour of the Terminal. You'll encounter a plethora of commands and applications on the command line. Whenever you need any help, try consulting the manual. Simply
type man (as in *manual*, not *oh, man!*), followed by the command name. Your
average manpage looks something like this:

```
MAN(1) BSD General Commands Manual MAN(1)

NAME
   man - format and display the on-line manual pages

SYNOPSIS
   man [-adfhkotw] [-m machine] [-p string] [-M path] [-P pager] [-S list]
   [section] name ...

DESCRIPTION
   Man formats and displays the on-line manual pages. This version knows
   about the MANPATH and PAGER environment variables, so you can have your
   own set(s) of personal man pages and choose whatever program you like to
   display the formatted pages. If section is specified, man only looks in
   that section of the manual. You may also specify the order to search the
   sections for entries and which preprocessors to run on the source files
```

```
via command line options or environment variables. If enabled by the
system administrator, formatted man pages will also be compressed with
the `/usr/bin/gzip -c' command to save space.

The options are as follows:

-M path Specify an alternate manpath. By default, man uses
:
```

Getting Off the Command Line

At any point, you can always close the Terminal window as you would close
any other window. However, it is far more polite—not to mention cleaner—
to log out of the shell session you're running by typing exit or logout:

```
$ logout
[Process completed]
```

Changing the Shell

If you do have a preference and want to use a different shell than what you
are currently using, simply open the Terminal Preferences (Terminal → Preferences) and specify the shell you want to use in the "Execute this command" text field, as shown in Figure 9-11.

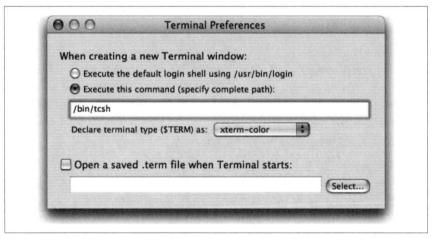

Figure 9-11. Changing the shell using the Terminal Preferences pane

Customizing the Terminal's Appearance

Over time, you'll no doubt become bored with the Terminal's default black-
on-white settings. You can change the colors and fonts used by the Terminal, as well as set a background image and even the window's transparency,

by using the Terminal Inspector (Terminal → Window Settings). Figure 9-12 shows the Display and Color panes of the Terminal Inspector.

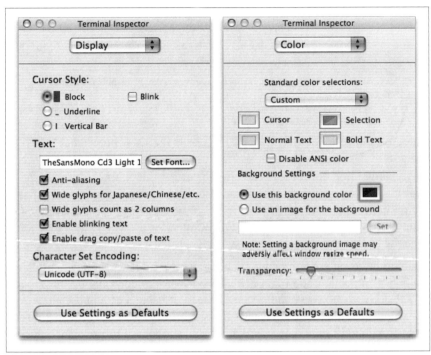

Figure 9-12. Tweaking the appearance of the Terminal window

Using the Terminal Inspector, you can change all the colors to whatever you want—even the traditional green-on-black settings from dumb terminal days. When you find a combination that pleases you, you can choose File → Use Settings as Defaults to have all future Terminal windows adopt the settings .

—*Wei Meng Lee, Rael Dornfest, and James Duncan Davidson*

Set Shell Environment Variables

HACK #92

An environment variable is a magical piece of invisible data that is acted upon by shell programs and utilities that look for its existence. They're innocent enough, and you rarely interact with them, but they can prove to be quite powerful and time-saving when used as part of your daily lifestyle.

Smart developers who care about code integrity use something called a *versioning system* to ensure a system of checks and balances, easy reversion to previous code, and preventive overwriting (by an automatic or manual merging process). It's such a common part of a developer's toolkit that the popular open source web IDE SourceForge.net (*http://www.sourceforge.net*) provides it as a default service.

One annoyance of Concurrent Versioning System (CVS)—longtime users can find many more—is the command line. Without an environment variable, you have to type your cvsroot each and every time you make any changes to your repository:

```
$ cvs -d:pserver:anonymous@cvs.amphetadesk.sourceforge.net:/cvsroot/¬
amphetadesk login
$ cvs -z3 -d:pserver:anonymous@cvs.amphetadesk.sourceforge.net:/cvsroot/¬
amphetadesk co AmphetaDesk
```

These two lines log you into a CVS server as the user *anonymous* and then check out the entire source tree of a program called AmphetaDesk. A cursory examination shows that the largest part of the command line is the -d flag; it's also repetitive, because it needs to be a part of every cvs command. It can make a person nuts when she has to worry about committing modifications to a dozen different files. Wouldn't it be great if you never had to type the -d flag and its heavy payload?

Thankfully, using environment variables, you don't. Think of an environment variable as a configuration file; the values are acted upon only by the application that knows how to handle them. Instead of being located in separate configuration files, they're loaded into the shell environment. You can think of them (roughly) as preferences for your shell (as opposed to preferences for the OS X Terminal application). The environment variable you want to set is called, semantically enough, CVS_ROOT (named after what the -d flag represents).

If you haven't been fiddling with the Terminal preferences, you're probably using the *bash* shell. There are lots of different types of shells, but *bash* is the default on OS X. How you set an environment variable varies according to which shell you're using, but under *bash*, enter the following:

```
$ export CVS_ROOT="-d:pserver:anonymous@cvs.amphetadesk.sourceforge.net:/¬
cvsroot/amphetadesk"
```

If, on the other hand, you've tweaked Terminal to use *tcsh*, enter the following instead:

```
% setenv CVS_ROOT "-d:pserver:anonymous@cvs.amphetadesk.sourceforge.net:/¬
cvsroot/amphetadesk"
```

With the preceding command, you'll notice that nothing seems to happen. That's because environment variables are invisible; they provide visual feedback only when you've screwed up the previous command (or if you've used a program that uses the variable). To make sure your variable was set properly, type printenv (for either shell). You'll see your CVS_ROOT, as well as a number of other variables already defined by OS X.

You can now enter the much smaller and more readable commands:

```
$ cvs login
$ cvs -z3 co AmphetaDesk
```

The problem with export and setenv is that they're both temporary; once you close the Terminal, your CVS_ROOT is forgotten and you're be back in the forest with a command line a mile long. What do you do? Make it permanent, of course.

Again, doing so differs depending on what shell you've chosen. Each shell has the ability to read a *startup file*: something you create that says "Hey, every time I start this shell, do the commands within this file." These files are located in your home directory and normally are not visible to the Finder. Under *bash*, the startup file is named *.bash_profile*. With the *tcsh* shell, the file is named *.tcshrc*. Creating those files, adding the matching command from before, and then starting a new Terminal window sets the CVS_ROOT at startup (you can check this with the printenv command).

Another alternative is to use the *plist* preference file format. Simply creating a file at ~/.MacOSX/environment.plist with the following contents would do it for you:

```
<?xml version="1.0" encoding="UTF-8"?>
<!DOCTYPE plist SYSTEM "file://localhost/System/Library/DTDs/PropertyList.
dtd">
<plist version="0.9">
<dict>
<key>CVS_ROOT</key>
<string>-d:pserver:anonymous@cvs.amphetadesk.sourceforge.net:/cvsroot/
amphetadesk</string>
</dict>
</plist>
```

See Also

- "Setting environment variables for user processes" (*http://developer. apple.com/qa/qa2001/qa1067.html*)

—Kevin Hemenway

HACK #93 A Security Primer

This hack provides a hands-on overview of the security tools built into your Mac OS X computer, including recommendations for best practices to protect your data and identity in a potentially dangerous world.

The recent security issues affecting Windows users have led the media—and sometimes even Mac-specialized publications—to talk about the shortcomings of the Windows security scheme and to provide surprisingly detailed advice.

So far, Mac users indeed have been luckier. Mac OS X is relatively secure out of the box, and Apple has been good about providing easily installable security updates as needed.

Unfortunately, some Mac users forget that security is more than just applying the occasional patch. It is a continuously evolving quest that requires additional steps to make their systems more secure. Luckily, the Unix foundation of Mac OS X, Darwin, has provided us with powerful tools that we can leverage to help our computers remain secure in an otherwise dangerous world.

In this hack, I'll take a hands-on approach to what I call *security through common sense*, the basic security steps that every single Mac user should take.

Disclaimer

Security is a touchy topic, and nobody owns a definitive security answer. This hack presents the steps that I recommend, but my views might differ from those of your network administrator, company, or school—either because you need a greater level of security, or because the organization relies on other, internally tested, solutions. In any case, please consult your IT department before implementing these steps.

If you handle sensitive data, I advise you to seek professional advice. Using a Mac is an excellent way to protect data—since they are extremely secure— but you might need to implement industrial-strength firewalling and intrusion-detection software. This is obviously out of the scope of this hack.

I have tested the third-party software I link to on my own machines. However, please understand that I have no insider knowledge about these applications and that I cannot endorse them.

Why Protect Your Mac?

Many Mac users, and computer users in general, do not take additional security steps to protect their data because they have the feeling that they have "nothing to hide" or that they do not store any valuable information on their computers.

Unfortunately, this comforting theory overlooks the fact that most of the time, hackers don't try to attack your computer or your network because of who you are. Indeed, most of the time, attacked computers are chosen semi-randomly: because they have detected that you have an unusual amount of traffic, because you run an unprotected Windows 95 computer somewhere on your network that makes it easy to crack, and so on.

Some people will try to break into your computer "for fun." However, nowadays, many exploits have a unique goal: turn the computer into some kind of zombie from which the attacker will be able to steal confidential information (can you swear that your credit card number isn't stored somewhere on your computer?) or perform illegal actions in your own name. Therefore, in most cases, hacking a computer is worth the time and effort spent, even if the person who tries to break in has no idea who you are.

Even worse, in some countries, not having any protection in place can be seen by the law as an implicit approbation of what other people could do on your computer without your knowledge—the good old "This person wasn't protected; this shows that he didn't mind what could happen." Were something to go wrong, being able to prove that your computer was indeed protected might be a good way to show your true intentions.

The Basics

Now that we have discussed a bit about why security is important, I'm going to walk you through the basic steps of securing your Mac. This first part will give you an overview of things you might know already, but it might include a new wrinkle or two.

Know your computer. Most security issues nowadays rely on simple social-engineering techniques: convince a user to download an application or run a special command that opens a breach in the security systems that have been set up. That's how most Windows viruses propagate, and we've all seen how effective this approach is.

By knowing Mac OS X better, you will be able to avoid common mistakes, such as turning on Windows file sharing and FTP services "just in case." This might sound silly, but this is the most essential step toward good security and allows you to react in an efficient manner to incidents and potential issues.

Of course, I assume you already know that you are not supposed to open unknown email attachments, run strange applications, and so on. You should exercise the same caution on your computer that you would use in the real world when dealing with strangers, let's say, on a dark street at around 3:00 a.m.

Stay up-to-date with security news. As a concerned citizen of your country, you are already trying to keep up with current events on a local, national, and international scale. That's great! But do you do the same when it comes to computer-related news?

Indeed, the best way to defeat social engineering and avoid attacks is to be aware of what's going on in the security world.

Luckily, you can do this easily in a variety of ways. The Apple Product Security page (*http://www.info.apple.com/usen/security*) provides you with simple tips to learn more about security issues as soon as they are discovered. I highly recommend you subscribe to Apple's security-announce mailing list as well.

Also, you might want to keep an eye on the recent virus outbreaks and security issues. Indeed, even reading about Windows- and Linux-only viruses and Trojan horses will give you a good idea of what's happening on the network and how social engineering works. The Symantec Security Response site (*http://securityresponse.symantec.com*) is a good place to start.

Were a Mac virus to be discovered, you would notice it immediately and be able to take the appropriate steps.

Ensure local security. In this hack, we're focusing on network-born threats. However, there can be no network security if anyone can sit in front of your screen, alter your settings, and then use the new setup to attack you remotely.

Therefore, I recommend you take a look the Mac DevCenter article "Securing Your TiBook (or Any Other Mac OS X Machine)" (*http://www.macdevcenter.com/pub/a/mac/2003/02/18/secure_tibook.html*), which shows how to set up a firmware password.

You should also turn off automatic login and make sure that authentication is required to alter the settings of most Preferences panes; you can do all of this through the Security Preferences pane. Also, get into the habit of using the "Lock screen" feature—available through the Keychain menu—whenever you step away from your keyboard, even for a few minutes.

Finally, you might want to take a look at FileVault (*http://www.macdevcenter.com/pub/a/mac/2003/12/19/filevault.html*) and decide whether you want to run it.

Keep your system up-to-date. The Mac OS X development team does its absolute best to provide you with a secure operating system and might release, from time to time, security updates—even when there's no known exploit.

I recommend you apply these updates as soon as they are released, to make sure you do not give time to attackers to exploit a known vulnerability. Indeed, it is now quite easy to find software on the Internet that automatically tries to break into computers and reports all the vulnerabilities found in a specific machine, along with tips about how to exploit them. In many countries, such software is perfectly legal and some authors update their applications daily!

The most convenient way to update your applications is, of course, to use the Software Update Preferences pane, available through the System Preferences application. It takes care of finding the updates you need and then downloads and installs them, which makes securing your computer easy. Unlike some update mechanisms featured by other operating systems, Software Update checks that the files it downloads indeed come from the Apple servers, not from any server that claims to be Apple.

For maximum security, you might want to download updates manually from the recently redesigned Apple Support Downloads page (*http://www.apple.com/support/downloads*). The main advantage is that you have the option to manually test the authenticity of the file you download (an added security) by using the md5 utility. The main drawback is that updates are usually posted on the download site with a slight delay—24 hours in most cases.

md5 is a Unix command-line utility that allows you to read the *checksum* of a file. Like fingerprints, checksums are unique identifiers that correspond to a specific file, and it is highly unlikely—some say virtually impossible—to find two different files with the same checksum. If the checksum provided by md5 on your Mac and the one provided by Apple on the download site match, you can be virtually sure that you have downloaded the right file and that it has not been altered during the download.

To check a file's md5 checksum, simply open a Terminal window [Hack #91] and type the following command: md5 */path/to/the/file*. Press Return and compare the string returned with the one displayed on the download page.

md5 checksums now have known flaws that could potentially allow someone to forge an altered file with the same checksum. This is, however, unlikely and md5 is still widely seen as a safe way to check the integrity of files—provided, of course, that the web site used as a reference hasn't been hacked too!

Keep your applications up-to-date. As important as it is to keep your operating system up-to-date, you should also not forget to update your applications. Many applications are updated frequently for security reasons, including third-party web browsers, email readers, and Microsoft Office. As long as you are running them, it is extremely important to update them too, since they could potentially allow an attacker to run malicious code on your computer; consider macro viruses, for example.

Many software authors now provide Software Update–like features, but, unfortunately, few have actually implemented security checks in them. Therefore, I recommend you use these features to check whether an update is available on a regular basis but go to the actual application site to download it. If the authors do not provide an md5 checksum, you might want to ask them to get into the habit of posting one.

Software Update usually notifies you about updates to the Apple applications you have installed on your computer, even if they are not bundled with the standard Panther installation.

Pick a good password. It might sound silly, but the easiest way to break into most computers is to politely ask the computer to give permission to enter! And how do you do that? By guessing the passwords set by the authorized users. Indeed, in most cases, computer users use relatively weak passwords that do not protect them efficiently and that can be guessed easily. Remember that hackers can use programs that try a few thousand passwords per minute!

When an attacker uses this method, no firewall or security system can really detect its presence and stop him, because, as far as the computer is concerned, this person is you.

Luckily, picking a good password isn't too difficult, as long as you at least follow some basic guidelines:

- It is not a word (or words) that can be found in a dictionary, regardless of the language or how complex the word is.
- It is not a word followed or preceded by random characters, numbers or signs.
- It is not a number-only code.
- It is not your computer's hostname or the name of an account.
- It is not an alteration (doubled, reversed, etc.) of the previous categories.
- It is longer than 8 characters; longer than 12 is even better.
- It contains uppercase and lowercase letters, punctuation, symbols, and numbers.
- It isn't any sensitive information, such as your Social Security Number.
- It cannot be easily guessed (i.e., it's not the name of your dog, favorite dish, or favorite celebrity).
- It is not listed as a "good password" on a web site or in a book—including this one!
- It is not something you send in the clear, such as your username, email address, an account number, and so on.

As surprising as it might seem, the user password is, in many cases, the weakest link in a security system.

Of course, if you rely on the Keychain to hold your various passwords securely, you should be extra careful when picking the password used to lock the Keychain. It should not be the same as any of the passwords that are stored inside of the Keychain. Panther users will notice that the New Keychain creation dialog now features a password checker, available through the I button.

To use the password-checker dialog, click the OK button once you have entered the password in the Password field; you do not need to enter it twice at this stage. You can then alter your password and see the new security rating appear in the password-checker window. Follow the recommendations until the bar turns completely green (there should be no remaining trace of red, orange, or yellow) and there are no recommendations in the lower part of the window.

Protect your password. Now that you have created a relatively secure password, you should also make sure that nobody knows it. The same applies to your other accounts, since a malicious user could try to use them to break into your computer—for example, by putting a malicious program in your email inbox—or steal your identity.

The first rule is to have separate passwords for everything. If you can't remember your various passwords, rely on the Keychain application to provide them to the applications or online forms that need them, but make sure that someone who has your AIM password (never encrypted) cannot log into your computer remotely or check your email!

Never reveal this password to anyone, especially if you are requested to send it through an unencrypted channel (e.g., via web page, email, instant message, phone, etc.) or receive a message with links to follow; these are usually scams that attempt to redirect you to a fraudulent site. You should not send passwords via a network, even to trusted individuals, because the passwords can be easily sniffed during the transfer over the wire—or worse, over a wireless network.

Do not write down your passwords. If you absolutely must write them down, lock them in a safe-deposit box, where you will be able to find them if you need to, but do not keep them on you or around your computer. No, not even under the keyboard!

If possible, try to create multiple keychains [Hack #94] on your Mac to group passwords and unlock the password sets on an as-needed basis. To create multiple keychains, use the Keychain Access utility (*Applications/Utilities/Keychain Access*). While you create and manage your keychains, be sure to use the View menu to display the Keychain menu item in your menu bar;

that way, you can lock and unlock keychains on the fly. Once a keychain is locked, your passwords are safely stored into an encrypted file.

Protecting passwords in a locked file prevents not only local and remote malicious users from using them but also potential Trojan horses, since you are required to provide your password to decrypt a keychain. Of course, as soon as you decrypt a keychain file to use a password, your password is at risk, but this limits the periods of exposure—and limits the exposure to only the application that accesses it.

Inside a keychain, you should also set up strict access rules for the various items and restrict their use as much as possible. Such settings can be found in the lower half of the Keychain window.

The Keychain application has a frequently forgotten feature: secure notes. Secure notes work exactly as password items and enjoy the same level of protection, but they allow you to enter an unlimited amount of text. To create one, simply use the Note button or the File menu. Notes are a good way to store relatively sensitive information, but you might want to create Notes-only keychains for the sake of organization and security.

 For more on using the Keychain to stow useful personal information, see "Stash Data in the Keychain" **[Hack #94]**.

A common password security issue is posed by mail readers that do not use SSL to connect to the server. You might want to take a look at "Secure Mail Reading on Mac OS X" (*http://www.macdevcenter.com/pub/a/mac/2002/03/19/secure_mail.html*) by Jason McIntosh. If you find that your provider does not support any kind of secure mail reading (a surprisingly common situation), consider switching to another provider as soon as possible. Apple's own .Mac mail services do offer secure mail reading through SSL and are fully integrated with Panther's Mail.

Passwords can be sniffed and intercepted in countless ways, and you should never trust the same password over a long period of time. Change your password regularly, and try to create new ones each time. For example, avoid sequential passwords such as Password01, Password02, and so on. These are easily cracked.

Make sure you do not allow in intruders. Unlike many other Unix (and especially Linux) distributions, Mac OS X ships with all network services and potentially dangerous daemons turned off by default. Most of them can be turned on by using the Sharing Preferences pane, available through the System Preferences application.

As soon as you turn a service on, you start a daemon that continuously listens for connections on a given port and replies to them. For example, turning on "Remote login" launches the sshd daemon that allows anyone to establish a connection to your Mac through port 22. If a malicious user knows your password, he can get in—and legally!

Some of these services turn your Mac into a server, raising a new class of potentially important security issues. Therefore, you should not turn on these services unless you really need them.

Of course, most of these daemons run as nonhuman users on Mac OS X. In other words, they run as if they were a separate user on your machine with limited privileges. This makes using them to break into your computer more difficult, especially if you make sure that you always use the latest versions of them.

However, such daemons can always be used to gain some interesting information about your computer and launch denial-of-service (DoS) attacks quite easily (e.g., repeatedly request SSH logins or file sharing to slow down your computer).

If you need to run a *dangerous* service (i.e., a widely known, insecure one, such as FTP or Windows File Sharing), you might want to dedicate a specific machine on your network to use as a file server. On properly firewalled networks, place this machine outside the firewalled zone, provided that you would like the whole world to know its contents, of course; this makes connecting it to the Internet and serving data much easier, while protecting the rest of your network.

For the same reason, avoid sharing your Internet connection through the Internet tab, because doing so grants legitimate access to other computers on your network and launches server daemons on your Mac too. Of course, this is not an issue when working with trusted computers and individuals, but it should also not become a common practice in public places.

Ensure security at the application level. However, making sure you didn't turn on any dangerous service at the operating-system level is sometimes not enough, because some applications can run their very own server services.

Some workgroup applications can turn your Mac into a file-sharing server, for example. Some webcam drivers have a web-server function that allows remote users to connect to your machine to see the images you publish. Of course, some of these applications are well written, but you should always consider the security risk associated with running servers, even if this does not happen at the OS level, because the effect is, ultimately, the same or worse.

Without discussing the legal aspects associated with peer-to-peer networks, let's not forget that many such applications have been known for installing spyware or featuring flawed security systems. If you insist on using them (to share files legally, of course), you might want to follow the procedure for running dangerous services, mentioned previously.

Some applications are known to raise constant security issues; I won't give names, but I am sure you see what I mean. Whenever possible, try to avoid these applications and rely on more secure alternatives. The open source community has released some great, fully functional alternative applications that can integrate perfectly into your existing workflow.

Wireless networks protected by WEP are inherently insecure, as described in Rob Flickenger's article "Dispelling the Myth of Wireless Security" (*http://www.oreillynet.com/pub/a/wireless/excerpt/wirlsshacks_chap1/index.html*). Please, do not attempt to reproduce the steps outlined in that article before making sure that it is legal in your country, even on your own network. Therefore, you might want to rely on better methods, such as WPA [Hack #65]. Apple recently released an AirPort update that allows you to use this updated security method, even in mixed AirPort/AirPort Extreme environments.

Better yet, lock them out. Now that you are sure you do not allow people in too easily, you might want to make sure that you lock them out, by using a firewall. As silly as it might seem, a software firewall is no stronger than the operating system on which it runs, as the ever-increasing Windows security issues show.

Therefore, it is important to get a hardware firewall that provides a first layer of security for your network by making it *stealth* (i.e., not responding to various probes, and warning you if someone really tries to break in).

No hardware firewall is 100% secure, but by applying the security updates provided by your vendor, you should be able to keep most wannabe evildoers out of your LAN. Also, using a hardware firewall to protect your network allows you to worry less about the security mistakes that some users might commit on their Macs, though this should not give a false sense of security either.

There are many, many types of firewalls, and all of them have their strengths and weaknesses. However, you might want to make sure that you follow these rules:

- Your external firewall should not require that you install any software of any kind on your Mac. Most firewalls now use a web-based interface, which solves most compatibility issues. However, all web-based interfaces are not created equal, and you should try to avoid the ones that have been "optimized for Internet Explorer 6 or better"; this usually indicates a PC-centric vendor and is in no way a warrantee that the interface is better, even if you plan to set it up from a Windows computer.

- Your firewall should provide you with detailed logs and should be able to warn you—by sending a mail, a page or a phone call—if it detects something abnormal. Even entry-level firewalls do that now (to some extent, of course), and it can be a valuable help.

- Your firewall should use a stateful packet-inspection system or better (i.e., a system that allows remote packets that come as a reply to a request you sent). Network Address Translation (NAT) is a first step toward security but does not a firewall make, although it is essential if you need to connect multiple computers on your LAN with one ISP-provided IP address.

- Your firewall should come with default settings that provide maximum security and should not require you to be an iptables expert!

- Ideally, your firewall should have demilitarized zone (DMZ) capabilities. A DMZ is an area of your network that is isolated from the firewalled computers and that can be connected directly to the Internet. This is the place where you place all your public servers and computers. It is not protected but, in case something goes wrong, the computers that contain your sensitive data are safe.

Some firewalls can act as routers and modems, which makes creating a network easy. Of course, you should pick one that uses Ethernet; I still have to see one that doesn't, but you never know what can pop up at a computer store.

Use a software firewall. Surprisingly, few Mac OS X users know that their operating system of choice comes with a built-in, time-tested, industrial-strength firewall that they can turn on by simply using the Sharing Preferences pane.

Just follow these steps:

1. Open System Preferences.
2. Open the Sharing Preferences pane and select the Firewall tab.
3. Make sure that no box is checked in the Allow list.
4. Click Start to start the firewall.

The firewall used by Mac OS X is called *ipfw* (which stands for *IP firewall*). Its job is fairly simple: close ports and prevent remote hosts and applications from connecting to them. Some users might argue that the interface provided by Apple does not allow a lot of fine-tuning. This is true, but this restriction is intentional; it allows even newcomers to benefit from reliable security settings, without having to worry too much about settings.

Of course, by turning your firewall on, you prevent some applications from establishing a connection with your computer. This is not likely to interfere with most of your workflow but can, under some circumstances, prevent a few network-aware applications from working, especially Rendezvous-enabled ones—iChat over Rendezvous, for example. To avoid this, you can open the necessary ports by checking the corresponding box in the Allow list. Just keep in mind that the more ports you open, the less effective your firewall will be. But it sure is far better than disabling the firewall altogether.

Unfortunately, *ipfw* does not feature instant warning and only writes its warning messages to a log, which is accessible through the Console utility. This has the advantage of not disrupting your workflow but, unfortunately, does not allow you to react in a timely manner to some attacks, because you are probably not constantly monitoring the logs.

Many companies now sell third-party firewalling solutions that do not rely on *ipfw* in any way. These firewalls provide you with instant-notification systems and are generally more friendly for a new user. However, they need to add *kernel extensions* (files that act as a low level in your operating system to add features) to your installations. While a well-written kernel extension can work perfectly, be aware that you need to update them frequently and pay attention to potential compatibility and stability issues.

Many firewall companies provide online tests that try to test your firewall—for example, Symantec Security Check (*http://security.symantec.com*). Of course, most of these tests are linked to advertisements for the company's products, and none of them replace a good security audit. However, they still can provide you with some valuable information.

Use and maintain antivirus software. Unfortunately, a few Mac users sometimes think they do not need to worry about viruses because "there are no viruses for Mac OS X."

First of all, this is not entirely true, and some macro viruses can travel across platforms. However, even if this really were the case, you should still scan your computer regularly. That way, you not only will you be able to stop PC viruses before you inadvertently forward them to your PC friends, but you also will be able to react quickly in the event of a massive Mac-compatible infection.

Again, there are many antivirus solutions out there, and many companies sell antivirus software with more or less identical features. However, since many .Mac members use Virex, this is the program I will focus on. If you already rely on another product, you should be able to adapt most of this advice.

The default Virex preferences are curiously set up, and you might want to change them a bit. First, make sure that Virex performs an "advanced scan of applications and macros." *Heuristic scanning* is a method of scanning files that attempts to recognize the characteristics of viruses, even if they are not listed in the virus definitions. This slows the scan down a bit but definitely provides an extra layer of security you shouldn't live without.

Of course, no antivirus software, even with the best heuristic-scanning capabilities, can protect you in an efficient manner if you do not update your antivirus definitions. McAfee, like most antivirus companies, updates its Mac definitions once a month, and, let's face it, this is not enough to stop PC or Unix viruses. If you're ready to use the Terminal, there is a way to update your definitions a lot more often:

1. Open Virex and click the "Virus info" button in the toolbar to open the Network Associates Virus Information Library in your default web browser.

2. Using the navigation bar on the left, click Downloads.

3. On the page that appears, click DATs.

4. Click "Weekly v.4.x (DAT only)."

5. Click the link next to Unix to download a compressed file called *dat-xxxx.tar* to your Desktop. Double-click it to decompress its contents.

6. Now, open the Terminal, type cd */path/to/dat/folder* (replacing the path with the real path to the folder you just decompressed on your Desktop), and press Return to navigate there.

7. Type: sudo cp *.dat /usr/local/vscanx and press Return. You will be asked to type your password **[Hack #88]**.

8. You should now be able to quit and relaunch Virex to use the latest definitions. To make sure that the upgrade was successful, just have a look at the Results field. It should state that your virus definitions have been updated recently.

Scan on the command line with Virex. Virex allows you to automate scanning each time you log in. This might be convenient for some users, but you might want to scan your hard drive at a different time each day. Ideally, you should scan your hard drive every day during your lunch hour; at this time, the computer is probably almost idle, so the scan can go more quickly and it won't interfere with your daily routine. Also, if Virex finds an infected file, you can see it almost immediately and take the appropriate steps.

Since Mac OS X is a Unix-based operating system, it allows you to auto-mate tasks by using cron [Hack #98]. You need to edit the system's *cron* file to automate Virex. Since this file already contains some important system information, you might want to use caution while you edit it. You definitely don't want to disable the Mac OS X maintenance tasks. Add the following line to the end of the existing list of cron events:

```
0 13 * * * root /usr/local/vscanx/vscanx -rv --secure / >/Applications/
virexreport.txt
```

Save the crontab.

Hereafter, every day at 1:00 p.m., Virex will run in the background as root and scan your computer. Once it is done, it creates a text file that contains the report in your Applications folder. Make sure you read it carefully every day to make sure that your system wasn't infected and to know more about what has happened. Once you have read it, delete it. That way, if the test crashes the next day and does not produce a report, you will notice it's miss-ing, rather than read the old one and think that it is the latest status of your system!

Do not enable the root user. Since the root user is, according to the Unix per-mission scheme, all-powerful, most attacks and exploits are targeted at it. Therefore, for security reasons, Apple has disabled it and allows you to gain root privileges only temporarily by entering your administrator password.

Some advanced Unix users might need to enable the root account to per-form some complex administrative tasks, but you should not do so, even if some tutorials suggest it. Doing so does not create a security issue in itself, but it makes breaking into your system much more rewarding!

To temporarily execute commands in the Terminal with root privileges, sim-ply add sudo in front of all the commands you want to execute with super-user privileges.

Some security tutorials even recommend you create another, simple-user account for your everyday work. If you feel comfortable about doing so, it might indeed be a good idea. However, it can be a real issue for users who often install or compile applications on their Macs, because such operations require administrative privileges.

Going Further

Now that your computer is properly firewalled, you have solid antivirus pro-tection, and you use secure passwords, you have achieved a security level that every single Mac user—and every computer user in general—should at least have.

However, there are still ways to go a bit further without disturbing your workflow too much. If you are willing to have a look at a few other cool applications and technologies, here we go!

Use a reverse firewall. While you are using your Mac, many, many applications constantly try to access the Internet, either to get information or to send some. The problem is that some of them might, along the way, send some details that you deem confidential (or they might simply be Trojan horses).

To avoid this, you can install *reverse firewalls* that monitor outgoing connections and provide you with live alerts, which allows you to accept or deny attempts. Of course, such third-party products are not perfect, because you must trust the authors and they too install kernel extensions to provide you with alerts.

However, the best of them can be a real help. Give it a try, and you will be surprised to see how many applications try to establish connections without your permissions!

One application in this category that is widely known in the Mac community is Little Snitch (*http://www.obdev.at/products/littlesnitch*), but it's not the only one, and you might want to look at other options and their various feature sets first.

Before installing them, you should be aware that such products might sometimes interfere with Mac OS X in itself; for example, they can prevent fast user switching from working. Luckily, since their authors are hard at work to improve them, compatibility issues disappear pretty quickly.

On a more legal note, keep in mind that preventing some applications from connecting to their authors' site for registration and license-controlling purposes might be unlawful in your country. Check with your legal advisor or the authors of the application first.

Reverse firewalls often generate many alerts when you first install them. You should take the time to fine-tune their rules to ensure maximum security. For example, allowing an application to establish "any connection" can be tempting, but it entirely disables the protection that you could enjoy against this application. Even if the application is trusted, remember that everything is hackable.

An important point to check is whether your reverse firewall can protect itself against malicious applications that might try to alter its database. Most of them won't have a very secure self-check system, but you should make sure that there is one to increase your security.

Use a tripwire-like system. Let's say that someone has broken into your computer and has begun to alter various configurations files to use your computer as a base for his unlawful activities.

Luckily, some applications out there can regularly calculate the checksum of your files (see the previous information on md5 in this hack) and compare it with a list of known good files. Such a system can certainly be defeated by altering the reference database, but it provides you with an extra layer of security, and can be a real lifesaver under certain circumstances.

Brian Hill, author of the world-famous Brickhouse (*http://brianhill.dyndns.org/*), has released an application called CheckMate that acts the same way and can check on a regular basis to see if any of your system files (or data files of your choice) have been altered without your consent.

Here is how to use CheckMate:

1. Download it from *http://brianhill.dyndns.org/*.

2. Launch the installer and read carefully the information printed on the screen. Do not install it systemwide; instead, install it on a per-user basis. That way, the installer won't ask you for your password.

3. To install CheckMate, click the Install button.

4. To set up CheckMate, open System Preferences and visit the Check-Mate Preferences pane.

5. Once you have authenticated, set up the check schedule and your notification options. I recommend you avoid sending an email (unless you work remotely), but be sure to both log it and display an alert dialog.

6. In the Files tab, click the "Update checksums" button; this creates a database of checksums the application considers good. If a file were already corrupted, CheckMate wouldn't notice the issue at this point. If you see files for which no checksum appears, this might mean that they do not ship with Panther anymore. Simply remove the file from the list. Add any files you deem important or that might hold critical data.

7. Click Apple Settings and exit CheckMate.

8. To test CheckMate, reopen it and launch a manual scan from the Scan tab. In my test, CheckMate sometimes ran into an infinite loop when multiple manual scans were performed in a row, but the application never had an issue with background scanning, and that's the important part.

To make sure that CheckMate runs normally, you can have a look at the system log via the Console (*Applications/Utilities/Console*).

The fact that an application such as CheckMate reports an integrity-check error does not necessarily mean you have been hacked. Indeed, updating the prebinding of files (a task commonly performed by an installer) can alter the checksum and cause an alert to appear.

Before worrying about an alert, you should always ask yourself whether there was a reason the file was modified.

There are many applications like CheckMate, and each has its own strengths and weaknesses. By going through their respective feature sets, you will be able to find the one that best fits your needs. For example, do you need a GUI, or do you prefer the Terminal? How secure should the application be? And how easy to use?

Final Thoughts

Security is a never-ending quest, but, thanks to Apple's attention to detail and commitment to security, we Mac users enjoy one of the most secure operating systems in the world. By following a few simple steps, we can go even further and make sure that even if the worse happens, we will remain safe and secure. By applying the same principles to online security that you would in real life, you can avoid many, if not most issues. Have the right attitude, use the right tools, and you should be safe.

—François Joseph de Kermadec

Stash Data in the Keychain

An overlooked location to store personal data securely is in the same place that the system uses to store your passwords: the Keychain.

One of the many nice features of Mac OS X is the Keychain that manages usernames and passwords for many applications, such as iChat and Mail. When you log into your computer, your system password unlocks your Keychain, making it available to these applications to use so that you don't have to take the time to enter (or remember) your passwords. But you can use the Keychain for more than this. You can store the usernames and passwords for the web sites you visit and even store arbitrary data if you like—all secure from prying eyes.

Using Safari AutoFill

As nice as it is to use all the various web applications out there, the side effect is that you now have to manage a long list of usernames and passwords for all the web sites you visit. Many users take the easy way out and use the same password for all their web sites, but this isn't very secure. After all, if your password on one site is compromised and you use the same password everywhere, then whoever has it can now access all of your sites. The solution is to use a different password for each site, but then you have to manage all of them.

Safari's AutoFill can take care of this for you. To let Safari work its magic, open its Preferences pane, go to the AutoFill section, and check the "User names and passwords" checkbox, as shown in Figure 9-13.

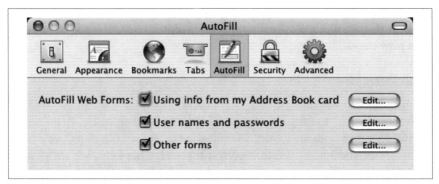

Figure 9-13. Enabling Safari AutoFill for usernames and passwords

Now, when you log into a site, Safari offers to save the data. If you let it, the next time you visit the site, Safari automatically fills out the login form for you.

To take a look at the passwords that Safari (and all the other apps on your system) store in the Keychain, use the Keychain Access (/Applications/Utilities) application, as shown in Figure 9-14. As you can see, the various passwords are saved in various entries, each of which can be edited.

Storing Personal Data

Using the Keychain to store passwords is great and a real boon. But what about the other kinds of data you want to keep nearby but don't want to leave in a plain-text file somewhere on your computer? For example, having your credit card numbers on your computer can be quite handy if you need to use your credit card but don't have access to your wallet. Or even better, having your account numbers saved can be quite handy if you ever lose them.

To store this kind of data, use the File → New Secure Note Item (or just use the Note button in the toolbar). The dialog shown in Figure 9-15 then allows you to save your data.

Of course, you're not limited to storing just credit-card data in the Keychain. You can store anything you like. Just remember, if you store anything

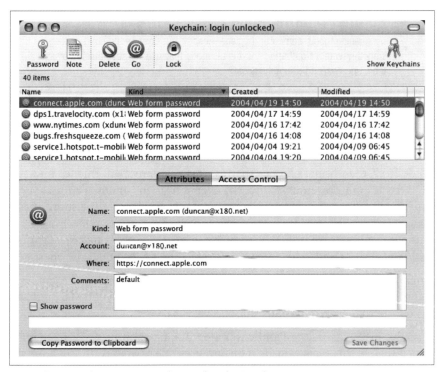

Figure 9-14. Looking at passwords stored in the Keychain

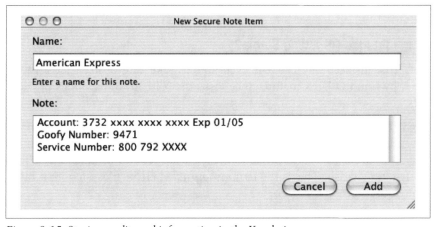

Figure 9-15. Storing credit card information in the Keychain

in here that's really important, you should make sure the Keychain (stored in *~/Library/Keychains*) is backed up regularly.

—*Wei Meng Lee and James Duncan Davidson*

Panther Maintenance

Maintaining good computer hygiene keeps your system humming along smoothly without gathering the digital moss that usually accumulates over time, updates, and everyday usage.

Have you noticed that over the life span of a system-software release, such as Jaguar, things just don't run as smoothly as in the beginning? At some point, we become thankful that a new release is on the way so that we can just *start over*.

Aside from the normal glitches that can occur, many performance and stability issues are preventable. Indeed, over weeks and months of use, users often neglect important maintenance tasks or, even worse, perform operations that are likely to damage their computers, such as disconnecting drives without ejecting them or installing many third-party tools on their machines without fully understanding the impact they might have under the hood.

After all, why not? Computers (especially Macs) are here to be enjoyed, right? The good news is that you can continue to enjoy your Mac and still make sure that everything runs smoothly.

If you've just upgraded to Panther, or are thinking about it, then the maintenance tips in this hack will help ensure good performance throughout the life of this OS release. Some of these tips will be reminders and others might be new to you, but combined, they will help you run a lean, mean computing machine.

I Thought Mac OS X Was Stable?

Yes, it is! In fact, Mac OS X is even able to take care of itself most of the time, by running Unix maintenance tasks that discard unused logs or cache files.

Even better, the latest release of Mac OS X, Panther, includes a powerful new feature, previously reserved for super-serious servers: it keeps a diary of what it does on your hard drive, so that you can recover instantly and effortlessly after a crash. This is the famous *journaled* HFS+ filesystem that raises many questions on the Web.

However, some poorly written applications might damage your file structure, or a clunky installer can ruin the permissions of what it installs. These small errors often go unnoticed; we quit the installer, reboot, and everything behaves normally.

The fact that you do not immediately notice symptoms does not mean that you do not have issues. Most of the time, Panther deals with them, logging the errors and going forward. For example, slight permissions issues slow your computer down a tiny bit, but they don't prevent it from running.

But when you run an update or install an application, the installer expects files to be in a certain place and directories to have a certain owner. If these issues interfere with the installation process, you might discover, upon reboot, that you cannot log in any more or that the Finder doesn't start up.

Following are the most common Mac OS X maintenance steps and how to perform them.

Repairing Privileges

Repairing the privileges of a file or folder is one of the most nonintrusive Mac OS X maintenance tasks; you can launch a utility and let it run in the background while you continue to work.

Open the Disk Utility (located in your Utilities folder) and click on the First Aid tab (see Figure 9-16). Then, select the Mac OS X partition (not the whole hard drive) and click Repair Permissions. You do not need to verify first.

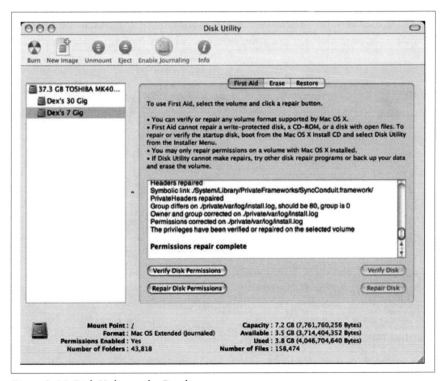

Figure 9-16. Disk Utility under Panther

By doing this, you ensure that installers will be able to install the right files in the right places and that they won't be denied access when they shouldn't. The reverse is also true: this makes sure that the parts of your installation that should be locked are indeed locked, and it prevents some applications from writing files where they shouldn't.

The new Panther Disk Utility has greatly improved the speed of the repair process. That's another reason to do it on a regular basis! The messages it prints to the window are also better formatted, making it easier to understand for beginners.

Repairing the Disk

You can run your computer on a hard drive with a damaged filesystem until, one day, it simply crashes without any warning.

To prevent that from happening, boot from the Mac OS X Install CD 1 and use the Installer menu to open the Disk Utility. Then, click on the First Aid tab, select your hard drive and repair it until you receive the message "Appears to be OK." You might have to repeat this step a few times on heavily damaged installations.

However, no amount of software maintenance will protect you in any way against hardware failures. So, please, have a good backup system in place too!

> In Panther only, at the bottom of the Disk Utility window, you will see a line called S.M.A.R.T status. No, this doesn't check your disk's IQ! S.M.A.R.T technology is a monitoring system that allows your hard drive to perform self-checks and to warn you when it is about to fail. If you see "verified," your disk is doing well. Perform your regular backups and continue reading this page. If you see "About to fail," your disk *will* fail and will do so sooner than later. Immediately back up your files and replace the hard drive, or contact your nearest Apple Store or Apple Authorized Service Provider.

As a general rule, you should monitor the status of your disk once a week— once a month, at least. Hard-drive failures happen to everyone sooner or later. Be prepared so that you can minimize data loss.

Forcing Periodic Maintenance

You might know that Mac OS X runs periodic maintenance tasks every night to get rid of unused logs and cache files. It also backs up some Unix files. However, these maintenance tasks were programmed to run at night—at 3:00, 4:00, or 5:00 a.m., depending on what they do—that is, unless your computer is turned off or asleep.

The good news is that not running these tasks is incredibly unlikely to cause instability. However, running them might free some of your disk space and make logs easier to read over the time.

To perform force these maintenance tasks to run on Jaguar or Panther, open your Terminal and type:

```
sudo periodic daily
sudo periodic weekly
sudo periodic monthly
```

Press Return between each line, and wait until the first command has completed to start the second one.

Updating the Prebinding

Sometimes, for some (apparently) inexplicable reason, your computer slows down to a crawl after you have installed a big application.

In that case, you might want to *update the prebinding*. This means forcing Mac OS X to go through all the application files and make sure that they are correctly linked together. The Mac OS X default installer usually takes care of this by itself, but some third-party installers might be less cautious.

To update the prebinding manually, simply open your Terminal and type:

```
sudo update_prebinding -root / -force
```

Then, press Return, type your password, and press Return again. Don't worry about the lines of text that scroll on your Terminal. This simply means that the command is doing its work.

The whole process should take only a few minutes. However, it will considerably slow down your computer. For maximum efficiency, you should not use it at the same time as you are performing other tasks. Once the command has exited, immediately reboot your computer.

 Users who still have Classic applications and a Mac OS 9 system folder on their computers do not need to worry: the command simply ignores those files and doesn't damage them.

Now that you know what these maintenance steps are, you might wonder when you should perform them.

What to Do and When to Do It

Now. Now would be a good time to back up your data and perform all these steps, just to give a boost to your Mac and—who knows?—perhaps even make things better and solve a few issues you might be having. Here are a few more specific times when you should perform specific maintenance tasks:

When you don't do any special installs

- Once a month:
  - Repair the privileges.
  - Repair the drive.
  - Force the periodic maintenance.

After an application crash, a power failure or a force reboot

- Immediately:
  - Repair the drive.
  - Repair the privileges.
- Then, if the computer slows down:
  - Force the periodic maintenance.
  - Update the prebinding.

When installing a big, new application or a system upgrade

- Before, do this:
  - Repair the privileges.
  - Repair the disk.
- After, do this: if this is more than a simple incremental OS update, repair the privileges and the filesystem again with the new, updated Disk Utility.

Now that you know what to do and when to do it, you might want to read about a few maintenance misconceptions that often cause issues to appear on even the best-kept machines.

A Few Maintenance Don'ts

Performing maintenance is a great idea, and it should be done often. However, taking care of a computer is like taking care of an old painting. Would you put too much product on it to make it shinier? You might actually damage it!

A Note About Upgrading to Panther

Upgrading your computer to Panther, even from Jaguar, is a complex task for the Installer: it has to look for certain files and either replace or update them. Following our maintenance agenda should allow you to avoid most problems easily.

However, you might feel that it's time for a *clean install*. Sure, it's a bit more time-consuming, but the Installer will run up to five times faster, the resulting installation will be snappier, and all freshly installed applications will behave wonderfully.

Tempting, isn't it? For once, you might want to forget about traditional maintenance, take the plunge, and initialize your hard drive. You'll find all the information you need at *http://discussions.info.apple.com/WebX?14@@.599b3b48*.

Using certain third-party disk utilities. Certain disk utilities are amazingly efficient and safe, while some others (though sold at your nearest computer shop) might harm your installation more that they will repair it.

Before using a third-party disk utility, you might want to check a few forums and ask users for their personal opinions, or simply search the existing database. That way, you should be able to buy a trusted application.

As a general rule, if a disk utility asks you to boot into Mac OS 9 to solve Mac OS X issues, use caution! If it doesn't clearly state on the box that it is compatible with your 10.x version, or if it says only "Mac OS X," check with the authors and ask them for some details.

Also, keep in mind that the disk utilities provided by Apple are the safest, and they're always the ones you should use first. They might not be all-powerful or repair some heavily damaged disks, but they will never prevent stronger utilities from working. The reverse, however, is not true: when a third-party disk utility has damaged your disk, don't expect Apple's Disk Utility to fix it.

Of course, keep in mind that Apple updates its disk utilities too. Using the Jaguar Disk Utility to repair a Panther installation might help if you are stuck in the middle of the Pacific Ocean with an unreadable hard drive, but this definitely isn't something you want to do otherwise.

Defragmenting too often. Defragmenting a hard drive is a way to make a computer go a bit faster by rearranging the information that is written on it.

Some Mac OS 9 users and PC switchers remember that defragmenting was an essential step in their maintenance processes.

However, the Mac community now seems to agree that Mac OS X is able to handle normally fragmented disks well, without any noticeable slowdown. The news gets better with Panther. It defragments reasonably sized files (i.e., all files smaller than 20 MB, which should be most of yours) on the fly.

Given the fact that forced defragmenting with third-party utilities can be a risky procedure—data is moved all around the drive—and that it might be demanding for tired or defective mechanisms, it should not be performed without good reasons to do so.

Panther users should take this maintenance step off their list and simply let their OS do the work.

Updating to fix. Some Panther users who experience problems think that updating their operating system or specific applications will fix things and allow them to go back to a default state that isn't affected by a specific issue.

However, unless a problem really is caused by an update in itself, which is uncommon, a faulty or damaged installation is likely to make things even worse. The maintenance steps listed at the beginning of this hack should allow you to solve most issues before you go forward.

If it ain't broke, don't fix it. Updates should not be applied carelessly on mission-critical computers. Computers that need an uptime of 100% should be treated with the greatest care and be backed up by a properly configured network.

However, some users sometimes do not apply recommended or critical security updates, thinking that they can only create problems on their Macs. Simply follow the upgrade advice in this hack or ask your network administrator before upgrading. Things are likely to go a lot smoother than you think. Keep in mind that the new Panther Disk Utility contains a new Restore feature that you might find useful when you're planning your backups and emergency boot drives for your most important Macs.

Summary

Mac OS X Panther is a great, easy-to-use, and powerful operating system. However, like any OS, it needs to be taken care of to make sure that things will run smoothly. This hack should help you to keep your computer in a safe state and avoid most of the common pitfalls.

—*François Joseph de Kermadec*

Use iCal to Schedule Tasks

iCal can keep not only your appointments in check, but also the appointments of your system.

The first tool old-school Unix hands reach to when they need to schedule something to run on a schedule is cron [Hack #98]. However, you don't have to go to the command line to schedule tasks. You can use iCal, the personal calendaring application that comes with Mac OS X. iCal features multiple calendars that can be published to other computers and synchronized with . Mac. To schedule something in iCal, you create an *event*: an entry on the calendar that is at a specific time with a specific duration. Events can be one-time occurrences or they can repeat.

Each event can have an alarm that displays a notice on your computer screen, opens a file, or even launches an application at a certain time prior to the event so that it can be ready for you. In addition, alarms can go off even if iCal is not running. iCal uses the iCal Helper application (stored in */Applications/ iCal.app/Contents/Resources*) to keep track of events and fire them off on schedule whether or not iCal itself is running.

You can use iCal's alarms along with AppleScript to execute just about any kind of task you like. To do so requires only three simple steps:

1. Create an AppleScript application that performs the functionality you want and save it somewhere.

2. Create a one-time or repeating event in iCal.

3. Set the alarm properties on that event to open your AppleScript application.

> One logical place to store your scripts is in *~/Library/Scripts*. Anything you store here shows up in the Script menu, if you've enabled it. To enable the Script menu, go to */Applications/ AppleScript* and double-click Install Script Menu. You can store almost anything here, including AppleScripts, shell scripts, and even application aliases. (If you're a former Mac OS 9 user, now you have a replacement for your unconfigurable Apple menu.)

For example, if you want to email a listing of all the files in your Home directory every week, you can create the following AppleScript with the Script Editor (*/Applications/AppleScript*) that scans the directory and emails the results:

```
set listing to (do shell script "/bin/ls -l $HOME")
tell application "Mail"
```

```
set the newMessage to (make new outgoing message with properties ¬
{subject:"Home dir ls output", content:listing})
tell newMessage
make new to recipient with properties {address:"you@somewhere.com"}
end tell
send newMessage
end tell
```

Once you have saved this script as an AppleScript application named
ListHomeDir, you can set it up to run in response to an event. The key to
running an application when an event is scheduled is to have the alarm set
to "Open file" and then select the application as the file to open, as shown
in Figure 9-17.

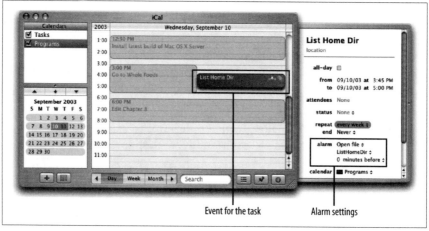

Event for the task   Alarm settings

Figure 9-17. Setting a repeating event in iCal to execute a task

Once the alarm has been set, as long as you are logged into the computer at
the time the event is scheduled for, the AppleScript application executes. For
many tasks, this sort of scheduling works out just fine. But if you want to
run a task every hour, or when you aren't logged in to your Mac, you'll need
to go to the command line and use the Unix scheduling tools.

HACK #97   Use periodic to Schedule Tasks

periodic, as the name suggests, makes sure important system tasks run on a
regular basis.

The periodic tool is designed to organize administrative tasks that need to
be performed over and over again at regular intervals; periodic supports

daily, weekly, and monthly intervals. Mac OS X itself has a set of tasks it runs using the periodic system, including the following:

- Tidy up log files and remove scratch files every day
- Rebuild the locate database and rotate log files every week
- Perform log-file rotation and login accounting every month

The tasks that periodic executes are a set of scripts in the /etc/periodic/daily, /etc/periodic/weekly, and /etc/periodic/monthly directories. To have periodic run your own script, simply add it to one of these directories. For example, if you have a batch of sales reports that you'd like to make a daily snapshot of, you could add the following script to the /etc/periodic/daily directory:

```
#!/bin/bash
echo Making daily backup of sales reports
DATE=`/bin/date +%Y-%m-%d`
/bin/mkdir -p /SalesBackups/$DATE
/bin/cp -R /Users/Shared/SalesData/* /SalesBackups/$DATE
```

periodic also gives you a way to control the order in which scripts run. If you look in the /etc/periodic/daily directory, you'll notice that scripts that come with the system start with a number. To have your scripts execute in a particular order, simply prefix them with a number and periodic takes care of ordering their execution:

```
$ ls -l /etc/periodic/daily/
total 24
-r-xr-xr-x 1 root wheel 1389 30 Aug 20:36 100.clean-logs
-r-xr-xr-x 1 root wheel 3529 30 Aug 20:36 500.daily
```

The number in the filename controls the execution order of the scripts. The lower the number, the earlier it executes, compared to other scripts in the directory. For example, to have the sales backup script in our example execute after the rest of the daily tasks, you could save it as /etc/periodic/daily/700.salesbackup.

Viewing the Output from periodic

Since periodic runs in the background, any output produced by the scripts is hidden from view. To see what happens, periodic saves the output in the /var/log directory. Daily output is saved to /var/log/daily.out, weekly output is saved in /var/log/weekly.out, and monthly output is saved in /var/log/monthly.out.

Changing periodic's Execution Time

By default, periodic runs daily tasks at 3:15 a.m., weekly tasks at 4:30 a.m., and monthly tasks at 5:30 a.m., because these are the hours when your system should be idle (while you are sound asleep). If your system isn't on 24 hours a day, you might consider changing the times that these tasks run to a time when your Mac will be powered on and somewhat idle. For example, if you want the daily tasks to run during your lunch hour, the weekly tasks on Monday at 10:00 a.m. while you're in a meeting, and the monthly tasks at 10:30 a.m., edit the */etc/crontab* file as follows.

```
15 12 * * * root periodic daily
0 10 * * 2 root periodic weekly
30 10 1 * * root periodic monthly
```

Since the system crontab doesn't belong to a user, you can't use crontab -e. Instead, you must edit the file directly.

Use cron to Schedule Tasks
#98
Use the venerable built-in scheduling tool to execute various tasks when you want them to run.

The primary tool for scheduling tasks on the command line is the venerable cron. This tool is started automatically by SystemStarter at boot time and runs continuously in the background. Every minute, cron wakes up, consults a set of tables to see if there is anything to be executed at that time, and, if so, takes care of executing it. These tables, known as *crontab files*, are located in two places on the filesystem:

/etc/crontab

> The crontab file for the system at large. Each entry in this table represents a command that the root user will run and the time that it will run. Anybody can read this file, but only the root user can edit it.

/var/cron/tabs/

> This directory contains the user crontab files for each user on the system who is using cron. These files are hidden and are visible only to the root user, so that other users on the system can't look at each other's crontab files.

The System crontab File

The following listing shows the contents of the system crontab as it appears in a default installation. While this file is for system tasks, you should always use the crontab file for your user.

```
# /etc/crontab
SHELL=/bin/sh
PATH=/etc:/bin:/sbin:/usr/bin:/usr/sbin
HOME=/var/log
#
# minute hour mday month wday who command
#
# */5 * * * * root /usr/libexec/atrun
#
# Run daily/weekly/monthly jobs.
15 3 * * * root periodic daily
30 4 * * 6 root periodic weekly
30 5 1 * * root periodic monthly
```

The crontab file format is similar to that of many other Unix utilities. Any line beginning with the hash character (#) is a comment. The first three uncommented lines of the file set the environment with which cron runs. The remaining lines of the crontab file consist of five numbers that define the interval at which a particular task is to run. The end of the line contains the command to run. In the case of the system crontab, the command also contains the name of the user under which to run the command. As the file itself indicates, each of the five numbers corresponds to a different interval, arranged in order of finer to larger granularity. Figure 9-18 describes the settings for each of these fields. In addition to numbers, each field can contain an asterisk (*) character, which means match every possibility for that field.

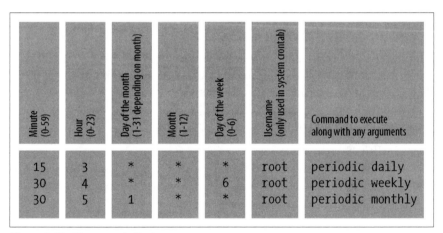

Figure 9-18. The crontab file format

To interpret the lines in the crontab file, read the fields for each line from left to right. For example, the first field (after the comments) in the system crontab indicates that periodic daily should run on the 15th minute of the third hour on any day of the month, in any given month, on any day of the week. This means that periodic daily will run at 3:15 a.m. every day. The second line indicates that the periodic weekly command will run on the 30th minute of the fourth hour of any Sunday; that is, it runs every Sunday at 4:30 a.m.

For each of the fields, you can also specify a list or range of numbers. For example, if you want to run a command every 15 minutes, you can use the following line:

```
0,15,30,60 * * * * command
```

Or, if you want a command to run only at 5:00 p.m. on weekdays, you can use the following:

```
0 5 * * 1-5 command
```

The User crontab

To set up tasks to get executed, you must edit your own personal crontab. You can take a look at what you already have in your crontab file by using the crontab command:

```
$ crontab -l
crontab: no crontab for duncan
```

This output means nothing has been scheduled yet. By default, a user account doesn't have a crontab.

Editing a User crontab

There are two ways to edit your crontab. The first involves using whatever editor you've set up on the command line (for example, vi, Emacs, or pico). The second involves using any editor you want (such as TextEdit or BBEdit) and loading a text file as your crontab. To edit your file on the command line, use the following command:

```
$ crontab -e
```

For your first crontab entry, add a line that makes your computer say "hello" every minute. To do this, add the following line to your crontab file:

```
* * * * * osascript -e 'say "hello"'
```

> If you get stuck in an unfamiliar editor, remember that you can get out of vi by typing :q!, and you can get out of Emacs by pressing Control-X and then Control-C.

Now, every minute of every day that your machine is on, it will say "hello" to you, which could become annoying indeed. There are a couple things going on here:

- The osascript -e 'say "hello"' command is issued by your system every minute, based on the five preceding asterisks.

- The command uses the default system voice set in the Speech Preferences panel to speak the word "hello" on cue.

But now that you have installed a crontab file, you can use crontab to list the file:

```
$ crontab -l
* * * * * osascript -e 'say "hello"'
```

The other way to create a crontab file is to use an editor such as TextEdit or BBEdit. To get the current crontab out in a form that you can open with any editor, save the file on your hard drive and then execute the crontab command as follows:

```
$ crontab mycrontabfile
```

This also gives a way to reset the crontab file quickly for a user. Passing the /dev/null file into crontab sets the user's crontab to an empty file.

Using the crontab comment to specify a file is also a good way to accidentally lose any cron settings that you have in place. Be sure to check your crontab before loading a new crontab file.

To retrieve your crontab for editing, you can direct the output using the following command:

```
$ crontab -l > mycrontabfile
```

Running Virex from cron

If you've installed the McAfee Virex virus scanner from .Mac, the vscanx command-line virus scanner is installed at /usr/local/vscanx/vscanx. You can take advantage of this and have your disk scanned for viruses from cron instead of from the GUI. This is a bonus that the virus scanner runs regardless of who's logged into the computer or even if nobody is.

To enable virus scanning from cron, delete the .VirexLogin item from the list of your Startup Items in the Accounts Preferences panel. Then, add a line to your crontab to execute /usr/local/vscanx/vscanx whenever you like. Note that you need to give the full path to the executable.

Additional Configuration Settings

The cron command on Mac OS X has been enhanced compared to the version found on some other Unix variants. For example, you can use the following more readable entries in the time field:

- Days of the week can be indicated by their abbreviated name: sun, mon, tue, wed, thu, fri, and sat.

- Months can be indicated by their abbreviated name: jan, feb, mar, apr, may, jun, jul, aug, sep, oct, nov, and dec.

You can indicate step values by using a fraction notation, such as 8-17/2, which, when used in the hours field, means "every two hours between the hours of 8 a.m. and 5 p.m."

Table 9-1 lists some special strings that can be used in crontab files.

Table 9-1. Special strings that can be used in a crontab

String	Description	Equivalent
@reboot	Run when system reboots	
@yearly	Run on midnight of January 1	0 0 1 1 *
@monthly	Run at midnight on the first of each month	0 0 1 * *
@weekly	Run at midnight each Sunday	0 0 * * 0
@daily	Run every day at midnight	0 0 * * *
@hourly	Run every hour at the top of the hour	0 * * * *
@AppleNotOnBattery	Prevent command from running if the system is on battery	

With the exception of @AppleNotOnBattery, all of the special strings in Table 9-1 replace the time fields. You can use @AppleNotOnBattery in front of a command to prevent the command from running when your laptop is disconnected from AC power. This ensures that you don't run disk-intensive tasks when you need your battery the most. For example, if you write a script that copies all your files from your ~/Documents folder to some safe storage location that you want to run only when your PowerBook is plugged in, you would use the following crontab entry:

```
0 * * * * @AppleNotOnBattery ~/bin/copyfiles
```

Sleep and cron

The cron system doesn't execute while your system is asleep, because the CPU is powered down and there's just enough happening in your machine to keep the contents of memory ready when you want to wake the system up.

Sometimes this isn't a big deal. For example, if you use a crontab line to remind you to stretch every hour, you won't mind if it's not running. However, for other tasks that you really need to have run, it can create a bit of a problem. The best piece of advice is to time tasks that need to run for when your system is less likely to be in sleep mode.

Reinstall Mac OS X
#99

One of the least appealing system administration tasks is reinstalling the operating system. Here's a checklist for you to use when you have to perform this tedious chore.

Sooner or later, the urge or need to reinstall your system will strike. Maybe you want to put in a faster and larger new hard drive. Maybe you bought a used machine that you want to start with a clean and known state. Or maybe you've screwed up your machine by hacking with things too much (yes, it's happened to the best of us). No matter what, before you scrape your hard drive off and install a fresh system, there are a few things you should think about. And the first thing you should do is back up your data.

Here is a list of things you should seriously consider backing up before you thrash your system:

- Address Book data (*~/Library/Application Support/AddressBook*)
- iCal data (*~/Library/Calendars*)
- Safari bookmarks (*~/Library/Safari*; but don't back up the Icons folder, because that just contains the browser's cache files)
- Preferences (*~/Library/Preferences*)
- Keychains (*~/Library/Keychains*)
- Email from Mail (*~/Library/Mail*)
- Stickies (*~/Library/StickiesDatabase*)
- Anything stored in these folders in your Home folder:
  - Documents (files you've created and saved locally)
  - Movies (movies you've saved or created with iMovie, Final Cut Express, or Final Cut Pro)
  - Music (music stored in iTunes)
  - Pictures (pictures stored in iPhoto)
  - Sites (any local web site you've created and are serving from your Mac)
- Files saved to your Desktop
- QuickTime Pro's registration number (*~/Library/QuickTime*)

- Fonts you've added to the system, either in your local domain (*~/Library/Fonts*) or for global use on your system (*/Library/Fonts*)
- Any shell scripts you have created
- Any AppleScripts you have created
- Any databases you run and access frequently, including FileMaker Pro and MySQL databases

Again, this is just a rough list. You should use this as a guide and then look good and hard at all the data stored on your Mac before you back it up. Once you've started installing Mac OS X on your Mac, there's no going back to recover the data; everything will be overwritten. Make sure you have a good, solid backup before you pop in the first install disc and restart while holding down the C key.

Installing Panther

Assuming you've taken the time to back up your data and check it to make sure that everything you need is there, it's now time to think about installing Panther on your Mac. The important word there is "think"; not that there's anything wrong with Panther, it's just that you should really think about how you're going to use your Mac.

- Are you going to run Classic? If so, you should consider setting up a separate partition in which to install Mac OS 9.
- Are you going to run more than one version of Mac OS X on your Mac, for testing purposes? If so, you'll need separate partitions for them too.
- Running an application that requires a scratch disk, such as Final Cut Pro or Photoshop? Consider setting aside part of your hard drive as a partition just for that purpose.
- How will you install Panther: clean or archive? A clean install is recommended, because it wipes your drive and checks it for errors (and attempts to fix said errors) before installing the operating system.

  If you opt to archive and install, all of the data in the */Users* directory will be archived and retained in a buffer during the install, then dropped back into the */Users* directory once the operating system has completed. Then, it's up to you to go back and pull what you want out of the archive and trash the rest.

Once you've given this some thought, make notes on what you plan to do. It's good to have a plan.

Partitioning Your Hard Drive

If you're planning partition your hard drive, you should jot down how big you want those partitions to be, keeping in mind that the largest partition should be used for the system you boot into. For example, say you have a 30 GB drive and you want to have separate partitions for Panther, Jaguar, Classic, and a scratch disk for Photoshop. If you won't be using Jaguar or Classic for much else than testing, you can get away with devoting a bare minimum of about 2 to 3 GB each for them. And, depending on how much you need to do with Photoshop, you might want to set that up with 1 to 2 GB as well. So, for this example, the partitioning scheme might look similar to Table 9-2.

Table 9-2. Possible partitioning scheme of a 30 GB hard drive

Partition number	Use	Amount of space
1	Panther (Mac OS X 10.3)	23 GB
2	Jaguar (Mac OS X 10.2.8)	3 GB
3	Classic (Mac OS 9.2.2)	2 GB
4	Scratch disk	2 GB

If you want to run different versions of Mac OS X (e.g., Jaguar and Panther), or if you need to run Mac OS 9 applications in Classic mode on your Mac, you need to partition your drive during the installation process. If you wait until after you finish, it's too late; you'll have to go back and reinstall.

Insert Install Disc 1 and reboot your Mac while holding down the C key. From the menu bar, select Installer → Open Disk Utility; this launches the Disk Utility program from the installation CD. In the left pane, select the hard drive you want to partition. Click on the Partition button to the right to examine the partitioning scheme for the hard drive.

In the Volume Scheme section, the pop-up menu should probably be set to Current. From this, select the number of partitions you want to create on your hard drive. You can have up to 16 partitions on a single drive. Set up your partitions by grabbing the slider bar either between the partitions in the Volume Scheme side or in the Volume Information section to the right.

In the Volume Information section, make sure you install the Mac OS 9 drivers if you plan to install Mac OS 9 to run Classic. Depending on how much space you need for Classic, give yourself at least 3 GB of space for installing Mac OS 9 and the apps you'll need to run in Classic mode. If you think you'll need more space for Mac OS 9, allocate the amount of space the apps require.

When you click a partition in the Volume Scheme section, details about that partition show up in the Volume Information section, including its Name, Format, and Size. For example, when you set up new partitions, the partitions have a name of Untitled 1, Untitled 2, and so on. If you want to change the name of a partition, click the partition block in the Volume Scheme section and then give the partition a new name by typing something into the Name field (for example, Panther).

For Mac OS X partitions, set the Format to Mac OS Extended (Journaled). For Mac OS 9 partitions, set the Format to Mac OS Extended.

When you're done changing the information in the Volume Information section, click the Partition button. A warning sheet pops up, letting you know that partitioning will destroy all of the information on the drive. If you're certain that you have a good backup from which to reload your data, click the Partition button on the sheet to split your drive up.

Your hard drive will be erased and the drive will be reformatted with the number of partitions you selected. You'll know Disk Utility is done when you see the partitions show up in the left side of the window.

Now that your drive has successfully been partitioned, quit Disk Utility (⌘-Q) to resume the installation process.

The Installation Itself

Okay, so you've backed up your data, you've figured out how you're going to install Panther (clean, right?), and you've evaluated how you need to slice up your hard drive for during the installation. This part is really pretty easy.

Selecting Easy Install installs all the standard applications (such as iCal, iSync, iPhoto, iMovie, Internet Explorer, and all the possible language support packages) on your Mac. The one thing that doesn't get installed on your Mac with the Easy Install method is Apple's version of X11; if you want that, you'll need to click the Customize button (or install it later from Install Disc 3).

Clicking the Customize button takes you to another screen that's labeled Customize Install on <HardDiskName>. Below that, you'll see a list of the packages that you can install. Items that have a checkmark in their box will be installed as part of the Easy Install. These items include:

- Essential System Software (this item is grayed out and cannot be unchecked)
- BSD Subsystem

- Additional Applications (these include Internet Explorer, StuffIt Expander, iTunes, iMovie, iPhoto, iCal—which is selected but grayed out—and iSync)
- Printer Drivers (all but Epson Printer Drivers 2 are selected)
- Additional Speech Voices
- Fonts (all but Fonts for Additional Languages are selected)
- Language Translations

And the following items are deselected by default; if you want to install these, you need to place a check in their checkbox:

- Epson Printer Drivers 2
- Fonts for Additional Languages
- X11

You can uncheck the following items:

Language Translations
> The language you've selected at the beginning of the installation process is installed by default, but why install Dutch, Japanese, and French (among a few) if you don't need them? By deselecting this item, you free up 695 MB of hard-drive space for better things.

Printer drivers you won't need
> If you have only one brand of printer attached to your Mac, there really isn't a need to install all the other brands.

Any of the Additional Applications, particularly Internet Explorer
> After all, Mac OS X comes with Safari, so why install Microsoft's browser when you really don't need it?

When you've finished selecting the items you want to install, click the Install button to begin the installation process. It'll take about an hour or so—maybe not so long if you are lucky enough to have a fast system with fast disks. And then you'll have a brand-spanking-new system.

—*Chuck Toporek*

Bypass the GUI

Bypass the beautiful Aqua GUI for those die-hard command-line fans.

You can keep the Mac OS X GUI, Aqua, from loading by making two simple changes on your Macintosh. The first involves manipulating the Open Firmware; the second involves manuplating a BSD configuration file. Both of these changes require you to have administrator access [Hack #88].

Please keep in mind that working with the Open Firmware can be dangerous. Be sure to type all commands exactly as they appear in this hack. You'll
need to use the Terminal application (*/Applications/Utilities*) to access the
command line.

Verbose Booting

Verbose booting shows you the actual process of Mac OS X's startup. You'll
see drivers get loaded and services launch. This command should work on
any recent (New World) Macintosh:

```
$ sudo /usr/sbin/nvram boot-args="-v"
```

The -v flag tells the system to boot verbosely. You can get the same result by
holding down ⌘-V at boot time, but that works only the one time. Modifying boot-args causes Mac OS X to boot verbosely every time from now on.

To resume normal booting, use the following command:

```
$ sudo /usr/sbin/nvram boot-args=""
```

Bypassing the GUI Login Window

If you are at the login window and want to bypass it to get straight to the
command line, there's a quick and easy way to do so. Simply enter >console
(including the greater-than symbol) as your username in the login dialog
box. The GUI exits and dumps you off at the black-and-white text-based
console and lets you log in with the shell. After your are done with your
shell session, the GUI comes back.

The only catch to this trick is that you must have your login screen set to
display only a username and password box, instead of a list of users, so that
you have a place to enter >console.

> If your login screen instead displays a list of users, you can
> access the username and password box by hitting Option-up
> arrow, then Return.

—Jason Deraleau

Index

We'd like to hear your suggestions for improving our indexes. Send email to *index@oreilly.com*.

OPML, 64
organized, keeping information, 7–12
Orinoco cards, 373
OSA (Open Scripting Architecture), 92
osascript tool, 63, 76
oscillating fan and iSight
        camera, 348–351
OSXvnc, 386
    wrapper application for, 391
outliners, 451

P

pairing
    iSync with Bluetooth devices (see
        iSync, pairing with Bluetooth
        devices)
    Macs with another
        Bluetooth-enabled
        device, 301–308
    when unnecessary, 300
Panic, 6
Panther
    installing, 542, 544–545
    upgrading to, 531
Parks, Graham, 178
Partition tab button, 543
partitioning hard drive, 543
Pashua, 126–132
    installing, 126
    overview, 127
    self-contained, double-clickable
        application, 136–142
    simple dialog, 131
    wizard generated with, 132–136
    (see also Perl; Python; shell
        scripts), 126
passive network scanners, 373
password-checker dialog, 513
passwords
    firmware, 510
    picking good, 512
    protecting, 513
PC Card, 447
PC-to-PC over crossover RJ-45, 347
PDAs
    controlling Mac with, 326–333
    iSync and, 358
PDF e-books, 49
PDF files
    storing and searching, 449–450

types of documents to store as, 450
    viewing in Safari, 157
performance slowing down after
        installing application, 529
periodic maintenance, 528
periodic tool
    changing execution time, 536
    tasks, 535
    using to schedule tasks, 534–536
    viewing output from, 535
Perl
    hacking Address Book
        with, 102–105
    under Mac OS X, 263
    web photo gallery, building, 261,
        262–270
    (see also Mac::Glue; Pashua)
PerlPad, 40
phone numbers, remembering, 308
PhotoRescue, 447
PHP, 410–411
    web site, 411
Pico, 440–443
    deleting characters, 443
    exiting, 443
    interface, 440
    moving around in, 441
    opening files, 442
    saving files, 441
    selecting text, 442
pictures
    storing in iPod, 285–287
    transferring with
        Rendezvous, 275–282
Pine email, 228–232
    traversing Mail mailboxes
        for, 229–231
    using, 231
pipe (|) character, 500
piping, 500
PithHelmet, 167
Pittenauer, Martin, 361
playlists
    Clutter, 240
    iTunes, 236
plist files, editing, 440
plist preference file format, 507
PNG files, recovering, 448
Pod2Go, 253–255
    grabbing subscriptions in
        NetNewsWire for, 254

Colophon

Our look is the result of reader comments, our own experimentation, and feedback from distribution channels. Distinctive covers complement our distinctive approach to technical topics, breathing personality and life into potentially dry subjects.

The tool on the cover of *Mac OS X Panther Hacks* is a pipe wrench, an adjustable tool that uses two serrated jaws for gripping and turning a pipe. In 1870, U.S. Patent #184,993 was issued for this type of wrench to inventor Daniel C. Stillson (pipe wrenches are also known as "Stillsons") of J.J. Walworth & Co., a Boston-area heating and plumbing company. Frustrated by existing pipefitting tools, Stillson whittled an improved wrench model out of wood and showed it to his boss. Impressed with the mechanics of this hacked prototype, Stillson's supervisor authorized corporate payment to a blacksmith so that the wrench design could be forged in steel. The forged wrench was then shown to the company president, who instructed its inventor to test it in the company's pipe room: "Twist off the pipe or break the wrench," he said. "Put enough strength on the wrench to do one or the other." Half an hour later, Stillson returned with a twisted off piece of pipe in one hand and an intact wrench in the other. His patent has long since expired, but the pipe wrenches manufactured today remain nearly identical to Stillson's original design.

Genevieve d'Entremont was the production editor and proofreader, and Brian Sawyer was the copyeditor for *Mac OS X Panther Hacks*. Philip Dangler and Darren Kelly provided quality control. Julie Hawks wrote the index.

Emma Colby designed the cover of this book, based on a series design by Edie Freedman. The cover image is from the *Just Tools* collection of the CMCD Library. Emma Colby produced the cover layout with QuarkXPress 4.1 using Adobe's Helvetica Neue and ITC Garamond fonts.

Melanie Wang designed the interior layout, based on a series design by David Futato. This book was converted by Andrew Savikas to FrameMaker 5.5.6 with a format conversion tool created by Erik Ray, Jason McIntosh, Neil Walls, and Mike Sierra that uses Perl and XML technologies. The text font is Linotype Birka; the heading font is Adobe Helvetica Neue Condensed; and the code font is LucasFont's TheSans Mono Condensed. The illustrations that appear in the book were produced by Robert Romano and Jessamyn Read using Macromedia FreeHand 9 and Adobe Photoshop 6. This colophon was written by Philip Dangler.

Related Titles Available from O'Reilly

Hacks

Amazon Hacks

BSD Hacks

Digital Photography Hacks

eBay Hacks

Excel hacks

Google Hacks

Harware Hacking Projects for Geeks

Linux Server Hacks

Mac OS X Hacks

Spidering Hacks

TiVo Hacks

Windows Server Hacks

Windows XP Hacks

Wireless Hacks

Keep in touch with O'Reilly

1. Download examples from our books

To find example files for a book, go to:

www.oreilly.com/catalog

select the book, and follow the "Examples" link.

2. Register your O'Reilly books

Register your book at *register.oreilly.com*

Why register your books? Once you've registered your O'Reilly books you can:

- Win O'Reilly books, T-shirts or discount coupons in our monthly drawing.
- Get special offers available only to registered O'Reilly customers.
- Get catalogs announcing new books (US and UK only).
- Get email notification of new editions of the O'Reilly books you own.

3. Join our email lists

Sign up to get topic-specific email announcements of new books and conferences, special offers, and O'Reilly Network technology newsletters at:

elists.oreilly.com

It's easy to customize your free elists subscription so you'll get exactly the O'Reilly news you want.

4. Get the latest news, tips, and tools

http://www.oreilly.com

- "Top 100 Sites on the Web"—PC Magazine
- CIO Magazine's Web Business 50 Awards

Our web site contains a library of comprehensive product information (including book excerpts and tables of contents), downloadable software, background articles, interviews with technology leaders, links to relevant sites, book cover art, and more.

5. Work for O'Reilly

Check out our web site for current employment opportunities:

jobs.oreilly.com

6. Contact us

O'Reilly & Associates
1005 Gravenstein Hwy North
Sebastopol, CA 95472 USA

TEL: 707-827-7000 or 800-998-9938
      (6am to 5pm PST)

FAX: 707-829-0104

order@oreilly.com
For answers to problems regarding your order or our products.
To place a book order online, visit:

www.oreilly.com/order_new

catalog@oreilly.com
To request a copy of our latest catalog.

booktech@oreilly.com
For book content technical questions or corrections.

corporate@oreilly.com
For educational, library, government, and corporate sales.

proposals@oreilly.com
To submit new book proposals to our editors and product managers.

international@oreilly.com
For information about our international distributors or translation queries. For a list of our distributors outside of North America check out:

international.oreilly.com/distributors.html

adoption@oreilly.com
For information about academic use of O'Reilly books, visit:

academic.oreilly.com

O'REILLY®

Our books are available at most retail and online bookstores.
To order direct: 1-800-998-9938 • *order@oreilly.com* • *www.oreilly.com*
Online editions of most O'Reilly titles are available by subscription at *safari.oreilly.com*